Craig P. Lambert

Subject-Grouped
1016 KANJI IN CONTEXT
A Guide to Reading Japanese

分野別1016漢字ブック

Subject-Grouped
1016 KANJI IN CONTEXT
A Guide to Reading Japanese

分野別 1016 漢字ブック

by Taeko Kamiya

THE HOKUSEIDO PRESS

Subject-Grouped 1016 KANJI IN CONTEXT
A Guide to Reading Japanese
分野別 1016 漢字ブック

© 1997 Taeko Kamiya

ISBN4-590-01043-7

Published by The Hokuseido Press
3-32-4, Honkomagome, Bunkyo-ku, Tokyo

Foreword
❄❄❄❄❄❄❄❄❄❄❄❄

This book is intended for those who are eager to learn how to read the Japanese written language. You may wish to read store signs, the names of railroad stations, newspaper ads or even native Japanese publications. Whatever your aim might be, you must have a knowledge of the basic *kanji*, Chinese characters.

The book presents the 1016 characters currently taught in the six years of elementary school in Japan and their numerous compounds. The characters are numbered #1 through #1016. In order to present them in meaningful context, not as isolated items, the characters are grouped by subject and divided into twenty chapters. Chapter 3, for instance, describes the *kanji* related time expressions, Chapter 9 for those related to weather, Chapter 12 for education, Chapter 17 for economy and so forth.

Each chapter or section of a chapter consists of three parts: Reference, Vocabulary and Reading Exercises. In the Reference, each *kanji* is given its stroke order, *kun-yomi* (native Japanese reading), *on-yomi* (reading taken from Chinese), and English meanings. Example words and compounds are given using only the characters previously introduced except for some compounds in earlier chapters. The Vocabulary gives newly introduced *kanji*-based words related to the subject. If you are interested in some words regarding geography, just look at the vocabulary list of Chapter 8; if you want to learn words about sports, Chapter 13 will do. The Reading Exercises provide ample material for practice, presenting repeatedly not only the new but also the already-learned *kanji* and words. The practice sentences are arranged to their difficulty as well as connections in reading and meaning.

I hope that you may find the book helpful. You will be surprised how much you can do with the 1016 essential characters if you put them to work to the maximum capacity.

Finally, I wish to express my gratitude to the Hokuseido Press, for making this publication possible.

Taeko Kamiya
November 1997

Usage Notes
✷✷✷✷✷✷✷✷✷✷✷✷✷

1. *Kun* readings are written in small letters. *On* readings are in capital letters. Parentheses enclose *okurigana* and explanatory information.
Similar English meanings are separated by a comma, but different meanings are marked off by a semi colon.

    kun   *hiro(u)* pick up
    ON   SHŪ pick up; JŪ ten (in documents)

    ON   BAN number, order; one's turn; keeping watch

2. Readings which are infrequent are in brackets.

    kun   *mut(tsu)*, *mu(tsu)*, *mu*, [*mui*] six

    ON   EN, [ON] far, distant

3. Irregular (Ir.) readings are indicated by an asterisk [*]. If the item is listed later, its number is also shown.

kun   *hito* person Ir. *hito(ri)**; *futa(ri)**; *(o)tona** #170
一人 *hitori** 1 person. 二人 *futari** 2 people.

kun   *ō(kii)*, *ō-* big, large Ir. *o(tona)**; *yama(to)** #396
大人 *otona** adult.

4. When an unknown *kanji* is used for a compound, *furigana* is added with the number under which the word (or the entry *kanji*) appears.
万国 #299 *bankoku* all nations.
七月 #52 *shichigatsu* July. (listed under | #52 月 |)

5. The slash[/] is used to indicate alternative choices.
今年 *kotoshi/konnen* this year.

6. The apostrophe ['] is used to show a break between two syllables, when *n* is followed by a vowel (*a, i, u, e, o*) or a *y* within a word.
全員 *zen'in* all members
本屋 *hon'ya* bookstore
The apostrophe added to *on* readings indicates the first consonant of the double consonants (*kk, pp, ss, tt*) and a break between syllables within a word.
GA' 合唱 *gasshō* chorus.
[HA'] 法度 *hatto* law; ban.

7. The sign 「々」 is used to indicate a repetition of the same character.
人々 *hitobito* people.

8. The change from an unvoiced to a voiced consonant in word combinations may occur.

寺 *tera* temple → 山寺 *yamadera* mountain temple

立つ *tatsu* stand up → 目立つ *medatsu* stand out

9. When a noun can be used as a verb by adding *suru*, the sign ‹v› is added after the noun.

休息 ‹v› *kyūsoku* rest, repose.

  (kyūsoku means a rest or a repose and *kyūsoku suru* means to rest or to repose.)

10. The character not included in the 1016 *kyōiku kanji* is indicated by the mark [▲] with *furigana*.

唯▲一の *yuiitsu no* only, sole.

Contents
****

Foreword

Usage Notes

The Kanji List

1	Numbers #1 - #23 ··	1
2	Counters #24 - #43 ···	8
3	Time Expressions (1) ··	14
	Days #44 - #51 ··	14
	Months and Years #52 - #63 ···································	18
	Weeks #64 - #72 ··	23
	Seasons #73 - #79 ··	27
4	Time Expressions (2) ··	30
	Time and Hours #80 - #106 ····································	30
	Eras #107 - #117 ···	39
5	People ···	44
	Family Relations #118 - #149 ·································	44
	Friends #150 - #155 ··	54
	Personal Pronouns and Forms of Address #156 - #165 ·········	57
	Life #166 - #184 ···	61

6   Animals, Birds, Insects #185 - #207 ···················· 68
7   Plants and Colors ···································· 75
    Plants #208 - #228 ······························ 75
    Colors #229 - #237 ······························· 82
8   Geography ·· 86
    Lands #238 - #265 ······························· 86
    Waters #266 - #283 ······························ 94
    The Earth #284 - #311 ··························· 100
    Cities and Prefectures #312 - #334 ·············· 108
9   Weather and Universe ······························ 115
    Weather #335 - #372 ···························· 115
    Universe #373 - #394 ···························· 126
10 Food, Drink, Cooking ······························ 132
    Food #395 - #412 ······························· 132
    Drink #413 - #420 ······························ 138
    Cooking #421 - #443 ···························· 141
11 Stores, Goods, Business ··························· 148
    Stores #444 - #465 ····························· 148

	Goods #466 - #490	156
	Business #491 - #522	163
12	Education	173
	Schools #523 - #551	173
	Learning #552 - #596	182
	Languages #597 - #620	194
13	Sports #621 - #652	201
14	Arts	211
	Fine Arts #653 - #668	211
	Music #669 - #680	216
	Theater #681 - #698	220
	Literature #699 - #727	225
15	Body and Health	233
	Body #728 - #756	233
	Health #757 - #785	242
16	Transportation	250
	Vehicles and Roads #786 - #806	250
	Trains and Ships #807 - #821	257

17 Economy ·· 262
    Industry　#822 – #855 ····························· 262
    Trade　#856 – #868 ······························· 272
    Company and Bank　#869 – #898 ············· 277
18 Government ·· 286
    Diet　#899 – #928 ································· 286
    Defense　#929 – #944 ···························· 294
    Foreign Affairs　#945 – #971 ················· 299
19 Law and Crime　#972 – #992 ············· 307
20 Religion and Morality　#993 – #1016 ···· 313

ANSWERS ·· 321
INDEX by Readings ································· 369
INDEX by Stroke Count ··························· 391

1

****

Numbers

■ I. Reference ■

#1		
一	1 strokes	一

kun *hito(tsu)*, *hito-* one Ir. *tsui(tachi)**#44

一つ *hitotsu* 1; 1 thing. りんご一つ *ringo hitotsu* 1 apple. 一つ一つ *hitotsu hitotsu* one by one. もう一つ *mō hitotsu* one more. 一つまみ *hitotsumami* a pinch (of salt).

ON ICHI, ITSU one, first

一 *ichi* one. アメリカ一 *Amerika ichi* number one in America. 一々しらべる *ichiichi shiraberu* check one by one. 一にする *itsu ni suru* unify. 唯一の *yuiitsu no* only, sole.

#2		
二	2 strokes	一 二

kun *futa(tsu)*, *futa* two Ir. *futsu(ka)**#44; *ha(tachi)**#31

二つ *futatsu* 2; 2 things. 二つにする *futatsu ni suru* divide in 2. 二けた *futaketa* 2-digits.

ON NI two

二 *ni* two. 二メートル *ni-mētoru* 2 meters. 一、二をあらそう *ichi-ni o arasou* contend for the 1st place. 一も二もなく *ichi mo ni mo naku* readily, without hesitation.

#3		
三	3 strokes	一 二 三

kun *mit(tsu)*, *mi(tsu)*, *mi* three Ir. *sha(mi)**#422

三つ *mittsu* 3; 3 things. 三つぞろい *mitsuzoroi* 3-piece suit. 三晩#96 *miban* 3 nights.

ON SAN three

三 *san* three. 一、二、三 *ichi, ni, san* 1, 2, 3. 三ページ *san-pēji* 3 pages; page 3. 二、三の *nisan no* 2 or 3, a few.

#4 四	5 strokes	丨 冂 冂 阴 四

kun **yot(tsu), yo(tsu), yo, yon** four
四つ *yottsu* 4; 4 things.　四つ角 #460 *yotsukado* street corner.　四人 #25 *yonin* 4 people.　四 *yon* four.　四ドル　yon-doru 4 dollars.

ON **SHI** four
四 *shi* four.　一、二、三、四 *ichi, ni, san, shi* 1, 2, 3, 4.　四季 #78 *shiki* 4 seasons.

#5 五	4 strokes	一 丁 五 五

kun **itsu(tsu), itsu** five Ir. *sa(tsuki)* * #52
五つ *itsutsu* 5; 5 things.　五日 #44 *itsuka* 5 days; 5th of the month.

ON **GO** five
五 *go* five.　四、五メートル *shigo-mētoru* 4 or 5 meters.　三々五々 *sansan-gogo* by twos and threes; in samll groups.

#6 六	4 strokes	丶 亠 亣 六

kun **mut(tsu), mu(tsu), mu, [mui]** six
六つ *muttsu* 6; 6 things.　六つ子 #121 *mutsugo* sextuplets.　六部屋 #448 *muheya* 6 rooms.　六日 #44 *muika* 6 days; 6th of the month.

ON **ROKU** six
六 *roku* six.　六マイル *roku-mairu* 6 miles.　六月 #52 *rokugatsu* June.

#7 七	2 strokes	一 七

kun **nana(tsu), nana, [nano]** seven Ir. *nanu(ka)* * #44; *tana(bata)* * #97
七つ *nanatsu* 7; 7 things.　七 *nana* seven.　七日 #44 *nanoka* 7 days; 7th of the month.

ON **SHICHI** seven
七 *shichi* seven.　七月 #52 *shichigatsu* July.　七五三 *shichigosan* festival day for 3-, 5-, and 7-year olds (Nov. 15).

#8 八	2 strokes ノ 八

kun   *yat(tsu)*, *ya(tsu)*, *ya*, [*yō*] eight

八つ *yattsu* 8; 8 things.   お八つ *oyatsu* afternoon refreshments. 八百屋 #448 *yaoya* vegetable store.   八日 #44 *yōka* 8 days; 8th of the month.

ON   HACHI eight

八 *hachi* eight.   八ミリ *hachi-miri* 8 mm cinecamera.   一か八かだ *Ichi ka bachi ka da* It's hit or miss.

#9 九	2 strokes ノ 九

kun   *kokono(tsu)*, *kokono* nine

九つ *kokonotsu* 9; 9 things.   九日 #44 *kokonoka* 9 days; 9th of the month.

ON   KYŪ, KU nine

九 *kyū/ku* nine.   九ドル *kyū-doru* 9 dollars.   九々 *kuku* multiplication table.   九月 #52 *kugatsu* September.

#10 十	2 strokes 一 十

kun   *tō, to* ten Ir. *(ha)ta(chi)** #31; *(ha)tsu(ka)** #44

十 *tō* 10; 10 things.   十月 #52 *totsuki* 10 months.

ON   JŪ, [JI'] ten

十 *jū* ten.   十グラム *jū-guramu* 10 grams.   二十 *nijū* 20.   三十五 *sanjūgo* 35.   十セント *jus-sento/jis-sento* 10 cents.

#11 百	6 strokes 一 丆 丆 百 百 百

kun   Ir. *(ya)o(ya)** #448
ON   HYAKU hundred

百 *hyaku* 100.   三百 *sanbyaku* 300.   四百 *yonhyaku* 400.   九百 *kyūhyaku* 900.   うそ八百 *uso happyaku* a pack of lies.

#12 千	3 strokes	ノ 二 千

kun   *chi* thousand
千草 #208 *chigusa* various flowering plants.   千葉 #210 *Chiba* Chiba (Place)

ON   SEN thousand
千 *sen* 1,000.   一千 *issen* 1,000.   三千 *sanzen* 3,000.   四千 *yonsen* 4,000.   七千 *nanasen* 7,000.   九千 *kyūsen* 9,000

#13 万	3 strokes	一 フ 万

ON   MAN ten thousand; BAN many, all
一万 *ichiman* 10,000.   百万 *hyakuman* 1 million.   一千万 *issenman* 10 million.   万一 *man'ichi* by any chance.   万国 #299 *bankoku* all nations.

#14 億	15 strokes	イ 广 俨 倍 億 億

ON   OKU 100 million
一億 *ichioku* 100 million.   五億六千万 *gooku rokusenman* 560 million.   億万 *okuman* billions.   億万長者 #161 *okuman chōja* billionaire.

#15 兆	6 strokes	ノ ヲ 丬 汁 兆 兆

kun   *kiza(shi)* sign, omen; *kiza(su)* show signs
兆し *kizashi* sign, omen.   あらしを兆す *arashi o kizasu* show signs of a storm.

ON   CHŌ trillion; sign, omen
一兆 *itchō* 1 trillion.   億兆 *okuchō* the people, the multitude.   兆候 #337 *chōkō* sign, symptom.

#16 壱	7 strokes	十 士 卢 卢 声 壱

ON   ICHI one (in documents)
壱千 *issen* 1,000.   壱万 *ichiman* 10,000.

#17 弐	6 strokes	一　二　三　三　弐　弐

ON　NI two (in documents)

弐百 *nihyaku* 200.　弐千 *nisen* 2,000.　弐億 *nioku* 200 million.　壱億弐千万 *ichioku nisenman* 120 million.

#18 参	8 strokes	厶　厸　矢　夅　参　参

kun　*mai(ru)* go, come, visit a temple/shrine; be beaten

すぐ参ります *Sugu mairimasu* I'm going right away.　お参り *omairi* visiting a temple/shrine.　参る *mairu* be beaten (by the heat).

ON　SAN three (in documents); participate

参千 *sanzen* 3,000.　参加^か <v> #426 *sanka* participation.

#19 拾	9 strokes	扌　扩　扚　拾　拾　拾

kun　*hiro(u)* pick up

拾う *hirou* pick up; find (a purse).　拾い物^{もの} #205 *hiroimono* a find.

ON　SHŪ pick up; JŪ ten (in documents)

拾万 *jūman* 100,000.　拾得物^{とくぶつ} #500 *shūtokubutsu* a find.

#20 数	13 strokes	ヽヽ　半　米　娄　娄　数

kun　*kazu* number; *kazo(eru)* count

数 *kazu* number.　数々の *kazukazu no* various.　数える *kazoeru* count.

ON　SŪ, [SU] number; (prefix) several

数 *sū* number.　数学^{がく} #523 *sūgaku* mathematics.　数百 *sūhayku* hundreds (of something).　数千 *sūsen* thousands (of something).

#21 第	11 strokes	⺮　竺　竺　竺　第

ON　DAI (prefix for ordinals)

第一 *daiichi* No.1, 1st.　第一に *daiichi ni* first, first of all.

#22 番	12 strokes	ノ　ニ　乎　乎　昏　番

ON BAN number, order; one's turn; keeping watch
一番 *ichiban* No.1, 1st.; most, best.　一番になる　*ichiban ni naru*
come out top.　あなたの番 *anata no ban* your turn.　番をする *ban o suru* tend (a shop).

#23 目	5 strokes	丨　冂　冃　目　目

kun *me*, [*ma*] eye; (suffix for ordinals)
目 *me* eye.　一目で *hitome de* at a glance.　目のあたり *ma no atari*
before one's eye.　二番目 *nibanme* 2nd.　三つ目 *mittsume* 3rd.

ON MOKU, [BOKU] eye
一目 *ichimoku* a glance.　面目 #260 *menboku* face, honor.

■ II. Vocabulary

一・一つ	*ichi/hitotsu*	1
二・二つ	*ni/futatsu*	2
三・三つ	*san/mittsu*	3
四・四つ	*shi/yon/yottsu*	4
五・五つ	*go/itsutsu*	5
六・六つ	*roku/muttsu*	6
七・七つ	*shichi/nana/nanatsu*	7
八・八つ	*hachi/yattsu*	8
九・九つ	*kyū/ku/kokonotsu*	9
十	*jū/tō*	10
百	*hyaku*	100
千	*sen*	1,000
一万	*ichiman*	10,000
一億	*ichioku*	100 million
一兆	*itchō*	1 trillion
壱万	*ichiman*	10,000
弐百	*nihyaku*	200
参千	*sanzen*	3,000
拾万	*jūman*	100,000

数	*kazu/sū*	number
数百	*sūhyaku*	hundreds
第一	*daiichi*	No.1,1st
一番	*ichiban*	No.1,1st;most, best
二番目	*nibanme*	2nd
三つ目	*mittsume*	3rd

■ III. Reading Exercises 1 ■

Read and translate the following.

1. りんごが**六**つあります。
2. オレンジが**八**つとレモンが**三**つあります。
3. ビルとトムはクラスで**一**、**二**をあらそっている。
4. あそこまで**五**、**六**マイルあります。
5. くりを**十**ばかり**拾**いました。
6. むすめは**九**つでむすこは**七**つです。
7. **十二**ページに**二**、**三**のミスがあります。
8. わたしの**番**です。あなたは**四番目**ですよ。
9. これは**二**つ**目**のハンバーガーです。
10. いすの**数**を**数**えてください。
11. **百五十**、**三千六百**、**五万四千**、**一億八千万**、**参兆**、**弐拾九万**、**壱千七百**、**数百**

2

****
Counters

■ I. Reference ■

#24 円	4 strokes	丨 冂 冂 円

kun *maru(i)* round
円い *marui* round.

ON EN circle; (counter for money)
円 *en* circle. 円をかく *en o kaku* draw a circle. 百円、千円、一万円 *hyakuen, sen'en, ichiman'en* 100, 1,000, 10,000 yen.

#25 人	2 strokes	ノ 人

kun *hito* person Ir. *(hito)ri**; *futa(ri)**; *(o)tona**[#170]
人 *hito* person. あの人 *ano hito* that person, he/she. 人々 *hito-bito* people. 一人 *hitori** 1 person. 二人 *futari** 2 people.

ON JIN, NIN person; (counter for people)
アメリカ人 *Amerika-jin* an American. 人数 *ninzu* number of people. 三人、四人、五人 *sannin, yonin, gonin* 3, 4, 5 people.

#26 名	6 strokes	ノ ク タ 夕 名 名

kun *na* name, fame
人の名 *hito no na* person's name. あだ名 *adana* nickname. 名のある *na no aru* famous.

ON MEI, MYŌ name, fame; (counter for people)
人名 *jinmei* person's name. 名人 *meijin* master, expert. 名目 *meimoku/myōmoku* name; pretext. 一名、二名、三名 *ichimei, nimei, sanmei* 1, 2, 3 people.

#27 本	5 strokes	一 十 オ 木 本

kun   *moto* origin
本 *moto* origin.   本をただす *modo o tadasu* trace to its origin.

ON   HON book; origin; main; real; (counter for slender objects)
本 *hon* book.   本人 *honnin* the person himself.   本名 *honmyō* real name.   本土 #72 *hondo* mainland.   一本、二本、三本 *ippon, nihon, sanbon* 1, 2, 3 bottles (of beer).

#28 冊	5 strokes	丨 冂 冊 冊 冊

ON   SATSU book; (counter for books); SAKU card
冊子 #121 *sasshi* booklet.   短冊 #104 *tanzaku* strip of fancy paper (for writing poetry).   一冊、二冊、三冊 *issatsu, nisatsu, sansatsu* 1, 2, 3 books.

#29 巻	9 strokes	丶 丷 凷 巻 巻 巻

kun   *maki* volume, roll; *ma(ku)* roll
一の巻 *ichi no maki* Volume 1.   一巻き *hitomaki* a roll (of silk).
巻く *maku* roll up (a carpet).

ON   KAN volume; (counter for volumes)
第一巻 *daiikkan* Volume 1.   一巻、二巻、三巻 *ikkan, nikan, sankan* 1, 2, 3 volumes.

#30 部	11 strokes	亠 产 音 音 音 部

ON   BU part, section; (counter for copies) Ir. *he(ya)** #448
一部 *ichibu* a part, a section.   本部 *honbu* headquarters, head office.   一部、二部、三部 *ichibu, nibu, sanbu* 1, 2, 3 copies.

#31 才	3 strokes	一 十 才

ON   SAI talent; (counter for ages) Ir. *(hata)chi**
才能 #617 *sainō* talent.   天才 #335 *tensai* genius.   一才、二才、三才 *issai, nisai, sansai* 1, 2, 3 years old.   二十才 *hatachi** 20 years old.

#32 台 — 5 strokes

ON DAI, TAI stand, platform, base; (counter for machines)
台 *dai* stand, platform. テレビの台 *terebi no dai* TV stand. 百円台 *hyakuendai* 100-yen level. 台本 *daihon* script. 台風 #350 *taifū* typhoon. 一台、二台、三台 *ichidai, nidai, sandai* 1, 2, 3 mchines.

#33 足 — 7 strokes

kun *ashi* foot, leg; *ta(riru), ta(ru)* be enough; *ta(su)* add
足 *ashi* foot, leg. これで足りますか *Kore de tarimasu ka* Is this enough?. 足らない *taranai* be not enough. 一つ足す *hitotsu tasu* add one more.

ON SOKU foot, leg; be enough; (counter for pairs of shoes/socks)
遠足 #112 *ensoku* excursion. 満足 ‹v› #282 *manzoku* satisfaction. 不足 ‹v› #405 *fusoku* shortage. 一足、二足、三足 *issoku, nisoku, sanzoku* 1, 2, 3 pairs of shoes/socks.

#34 回 — 6 strokes

kun *mawa(ru)* go round; *mawa(su)* spin, pass round
回る *mawaru* go round, turn round. こまを回す *koma o mawasu* spin a top. バターを回す *batā o mawasu* pass the butter.

ON KAI, [E] turn; (counter for times)
回転 ‹v› #392 *kaiten* turning, rotation. 回向 #388 *ekō* Buddhist memorial service. 一回、二回、三回 *ikkai, nikai, sankai* 1, 2, 3 times.

#35 度 — 9 strokes

kun *tabi* time, occasion
この度 *kono tabi* this time. 度々 *tabitabi* frequently. 数える度に *kazoeru tabi ni* each time one counts.

ON DO, [TO], [TAKU] degree, measure; (counter for times/degrees).
度をすごす *do o sugosu* go too far. 支度 ‹v› #509 *shitaku* preparation. 法度 #599 *hatto* law; ban. 一度、二度、三度 *ichido, nido, sando* 1, 2, 3 times/degrees.

#36 機	16 strokes 木　杉　桜　桜　機　機

kun *hata* loom
機 *hata* loom.　機をおる *hata o oru* weave.

ON KI machine; occasion; (counter for aircrafts)
ジェット機 *jetto-ki* jet plane.　コピー機 *kopī-ki* copy machine.　機
会 #321 *kikai* opportunity, occasion.　一機、二機、三機 *ikki, niki,*
sanki 1, 2, 3 airplanes.

#37 着	12 strokes 　丷　羊　羊　羊　着

kun *tsu(ku)* arrive; *ki(ru)* wear
着く *tsuku* reach, arrive (at a station).　着る *kiru* wear (a coat).

ON CHAKU, [JAKU] arrival; (counter for clothes); (order for coming in).　シカゴ着 *Shikago-chaku* arriving at Chicago.　着々と *cha-*
kuchaku to steadily, step by step.　一着、二着、三着 *itchaku,*
nichaku, sanchaku 1, 2, 3 suits; 1st, 2nd, 3rd place (in a race).

#38 倍	10 strokes 亻　亻　位　位　倍　倍

ON BAI double; (counter for duplication)
倍 *bai* double, twice.　倍になる *bai ni naru* double.　一倍、二倍、
三倍 *ichibai, nibai, sanbai* 1, 2, 3 times.　数倍 *sūbai* several times.

#39 個	10 strokes 亻　亻　们　佃　個　個

ON KO individual; (counter for various objects)
個人 *kojin* an individual.　個々の *koko no* indivisual, separate.　一
個、二個、三個 *ikko, niko, sanko* 1, 2, 3 things.

#40 戸	4 strokes 一　ヲ　ヨ　戸

kun *to* door
戸 *to* door.　戸棚 *todana* cupboard.

ON KO (counter for houses)
戸数 *kosū* number of houses.　一戸、二戸、三戸 *ikko, niko, sanko*
1, 2, 3 houses.

#41 枚	8 strokes	十　木　朾　朾　杉　枚

ON　MAI (counter for thin, flat objects)
枚数 *maisū* number of sheets.　一枚、二枚、三枚 *ichimai, nimai, sanmai* 1, 2, 3 sheets (of paper).

#42 羽	6 strokes	丁　羽　羽　羽　羽　羽

kun　*ha, hane* feather, wing; (counter for birds)
羽 *hane* feather, wing.　羽のある *hane no aru* feathered, winged.
一羽、三羽、六羽 *ichiwa, sanba, roppa* 1, 3, 6 birds.

ON　U feather, wing
羽毛 #483 *umō* feathers, down.

#43 階	12 strokes	ﾉ　阝　阝ﾄ　阝比　阝比　階

ON　KAI stair, story, level; (counter for floors)
この階 *kono kai* this floor.　八階のビル *hachikai no biru* 8-story building.　一階、二階、三階 *ikkai, nikai, sangai* 1st, 2nd, 3rd floor.

■ II. Vocabulary ■

百円、千円、一万円	*hyakuen, sen'en, ichiman'en*	100, 1,000, 10,000 yen
一人、二人、三人	*hitori, futari, sannin*	1, 2, 3 people
一名、二名、三名	*ichimei, nimei, sanmei*	1, 2, 3 people
一本、二本、三本	*ippon, nihon, sanbon*	1, 2, 3 bottles (of beer)
一冊、二冊、三冊	*issatsu, nisatsu, sansatsu*	1, 2, 3 books.
一巻、二巻、三巻	*ikkan, nikan, sankan*	1, 2, 3 volumes
一部、二部、三部	*ichibu, nibu, sanbu*	1, 2, 3 copies
一才、二才、三才	*issai, nisai, sansai*	1, 2, 3 years old
一台、二台、三台	*ichidai, nidai sandai*	1, 2, 3 machines
一足、二足、三足	*issoku, nisoku, sanzoku*	1, 2, 3 pairs of shoes/socks
一回、二回、三回	*ikkai, nikai, sankai*	1, 2, 3 times
一度、二度、三度	*ichido, nido, sando*	1, 2, 3 times/degrees
一機、二機、三機	*ikki, niki, sanki*	1, 2, 3 airplanes

一着、二着、三着	*itchaku, nichaku, sanchaku*	1, 2, 3 suits; 1st, 2nd, 3rd place (in a race)
一倍、二倍、三倍	*ichibai, nibai, sanbai*	1, 2, 3 times
一個、二個、三個	*ikko, niko, sanko*	1, 2, 3 things
一戸、二戸、三戸	*ikko, niko, sanko*	1, 2, 3 houses
一枚、二枚、三枚	*ichimai, nimai, sanmai*	1, 2, 3 sheets (of paper)
一羽、三羽、六羽	*ichiwa, sanba, roppa*	1, 3, 6 birds
一階、二階、三階	*ikkai, nikai, sangai*	1st, 2nd, 3rd floor

■ III. Reading Exercises 2 ■

Read and translate the followeing.

1. 円いテーブルが二つといすが八つあります。
2. 本が三冊とノートが四、五冊あります。
3. オフィスにコピー機が二台あります。
4. 戸棚にさらが十枚と、コップが六個と、ナイフが十二本ある。
5. あそこにアメリカ人が二人います。
6. そのグループにカナダ人が数名いました。
7. ジムは十九才でサラは二十才です。
8. かもめが三羽えさをあさっています。
9. 戸数が二倍になった。
10. 台本を三部もらえませんか。
11. 本部はあのビルの十三階です。
12. メリーゴーランドが四回回って、ストップした。
13. このレポートをもう一度回してください。
14. 人数を数える度に一人足りません。
15. ジェット機が二機着いたところです。
16. ドイツ人がマラソンで一着になりました。
17. その人はスーツが六着と、くつが八足あります。
18. この本の第一巻は三千二百円で、第二巻は二千五百円です。

3

****

Time Expressions (1)

Days

■ **I. Reference** ■

| #44 | 日 | 4 strokes | 丨 冂 月 日 |

    kun   *hi* day; sun; *-ka* day Ir. *(tsui)tachi**; *Ni(hon/ppon)**; *(kyo)o** #45
(kino)o*#46; *(a)su** #47
日 *hi* day; sun. その日 *sono hi* that day. 日差し #362 *hizashi*
sunlight. 日々 *hibi* days. 一日 *tsuitachi** 1st of the month. 二日
futsuka* 2nd of the month; 2 days. 五日 *itsuka* 5th; 5 days. 六日
muika 6th; 6 days. 七日 *nanoka/nanuka** 7th; 7 days. 八日 *yōka*
8th; 8 days. 九日 *kokonoka* 9th; 9 days. 二十日 *hatsuka** 20th;
20 days.

    ON   NICHI, JITSU day; sun
一日 *ichinichi/ichijitsu* 1 day. 日光 #379 *nikkō* sunshine. 日本
Nihon*/*Nippon** Japan.

| #45 | 今 | 4 strokes | ノ 人 㕮 今 |

    kun   *ima* now Ir. *kyo(o)**; *ko(toshi)**#60; *ke(sa)** #93
今 *ima* now. 今のところ *ima no tokoro* for the time bing. 今日
kyō* today.

    ON   KON, KIN now
今日 *konnichi* today, nowadays. 今日は *Konnichi wa* Good day.
今度 *kondo* this time; next time. 今上陛下 #904 *kinjōheika* reigning emperor.

| #46 | 昨 | 9 strokes | 丨 冂 日' 旷 昨 昨 |

    kun   Ir. *kino(o)**
昨日 *kinō** yesterday.

ON　SAKU last, past

昨日 *sakujitsu* yesterday.　一昨日 *issakujitsu* day before yesterday.
昨今 *sakkon* these days.

#47 明	8 strokes　｜　冂　日　明　明　明

kun　*aka(ri)* light; *aka(rui)* bright; *aki(raka)* clear; *a(keru)* dawn
明かり *akari* light, lamp.　明るい *akarui* bright, light; cheerful.　明
らかな *akiraka na* clear, obvious.　明けましておめでとう *Ake-mashite omedetō* Happy New Year!　明日 *asu** tomorrow.

ON　MEI light; MYŌ light; next
明日 *myōnichi* tomorrow.　光明 #379 *kōmyō* light, rays.　未明 #178
mimei dawn.　照明 #349 *shōmei* lighting.

#48 休	6 strokes　ノ　イ　仁　什　休　休

kun　*yasu(mu)* rest, take a day off; *yasu(mi)* rest, vacation, holiday
休む *yasumu* rest; not attend.　休み *yasumi* rest, break; holiday.
一休み *hitoyasumi* short break.　休み明け *yasumiake* after the
vacation.

ON　KYŪ rest, vacation, holiday
休日 *kyūjitsu* holiday, day off.　休息 (い) #134 *kyūsoku* rest, repose.

#49 祭	11 strokes　ノ　夕　夕ヲ　夕又　祭　祭

kun　*matsu(ru)* enshrine, worship; *matsu(ri)* festival
祭る *matsuru* enshrine (a god), worship (one's ancestors).　祭り
matsuri festival.　きく祭り *kiku matsuri* chrysanthemum festival.

ON　SAI festival
祭日 *saijitsu* holiday, festival day.　文化祭 #723 *bunkasai* cultural
festival.

#50 祝	9 strokes　ラ　ネ　ネ　礻ㄱ　祀　祝

kun　*iwa(u)* celebrate; *iwa(i)* celebration Ir. *nori(to)**#603
祝う *iwau* celebrate.　お祝い *o-iwai* celebration.

ON　SHUKU, [SHŪ] celebration
祝日 *shukujitsu* national holiday.　祝言 #566 *shūgen* wedding.

連 10 strokes 一 一 亘 車 連 連

kun   *tsura(naru)* range; *tsu(reru)* take along; *tsu(re)* companion
連なる *tsuranaru* range, lie in a row.   連れていく *tsurete iku* take someone along.   連れ *tsure* companion.   二人連れ *futarizure* a couple, 2 people.

ON   REN group, accompaniment
連休 *renkyū* consecutive holidays.   連日 *renjitsu* everyday, day after day.   連名 *renmei* joint signature.   一連の *ichiren no* a series (of events).

■ II. Vocabulary ■

一日	*tsuitachi*	1st of the month
	ichinichi/ichijitsu	1 day
二日	*futsuka*	2nd; 2 days
三日	*mikka*	3rd; 3 days
四日	*yokka*	4th; 4 days.
五日	*itsuka*	5th; 5 days.
六日	*muika*	6th; 6 days.
七日	*nanoka/nanuka*	7th; 7 days.
八日	*yōka*	8th; 8 days.
九日	*kokonoka*	9th; 9 days.
十日	*tōka*	10th; 10 days.
十四日	*jūyokka*	14th; 14 days.
十八日	*jūhachinichi*	18th; 18 days.
二十日	*hatsuka*	20th; 20 days.
三十日	*sanjūnichi*	30th; 30 days.
今日	*kyō/konnichi*	today.
明日	*asu/myōnichi*	tomorrow.
昨日	*kinō/sakujitsu*	yesterday.
一昨日	*issakujitsu*	day before yesterday.
休み	*yasumi*	rest, break; holiday.
休日	*kyūjitsu*	holiday, day off.
連休	*renkyū*	consecutive holidays.
連日	*renjitsu*	everyday, day after day.

祭り	*matsuri*	festival.
祭日	*saijitsu*	holiday, festival day.
お祝い	*o-iwai*	celebration.
祝日	*shukujitsu*	national holiday

■ III. Reading Exercises 3 ■

Read and translate the following.

1. 今日は三日です。
2. 昨日は祝日でした。
3. 一昨日、お祝いのパーティーをしました。
4. 七日と二十日に祭りがあります。
5. 明日は祭日なので、休みます。
6. パリからのジェット機は今着いたところです。
7. 今度の休みは十四日です。
8. 休日は連れとテニスをします。
9. 二十九日から五日の連休です。
10. 日が明るいので、連日ゴルフをやっています。

Months and Years

#52 月	4 strokes	) 几 月 月

kun   *tsuki* month, moon Ir. *(sa)mi(dare)** #340

月 *tsuki* month, moon. この月 *kono tsuki* this month. 月日 *tsukihi* months and days; time. 五月 *satsuki** May. 三日月 *mikazuki* crescent.

ON   GETSU month, moon; GATSU month

今月 *kongetsu* this month. 一か月 *ikkagetsu̥* 1 month. 名月 *meigetsu* bright moon. 一月 *ichigatsu* January. 二月 *nigatsu* February.

#53 来	7 strokes	一 ㄇ 立 平 来 来

kun   *ku(ru)* come; *kita(ru)* coming

来る *kuru* come. 来る五日 *kitaru itsuka* coming 5th.

ON   RAI come; next, coming; since

来月 *raigetsu* next month. 数日来 *sūjitsurai* for the past few days. 来日‹v› *rainichi* coming to Japan. 本来 *honrai* originally.

#54 行	6 strokes	′ ⼃ 彳 彳 行 行

kun   *i(ku)*, *yu(ku)* go; *okona(u)* do, conduct Ir. *yuku(e)** #160

行く *iku/yuku* go. 来月行く *raigetsu iku* go next month. パリ行き *Pari-yuki* (a jet) bound for Paris. 行なう *okonau* do (business). 行い *okonai* act, behavior.

ON   KŌ, [AN] go; GYŌ line (of text)

一行 *ikkō* a party (of 5). 行進‹v› #831 *kōshin* march. 三行 *sangyō* 3 lines. 五行目 *gogyōme* 5th line.

#55 帰	10 strokes	） ）⼀ ）⼾ ）彐 帰 帰

kun   *kae(ru)* return

帰る *kaeru* return. 今月帰る *kongetsu kaeru* return this month. 日帰り ‹v› *higaeri* going and returning in one day. アメリカ帰り *Amerika-gaeri* one who returned from America.

ON   KI return

帰国 ‹v› #299 *kikoku* returning to one's own country.

#56

正   5 strokes   一　丁　下　正　正

kun   *tada(shii)* correct; *tada(su)* correct; *masa(ni)* exactly, indeed

正しい *tadashii* correct. 正す *tadasu* correct (an error). 正に *masa ni* exactly, indeed.

ON   SEI, SHŌ correct

正月 *shōgatsu* New Year; January. 正数 *seisū* positive number.

#57

先   6 strokes   ノ　←　┶　生　牜　先

kun   *saki* previous; ahead; future; destination; tip

先に *saki ni* previously, beforehand. 先程 #553 *sakihodo* a while ago. 行き先 *yukisaki* destination. ペン先 *pen-saki* tip of a pen.

ON   SEN previous; ahead; future

先月 *sengetsu* last month. 先々月 *sensengetsu* month before the last. 先日 *senjitsu* the other day. 先行 ‹v› *senkō* going ahead. 先着 ‹v› *senchaku* arriving before (others). 先見 #221 *senken* foresight.

#58

初   7 strokes   ラ　ネ　ネ　ネ　初　初

kun   *haji(me)* beginning; *haji(mete)* for the first time; *hatsu-, ui-* first; *-so(meru)* begin to

初め *hajime* beginning. 月初め *tsukihajime* beginning of the month. 初めて *hajimete* for the first time. 初物 #205 *hatsumono* first products of the season. 初々しい *uiuishii* innocent (maiden). 明け初める *akesomeru* begin to dawn.

ON   SHO beginning

初日 *shonichi* opening day, premiere. 初夏 #74 *shoka* early summer.

#59 末 5 strokes 一 二 十 才 末

kun   *sue* end

末 *sue* end. 六月の末 *rokugatsu no sue* end of June. 月末 *tsuki-zue* end of the month.

ON   MATSU, BATSU end

月末 *getsumatsu* end of the month. 三月末 *sangatsu matsu* end of March. 末席 #560 *basseki/masseki* lowest seat; bottom.

#60 年 6 strokes ノ ー 仁 仨 年 年

kun   *toshi* year

年 *toshi* year, age. 年の初め *toshi no hajime* beginning of the year. 年月 *toshitsuki* months and years, time. 今年 *kotoshi** this year.

ON   NEN year

年末 *nenmatsu* end of the year. 今年 *konnen* this year. 昨年 *sakunen* last year. 来年度 *rainendo* next fiscal year. 二千年 *nisennen* the year 2000. 年月 *nengetsu* months and years, time.

#61 去 5 strokes 一 十 土 去 去

kun   *sa(ru)* leave, depart; pass

去る *saru* leave (a place). 年月が去る *nengetsu ga saru* Time passes. 去る三月三日 *saru sangatsu mikka* last March 3.

ON   KYO, KO leave, depart; pass

去年 *kyonen* last year. 去来い *kyorai* coming and going. 過去 #176 *kako* past.

#62 翌 11 strokes フ ヲ ヲヨ 翌 翌 翌

ON   YOKU next, following

翌月 *yokugetsu* following month. 翌年 *yokunen* following year. 翌日 *yokujitsu* following day. 翌々日 *yokuyokujitsu* day after next.

#63 何	7 strokes ノ 广 仁 仁 何 何	

kun *nani, nan* what, how many

何 *nani* what. 何月 *nangatsu* what month. 何か月 *nankagetsu* how many months. 何年 *nannen* what year; how many years. 何日 *nannichi* what date; how many days. 何人 *nannin* how many people.

ON KA what
幾何 *kika* geometry.

■ II. Vocabulary

一月	*ichigatsu*	January
二月	*nigatsu*	Feburary
三月	*sangatsu*	March
四月	*shigatsu*	April
五月	*gogatsu*	May
六月	*rokugatsu*	June
七月	*shichigatsu*	July
八月	*hachigatsu*	August
九月	*kugatsu*	September
十月	*jūgatsu*	October
十一月	*jūichigatsu*	November
十二月	*jūnigatsu*	December
正月	*shōgatsu*	New Year; January
月初め	*tsukihajime*	beginning of the month
月末	*tsukizue/getsumatsu*	end of the month
今月	*kongetsu*	this month
来月	*raigetsu*	next month
先月	*sengetsu*	last month
翌月	*yokugetsu*	following month
一か月	*ikkagetsu*	1 month
年の初め	*toshi no hajime*	beginning of the year
今年	*kotoshi/konnen*	this year
去年	*kyonen*	last year
来年度	*rainendo*	next fiscal year

年末	*nenmatsu*	end of the year
何年	*nannen*	how many years; what year
来る・去る五日	*kitaru/saru itsuka*	coming/last 5th

■ III. Reading Exercises 4 ■

Read and translate the following.

1. 一月三日、四月六日、七月四日、八月八日、十一月十日、千九百八十五年
2. 今月の末にテストがあります。
3. 年末までにあと二、三日しかない。
4. 去年の六月にカナダへ行きました。
5. その一行は九日に着いて、翌日去りました。
6. 先月の初めにアメリカから帰りました。
7. すもうの初日は何日ですか。
8. 九月に祭日が二日あります。
9. 今年は初めて一か月の休みをとりました。
10. 昨年は二度パリへ行きました。
11. 来年の正月はハワイで祝います。
12. 来る二月四日、このホールでコンサートが行なわれます。
13. スミスさんが日本へ来てから何年になりますか。

Weeks

■ **I. Reference** ■

#64 週	11 strokes	ノ 月 冃 周 週 週

ON   SHŪ week

今週 *konshū* this week. 来週 *raishū* next week. 先週 *senshū* last week. 先々週 *sensenshū* week before the last. 週末 *shūmatsu* weekend. 来週末 *raishūmatsu* next weekend. 週日 *shūjitsu* weekday. 週休 *shūkyū* weekly holiday.

#65 間	12 strokes	l ｌ 門 門 問 間

kun   *aida* space, interval; *ma* space, interval, time; room.

間 *aida* space, interval. 一年の間 *ichinen no aida* for 1 year. 行と行の間 *gyō to gyō no aida* space between the lines. 間がある *ma ga aru* have time. 二間 *futama* 2 rooms.

ON   KAN, KEN space, interval

一週間 *isshūkan* 1 week. 三日間 *mikkakan* for 3 days. 年間 *nenkan* yearly, a year. 人間 *ningen* human being.

#66 毎	6 strokes	ノ ⌐ ⌐ 勹 勾 毎

ON   MAI every, each

毎週 *maishū* every week. 毎日 *mainichi* every week. 毎月 *maitsuki/maigetsu* every month. 毎年 *maitoshi/mainen* every year. 毎度 *maido* every/each time. 毎回 *maikai* every/each time.

#67 曜	18 strokes	冂 日ヨ 日ヨヨ 曜ヨ 曜丰 曜

ON   YŌ day of the week

月曜日 *gatsuyōbi* Monday. 毎月曜日 *maigetsuyōbi* every Monday. 第三日曜日 *daisan nichiyōbi* 3rd Sunday. 何曜日 *nan'yōbi* what day of the week.

#68 火	4 strokes	丶　丶丶　少　火

kun *hi, [ho]* fire

火 *hi* fire.　火鉢 *hibachi* charcoal brazier.　火影 *hokage* a flicker of light.

ON KA fire

火曜日 *kayōbi* Tuesday.　四月六日〔火〕 *shigatsu muika (ka)* (Tues) April 6.

#69 水	4 strokes	丿　刁　才　水

kun *mizu* water

水 *mizu* water.　水着 *mizugi* swimming suit.

ON SUI water

水曜日 *suiyōbi* Wednesday.　月・火・水 *getsu-ka-sui* Mon., Tues., Wed.

#70 木	4 strokes	一　十　才　木

kun *ki, [ko]* tree, wood Ir. *mo(men)*＊#486

木 *ki* tree.　木々 *kigi* trees.　木の葉 #210 *ko no ha* tree leaves.

ON BOKU, MOKU tree, wood

木曜日 *mokuyōbi* Thursday.　木刀 #941 *bokutō* wooden sword.

#71 金	8 strokes	丿　人　仐　余　金　金

kun *kane* money; metal; *kana* metal

金 *kane* money.　金の鉢 *kane no hachi* metal bowl.　金物 #205 *kanamono* hardware.

ON KIN, KON gold, metal

金 *kin* gold.　.　金曜日 *kin'yōbi* Friday.　金属 #762 *kinzoku* metal. 金色 #229 *konjiki* gold color.

#72 土	3 strokes	一　十　土

kun *tsuchi* earth, soil, ground Ir. *mi(yage)*＊#827

土 *tsuchi* earth, soil.　土をほる *tsuchi o horu* dig in the ground.

ON   DO, TO earth, soil, ground

土曜日 *doyōbi* Saturday.   本土 *hondo* mainland.   土人 *dojin* native.   土地 #246 *tochi* land.

■ II. Vocabulary ■

日曜日	*nichiyōbi*	Sunday
月曜日	*getsuyōbi*	Monday
火曜日	*kayōbi*	Tuesday
水曜日	*suiyōbi*	Wednesday
木曜日	*mokuyōbi*	Thursday
金曜日	*kin'yōbi*	Friday
土曜日	*doyōbi*	Saturday
何曜日	*nan'yōbi*	what day of the week
第三日曜日	*daisan nichiyōbi*	3rd Sunday
月・火・水	*getsu-ka-sui*	Mon., Tues., Wed.
今週	*konshū*	this week
来週	*raishū*	next week
先週	*senshū*	last week
先々週	*sensenshū*	week before the last
毎週	*maishū*	every week
毎月曜日	*maigetsuyōbi*	every Monday
週日	*shūjitsu*	weekday
週末	*shūmatsu*	weekend
来週末	*raishūmatsu*	next weekend
一週間	*isshūkan*	1 week

■ III. Reading Exercises 5 ■

Read and translate the following.
1. 今日は**何曜日**ですか。
2. 昨日は**火曜日**でした。
3. **金曜日**にピクニックがある。
4. **毎週**、**土曜日**か**日曜日**にテニスをします。
5. **先週**ゴルフのコンペがあった。

6. 一**週**間に三度クイズがあります。

7. **今週**は一度もジムへ行かなかった。

8. **月・火・水**にジョッギングをします。

9. デパートは**毎月曜日**に休みます。

10. **週日**はスーパーへ行く**間**がありません。

11. お**金**がないから、**来週末**はどこへも行けない。

12. コンサートは今月の第三**木曜日**に行なわれる。

Seasons

■ I. Reference ■

#73 春	9 strokes	一 丰 夫 夫 春 春

kun   *haru* spring
春 *haru* spring.   春休み *haruyasumi* spring vacation.

ON   SHUN spring
来春 *raishun* next spring.   今春 *konshun* this spring.   春分 #81 *shunbun* vernal equinox.

#74 夏	10 strokes	一 ア 百 頁 夏 夏

kun   *natsu* summer
夏 *natsu* summer.   夏休み *natsuyasumi* summer vacation.   夏着 *natsugi* summer clothes.

ON   KA, [GE] sumer
初夏 *shoka* early summer.   夏至 #805 *geshi* summer solstice.

#75 秋	9 strokes	二 禾 禾 秒 秋 秋

kun   *aki* autumn, fall
秋 *aki* autumn, fall.   秋祭り *akimatsuri* autumn festival.

ON   SHŪ autumn, fall
今秋 *konshū* this autumn.   初秋 *shoshū* early autumn.   春秋 *shunjū* spring and autumn; years.   秋分 #81 *shūbun* autumnal equinox.

#76 冬	5 strokes	ノ ク 冬 冬 冬

kun   *fuyu* winter
冬 *fuyu* winter.   冬休み *fuyuyasumi* winter vacation.   冬着 *fuyugi* winer clothes.   冬日 *fuyubi* winter sun.

ON   TŌ winter
初冬 *shotō* early winter.   春夏秋冬 *shunka shūtō* 4 seasons; all the year round.   冬至 #805 *tōji* winter solstice.

#77 立	5 strokes	` 一 亠 广 立 立

kun *ta(tsu)* stand (up); *ta(teru)* set up, raise

立つ *tatsu* stand (up).　立てる *tateru* set (a book on edge).　目立つ *medatsu* stand out, be conspicuous.

ON RITSU, [RYŪ] stand (up)

立春 *risshun* 1st day of spring.　立夏 *rikka* 1st day of summer.　立秋 *risshū* 1st day of autumn.　立冬 *rittō* 1st day of winter.　建立⟨v⟩ #534 *konryū* constructing (of a Buddhist temple).

#78 季	8 strokes	二 千 禾 禾 季 季

ON KI season

四季 *shiki* 4 seasons.　春季 *shunki* spring season.　夏季 *kaki* summer season.　秋季 *shūki* autumn season.　冬季 *tōki* winter season. 年季 *nenki* apprenticeship; experience.

#79 節	13 strokes	⺮ 竺 笁 笸 節 節

kun *fushi* joint; melody

節 *fushi* joint (in a bamboo/a body).　節々 *fushibushi* joints. かなしい節 *kanashii fushi* sad melody

ON SETSU, [SECHI] season; occasion; paragraph; moderation

季節 *kisetsu* season.　おひまの節は *o-hima no setsu wa* when you are free.　第二節 *dainisetsu* 2nd paragraph.　節度 *setsudo* moderation.　お節 *osechi* osechi cuisine (dishes for the New Year).

■ II. Vocabulary ■

季節	*kisetsu*	season
四季	*shiki*	4 seasons
春	*haru*	spring
夏	*natsu*	summer
秋	*aki*	autumn, fall
冬	*fuyu*	winter
夏季	*kaki*	summer season

冬季	*tōki*	winter season
来春	*raishun*	next spring
今秋	*konshū*	this autumn
立春	*risshun*	1st day of spring
立秋	*risshū*	1st day of autumn
春秋	*shunjū*	spring and autumn; years
春夏秋冬	*shunka shūtō*	4 seasons; all the year round
初夏	*shoka*	early summer
初冬	*shotō*	early winter
春分	*shunbun*	vernal equinox
秋分	*shūbun*	autumnal equinox
夏至	*geshi*	summer solstice
冬至	*tōji*	winter solstice

■ III. Reading Exercises 6 ■

Read and translate the following.

1. 秋はスポーツの季節です。
2. 日本には四季 —— 春、夏、秋、冬がある。
3. おひまの節は来てください。
4. 春休みは何週間ですか。
5. 今週の水曜日は春分です。
6. ブラウンさんは来春ヨーロッパから帰ります。
7. 冬にはスキーに行きます。
8. 今年の立冬は何日ですか。
9. かれは冬季オリンピックで金メダルを二つもらった。
10. まだ夏なのに初秋のようですね。
11. 今日から五月。もう初夏ですね。
12. 去年の夏至は八月の第三火曜日でした。

4

****

Time Expressions (2)

Time and Hours

■ I. Reference ■

#80 時	10 strokes	冂 日一 日土 昨 時 時

kun   *toki* time; hour Ir. *to(kei)* *#99; *shi(gure)* *#340
時 *toki* time; hour. 時がたつ *Toki ga tatsu* Time passes. どんな時にも *donna toki ni mo* at any time. 時々 *tokidoki* sometimes.

ON   JI time; hour
一時 *ichiji* 1 o'clock. 時間 *jikan* time; hour. 二時間 *nijikan* 2 hours. 何時 *nanji* what time. 何時間 *nanjikan* how many hours. 行く時間 *iku jikan* time to go.

#81 分	4 strokes	ノ 八 分 分

kun   *wa(keru)* devide; *wa(kareru)* be devided; *wa(karu)* understand
分ける *wakeru* devide (a thing). 分かれる *wakareru* be devided (into 2 parts). 分かる *wakaru* understand.

ON   BUN, BU part, share; FUN minute
春分 *shunbun* vernal equinox. 秋分 *shūbun* autumal equinox. 五分 *gofun* 5 minutes. 十分 *juppun/jippun* 10 minutes. 十分な *jūbun na* enough. 五分五分 *gobugobu* fifty-fifty.

#82 秒	9 strokes	二 禾 利 利 秒 秒

ON   BYŌ second (of time)
一秒 *ichibyō* 1 second. 数秒 *sūbyō* a few seconds. 二分三十秒 *nifun sanjūbyō* 2 minutes 30 seconds.

#83 半	5 strokes	丶　丷　⺌　⺍　半

kun *naka(ba)* half

三月の半ば *sangatsu no nakaba* mid-March.

ON HAN half

四時半 *yoji-han* half past 4.　半年 *hantoshi* a half year.　半日 *hannichi* a half day.　半分 *hanbun* half.

#84 前	9 strokes	丷　广　艹　肖　前　前

kun *mae* before, in front of

前 *mae* before, in front of.　八時前 *hachiji mae* before 8 o'clock. ビルの前 *biru no mae* in front of a building.　人前で *hitomae de* in public.　名前 *namae* name.　分け前 *wakemae* one's share.

ON ZEN before, in front of

前日 *zenjitsu* previous day.　前半 *zenhan* 1st half (of a game).　前回 *zenkai* last time.　目前に *mokuzen ni* before one's eyes.

#85 午	4 strokes	ノ　⺅　⺂　午

ON GO noon

午前 *gozen* morning.　午前九時半 *gozen kuji-han* 9:30 A.M.　正午 *shōgo* noon

#86 後	9 strokes	⺯　彳　彳　彳　彷　後　後

kun *nochi* after, later; *ushi(ro)* behind; *ato* afterward; back; *oku(reru)* be behind

後程 #553 *nochihodo* later.　三日後 *mikka nochi* 3 days later.　後ろ *ushiro* behind.　後で *ato de* later.　後にさがる *ato ni sagaru* stay back.　後れる *okureru* be behind (in one's work).

ON GO after, later; KŌ behind

午後 *gogo* afternoon.　午後二時 *gogo niji* 2 P.M.　今後 *kongo* hereafter.　明後日 *myōgonichi* day after tomorrow.　前後 *zengo* front and behind; before and after.　後方の #160 *kōhō no* rear.

#87 起	10 strokes	＋　　キ　　キ　　走　　起　　起

kun *o(kiru)* get up; occur; *o(koru)* occur; *o(kosu)* wake up (someone); give rise to

起きる *okiru* get up (at 6); (Accidents) occur.　起こる *okoru* occur.　起こす *okosu* wake up (someone); give rise to (a riot).

ON KI get up

起立 ‹v› *kiritsu* standing up.　起草 #208 ‹v› *kisō* drafting.

#88 中	4 strokes	｜　　冂　　口　　中

kun *naka* middle, inside, through

中 *naka* the inside, in the middle.　かごの中 *kago no naka* in the basket.　この中で *kono naka de* among these.

ON CHŪ middle, inside, through

午前中 *gozenchū* in the morning.　日中 *nitchū* in the daytime.　一日中 *ichinichijū* all day long.　日本中 *Nihonjū* throughout Japan.

#89 以	5 strokes	｜　　ｼ　　ㇱ　　ㇱ／　　以

ON I from

二時以後 *nijiigo* after 2 o'clock.　四月以来 *shigatsu irai* since April.　以前 *izen* formerly.

#90 上	3 strokes	一　　卜　　上

kun *ue* upper; [*uwa*] , *kami* upper part; *a(geru)* raise; give; *a(garu)*, *nobo(ru)* go up, rise

上 *ue* on, above; top.　上着 *uwagi* coat, jacket.　上回る *uwamawaru* surpass.　川上 #266 *kawakami* upstream.　上げる *ageru* raise (one's salary); give (a gift).　上がる *agaru* go up (a slope); (Prices) rise.　上る *noboru* go up (a slope).

ON JŌ, [SHŌ] upper, above

二時間以上 *nijikan ijō* more than 2 hours.　上部 *jōbu* upper part.　水上スキー *suijō sukī* water skiing.　上人 *shōnin* saint.

#91 下	3 strokes 一 丁 下

kun *shita* under; *shimo* lower part; *moto* under; *sa(geru)* lower; *sa(garu), ku(daru)* go down; *kuda(saru)* give; *o(riru)* get down Ir. *he(ta)**#440

下 *shita* under, beneath; bottom. 川下 #266 *kawashimo* downstream. 名人の下で *meijin no moto de* (study) under the expert. 下げる *sageru* lower (the price). 下がる *sagaru* (Prices) go down. 下る *kudaru* go down (a hill). 下さる *kudasaru* give (honorific). 下りる *oriru* get down (from a tree).

ON KA, GE under, below

二時間以下 *nijikan ika* less than 2 hours. 部下 *buka* subordinate follower. 上下に *jōge ni* up and down. 下水 *gesui* sewage

#92 丁	2 strokes 一 丁

ON CHŌ block (of a town); unit of length; TEI No. 4, D

六本木二丁目 *Roppongi ni-chōme* 2-chome, Roppongi. 丁度 *chōdo* exactly, just. 五時丁度 *goji chōdo* exactly 5 o'clock.

#93 朝	12 strokes 十 宁 古 卓 朝 朝

kun *asa* morning Ir. *(ke)sa**

朝 *asa* morning. 毎朝 *maiasa* every morning. 今朝 *kesa** this morning. 朝日 *asahi* morning sun.

ON CHŌ morning; dynasty

翌朝 *yokuchō* next morning. 来朝⟨v⟩ *raichō* coming to Japan. 帰朝⟨v⟩ *kichō* returning to Japan. 平安朝 #469 *Heianchō* Heian Dynasty/period.

#94 昼	9 strokes 一 尸 尺 尽 昼 昼

kun *hiru* daytime, noon

昼 *hiru* daytime, noon. 昼間 *hiruma* daytime. 昼休み *hiruyasumi* noon recess. 昼下がり *hirusagari* early afternoon.

ON CHŪ daytime, noon

昼間 *chūkan* daytime. 昼食 #395 *chūshoku* lunch.

#95 夜	8 strokes	亠 广 疒 厷 厷 夜

kun   *yo, yoru* night

夜 *yoru* night.   夜中 *yonaka* midnight.   夜明け *yoake* dawn.

ON   YA night

今夜 *kon'ya* tonight.   昨夜 *sakuya* last night.   夜間 *yakan* night-time.   昼夜 *chūya* day and night.   夜半 *yahan* midnight.

#96 晩	12 strokes	冂 日' 旷 旷 晄 晩

ON   BAN evening, night

晩 *ban* evening, night.   今晩 *konban* tonight.   明晩 *myōban* tomorrow night.   毎晩 *maiban* every night.   朝晩 *asaban* morning and night.   三晩 *miban* 3 night.   晩春 *banshun* late spring.

#97 夕	3 strokes	ノ ク 夕

kun   *yū* evening Ir. *(tana)bata**

朝夕 *asayū* morning and evening.   夕方 #160 *yūgata* evening.   夕日 *yūhi* evening/setting sun.   ショパンの夕べ *Shopan no yūbe* a Chopin evening.   七夕 *tanabata** Star Festival.

ON   SEKI evening

一朝一夕 *itchō isseki* in a day, in a short time.

#98 早	6 strokes	丨 冂 冃 日 旦 早

kun   *haya(i)* early

早い *hayai* early.   朝早く *asa hayaku* early in the morning.   早目に *hayame ni* a little earlier.   早起き *hayaoki* getting up early.

ON   SŌ, [SA'] early

早朝 *sōchō* early in the morning.   早春 *sōshun* early spring.   来月早々 *raigetsu sōsō* early next month.   早急に #809 *sōkyū/sakkyū ni* in a hurry.

| #99 計 | 9 strokes | 一 言 言 言 計 計 |

kun *haka(ru)* measure; plan
計る *hakaru* measure (the length); plan (a picnic).　計らい *hakarai* arrangement.

ON KEI measure; plan
時計 *tokei** watch, clock.　計二千円 *kei nisen'en* 2,000 yen in total.
一年の計 *ichinen no kei* plans for the year.

| #100 合 | 6 strokes | ノ 人 今 合 合 合 |

kun *a(u)* fit, be correct; *a(waseru)* put together; set
合う *au* fit, suit, match.　間に合う *ma ni au* be in time; be enough.　時計が合っている *Tokei ga atte iru* The clock is correct.
合わせる *awaseru* put together; set (a watch).

ON GŌ, GA', [KA'] put together Ir. *ga(ten)** #581
合計 *gōkei* total.　合唱 ⟨v⟩ #671 *gasshō* chorus.　合戦 #630 *kassen* battle.

| #101 止 | 4 strokes | 一 ト 止 止 |

kun *to(maru)* stop, halt; *to(meru)* stop, turn off Ir. *(ha)to(ba)** #354
止まる *tomaru* stop.　時計が止まる *Tokei ga tomaru* A clock stops.
止める *tomeru* stop, turn off (a machine).　行き止まり *yukidomari* dead end.

ON SHI stop, halt
中止 ⟨v⟩ *chūshi* suspension.　一時休止 *ichiji kyūshi* out of service for a time.

| #102 針 | 10 strokes | ノ 今 午 金 金 針 |

kun *hari* needle
針 *hari* needle.　時計の針 *tokei no hari* hands of a watch.　針金 *harigane* wire.

ON SHIN needle
分針 *funshin* minute hand.　秒針 *byōshin* second hand.

#103 長	8 strokes	丨 ｆ 巨 長 長 長

kun   *naga(i)* long

長い *nagai* long.   長年 *naganen* for many years.

ON   CHŌ long; chief, head

長針 *chōshin* minute hand.   年長の *nenchō no* older, senior.   長上 *chōjō* one's senior.   部長 *buchō* department head.

#104 短	12 strokes	㇑ 矢 知 知 知 短

kun   *mijika(i)* short

短い *mijikai* short

ON   TAN short

短針 *tanshin* hour hand.   短時間 *tanjikan* in short time.   長短 *chō-tan* length; merits and demerits.   短冊 *tanzaku* strip of fancy paper (for writing poetry).

#105 出	5 strokes	丨 屮 中 屮 出

kun   *de(ru)* go/come out; *da(su)* put out; send; submit

出る *deru* go/come out (of a place).   出す *dasu* put out (a magazine); send (a card); submit (a report).   日の出 *hi no de* sunrise. 出足 *deashi* start.   出前 *demae* home delivery (from a restaurant). 出来る *dekiru* can (do).   出回る *demawaru* come on (to the market).

ON   SHUTSU, [SUI] go/come out, put out; send; submit

出火 ⟨v⟩ *shukka* outbreak of fire.   提出 ⟨v⟩ #574 *teishutsu* presentation.   出納 #512 *suitō* receipts and disbursements.

#106 入	2 strokes	ノ 入

kun   *i(ru), hai(ru)* enter; *i(reru)* put in

入る・入る *iru/hairu* enter (a place).   入れる *ireru* put (a thing) in. 日の入り *hi no iri* sunset.   金入れ *kaneire* cashbox; wallet.

ON   NYŪ enter, put in

出入 ⟨v⟩ *shutsunyū* coming and going.   入学 ⟨v⟩ #523 *nyūgaku* entering a school.

■ II. Vocabulary ■

時	*toki*	time; hour
時間	*jikan*	time; hour
一時	*ichiji*	1:00
二時五分	*niji gofun*	2:05
三時半	*sanji-han*	half past 3
四時前	*yoji mae*	before 4 o'clock
五時丁度	*goji chōdo*	exactly 5 o'clock
二分三十秒	*nifun sanjūbyō*	2 minutes 30 seconds
正午	*shōgo*	noon
午前	*gozen*	morning
午後	*gogo*	afternoon
後程・後で	*nochihodo/ato de*	later
午前七時	*gozen shichiji/nanaji*	7 A.M.
午後八時	*gogo hachiji*	8 P.M.
午前中	*gozenchū*	in the morning
二時間以上・以下	*nijikan ijō/ika*	more/less than 2 hours
三月の半ば	*sangatsu no nakaba*	mid-March
時計	*tokei*	watch, clock
間に合う	*ma ni au*	be in time; be enough
長い針	*nagai hari*	minute hand
短針	*tanshin*	hour hand
朝	*asa*	morning
早朝	*sōchō*	early in the morning
早起き〈v〉	*hayaoki*	getting up early
昼	*hiru*	daytime, noon
夜	*yoru*	night
昼夜	*chūya*	day and night
今夜	*kon'ya*	tonight
晩	*ban*	night
毎晩	*maiban*	every night
朝夕	*asayū*	morning and evening
日の出	*hi no de*	sunrise
日の入り	*hi no iri*	sunset

■ III. Reading Exercises 7 ■

Read and translate the following.

1. **七時**、**三時十分**、**四時五分前**、**六時半**、**八時丁度**、**一分二十秒**
2. **昼休**みは**正午**から**一時**までです。
3. 先週末は**一日中**ゴルフをした。
4. **時計**の**秒針**が**止**まっています。
5. 明日の**日の出**は**何時**ですか。
6. 九月の**半**ばには**朝夕**すずしくなる。
7. **毎朝**早く**起**きて、**三十分以上**ジョッギングをします。
8. **午前中**はいそがしいから、**三時以後**に来て下さい。
9. **今晩**は**早目**にオフィスを**出**て、ショパンの**夕**べに行くつもりです。
10. デパートは火曜日をのぞいては、**午前十時半**から**午後七時**までです。
11. 昨今、**夜**が**長**く、**昼**が**短**くなった。
12. 今から行っても、**二時**のバスには間に**合**いませんよ。

Eras

■ I. Reference ■

#107 代	5 strokes	ノ　イ　仁　代　代

kun   *kawa(ri)* substitute; *ka(waru)* be substituted; *ka(eru)* replace; *yo* generation; *shiro* price

代わり *kawari* substitute, deputy. 代わる *kawaru* be substituted (for a person). 代える *kaeru* replace (one thing with another). 君が代 #162 *Kimi ga yo* Thy Glorious Reign (Japanese anthem). 身の代金 #728 *minoshirokin* ransom.

ON   DAI generation; age; price; TAI substitution

時代 *jidai* era, period. 年代 *nendai* age, period. 六十年代 *rokujū nendai* the 60's. 代々 *daidai* generation after generation. 代金 *daikin* price, charge. 交代⟨v⟩ #789 *kōtai* taking turns.

#108 世	5 strokes	一　十　世　世　世

kun   *yo* world, age

世の中 *yo no naka* world, life. 今の世 *ima no yo* this age. 明治の世 #900 *Meiji no yo* Meiji era.

ON   SEI, SE world, age

世代 *sedai* generation. 二世 *nisei* 2nd generation. 後世 *kōsei* future generation. 中世 *chūsei* Middle Ages. 世間 *seken* world. 出世⟨v⟩ *shusse* success in life.

#109 紀	9 strokes	く　幺　乡　糸　紀　紀

ON   KI period, era; record

世紀 *seiki* century. 今世紀 *konseiki* this century. 前世紀 *zenseiki* last century. 二十一世紀 *nijūisseiki* 21st century. カナダ紀行 *Kanada kikō* account of the Canadian journey.

#110 近	7 strokes	′ 　丆 　斤 　乒 　近 　近

kun   *chika(i)* near, recent

近い *chikai* near.   近いうちに *chikai uchi ni* one of these days.
近々 *chikajika* shortly.   近づく *chikazuku* approach.

ON   KIN near, recent

近年 *kinnen* recent years.   近代 *kindai* modern ages; Meiji and
Taisho eras (Japanese history).   近世 *kinsei* recent ages; Edo era
(Japanese history).   近日中に *kinjitsuchū ni* one of these days.

#111 昔	8 strokes	一 　艹 　芦 　芐 　昔 　昔

kun   *mukashi* ancient times, long ago

昔 *mukashi* ancient times, long ago.   昔々 *mukashimukashi* once
upon a time.

ON   SEKI, [SHAKU] ancient times, long ago

昔日 *sekijitsu* old days.   今昔 *konjaku* present and past.

#112 遠	13 strokes	土 　寺 　声 　袁 　袁 　遠

kun   *tō(i)* far, distant

遠い *tōi* far, distant.   遠い昔 *tōi mukashi* long time ago.   遠回りす
る *tōmawari suru* make a detour, go a long way about.

ON   EN, [ON] far, distant

遠足 *ensoku* excursion.   遠近 *enkin* far and near, distance.   久遠
の #957 *kuon no* eternal.

#113 将	10 strokes	⺀ 　扩 　扩 　扦 　将 　将

ON   SHŌ be about to; commander, general

将来 *shōrai* future.   近い将来 *chikai shōrai* near future.   将校 #525
shōkō officer.   将軍 #930 *shōgun* general.

#114 新	13 strokes	亠 立 亲 亲ノ 新ノ 新

kun *atara(shii), ara(ta), nii-* new
新しい *atarashii* new. 新たな *arata na* new. 新妻#136 *niizuma* newly married woman.

ON SHIN new
新時代 *shinjidai* new era. 新年 *shinnen* New Year. 新春 *shin-shun* New Year. 一新⟨ʋ⟩ *isshin* renewal.

#115 古	5 strokes	一 十 十 古 古

kun *furu(i)* old
古い *furui* old. 古本 *furuhon* used book.

ON KO old
古代 *kodai* ancient times. 古代人 *kodaijin* ancient people. 古来 *korai* from ancient times.

#116 現	11 strokes	丁 王 珂 玧 玾 現

kun *arawa(reru)* appear, come out; *arawa(su)* show
現れる *arawareru* appear, come out. 現す *arawasu* show (one's talent).

ON GEN present; appearance
現代 *gendai* present age. 現代人 *gendaijin* a modern. 現金 *gen-kin* cash. 出現⟨ʋ⟩ *shutsugen* appearance.

#117 在	6 strokes	一 ナ ナ 右 在 在

kun *a(ru)* exist
在る *aru* exist.

ON ZAI exist; outskirts, country
現在 *genzai* present time, nowadays. 在日アメリカ人 *zainichi Amerika-jin* Americans staying in Japan. 在世中に *zaiseichū ni* during one's lifetime. 近在 *kinzai* neighboring districts.

■ II. Vocabulary ■

時代	*jidai*	era, period
年代	*nendai*	age, period
世代	*sedai*	generation
代々	*daidai*	generation after generation
二世	*nisei*	2nd generation
世紀	*seiki*	century
今世紀	*konseiki*	this century
二十一世紀	*nijūisseiki*	21st century
近年	*kinnen*	recent years
近代	*kindai*	modern ages; Meiji & Taisho eras
近世	*kinsei*	recent ages; Edo era
中世	*chūsei*	Middle Ages
新しい	*atarashii*	new
新時代	*shinjidai*	new era
古い	*furui*	old
古代	*kodai*	ancient times
現代	*gendai*	present age
現在	*genzai*	present time, nowadays
将来	*shōrai*	future
近い将来	*chikai shōrai*	near future
昔	*mukashi*	ancient times, long ago
遠い昔	*tōi mukashi*	long time ago
昔日	*sekijitsu*	old days
今昔	*konjaku*	present and past

■ III. Reading Exercises 8 ■

Read and translate the following.

1. 長い冬が去り、アフリカに**新時代**がやって来た。
2. わたしの**新しい**オフィスは六本木三丁目に**在り**ます。
3. **近い将来**、かれのカナダ**紀行**が出るそうです。
4. **近年**、**在日**アメリカ人の数が三倍になった。
5. 円い月がビルの上に**現**われました。
6. **現代人**にはそんな**古い**アイディアは分からない。

7. **古代**の人々は何で時間を計りましたか。

8. これは**遠い昔**、土人が着ていたものです。

9. 今の**世代**と前の**世代**の間にはかなりのギャップが**在**る。

10. あと数年で二十一**世紀**になります。

11. かれは**前世紀**の半ばに度々来日しました。

12. **遠回**りしたので、そこへ行くのに一時間以上かかった。

13. **中世**のおもかげのあるチャペルに入って、スナップを数枚とった。

5
✳✳✳✳✳✳✳✳✳✳✳✳✳✳✳✳✳✳✳✳
People

Family Relations

■ I. Reference ▬▬▬▬▬▬▬▬▬▬▬▬▬▬▬▬▬

#118 男	7 strokes	丨 冂 田 田 男 男 男

kun   *otoko* man, male
男 *otoko* man.   男の人 *otoko no hito* man.   中年男 *chūnen'otoko*
middle-aged man.   男らしい *otokorashii* manly.

ON   DAN, NAN man, male
長男 *chōnan* oldest son.   三男 *sannan* 3rd son.

#119 女	3 strokes	〈 女 女

kun   *onna* woman, female; *me* feminine Ir. *(a)ma** #268
女 *onna* woman.   女の人 *onna no hito* woman.   中年女
chūnen'onna middle-aged woman.   女らしい *onnarashii* womanly,
ladylike.   女々しい *memeshii* unmanly.

ON   JO, NYO, [NYŌ] woman, female
男女 *danjo* man and woman.   長女 *chōjo* oldest daughter.   三女
sanjo 3rd daugher.   一男二女 *ichinan nijo* 1 son and 2 daughters.

#120 性	8 strokes	丶 忄 忄 忤 忰 性

ON   SEI sex; nature; SHŌ nature, temperament
男性 *dansei* man, male.   女性 *josei* woman, female.   中性 *chūsei*
neuter gender.   人間性 *ningensei* humanity.   将来性 *shōraisei*
prospect.   本性 *honshō* real nature.   性分 *shōbun* nature, disposition.

#121 子

3 strokes ア 了 子

kun   *ko* child
子ども *kodomo* child, son/daughter. 男の子 *otoko no ko* boy. 女
の子 *onna no ko* girl. 末っ子 *suekko* youngest child.

ON   SHI, SU child; tiny thing
男子 *danshi* boy, man, male. 女子 *joshi* girl, woman, female.
分子 *bunshi* molecule. 冊子 *sasshi* booklet. 様子 #163 *yōsu* state
of affairs, appearance.

#122 供

8 strokes イ 亻 仁 仹 供 供

kun   *tomo* companion; *sona(eru)* offer
供 *tomo* companion, attendant. 子供 *kodomo* child, son/daugh-
ter. 供をする *tomo o suru* accompany (a person). 供える *sonaeru*
offer (flowers on a tomb).

ON   KYŌ, [KU] offer, supply
供出 ⟨い⟩ *kyōshutsu* delivery. 供物 #205 *kumotsu* votive offering.

#123 次

6 strokes ` シ ソ 汐 汐 次

kun   *tsugi* next; *tsu(gu)* rank next
次の *tsugi no* next, following. 次々 *tsugitsugi* one after another.

ON   JI, SHI next
次女 *jijo* 2nd daughter. 次男 *jinan* 2nd son. 次回 *jikai* next
time. 第一次 *daiichiji* 1st. 次第に *shidai ni* gradually. 年の明け
次第 *toshi no akeshidai* as soon as the new year comes. 目次
mokuji table of contents.

#124 父

4 strokes ノ ハ ク 父

kun   *chichi* father Ir. *tō(san)**
父 *chichi* father. お父さん *o-tōsan** father (polite)

ON   FU father
父子 *fushi* father and son/daughter.

#125 母

5 strokes　　㇄　𠃌　𠃌　𠃌　母

kun　　*haha* mother Ir. *kā(san)**; *omo(ya)**#139; *(u)ba**#415
母 *haha* mother.　お母さん *o-kāsan** mother (polite)

ON　　BO mother
父母 *fubo* father and mother.　母子 *boshi* mother and child.　母性
bosei motherhood.

#126 親

16 strokes　　亠　立　辛　亲　亲斤　親

kun　　*oya* parent; *shita(shii)* intimate; *shita(shimu)* become intimate
親 *oya* parent(s).　父親 *chichioya* father.　母親 *hahaoya* mother.
親子 *oyako* parent(s) and child(ren).　親しい *shitashii* intimate.
親しむ *shitashimu* become intimate (with people).

ON　　SHIN parent; intimacy
近親 *kinshin* close relative.　親日の *shinnichi no* pro-Japanese

#127 両

6 strokes　　一　厂　冂　帀　両　両

ON　　RYŌ both, two; old unit of money
両親 *ryōshin* parents.　両足 *ryōashi* feet, legs.　両立〈ﾘ〉 *ryōritsu*
coexistence.　千両 *senryō* 1 thousand ryō.

#128 祖

9 strokes　　⼆　ネ　礻　初　祀　祖

ON　　SO ancestor
祖父 *sofu* grandfather.　祖母 *sobo* grandmother.　祖父母 *sofubo*
grandparents.　祖先 *sosen* ancestor.　先祖 *senzo* ancestor.

#129 兄

5 strokes　　丨　冂　口　尸　兄

kun　　*ani* older brother Ir. *nī(san)**
兄 *ani* older brother.　お兄さん *o-nīsan** older brother (polite).

ON　　KEI, [KYŌ] older brother
父兄 *fukei* parents.　長兄 *chōkei* oldest brother.　次兄 *jikei* 2nd
older brother.

#130 弟	7 strokes	丶　丷　坐　峃　弟　弟

kun *otōto* younger brother
弟 *otōto* younger brother.

ON TEI, [DAI], [DE] younger brother
兄弟 *kyōdai* brothers, siblings.　末弟 *mattei* youngest brother.
子弟 *shitei* children.　弟子 *deshi* pupil, disciple.

#131 姉	8 strokes	く　女　女'　妒　姉　姉

kun *ane* older sister Ir. *nē(san)**
姉 *ane* older sister.　お姉さん *o-nēsan** older sister (polite).

ON SHI older sister
姉妹 #132 *shimai* sisters.

#132 妹	8 strokes	く　女　女'　妌　姝　妹

kun *imōto* younger sister
妹 *imōto* younger sister

ON MAI younger sister
姉妹 *shimai* sisters.　姉妹都市 #320 *shimai toshi* sister city.

#133 孫	10 strokes	了　子　孑　孫　孫　孫

kun *mago* grandchild
孫 *mago* grandchild.　初孫 *hatsumago* one's 1st grandchild.
孫子の代まで *magoko no dai made* to the generations of one's descendants.

ON SON grandchild
子孫 *shison* offspings, posterity.

#134 息	10 strokes	亻　白　自　自　息　息

kun *iki* breath Ir. *musu(ko)**
息 *iki* breath.　一息に *hitoiki ni* in a breath.　息子 *musuko** son.

ON SOKU son; breath
ご子息 *go-shisoku* son (polite).　休息 ⟨v⟩ *kyūsoku* rest, repose.

#135 夫	4 strokes	一　二　𠃌　夫

kun *otto* husband
夫 *otto* husband

ON FU, [FŪ] husband; worker
夫人 *fujin* one's wife.　三木夫人 *Miki-fujin* Mrs. Miki.　前夫 *zenpu* former husband.　水夫 *suifu* sailor.　人夫 *ninpu* laborer.

#136 妻	8 strokes	ラ　ヲ　ヺ　㞢　妻　妻

kun *tsuma* wife
妻 *tsuma* wife.　新妻 *niizuma* newly married woman.

ON SAI wife
スミス夫妻 *Sumisu-fusai* Mr. and Mrs. Smith.　妻子 *saishi* wife and child(ren).　先妻 *sensai* one's former wife.

#137 婦	11 strokes	女　女ㄱ　女ㅋ　婦　婦　婦

ON FU woman, wife
婦人 *fujin* woman, lady.　婦女子 *fujoshi* women and children.　夫婦 *fūfu* husband and wife.　新婦 *shinpu* bride.　一夫一婦 *ippu ippu* monogamy.

#138 主	5 strokes	丶　二　亠　主　主

kun *nushi* master, owner; *omo(na)* main
主 *nushi* master, owner.　主のない *nushi no nai* ownerless (cat)
主な *omo na* main (thing).

ON SHU, [SU] master, owner
主人 *shujin* one's husband; master.　主婦 *shufu* housewife.　主将 *shushō* captain (of a team).

#139 家	10 strokes	丶　宀　宁　㝛　冢　家

kun *ie, ya* house
家 *ie* house.　家主 *yanushi* landlord, house owner.　母家 *omoya** main building of a house.

ON   KA, KE house; family

一家 *ikka* family, household.   家計 *kakei* household economy.
水木家 *Mizuki-ke* the Mizuki family.

| #140 内 | 4 strokes | 丨 冂 内 内 |

kun   *uchi* inside, within

内 *uchi* inside.   内の人 *uchi no hito* my husband.   内金 *uchikin* bargain money.

ON   NAI, [DAI] inside, within

家内 *kanai* my wife; family, household.   内部 *naibu* inside.   一週間以内 *isshūkan inai* within a week.   年内に *nennai ni* within the year.   参内 ⟨v⟩ *sandai* going to the Imperial Palace.

| #141 族 | 11 strokes | 亠 ナ 方 疒 㫃 族 |

ON   ZOKU family, tribe, clan

家族 *kazoku* family.   一族 *ichizoku* whole family.   親族 *shinzoku* relative, kin.   部族 *buzoku* tribe.

| #142 庭 | 10 strokes | 亠 广 庀 庭 庭 庭 |

kun   *niwa* garden

庭 *niwa* garden, yard.   中庭 *nakaniwa* courtyard.

ON   TEI garden

家庭 *katei* family, home.   家庭人 *kateijin* family man.   家庭着 *kateigi* home dress.

| #143 宅 | 6 strokes | 丶 宀 宀 宀 宅 宅 |

ON   TAKU home, house; husband

宅 *taku* my home; my husband.   家宅 *kataku* house.   三木宅 *Mikitaku* the Miki's house.   本宅 *hontaku* principal residense. 帰宅 ⟨v⟩ *kitaku* going/coming home.

#144 類	18 strokes	ヽ ヽ 米 米 类 類 類

ON RUI kind, type

親類 *shinrui* relative.　人類 *jinrui* mankind.　下着類 *shitagirui* underwear.　分類 ‹v› *bunrui* classification.

#145 養	15 strokes	亠 ⺍ 羊 养 養 養

kun *yashina(u)* bring up; adopt; support

養う *yashinau* bring up (children); support (one's family).

ON YŌ bring up; adopt; support

養子 *yōshi* adopted child.　養女 *yōjo* adopted daughter.　養父 *yōfu* foster father.　養分 *yōbun* nourishment.　休養 ‹v› *kyūyō* rest.

#146 有	6 strokes	ノ ナ 冇 冇 有 有

kun *a(ru)* exist, have

有る *aru* exist, have.　子供が有る *kodomo ga aru* have a child.　名の有る *na no aru* famous.

ON YŌ, U exist, have

有名な *yūmei na* famous.　有無 #868 *umu* existence; yes or no.

#147 居	8 strokes	一 尸 尸 居 居 居

kun *i(ru)* be, exist

居る *iru* be, exist.　人が居る *Hito ga iru* There are people.

居間 *ima* living room.　長居 ‹v› *nagai* staying long.

ON KYO be, exist

新居 *shinkyo* new house.　入居 ‹v› *nyūkyo* moving into (a house).

起居 *kikyo* one's daily life.

#148 住	7 strokes	亻 亻 亻 亻 亻 住

kun   *su(mu)*, *su(mau)* live, reside
           住む・住まう *sumu/sumau* live, reside.   住まい *sumai* house, residence.
ON   JŪ live, reside
           住居 *jūkyo* house, residence.   住宅 *jūtaku* house, residence.
           住人 *jūnin* inhabitant, resident.   居住〈い〉 *kyojū* residence.

#149 暮	14 strokes	艹 芦 苜 莫 幕 暮

kun   *ku(rasu)* live; *ku(reru)* grow dark, come to end; *ku(re)* end
           暮らす *kurasu* live.   一人暮らし *hitorigurashi* living alone.
           暮れる *kureru* grow dark.   夕暮れ *yūgure* evening, twilight.
           年の暮れに *toshi no kure ni* at the year-end.
ON   BO grow dark, come to end.
           暮春 *boshun* late spring.   暮秋 *boshū* late autumn

■ II. Vocabulary ■

男	*otoko*	man
女	*onna*	woman
男女	*danjo*	man and woman
男性	*dansei*	man, male
子供	*kodomo*	child, son/daughter
男の子	*otoko no ko*	boy
女の子	*onna no ko*	girl
息子	*musuko*	son
長男	*chōnan*	oldest son
次女	*jijo*	2nd daughter
養子	*yōshi*	adopted child
父	*chichi*	father
母	*haha*	mother
父母	*fubo*	father and mother
親	*oya*	parent(s)
両親	*ryōshin*	both parents

祖父	*sofu*	grandfather
祖母	*sobo*	grandmother
祖先・先祖	*sosen/senzo*	ancestor
孫	*mago*	grandchild
子孫	*shison*	offsprings, posterity
兄	*ani*	older brother
弟	*otōto*	younger brother
兄弟	*kyōdai*	brothers, siblings
姉	*ane*	older sister
妹	*imōto*	younger sister
姉妹	*shimai*	sisters
夫	*otto*	husband
妻	*tsuma*	wife
スミス夫妻	*Sumisu-fusai*	Mr. and Mrs. Smith
夫婦	*fūfu*	husband and wife
夫人	*fujin*	one's wife
婦人	*fujin*	woman, lady
主人	*shujin*	one's husband; master
宅	*taku*	my home; my husband
家	*ie*	house
家内	*kanai*	my wife; household
家族	*kazoku*	family
庭	*niwa*	garden, yard
家庭	*katei*	family, home
親類	*shinrui*	relative
住まい・住居	*sumai/jūkyo*	house, residence
一人暮らし	*hitorigurashi*	living alone

■ III. Reading Exercises 9 ■

Read and translate the following.

1. 木の下に**男**の子と**女**の子が**居**ます。
2. **男性**と**女性**が二つのチームに分かれました。
3. **姉**の**長女**は十五才ですが、**次男**はまだ三つです。
4. **兄**のオフィスはビルの八階に**在**る。
5. トムは**兄弟**が六人**有**ります。お**兄**さんが二人と、**弟**さんが三人と**お姉**さんが

一人です。

6. **息子**は毎晩七時に**帰宅**します。

7. **主人**が帰り**次第**、出かけます。

8. スミス**夫妻**は明日の午後四時に着きます。

9. その二人は二十才で**夫婦**になった。

10. **妹**の**家族**は庭のある**家に**住みたがっています。

11. **家庭**の**主婦**は年の暮れにはとてもいそがしいです。

12. **祖父**は**孫**を連れて、ディズニーランドへ行った。

13. **家内**の**父親**は八十才まで一人暮らしでした。

14. お**母**さん、今日は**母**の日だから、どこへでも**お供**しますよ。

15. **子供**のころ、時々**両親**と**親類**の**家**へ行きました。

Friends

■ I. Reference ■

#150 友	4 strokes	一　ナ　方　友

kun *tomo* friend
友 *tomo* friend, companion.　友だち *tomodachi* friend.　親しい友 *shitashii tomo* close friend.

ON YŪ friend
友人 *yūjin* friend.　親友 *shin'yū* close friend.

#151 達	12 strokes	十　寺　幸　達　達　達

kun *tas(suru)* reach, attain; *-tachi* (for plurality) Ir. *(tomo)dachi**
達する *tassuru* reach (the age of 80).　子供達 *kodomo-tachi* children.　友達 *tomodachi** friend.

ON TATSU reach, attain
達人 *tatsujin* expert, master.　上達 ⟨v⟩ *jōtatsu* improvement.

#152 仲	6 strokes	ノ　イ　亻　仲　仲　仲

kun *naka* relation, relationship Ir. *nakō(do)**
仲 *naka* relation, relationship.　仲がいい *naka ga ii* be on good terms.　仲間 *nakama* companion.　仲立ち *nakadachi* mediation.　仲人 *nakōdo** go-between.

ON CHŌ relation, relationship
仲裁 ⟨v⟩ #975 *chūsai* arbitration.　仲春 *chūshun* 2nd month of the lunar year.　中秋の名月 *chūshū no meigetsu* harvest moon.

#153 知	8 strokes	广　乍　矢　知　知　知

kun *shi(ru)* know
知る *shiru* know.　知らせる *shiraseru* inform a person (of).　知り合い *shiriai* acquaintance.

ON CHI know
知人 *chijin* acquaintance. 知名人 *chimeijin* well-known person.
知性 *chisei* intelligence.

#154 他	5 strokes	ノ イ 竹 仲 他

ON TA another, other
他の *ta no* another, other. 他の人々 *ta no hitobito* other people;
the rest. 他に *ta ni* besides. その他 *sono ta* and so on.
他人 *tanin* stranger; other people. 他日 *tajitsu* some other day.

#155 外	5 strokes	ノ ク タ 夘 外

kun *soto* outside; *hoka* another; *hazu(su)* remove, undo
外 *soto* outside. 家の外 *ie no soto* outside the house. 外の *hoka*
no another. 外の人 *hoka no hito* someone else.

ON GAI, GE outside
外人 *gaijin* foreigner. 外部 *gaibu* outside. 外部の人 *gaibu no hito*
outsider. 週末以外 *shūmatsu igai* except for weekends.
外出 ⟨v⟩ *gaishutsu* going out. 外題 #575 *gedai* title of a play.

■ II. Vocabulary ■

友達	*tomodachi*	friend
友人	*yūjin*	friend
親友	*shin'yū*	close friend
仲間	*nakama*	companion
知り合い	*shiriai*	acquaintance
知人	*chijin*	acquaintance
知名人	*chimeijin*	well-known person
他人	*tanin*	stranger; other people
他の人々	*ta no hitobito*	other people; the rest
外の人	*hoka no hito*	someone else
外人	*gaijin*	foreigner
外部の人	*gaibu no hito*	outsider

Read and translate the following.

1. 兄は**外人**の**友達**が五、六人有ります。

2. 水木さんは妹の昔からの**知**り合いです。

3. あの人は兄弟も親類も**知人**もいません。

4. 姉は**親友**の子供を養子にしました。

5. 先週末、古い**仲間**とゴルフをしました。

6. 三木さんはまだ居ますが、**他**の人々はもう帰りました。

7. あの二人は**他人**なのに、姉妹のように**仲**がいい。

8. スミス夫人の代わりに**外**の人が来ました。

9. あの人が**外部**の人か内部の人か**知**りません。

10. かれは**知名人**だけあって、どこへ行っても**友人**や**知人**が居ます。

Personal Pronouns and Forms of Address

#156 私	7 strokes	ノ 二 千 禾 私 私

kun *watakushi, watashi* I, private
私 *watakushi, watashi* I.   私達 *watakushi/watashi-tachi* we.

ON SHI private
私立の *shiritsu/watakushiritsu no* privately-established (clinic).
私有の *shiyū no* privately-owned (building).

#157 自	6 strokes	′ ⺆ 冂 白 自 自

kun *mizuka(ra)* self, in person
自ら *mizukara* oneself, in person.   自ら名のる *mizukara nanoru* introduce oneself.

ON JI, SHI self, in person
自分 *jibun* oneself, I.   自分で *jibun de* by oneself, personally.
自立 ⟨v⟩ *jiritsu* independence.   自供 ⟨v⟩ *jikyō* confession of crime.   自然 #283 *shizen* nature.

#158 己	3 strokes	フ コ 己

kun *onore* self
己 *onore* self, myself, oneself.   己をすてる *onore o suteru* rise above self.

ON KO, KI self
自己 *jiko* ego, self.   自己を知る *jiko o shiru* know oneself.
私一己としては *watakushi ikko to shite wa* as for myself.   知己 *chi-ki* acquaintance.

#159 我	7 strokes	二 千 手 我 我 我

kun *ware* I, oneself; *wa(ga)* my, our
我 *ware* I, oneself.   我々 *wareware* we.   我が家 *waga ya* my

house/home.

ON　　GA I, oneself
我 *ga* self, ego.　　我のつよい *ga no tsuyoi* obstinate, egoistic
自我 *jiga* self, ego.

#160　方　4 strokes　　`　亠　亍　方

kun　　*kata* person; direction; method Ir. *(yuku)e**
あの方 *ano kata* (polite) that person.　　あなた方 *anata-gata* (polite)
you all.　　父方の親類 *chichikata no shinrui* relative on father's side.
やり方 *yarikata* method.　　夕方 *yūgata* evening.　　行方 *yukue**
whereabouts.

ON　　HŌ direction, side
両方 *ryōhō* both, both sides.　　一方 *ippō* one side, one way.　　方々
hōbō various places.　　後方の *kōhō no* rear.　　方針 *hōshin* policy.

#161　者　8 strokes　　十　歩　耂　者　者　者

kun　　*mono* person
家族の者 *kazoku no mono* (humble) member of one's family.　　目下
の者 *meshita no mono* one's subordinate.　　よその者 *yoso no mono*
outsider to one's family/group.

ON　　SHA person
第三者 *daisansha* 3rd person, outsider.　　億万長者 *okuman chōja*
multimillionair.　　前者 *zensha* the former.　　後者 *kōsha* the latter.

#162　君　7 strokes　　フ　ヲ　尹　尹　君　君

kun　　*kimi* you; lord
君 *kimi* you.　　我が君 *waga kimi* my lord.　　君が代 *Kimi ga Yo*
Thy Glorious Reign (Japanese national anthem).

ON　　KUN lord; (familiar suffix)
スミス君 *Sumisu-kun* Mr. Smith.　　トム君 *Tomu-kun* Tom.　　君主
kunshu monarch, ruler.　　名君 *meikun* wise ruler.

#163　様　14 strokes　　十　木　木゙　杧　様　様

kun　　*sama* condition; (polite suffix)

お父様 *o-tōsama* father.　水木様 *Mizuki-sama* Mr./Mrs./Miss Mizuki.

四名様 *yonmei-sama* 4 customers.　有様 *arisama* state, condition.

様々な *samazama na* all sorts of (things).

ON　YŌ appearance, state

様子 *yōsu* state of affairs, appearance.

#164 氏	4 strokes	´ ⺁ ⻏ 氏

kun　*uji* family, lineage

氏 *uji* family, lineage.　氏なき者 *uji naki mono* lowborn person.

氏子 *ujiko* people under the protection of a community deity.

ON　SHI family, surname; (formal suffix for 3rd person)

三木氏 *Miki-shi* Mr/Ms. Miki.　正木、今中両氏 *Masaki, Imanaka ryōshi* both Mr/Ms. Masaki and Imanaka.　氏名 *shimei* full name.

氏族 *shizoki* family, clan.

#165 諸	15 strokes	言 言 計 訝 諸 諸

ON　SHO all, various

諸君 *shokun* gentlemen, you all.　諸氏 *shoshi* gentlemen, you all.

諸子 *shoshi* you all.　諸方 *shohō* all directions.

■ II. Vocabulary ■

私	*watakushi/watashi*	I
私達	*watakushi/watashi-tachi*	we
我	*ware*	I, oneself
我々	*wareware*	we
我が家	*waga ya*	my house/home
あなた達	*anata-tachi*	you all
あなた方	*anata-gata (polite)*	you all
あの人	*ano hito*	that person
あの方	*ano kata (polite)*	that person
君	*kimi (familiar)*	you
自分	*jibun*	oneself, I
己	*onore*	self, myself, oneself

自己	*jiko*	ego, self
家族の者	*kazoku no mono (humble)*	member of one's family
様	*-sama*	(polite suffix)
お父様	*o-tōsama*	father
水木様	*Mizuki-sama*	Mr./Mrs./Miss Mizuki
四名様	*yonmei-sama*	4 customers
君	*-kun*	(familiar suffix)
スミス君	*Sumisu-kun*	Mr. Smith
トム君	*Tomu-kun*	Tom
諸君	*shokun*	gentlemen, you all
氏	*-shi*	(formal suffix for 3rd person)
三木氏	*Miki-shi*	Mr./Ms. Miki
正木、今中両氏	*Masaki, Imanaka ryōshi*	both Mrs. Masaki and Imanaka
諸氏	*shoshi*	gentlemen, you all

■ III. Reading Exercises 11 ■

Read and translate the following.

1. あの方はどなた様でいらっしゃいますか。
2. 君達はトム君を知っていますか。
3. 諸君の間で何かいいアイディアはありませんか。
4. 私達は週末以外には外出しません。
5. 我々のゴルフ仲間には男性も女性もいます。
6. 弟の長男はまだ四才ですが、何でも自分でやりたがります。
7. あの男は自己も知らず、自我ばかりつよい。
8. 三木氏は去年の夏、三か月カナダで暮らした。

Life

■ I. Reference ■

#166 生 — 5 strokes ノ ヒ 牛 牛 生

kun *i(kiru)* live; *u(mareru)* be born; *u(mu)* give birth; *ha(eru)* grow, come out; *o(u)* grow; *nama* raw; *ki-* pure 、
生きる *ikiru* live. 生まれる *umareru* be born. 生む *umu* give birth. 生える *haeru* cut (a tooth). 生い立ち *oitachi* growth, bringing-up. 生ビール *nama bîru* draft beer. 灘の生一本 *Nada no kiippon* pure undiluted sake from Nada.

ON SEI, SHŌ life
人生 *jinsei* human life. 一生 *isshō* one's whole life. 生年月日 *seinen gappi* birth date. 先生 *sensei* teacher.

#167 命 — 8 strokes 人 亼 合 合 合 命

kun *inochi* life
命 *inochi* life. 命拾いをする *inochibiroi o suru* have a narrow escape (from death).

ON MEI life; command; MYŌ life
生命 *seimei* life. 人命 *jinmei* human life. 長命 *chōmei* long life. 命にしたがう *mei ni shitagau* obey a command.

#168 誕 — 15 strokes 言 言 訂 証 誕 誕

ON TAN birth
誕生 *tanjō* birth. 誕生日 *tanjōbi* birthday. 生誕百年祭 *seitan hyakunensai* a centenary of a person's birth.

#169 育 — 8 strokes 亠 云 宀 育 育 育

kun *soda(tsu)* grow up; *soda(teru)* raise
育つ *sodatsu* grow up. 育てる *sodateru* raise (a child). 育ての親 *sodate no oya* foster parent.

ON   IKU raise

養育 ⟨い⟩ *yōiku* bringing up (a child).   養育者 *yōikusha* fosterer.

#170 大	3 strokes	一 ナ 大

kun   *ō(kii)*, *ō-* big, large Ir. *o(tona)**; *yama(to)* #396*

大きい *ōkii* big, large.   大時計 *ōdokei* big clock.   大水 *ōmizu* flood.   大人 *otona** adult.

ON   DAI, TAI big, large

大家 *taika* great master.   大半 *taihan* majority.   大金 *taikin* large sum of money.   短大 *tandai* 2-year college.

#171 小	3 strokes	亅 小 小

kun   *chii(sai)*, *ko-*, *o-* small Ir. *a(zuki)* #410*

小さい *chiisai* small, little.   小人 *kobito* dwarf.   小川 #266 *ogawa* creek.

ON   SHŌ small

小人 *shōnin* children (used in fares).   小人 *shōjin* small-minded person.   大小 *daishō* large and small; size

#172 幼	5 strokes	乚 幺 幺 幻 幼

kun   *osana(i)* infant, infantile

幼い *osanai* young (child), infantile.   幼子 *osanago* infant.   幼友達 *osanatomodachi* childhood friend.

ON   YŌ infant, infantile

幼年 *yōnen* infancy.   幼年時代 *yōnen jidai* early childhood. 幼女 *yōjo* little girl.   幼名 *yōmei/yōmyō* childhood name.

#173 児	7 strokes	丨 冂 𯾫 日 尸 児

ON   JI, [NI] infant, child

幼児 *yōji* infant.   男児 *danji* boy.   女児 *joji* girl.   育児 *ikuji* child care.   小児 *shōni* infant.

#174 期	12 strokes	十　卄　甘　其　期　期

ON　KI, [GO] period, term
幼児期 *yōjiki* babyhood.　幼年期 *yōnenki* early childhood.　期日 *kijitsu* fixed date.　その期間中 *sono kikanchū* during that period.　短期 *tanki* short term.　末期 *matsugo* one's dying hour.

#175 少	4 strokes	丿　小　小　少

kun　*suku(nai)* few; *suko(shi)* a little, a few
少ない *sukunai* few.　少なくとも *sukunaku tomo* at least.　少し *sukoshi* a little, a few.

ON　SHŌ a little, a few
少年 *shōnen* boy.　少女 *shōjo* girl.　少年期 *shōnenki* boyhood.　年少者 *nenshōsha* youth; minor.　少々 *shōshō* a little, a bit.

#176 過	12 strokes	冂　冋　咼　渦　渦　過

kun　*su(giru)* pass, exceed; *su(gosu)* spend (time); *ayama(tsu)* err; *ayama(chi)* error
過ぎる *sugiru* pass (the noon).　大き過ぎる *ōkisugiru* too big.　少年期を過ごす *shōnenki o sugosu* spend one's boyhood.　過つ *ayamatsu* err (in one's judgment).　過ち *ayamachi* error.

ON　KA pass, exceed
過去 *kako* past.　過半数 *kahansū* majority, more than half.

#177 成	6 strokes	丿　厂　厉　成　成　成

kun　*na(ru)* become, be completed, consist of; *na(su)* do, form
成る *naru* become (an adult); consist of (3 parts).　成り行き *nariyuki* course (of events).　名を成す *na o nasu* make a name.

ON　SEI, [JŌ] become, be completed, consist of
成年 *seinen* full age.　成人 *seijin* adult.　成長 ⟨v⟩ *seichō* growth.　養成 ⟨v⟩ *yōsei* training.　成仏 ⟨v⟩ #1000 *jōbutsu* dying in peace.

#178 未	5 strokes	一　二　キ　オ　未

ON　MI not yet
未成年者 *miseinensha* minor.　未来の妻 *mirai no tsuma* one's future wife.　未知の人 *michi no hito* stranger.　未明 *mimei* early dawn.

#179 青	8 strokes	十　丰　青　青　青　青

kun　*ao, ao(i)* blue, green; unripe Ir. *(mas)sao* #662
青·青い *ao/aoi* blue, green.　青いりんご *aoi ringo* green apple.
青二才 *aonisai* green youth, greenhorn.

ON　SEI, [SHŌ] blue, green; unripe
青年 *seinen* young man.　青年男女 *seinen danjo* young men and women.　青春時代 *seishun jidai* springtime of life.　緑青 #235 *rokushō* green rust.

#180 思	9 strokes	冂　甩　甲　思　思　思

kun　*omo(u)* think, believe
思う *omou* think, belive.　思い出す *omoidasu* recall, remember.
思い出 *omoide* reminiscences.

ON　SHI think, believe
思春期 *shishunki* puberty.

#181 若	8 strokes	一　ア　芋　芋　若　若

kun　*waka(i)* young; *mo(shiku wa)* or, otherwise Ir. *wakō(do)**
若い *wakai* young.　若々しい *wakawakashii* young-looking.　若者 *wakamono* young person.　若人 *wakōdo** youth.　若しくは *moshiku wa* or, otherwise.

ON　JAKU, [NYAKU] young
若年 *jakunen* youth, early age.

#182 老	6 strokes	一 十 土 耂 芳 老

kun   *o(iru)*, *fu(keru)* grow old
老いる・老ける *oiru/fukeru* grow old.

ON   RŌ old
老人 *rōjin* old person.   老年 *rōnen* old age.   老夫婦 *rōfūfu* old married couple.   老若男女 *rōnyaku nannyo* men and women of all ages.   養老年金 *yōrō nenkin* old-age pension.

#183 死	6 strokes	一 ァ 歹 歹 歹ﾞ 死

kun   *shi(nu)* die
死ぬ *shinu* die.   若死〈v〉 *wakajini* dying young.

ON   SHI death
死 *shi* death.   死者 *shisha* the dead.   死去〈v〉 *shikyo* death.

#184 亡	3 strokes	丶 亠 亡

kun   *na(i)* dead, deceased
亡くなる *nakunaru* die, pass away.   亡き友人 *naki yūjin* one's late friend.

ON   BŌ, [MŌ] die
死亡〈v〉 *shibō* death.   死亡者 *shibōsha* the dead.   亡父 *bōfu* one's late father.   未亡人 *mibōjin* widow.   亡命〈v〉 *bōmei* seeking refuge.

■ II. Vocabulary. ■

人生	*jinsei*	human life
一生	*isshō*	one's whole life
命	*inochi*	life
生命	*seimei*	life
生年月日	*seinen gappi*	birth date
誕生日	*tanjōbi*	birthday
育ての親	*sodate no oya*	foster parent
養育〈v〉	*yōiku*	bringing up

大人	*otona*	adult
小人	*shōnin*	children (used in fares)
幼子	*osanago*	infant
幼児	*yōji*	infant
少年	*shōnen*	boy
少女	*shōjo*	girl
青年	*seinen*	young man
若者	*wakamono*	young person
若年	*jakunen*	youth, early age
成年	*seinen*	full age
成人	*seijin*	adult
未成年者	*miseinensha*	minor
老人	*rōjin*	old person
老年	*rōnen*	old age
幼児期	*yōjiki*	babyhood
幼年期	*yōnenki*	carly childhood
少年期	*shōnenki*	boyhood
思春期	*shishunki*	puberty
青春時代	*seishun jidai*	springtime of life
亡き友人	*naki yūjin*	one's late friend
死亡‹v›	*shibō*	death

■ III. Reading Exercises 12 ■

Read and translate the following.

1. 先月、友人の妹さんに二番目の女の子が**生**まれました。
2. 今や、**人生**八十年の時代になった。
3. その女性は親のない**幼児**の養育に**生命**をささげました。
4. あの**老人**は自分の名前も**生年月日**も知らない。
5. 来週の木曜日に私達の**先生**の**誕生日**を祝います。
6. その兄弟は**少年期**をドイツで**過**ごした。
7. このクラブのメンバーの**過半数**は若い女性です。
8. **若年**ながら弟は**大**きいホテルのマネージャーです。
9. ここは**大人**しか入れません。**未成年者**はだめです。
10. 父は六十才で**亡**くなり、母は五十二才で**未亡人**になった。

11. 昨日のアクシデントで、**死者**の数は百人以上に達しました。
12. 兄の息子は二人とも今が**思春期**です。
13. 姉は子供達が**成長**した後、**青春**の思い出のあるパリへ去った。

6

Animals, Birds, Insects

■ I. Reference ■

#185

犬	4 strokes	一　ナ　大　犬

kun	*inu* dog
	犬 *inu* dog.　小犬·子犬 *koinu* puppy.
ON	KEN dog
	番犬 *banken* watchdog.

#186

遊	12 strokes	亠　方　ガ　斿　游　遊

kun	*aso(bu)* play, enjoy oneself
	遊ぶ *asobu* play, enjoy oneself.　犬と遊ぶ *inu to asobu* play with a dog.　遊び時間 *asobijikan* playtime.　遊び着 *asobigi* playsuit.
ON	YŪ, [YU] play, enjoy oneself
	外遊 ⟨v⟩ *gaiyū* foreign trip.　回遊 ⟨v⟩ *kaiyū* excursion, round trip
	遊山 #238 *yusan* picnic, excursion.

#187

牛	4 strokes	ノ　ᅩ　二　牛

kun	*ushi* cow, bull, cattle
	牛 *ushi* cow, bull, cattle.　小牛·子牛 *koushi* calf.
ON	GYŪ cow, bull, cattle
	水牛 *suigyū* water buffalo.

#188

馬	10 strokes	丨　厂　厈　馬　馬　馬

kun	*uma*, [*ma*] horse
	馬 *uma* horse.　小馬·子馬 *kouma* pony.　馬が合う *uma ga au* get along well.　馬子 *mago* road-horse man.

ON   BA horse

牛馬 *gyūba* oxen and horses.   木馬 *mokuba* rocking horse.   馬丁 *batei* stableman.   出馬 ‹v›*shutsuba* standing as a candidate.

#189 歩	8 strokes	ト	ﻟ	止	牛	歩	歩

kun   *aru(ku), ayu(mu)* walk

歩く・歩む *aruku/ayumu* walk.   歩み *ayumi* walking; history (of a school).   牛の歩みのごとく *ushi no ayumi no gotoku* at a snail's pace.   歩み合い *ayumiai* compromise.

ON   HO, BU, [FU] walk

歩行者 *hokōsha* pedestrian.   初歩 *shoho* rudiments.   第一歩 *daiippo* first step.   歩合 *buai* percentage; commission.

#190 走	7 strokes	十	土	牛	牛	走	走

kun   *hashi(ru)* run Ir. *(shi)wasu** #558

走る *hashiru* run.   馬が走る *Uma ga hashiru* Horses run.   走り回る *hashirimawaru* run around.

ON   SŌ run

走者 *sōsha* runner.   走行中 *sōkōchū* while (a bus is) running.

#191 飼	13 strokes	𠆢	今	食	飣	飣	飼

kun   *ka(u)* raise, keep

飼う *kau* raise, keep (animals).   飼い犬 *kaiinu* pet dog.   飼い主 *kainushi* pet owner.

ON   SHI raise

飼育 ‹v›*shiiku* raising.   飼養 ‹v›*shiyō* breeding.

#192 羊	6 strokes	丶	丷	꾸	꾸	兰	羊

kun   *hitsuji* sheep

羊 *hitsuji* sheep.   小羊・子羊 *kohitsuji* baby sheep.

ON   YŌ sheep

羊毛 #483 *yōmō* wool.

#193 群 | 13 strokes 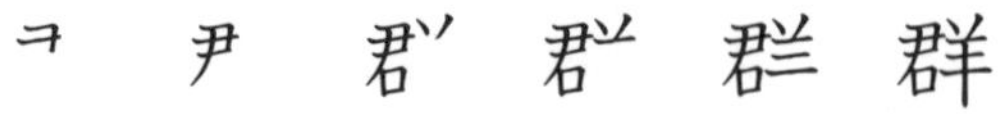

kun *mu(re)*, [*mura*] herd, flock, group; *mura(garu), mu(reru)* crowd, flock

群れ *mure* herd, flock, group. 羊の群れ *hitsuji no mure* a flock of sheep. 群すずめ *murasuzume* a flock of sparrows. 群がる·群れる *muragaru/mureru* crowd, flock.

ON GUN herd, flock, group

一群 *ichigun* a herd/flock/group. 馬の一群 *uma no ichigun* a herd of horses. 群生 ‹v› *gunsei* growing gregariously.

#194 象 | 12 strokes 

ON SHŌ image, shape; ZŌ elephant

象 *zō* elephant. 象の大群 *zō no taigun* large group of elephants. 現象 *genshō* phenomenon. 万象 *banshō* all things in the universe.

#195 魚 | 11 strokes 

kun *sakana, uo* fish Ir. *(za)ko** #706

魚 *sakana* fish. 魚釣▲り(つ) *sakanatsuri/uotsuri* fishing. 魚河岸(がし) #274 *uogashi* riverside fish market.

ON GYO fish

金魚 *kingyo* goldfish. 魚類 *gyorui* fishes.

#196 貝 | 7 strokes 

ON KAI shellfish

貝 *kai* shellfish. 貝類 *kairui* shellfish. 二枚貝 *nimaigai* bivalve. 巻き貝 *makigai* spiral shell.

#197 泳 | 8 strokes 

kun *oyo(gu)* swim

泳ぐ *oyogu* swim. 魚が泳いでいる *Sakana ga oyoide iru* Fish are swimming. 立ち泳ぎ ‹v› *tachioyogi* standing stroke.

ON   EI swim

水泳 *suiei* swimming.   遠泳 *en'ei* long-distance swimming.

#198 鳥	11 strokes	ノ 冂 臼 烏 鳥 鳥

kun   *tori* bird

鳥 *tori* bird.   小鳥 *kotori* little bird.   鳥の羽 *tori no hane* bird's feather.   鳥居 *torii* Shinto shrine archway.

ON   CHŌ bird

鳥類 *chōrui* birds, fowls.   白鳥 #230 *hakuchō* swan.

#199 巣	11 strokes	⺌ ⺍ 岁 単 単 巣

kun   *su* nest

巣 *su* nest.   鳥の巣 *tori no su* bird nest.   古巣 *furusu* old nest.
ギャングの巣 *gyangu no su* haunt of gangsters.   巣立つ *sudatsu* leave one's nest.

ON   SŌ nest

帰巣 ⟨ᵥ⟩ *kisō* homing (of birds).   巣くつ *sōkutsu* haunt.

#200 飛	9 strokes	飞 飞 飛 飛 飛 飛

kun   *to(bu)* fly; *to(basu)* fly; skip

飛ぶ *tobu* fly.   飛ばす *tobasu* fly (a bird); skip (pages).   飛び火 flying sparks.

ON   HI fly

飛鳥 *hichō* flying bird.   飛行機 *hikōki* airplane.   飛来 ⟨ᵥ⟩ *hirai* coming by air.

#201 虫	6 strokes	` 冂 口 中 虫 虫

kun   *mushi* insect, bug

虫 *mushi* insect, bug.   本の虫 *hon no mushi* bookworm.

ON   CHŪ insect, bug

昆虫 *konchū* insect.   幼虫 *yōchū* larva.   成虫 *seichū* imago.

#202 蚕	10 strokes	一 Ｆ 天 吞 蚕 蚕

kun　*kaiko* silkworm
　　　蚕 *kaiko* silkworm.

ON　SAN silkworm
　　　養蚕 *yōsan* sericulture.　春蚕 *shunsan* spring breed of silkworms.

#203 鳴	14 strokes	口 叮 呚 呜 鳴 鳴

kun　*na(ku)* sing, chirp, howl; *na(ru)* ring
　　　鳴く *naku* sing, chirp, howl.　鳥が鳴く *Tori ga naku* A bird sings.
　　　犬が鳴く *Inu ga naku* A dog howls.　鳴る *naru* ring.

ON　MEI make a sound
　　　共鳴 ⟨v⟩ #524 *kyōmei* resonance; sympathy.　悲鳴 #684 *himei* scream.

#204 動	11 strokes	二 台 車 重 動 動

kun　*ugo(ku), ugo(kasu)* move
　　　動く *ugoku* move.　動かす *ugokasu* move (furniture).　時代の動き
　　　jidai no ugoki movement of the times.

ON　DŌ move
　　　行動 ⟨v⟩ *kōdō* act, conduct.　動機 *dōki* motive.　自動の *jidō no*
　　　automatic.

#205 物	8 strokes	′ 牛 牛 牜 物 物 物

kun　*mono* thing, article
　　　物 *mono* thing, article.　本物 *honmono* real thing.　金物 *kanamo-*
　　　no hardware.　拾い物 *hiroimono* a find.　初物 *hatsumono* 1st
　　　products of the season.

ON　BUTSU, MOTSU thing, article
　　　動物 *dōbutsu* animal.　人物 *jinbutsu* person.　名物 *meibutsu* noted
　　　product.　供物 *kumotsu* votive offering.

#206 園	13 strokes	冂 冂 冃 冐 園 園

kun   *sono* garden
        園 *sono* garden.   花園 #209 *hanazono* flower garden.

ON   EN garden
        動物園 *dōbutsuen* zoo.   日本庭園 *Nihon teien* Japanese garden.
        名園 *meien* famous garden.   園児 *enji* kidergarten children.

#207 館	16 strokes	𠆢 㑒 食 飣 飦 館

ON   KAN building, hall
        水族館 *suizokukan* aquarium.   月曜休館 *getsuyō kyūkan* Closed on
        Mondays.   本館 *honkan* main building.   新館 *shinkan* new
        building.

■ II. Vocabulary ■

犬	*inu*	dog
番犬	*banken*	watchdog
牛	*ushi*	cow, bull, cattle
馬	*uma*	horse
牛馬	*gyūba*	oxen and horses
飼い犬	*kaiinu*	pet dog
飼育‹v›	*shiiku*	raising
羊	*hitsuji*	sheep
羊毛	*yōmō*	wool
群れ	*mure*	herd, flock, group
大群	*taigun*	large group
象	*zō*	elephant
魚	*sakana*	fish
金魚	*kingyo*	gold fish
貝類	*kairui*	sellfish
鳥	*tori*	bird
飛鳥	*hichō*	flying bird
巣	*su*	nest
帰巣‹v›	*kisō*	homing

虫	*mushi*	insect, bug
昆虫	*konchū*	insect
蚕	*kaiko*	silkworm
養蚕	*yōsan*	sericulture
動物	*dōbutsu*	animal
動物園	*dōbutsuen*	zoo
水族館	*suizokukan*	aquarium

■ III. Reading Exercises 13 ■

Read and translate the following.

1. 幼い子供が**小犬**と**遊**んでいます。
2. 我が家で大きい**番犬**を**飼**っています。
3. この**牛**もその**馬**も父が育てたのです。
4. 祖父は長年**牛馬**の**飼育**をやっていました。
5. アフリカには**象**や**水牛**などの**動物**が居ます。
6. 私達は**動物園**まで歩きました。
7. 庭のどこかで**虫**が**鳴**いています。
8. 次男は今朝早く、友達と**昆虫**をとりに出かけた。
9. **羊**の**群**れがゆっくりと**動**いています。
10. 魚の**大群**が水の中を**泳**いでいます。
11. この本にはめずらしい**魚類**や**貝類**のことが出ている。
12. **鳥**が三羽**飛**んでいる。**飛行機**は二機**飛**んでいる。
13. ある**鳥類**は毎年、**古巣**に帰るそうです。
14. 昔は**蚕**を**飼**っていましたが、現在**養蚕**は行なわれていません。
15. この**水族館**は月曜**休館**です。

7
****
Plants and Colors

Plants

■ I. Reference ■

#208 草	9 strokes	一　艹　艹　昔　苩　草

kun　*kusa* grass, weed, plants
草 *kusa* grass, weed.　草木 *kusaki* trees and plants.　千草 *chigusa* various flowering plants.　草分け *kusawake* pioneer.

ON　SŌ grass, weed, plants
草木 *sōmoku* trees and plants.　起草 ⟨v⟩ *kisō* drafting.

#209 花	7 strokes	一　艹　艼　花　花

kun　*hana* flower
花 *hana* flower.　草花 *kusabana* flowering plant.　花園 *hanazono* flower garden.　花火 *hanabi* fireworks.

ON　KA flower
花瓶▲ *kabin* flower vase.　造花 #847 *zōka* artificial flower.

#210 葉	12 strokes	艹　芏　苹　苺　葦　葉

kun　*ha* leaf, foliage Ir. *(momi)ji** #232
葉 *ha* leaf.　木の葉 *ko no ha* tree leaves.　若葉 *wakaba* young leaves.　千葉 *Chiba* Chiba (place).

ON　YŌ leaf, foliage
紅葉 #232 *kōyō* autumn/colored leaves.　中葉 *chūyō* middle (of the century).　末葉 *matsuyō* end.

#211 芽	8 strokes	艹 芇 芇 芒 芽 芽

kun *me* bud, sprout
芽 *me* bud, sprout.　新芽 *shinme* bud, spout.

ON GA bud, sprout
葉芽 *yōga* leaf bud.　幼芽 *yōga* germ.

#212 枝	8 strokes	十 木 杉 杉 枝 枝

kun *eda* branch
枝 *eda* branch.　小枝 *koeda* twig.　大枝 *ōeda* bough.　枝葉 *edaha* branches and leaves; unessentials.

ON SHI branch
枝葉 *shiyō* branches and leaves; unessentials　枝葉末節にこだわる *shiyō massetsu ni kodawaru* be particular about trivial details.

#213 幹	13 strokes	十 古 直 軡 軡 幹

kun *miki* tree trunk
幹 *miki* tree trunk.

ON KAN main part
幹部 *kanbu* executives, key officers.　主幹 *shukan* chief editor.　才幹 *saikan* ability, talent.

#214 根	10 strokes	十 木 杪 杪 根 根

kun *ne* root
根 *ne* root.　草の根 *kusa no ne* grass root.　根も葉もない *ne mo ha mo nai* groundless (rumor).　根回し *nemawashi* digging around the root of a tree; maneuvering behind the scenes.

ON KON root
大根 *daikon* Japanese radish.　根本 *konpon* origin, source.　根幹 *konkan* basis, root.　根性 *konjō* nature, disposition.

#215 種	14 strokes	千 禾 秈 稆 稆 種

kun *tane* seed
種 *tane* seed.　種馬 *taneuma* studhorse.　種本 *tanehon* source book.

ON   SHU seed; species

種子 *shushi* seed.   種類 *shurui* kind.   種々の *shuju no* all kinds of (trees).   人種 *jinshu* human race.

#216 樹	16 strokes	木	术	桔	椊	桔	樹

ON   JU tree

樹木 *jumoku* tree.   樹幹 *jukan* tree trunk.   針葉樹 *shin'yōju* needle-leaf tree.   樹立 ⟨v⟩ *juritsu* establishment (of a world record).

#217 竹	6 strokes	ノ	⺊	⺮	⺮	⺮	竹

kun   *take* bamboo Ir. *shi(nai)* * #941

竹 *take* bamboo.   竹の子 *take no ko* bamboo shoots.   竹馬 *takeuma* stilts.

ON   CHIKU bamboo

竹馬の友 *chikuba no tomo* childhood friend.

#218 松	8 strokes	十	木	术	杦	松	松

kun   *matsu* pine

松 *matsu* pine.   松の木 *matsu no ki* pine tree.   松葉 *matsuba* pine needle.   松の内 *matsu no uchi* 1st 7 days of the New Year.

ON   SHŌ pine

松竹梅 #219 *shōchikubai* pine-bamboo-plum.

#219 梅	10 strokes	十	术	杧	栴	栴	梅

kun   *ume* plum tree Ir. *tsu(yu)* * #340

梅 *ume* plum tree.   梅の花 *ume no hana* plum blossoms.

ON   BAI plum tree

松竹梅 *shōchikubai* pine-bamboo-plum.   梅花 *baika* plum blossoms.   梅園 *baien* plum orchard.   入梅 *nyubai* beginning of the rainy season.

#220 桜

10 strokes   十 才 杉 松 桜 桜

kun *sakura* cherry tree
桜 *sakura* cherry tree.   桜の花 *sakura no hana* cherry blossoms.
桜の園 *sakura no sono* garden for cherry trees.

ON Ō cherry tree
桜花 *ōka* cherry blossoms.   桜樹 *ōju* cherry tree.

#221 見

7 strokes | 冂 冃 目 見 見

kun *mi(ru)* see, look, view; *mi(eru)* be seen; *mi(seru)* show
見る *miru* see, look, view.   見える *mieru* be seen.   見せる *miseru* show.   花見 *hanami* cherry-blossom viewing.   見方 *mikata* viewpoint.   見出し *midashi* headline.   見下ろす *miorosu* look down.

ON KEN see, look, view
見物 ⑴ *kenbutsu* sightseeing.   見物人 *kenbutsunin* sightseer.
先見 *senken* foresight.

#222 植

12 strokes   木 杧 柿 柿 植 植

kun *u(eru)* plant
植える *ueru* plant.   植木 *ueki* garden plant, potted plant.

ON SHOKU plant
植物 *shokubutsu* plant.   植物園 *shokubutsuen* botanical garden.

#223 切

4 strokes   一 七 切 切

kun *ki(ru)* cut; *ki(reru)* cut well; run out of; *ki(re)* cuts, slices
切る *kiru* cut.   切り花 *kiribana* cut flower.   切れる *kireru* cut well; run out of (cash).   一切れ *hitokire* a slice of (meat).

ON SETSU, [SAI] cut
大切な *taisetsu na* important, precious.   親切な *shinsetsu na* kind.
一切 *issai* all, everything.

#224 実	8 strokes	丶 宀 宀 宀 宲 実

kun   *mi* fruit, nut; *mino(ru)* bear fruit
実 *mi* fruit, nut. 実る *minoru* bear fruit.

ON   JITSU reality, truth
実に *jitsu ni* truly. 実物 *jitsubutsu* real thing, original. 現実 *gen-jitsu* realities. 実行 ‹v› *jikkō* putting into practice.

#225 熟	15 strokes	亠 吉 享 剪 孰 熟

kun   *u(reru)* ripen
熟れる *ureru* ripen. 熟れたトマト *ureta tomato* ripe tomato.

ON   JUKU ripen, mature
熟す *jukusu* ripen. 熟した実 *jukushita mi* ripe fruit. 半熟の *han-juku no* soft-boiled (egg). 未熟な *mijuku na* inexperienced. 成熟 ‹v› *seijuku* maturation. 熟知 ‹v› *jukuchi* full knowledge.

#226 散	12 strokes	十 廿 昔 背 散 散

kun   *chi(ru)* fall, disperse, scatter
散る *chiru* fall, disperse, scatter. 花が散る *Hana ga chiru* Flowers fall. 三々五々に散る *sansan-gogo ni chiru* (people) disperse by tows and threes.

ON   SAN fall, disperse, scatter
散歩 ‹v› *sanpo* walk. 散在 ‹v› *sanzai* being found here and there. 散水 ‹v› *sansui* water sprinkling. 飛散 ‹v› *hisan* scattering.

#227 折	7 strokes	扌 扌 扩 扩 折 折

kun   *o(ru)* break; fold; *o(reru)* break; be folded; compromise; *ori* occasion
折る *oru* break; fold. 枝を折る *eda o oru* break off a branch. カードを折る *kādo o oru* fold a card. 折れる *oreru* break; be folded; compromise. その折り *sono ori* at that occasion. 折々 *oriori* occasionally.

ON   SETSU break; fold
折半 ‹v› *seppan* deviding into halves.

落

12 strokes 　一　艹　汔　莎　荶　落

kun　*o(chiru)* fall; *o(tosu)* drop; lose
落ちる *ochiru* fall.　落ち葉 *ochiba* fallen leaves.　落ち着く *ochitsu-ku* settle down.　落とす *otosu* drop (a cup); lose (a wallet).　落とし物 *otoshimono* lost article.

ON　RAKU fall
落葉樹 *rakuyōju* deciduous tree.　落下 ⟨v⟩ *rakka* falling.　落第 ⟨v⟩ *rakudai* failure in an examination.

■ II. Vocabulary

草	*kusa*	grass, weed
草木	*kusaki/sōmoku*	trees and plants
花	*hana*	flower
切り花	*kiribana*	cut flower
花見	*hanami*	cherry-blossom viewing
見物 ⟨v⟩	*kenbutsu*	sightseeing
枝	*eda*	branch
葉	*ha*	leaf, foliage
木の葉	*ko no ha*	tree leaves
枝葉	*edaha/shiyō*	branches and leaves; unessentials
芽	*me*	bud, sprout
幼芽	*yōga*	leaf bud
種	*tane*	seed
種子	*shushi*	seed
実	*mi*	fruit, nut
熟れた・熟した	*ureta/jukushita*	ripe (fruit)
根	*ne*	root
大根	*daikon*	Japanese radish
竹	*take*	bamboo
松	*matsu*	pine
梅	*ume*	plum tree
松竹梅	*shōchikubai*	pine, bamboo, plum
桜	*sakura*	cherry tree
桜花	*ōka*	cherry blossoms

樹木	*jumoku*	tree
幹	*miki*	tree trunk
樹幹	*jukan*	tree trunk
落ち葉	*ochiba*	fallen leaves
落葉樹	*rakuyōju*	deciduous tree
植木	*ueki*	garden plant, potted plant
植物	*shokubutsu*	plant
植物園	*shokubutsuen*	botanical garden

■ III. Reading Exercises 14 ■

Read and translate the following.

1. 庭に草が生えています。
2. 子供が竹を二つに折りました。
3. 男の人が松の枝を切っています。
4. 梅の花が散って、桜の花の季節が来た。
5. 今週末、花見に行きませんか。
6. 正月やその他のめでたい折に松竹梅をかざります。
7. 木の幹に大きい虫が止まっている。
8. 秋には木の葉が落ちます。
9. 葉の落ちる木を落葉樹といいます。
10. 枝葉にこだわらず、根幹を正すことが大切です。
11. 大根の種を植えましたが、まだ芽が出ません。
12. この実はまだ熟していないが、そちらはもう十分熟れている。
13. 種々の草木や樹木を見ながら、植物園の中を散歩した。

Colors

■ **I. Reference** ■

#229 色	6 strokes	ノ ク ク ク 色 色

kun *iro* color; erotic passion
色 *iro* color.   色々の *iroiro no* various.   金色 *kin'iro* gold color.
水色 *mizuiro* blue.   色男 *irootoko* lover, handsome man.   色っぽ
い *iroppoi* erotic, sexy.

ON SHOKU, SHIKI color
金色 *konjiki* gold color.   才色 *saishoku* wit and beauty.

#230 白	5 strokes	ノ イ 白 白 白

kun *shiro*, [*shira*], *shiro(i)* white
白·白い *shiro/shiroi* white.   白魚 *shirauo* whitebait.   色白の *irojiro
no* fair-skinned (girl).

ON HAKU, BYAKU white
白色 *hakushoku* white color.   白人 *hakujin* Caucasian.   白鳥
hakuchō swan.   白夜 *hakuya/byakuya* nights with the midnight sun.

#231 赤	7 strokes	一 十 土 ナ 赤 赤

kun *aka, aka(i)* red Ir. *(mak)ka**#662
赤·赤い *aka/akai* red.   赤ちゃん *akachan* baby.   赤の他人 *aka no
tanin* perfect stranger.

ON SEKI, [SHAKU] red
赤色 *sekishoku* red color.   赤銅色 #845 *shakudōiro* brown.

#232 紅	9 strokes	く 幺 幺 糸 紅 紅

kun *kurenai* crimson; *beni* rouge Ir. *momi(ji)**
紅 *kurenai* crimson.   紅 *beni* rouge.   紅色 *kurenaiiro/beniiro*
crimson.   紅葉 *momiji** maple tree; autumn/colored leaves.

ON   KŌ, [KU] crimson
紅葉 *kōyō* autumn/colored leaves.   紅梅 *kōbai* red plum blossom.
紅白 *kōhaku* red and white.   真紅 #662 *shinku* crimson.

#233 黄	11 strokes	⺧ 艹 芒 苗 黄 黄

kun   *ki, [ko]* yellow
黄色 *kiiro* yellow.   黄金色 *koganeiro* golden color.   黄ばむ *kiba-mu* grow yellowish.
ON   KŌ, Ō yellow
黄金色 *ōgonshoku* golden color.   黄色人種 *ōshoku jinshu* yellow race.   黄葉 *kōyō* golden leaves.

#234 茶	9 strokes	一 艹 芖 苯 茶 茶

ON   CHA, SA tea
茶 *cha* tea.   茶色 *chairo* brown.   日本茶 *Nihoncha* Japanese tea.
紅茶 *kōcha* black tea.   茶道 #301 *sadō* tea ceremony.

#235 緑	14 strokes	⸜ 纟 糸 糺 紀 緑

kun   *midori* green
緑 *midori* green.   緑色 *midoriiro* green.
ON   RYOKU, [ROKU] green
緑茶 *ryokucha* green tea.   新緑 *shinryoku* fresh verdure.   緑青 *rokushō* green rust.   緑青色 *rokushōiro* bluish green.

#236 黒	11 strokes	丶 口 甲 里 里 黒

kun   *kuro, kuro(i)* black
黒・黒い *kuro/kuroi* black.   白黒 *shirokuro* balck and white; right or wrong.
ON   KOKU black
黒白 *kokubyaku* black and white; right or wrong.   黒人 *kokujin* black person.

#237 変	9 strokes	一 ナ 亣 亦 亦 変 変

kun   *ka(waru)* change, be altered; *ka(eru)* change, alter
変わる *kawaru* change, be altered.   変える *kaeru* change (plans).
色変わり‹v› *irogawari* change of color.

ON   HEN change
変色‹v› *henshoku* change of color.   変動‹v› *hendō* change, fluctuation.   変人 *henjin* eccentric person.   大変な *taihen na* serious, terrible.

■ II. Vocabulary ■

色	*iro*	color
色々の	*iroiro no*	various
金色	*kin'iro/konjiki*	gold color
白・白い	*shiro/shiroi*	white
白色	*hakushoku*	white color
赤・赤い	*aka/akai*	red
赤色	*sekishoku*	red color
黒・黒い	*kuro/kuroi*	black
白黒	*shirokuro*	black-and-white; right or wrong
黒白	*kokubyaku*	black-and-white; right or wrong
紅	*kurenai*	crimson
紅色	*kurenaiiro/beniiro*	crimson
紅葉	*kōyō/momiji*	autumn/colored leaves
黄色	*kiiro*	yellow
黄金色	*koganeiro/ōgonshoku*	golden color
茶色	*chairo*	brown
紅茶	*kōcha*	black tea
緑・緑色	*midori/midoriiro*	green
緑茶	*ryokucha*	green tea
色変わり‹v›	*irogawari*	change of color
変色‹v›	*henshoku*	change of color

Read and translate the following.

1. 花園に**色々**の**色**の花がさいています。
2. 若葉に**金色**の日がさしています。
3. 少女が**赤い**花を折って来ました。
4. **白い**鳥が松の枝に止まっています。
5. **白鳥**が青い水の上を泳いで行く。
6. **紅**の夕日が実にうつくしい。
7. 庭園の**紅梅**が散りました。
8. 秋には木の葉が**紅葉**します。
9. **緑**の草の上を**茶色**の小馬が歩いている。
10. 私は**紅茶**がいいですが、母は**緑茶**の方がいいです。
11. この実は熟れると、**黄色**に**変色**します。
12. スミス夫人は**黄金色**のブラウスに黒のスカートをはいている。
13. アメリカには様々な人種が住んでいる。**白人**も、**黒人**も、**黄色人種**も居る。

8

Geography

Lands

I. Reference

#238 山	3 strokes 

kun — *yama* mountain Ir. *da(shi)** #786

山 *yama* mountain. 山々 *yamayama* mountains. 夏山 *natsuyama* mountains in summer.

ON — SAN mountain

エベレスト山 *Eberesuto-san* Mt. Everest. 火山 *kazan* volcano. 死火山 *shikazan* extinct volcano. 遊山 *yusan* picnic, excursion.

#239 頂	11 strokes 

kun — *itadaki* summit, top; *itada(ku)* receive

頂 *itadaki* summit, top. 頂く *itadaku* (humble) receive.

ON — CHŌ summit, top

山頂 *sanchō* mountain top. 頂上 *chōjō* summit, top.

#240 登	12 strokes 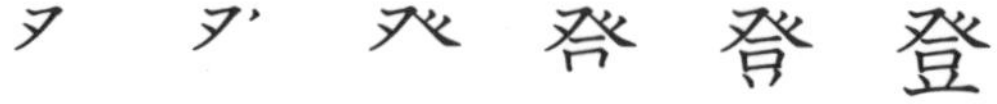

kun — *nobo(ru)* climb

登る *noboru* climb. 山登り ‹v› *yamanobori* mountain climbing.

ON — TŌ, TO climb

登山 ‹v› *tozan* mountain climbing. 登山者 *tozansha* mountain climber. 登頂 ‹v› *tōchō* reaching the summit.

#241 脈	10 strokes 

ON — MYAKU pulse, vein; geological vein

山脈 *sanmyaku* mountain range. 火山脈 *kazanmyaku* volcanic

mountain range. 脈 *myaku* pulse, vein. 動脈 *dōmyaku* artery.
脈動 ‹v› *myakudō* pulsation.

| #242 林 | 8 strokes | 十 才 木 朴 材 林 |

kun   *hayashi* woods, forest
          林 *hayashi* woods, small forest.   松林 *matsubayashi* pine woods.
ON   RIN woods, forest
          山林 *sanrin* mountain forest.   林立 ‹v› *rinritsu* standing close
together (like trees in a forest).

| #243 森 | 12 strokes | 十 木 木 朿 森 森 |

kun   *mori* forest
          森 *mori* forest.   青森 *Aomori* Aomori (Place).
ON   SHIN forest
          森林 *shinrin* forest.   森林動物 *shinrin dōbutsu* forest animal.

| #244 谷 | 7 strokes | ノ ハ 分 谷 谷 谷 |

kun   *tani* valley
          谷 *tani* valley.   谷水 *tanimizu* valley water.   谷間 *tanima* ravine.
ON   KOKU valley
          渓谷 *keikoku* gorge.

| #245 底 | 8 strokes | 亠 广 庀 庐 底 底 |

kun   *soko* bottom
          底 *soko* bottom.   谷底 *tanizoko* bottom of a valley.
ON   TEI bottom
          水底 *suitei* bottom of the water.   底本 *teihon* original text.   根底
kontei bottom, foundation.

| #246 地 | 6 strokes | 一 十 土 圵 坤 地 |

ON   CHI, JI earth, ground
          土地 *tochi* land.   山地 *sanchi* mountainous district.   地方 *chihō*
region.   地名 *chimei* place name.   地主 *jinushi* landlord.

#247 平	5 strokes	一 一 丆 丆 平

kun *tai(ra), hira* flat, even, ordinary
平らな *taira na* flat (land). 平家 *hiraya* one-story house. 平泳ぎ *hiraoyogi* breast stroke.

ON HEI, BYŌ flat, even, ordinary
平地 *heichi* flat ground. 平日 *heijitsu* weekday. 平年 *heinen* ordinary year. 平等 #526 *byōdō* equality.

#248 野	11 strokes	口 甲 里 野 野 野

kun *no* field, plain
野 *no* field, plain. 野山 *noyama* hills and fields.

ON YA field, plain
平野 *heiya* plain. 野鳥 *yachō* wild bird. 野生動物 *yasei dōbutsu* wild animal. 分野 *bun'ya* field (of study).

#249 原	10 strokes	一 厂 厂 所 原 原

kun *hara* field, plain
野原 *nohara* field. 草原 *kusahara* grassy plain.

ON GEN original; field, plain
草原 *sōgen* grassy plain. 原野 *gen'ya* wasteland. 原生林 *genseirin* virgin forest. 原子 *genshi* atom.

#250 広	5 strokes	丶 亠 広 広 広

kun *hiro(i)* broad, wide; *hiro(garu)* spread, expand; *hiro(maru)* spread
広い *hiroi* broad, wide, large. 広さ *hirosa* width; area. 広がる *hirogaru* spread, expand. 広まる *hiromaru* spread, become popular.

ON KŌ broad, wide
広大な *kōdai na* vast (plain). 広野 *kōya* vast plain.

#251 田	5 strokes	丨 冂 冊 田 田

kun *ta* rice field Ir. *i(naka)** #533
田 *ta* rice field. 田植え ‹v› *taue* rice planing.

ON DEN rice field
水田 *suiden* rice paddy. 田地 *denchi* rice paddy. 田園 *den'en* country side.

#252 畑	9 strokes	` ⺌ 灯 灯 炉 畑

kun *hata, hatake* field, farm
畑 *hatake* field, farm. 田畑 *tahata* fields, farm. 茶畑 *chabatake* tea field. 花畑 *hanabatake* flower field.

#253 耕	10 strokes	= 丰 耒 耒 耕 耕

kun *tagaya(su)* till, cultivate
耕す *tagayasu* till, cultivate (fields).

ON KŌ till, cultivate
耕地 *kōchi* cultivated field.

#254 作	7 strokes	ノ イ 亻 仁 仵 作 作

kun *tsuku(ru)* make, produce
作る *tsukuru* make, produce.

ON SAKU, SA make, produce
耕作 ‹v› *kōsaku* cultivation. 作物 *sakumotsu* crops. 名作 *meisaku* masterpiece. 作者 *sakusha* author. 動作 *dōsa* action.

#255 米	6 strokes	` ` 丷 平 米 米

kun *kome* rice
米 *kome* rice

ON BEI, MAI rice
米作 *beisaku* rice culture. 白米 *hakumai* polished rice. 新米 *shinmai* new rice; novice.

#256 麦	7 strokes	一　十　圭　声　考　麦

kun *mugi* wheat, barley
麦 *mugi* wheat, barley.　小麦 *komugi* wheat.　大麦 *ōmugi* barley.
麦畑 *mugibatake* wheat field.

ON BAKU wheat, barley
麦芽 *bakuga* malt.　麦秋 *bakushū* barley harvest season.

#257 穀	14 strokes	士　声　幸　幸　穀　穀

ON KOKU grain, cereals
穀物 *kokumotsu* grain.　米穀 *beikoku* rice.　穀類 *kokurui* grains.

#258 牧	8 strokes	⺧　牛　牛　牜　牧　牧

kun *maki* pasture
牧場 #259 *makiba* pasture.

ON BOKU pasture
牧草 *bokusō* grass, pasture.　遊牧 *yūboku* nomadism.　牧牛
bokugyū pasturing cattle.　牧夫 *bokufu* herdsman.

#259 場	12 strokes	士　圠　垍　垍　堨　場

kun *ba* place
牧場 *makiba* pasture.　広場 *hiroba* open ground; square.　立場
tachiba standpoint.　この場合 *kono baai* in this case.

ON JŌ place
牧場 *bokujō* pasture.　場内 *jōnai* inside the hall.　場外 *jōgai* outside the hall.

#260 面	9 strokes	一　厂　帀　而　面　面

kun *omote, omo, tsura* face
面を上げる *omote o ageru* look up.　面長な *omonaga na* oval-faced
(girl).　面白い *omoshiroi* interesting.　ふくれっ面 *fukurettsura*
sulky look.

ON   MEN mask, surface, aspect
面 *men* mask.   水面 *suimen* water surface.   地面 *jimen* ground.
千葉方面 *Chiba hōmen* Chiba districts.   面目 *menboku* face,
honor.

#261 積	16 strokes	千　禾　秮　秮　積　積

kun   *tsu(mu)* pile up, load; *tsu(moru)* be piled up; *tsu(mori)* intention;
estimate
積む *tsumu* pile up, load.   積もる *tsumoru* be piled up.   積もり
tsumori intention.   見積もり ‹v› *mitsumori* estimation.

ON   SEKI pile up, load
面積 *menseki* area.   山積 ‹v› *sanseki* piling up.

#262 層	14 strokes	一　尸　屈　屈　層　層

ON   SŌ layer, level
地層 *chisō* land stratum.   上層 *jōsō* upper layer/classes/floors.
下層 *kasō* lower layer/classes/floors.   若年層 *jakunensō* younger
generation.   一層 *issō* even more.

#263 石	5 strokes	一　厂　尤　石　石

kun   *ishi* stone
石 *ishi* stone.   小石 *koishi* pebble.

ON   SEKI, [SHAKU] stone; [KOKU] (unit of volume)
誕生石 *tanjōseki* birthstone.   石二鳥 *isseki nichō* killing 2 birds
with 1 stone.   磁石 #480 *jishaku* magnet.   百万石 *hyakuman-goku* 1
million koku of rice.

#264 岩	8 strokes	⺊　山　屵　岩　岩　岩

kun   *iwa* rock
岩 *iwa* rock.   岩山 *iwayama* rocky mountain.

ON   GAN rock
岩石 *ganseki* rock.   水成岩 *suiseigan* aqueous rock.

#265 砂	9 strokes	一 ｢ 石 石 砂 砂

kun   *suna* sand Ir. *ja(ri)* *#502

         砂 *suna* sand.   砂地 *sunaji* sandy soil.   砂場 *sunaba* sandbox.

ON   SA, SHA sand

         土砂 *dosha* earth and sand.   土砂くずれ *doshakuzure* landslide.

         砂金 *sakin* gold dust.

■ II. Vocabulary ■

山	*yama*	mountain
山脈	*sanmyaku*	mountain range
頂	*itadaki*	summit, top
山頂	*sanchō*	mountain top
山登り‹v›	*yamanobori*	mountain climbing
登山‹v›	*tozan*	mountain climbing
林	*hayashi*	woods, small forest
森	*mori*	forest
森林	*shinrin*	forest
谷	*tani*	valley
谷底	*tanizoko*	bottom of a valley
水底	*suitei*	bottom of the water
土地	*tochi*	land
野原	*nohara*	field
平野	*heiya*	plain
広野	*kōya*	vast plain
草原	*kusahara/sōgen*	grassy plain
牧場	*makiba/bokujō*	pasture
田	*ta*	rice field
水田	*suiden*	rice paddy
畑	*hatake*	field, farm
耕地	*kōchi*	cultivated field
耕作‹v›	*kōsaku*	cultivation
米	*kome*	rice
米作	*beisaku*	rice culture
麦	*mugi*	wheat, barley

麦芽	*bakuga*	malt
穀物	*kokumotsu*	grain
面積	*menseki*	area
地層	*chisō*	land stratum
石	*ishi*	stone
岩	*iwa*	rock
岩石	*ganseki*	rock
砂	*suna*	sand
土砂	*dosha*	earth and sand

■ III. Reading Exercises 16 ■

Read and translate the following.

1. 山の頂から、森や林が見えます。
2. 森林に種々の動物や鳥が住んでいる。
3. 来年はエベレスト山に登りたい。
4. 去年の夏休みに、四、五人の仲間と登山した。
5. 山頂から、谷底を見下ろした。
6. 水底を小さい魚が泳いでいる。
7. 田畑を耕して、色々の穀物を作る。水田に米を、畑に麦を作る。
8. その土地の面積の半分以上は耕地です。
9. この地方では一年に二度米作を行なっている。
10. 野原で野鳥が鳴いている。
11. 広い草原を一群の馬が走っている。
12. トンネルを出ると、目の前に広大な平野が広がった。
13. 緑の牧場で羊が草をたべています。
14. この植物は、砂地でも石や岩のある地面でも育たない。
15. 土砂や岩石が積みかさなって地層が出来る。

Waters

#266 川 | 3 strokes | ノ 川 川

kun   *kawa* river Ir. *ka(wara)**
川 *kawa* river.   小川 *ogawa* creek.   川上 *kawakami* upstream.
川下 *kawashimo* downstream.   川原 *kawara** dry riverbed.

ON   SEN river
山川 *sansen* mountains and rivers.   山川草木 *sansen sōmoku*
nature.

#267 河 | 8 strokes | ` 氵 氵 汀 河 河 河

kun   *kawa* river
河 *kawa* river.   河原 *kawara* dry riverbed.

ON   KA river
河川 *kasen* rivers.   山河 *sanga* mountains and rivers.   大河 *taiga*
large river.

#268 海 | 9 strokes | 氵 氵 汒 洨 海 海 海

kun   *umi* sea, ocean Ir. *a(ma)**; *una(bara)**
海 *umi* sea, ocean.   海女 *ama** female pearl diver.   海原 *unabara**
wide expanse of waters.

ON   KAI sea, ocean
日本海 *Nihonkai* Japan Sea.   海水 *kaisui* sea water.   海外 *kaigai*
overseas.   海底トンネル *kaitei tonneru* undersea tunnel.

#269 洋 | 9 strokes | ` 氵 氵 氵 洋 洋

ON   YŌ ocean; occidental
インド洋 *Indo-yō* Indian Ocean.   海洋 *kaiyō* ocean.   洋上 *yōjō* on
the sea.   洋間 *yōma* western style room.

#270 太	4 strokes	一　ナ　大　太

kun *futo(i)* fat, thick; *futo(ru)* get fat
太い *futoi* fat, thick.　太さ *futosa* thickness; size.　太る *futoru* get fat.

ON TAI, TA fat, thick
太平洋 *Taiheiyō* Pacific Ocean.　太古 *taiko* ancient times.　<ruby>丸<rt>まる</rt></ruby>太 #651 *maruta* log.

#271 池	6 strokes	丶　冫　氵　汋　沖　池

kun *ike* pond
池 *ike* pond.　古池 *furuike* old pond.

ON CHI pond
電池 #450 *denchi* battery.

#272 貯	12 strokes	冂　貝　貝'　貯　貯　貯

ON CHO reserve, save
貯水池 *chosuichi* reservoir.　貯木池 *chobokuchi* timber pond.
貯金 <v> *chokin* saving money.

#273 湖	12 strokes	氵　汁　沽　沽　湖　湖

kun *mizuumi* lake
湖 *mizuumi* lake.

ON KO lake
山中湖 *Yamanaka-ko* Lake Yamanaka.　湖水 *kosui* lake water.
湖面 *komen* surface of a lake.　湖底 *kotei* bottom of a lake.

#274 岸	8 strokes	丶　屵　屵　屵　岸　岸

kun *kishi* bank, shore, coast Ir. *(ka)shi**
岸 *kishi* bank, shore, coast.　川岸 *kawagishi* riverbank.　河岸 *kashi** riverbank.　魚河岸 *uogashi** riverside fish market.

ON　GAN bank, shore, coast

海岸 *kaigan* seashore.　河岸 *kagan* riverbank.　湖岸 *kogan* shore of a lake.

#275 沿　8 strokes　氵　シ　氵ハ　氵八　沿　沿

kun　*so(u)* stand along

沿う *sou* stand along.　海沿いの *umizoi no* along the sea.

ON　EN alongside

沿岸 *engan* coast, shore.　沿岸地方 *enganchihō* districts along the coast.　沿海 *enkai* sea along the coast.

#276 深　11 strokes　氵　氵　氵宀　氵冖　浭　深

kun　*fuka(i)* deep, profound

深い *fukai* deep, profound.　深さ *fukasa* depth.

ON　SHIN deep, profound

水深 *suishin* water depth.　深海 *shinkai* deep sea.　深夜に *shin'ya ni* late at night.

#277 浅　9 strokes　氵　氵　浐　浅　浅　浅

kun　*asa(i)* shallow

浅い *asai* shallow.　遠浅 *tōasa* shoal.

ON　SEN shallow

深浅 *shinsen* depth.　浅海 *senkai* shallow sea.　浅見 *senken* superficial view.

#278 泉　9 strokes　ノ　白　帛　臬　泉　泉

kun　*izumi* spring, fountain

泉 *izumi* spring, fountain.　青春の泉 *seishun no izumi* fountain of youth.

ON　SEN spring, fountain

泉水 *sensui* artificial pond, fountain.　温泉 #359 *onsen* hot spring.

#279 潮	15 strokes	氵 汀 浐 浐 潮 潮

kun   *shio* tide, current

潮 *shio* tide, current.   上げ潮 *ageshio* flowing tide.   朝潮 *asashio* morning tide.   潮時 *shiodoki* chance, opportunity.

ON   CHŌ tide, current

思潮 *shichō* current ideas.   紅潮 ⟨v⟩ *kōchō* flushing, blushing.

#280 流	10 strokes	氵 汀 浐 浐 浐 流

kun   *naga(reru)* flow; *naga(su)* let flow; *naga(re)* stream, current

流れる *nagareru* flow.   流す *nagasu* let (water) flow.   流れ *nagare* stream, current.   潮の流れ *shio no nagare* tidal current.

ON   RYŪ, [RU] current; rank

潮流 *chōryū* tidal current.   海流 *kairyū* ocean current. 一流の *ichiryū no* top-ranking.   流行 ⟨v⟩ *ryūkō* fashion.   自己流 *jikoryū* one's own style.   流布 ⟨v⟩ #484 *rufu* circulation, spreading.

#281 干	3 strokes	一 二 干

kun   *hi(ru)* get dry; *ho(su)* dry; drink up

干る *hiru* get dry.   潮干 *shiohi* ebb tide.   干物 *himono* dried fish. 干す *hosu* dry (a thing); empty (one's glass).

ON   KAN dry

干潮 *kanchō* ebb tide.   若干の *jakkan no* a few (people).

#282 満	12 strokes	氵 汒 汢 満 満 満

kun   *mi(chiru)* become full; *mi(tasu)* fill

満ちる *michiru* become full.   満ち潮 *michishio* full tide.   満たす *mitasu* fill (a glass).

ON   MAN full

満潮 *manchō* full tide.   満月 *mangetsu* full moon.   円満な *enman na* harmonious (family).   満足 ⟨v⟩ *manzoku* satisfaction.

| #283 然 | 12 strokes | ノ | 夕 | 歼 | 殊 | 殊 | 然 |

ON ZEN, NEN as, like; (suffix for state)

自然 *shizen* nature.   自然現象 *shizen genshō* natural phenomenon.
未然に *mizen ni* beforehand.   平然と *heizen to* calmly.   天然水 #335
tennensui natural water.

■ II. Vocabulary

川・河	*kawa*	river
河川	*kasen*	rivers
山河	*sanga*	mountains and rivers
川原・河原	*kawara*	dry riverbed
海	*umi*	sea, ocean
日本海	*Nihonkai*	Japan Sea
太平洋	*Taiheiyō*	Pacific Ocean
池	*ike*	pond
貯水池	*chosuichi*	reservoir
湖	*mizuumi*	lake
山中湖	*Yamanaka-ko*	Lake Yamanaka
岸	*kishi*	bank, shore, coast
川岸	*kawagishi*	riverbank
海岸	*kaigan*	seashore
海沿いの	*umizoi no*	along the sea
沿岸	*engan*	coast, shore
深い	*fukai*	deep, profound
浅い	*asai*	shallow
深浅	*shinsen*	depth
泉	*izumi*	spring, fountain
泉水	*sensui*	artificial pond, fountain
潮の流れ	*shio no nagare*	tidal current
潮流	*chōryū*	tidal current
潮干	*shiohi*	ebb tide
干潮	*kanchō*	ebb tide
満ち潮	*michishio*	full tide
満潮	*manchō*	full tide
自然	*shizen*	nature

Read and translate the following.

1. **川岸**に緑の松が生えている。
2. **川原（河原）**で子供が数人遊んでいる。
3. 春と秋には**山河**がうつくしい。
4. 夏には、人々は**海**で泳いだり、**海岸**を散歩したりする。
5. 原生林の中に**泉**がわき出ている。
6. 庭の**泉水**に赤い金魚が居る。
7. この植物は**深い池**には見られるが、**浅い池**には見られない。
8. あの人達は**川**や、**海**や、**湖**の**深浅**をしらべている。
9. **貯水池**の水が半分しかない。
10. その五つの**湖**の中で、**山中湖**が一番大きい。
11. 日本**海流**は**太平洋**を**流**れている。
12. **満ち潮**の時には、**水深**が十メートル以上になる。
13. **干潮**は午後六時ごろで、**若干**の人が貝を拾いに出る。
14. **海沿**いに数戸の家が散在している。
15. 時々、その**沿岸地方**にめずらしい**自然現象**が起こっている。

The Earth

■ I. Reference ■

#284 図	7 strokes	丨 冂 冂 冈 図 図

kun *haka(ru)* plan, devise
図る *hakaru* plan, devise.

ON ZU sketch, diagram; TO plan, devise
図 *zu* sketch, diagram.　地図 *chizu* map.　合図 *aizu* signal, sign.
意図 ⟨い⟩ #369 *ito* intention.　図書館 #447 *toshokan* library.

#285 理	11 strokes	丁 丑 珏 珇 理 理

ON RI reason, logic, principle
地理 *chiri* geography.　物理 *butsuri* physics.　理性 *risei* reasoning
power.　原理 *genri* principle.

#286 勢	13 strokes	土 去 坴丿 坴九 勢 勢

kun *ikio(i)* power, force; trend
勢い *ikioi* power, force.　自然の勢い *shizen no ikioi* natural
tendency.　勢いよく *ikioiyoku* forcibly.

ON SEI power, force; trend
地勢 *chisei* geographical position.　地勢図 *chiseizu* topographic
map.　大勢 *taisei* general trend.　大勢 *ōzei* many people.

#287 界	9 strokes	冂 冂 田 畀 界 界

ON KAI world
世界 *sekai* world.　世界地図 *sekai chizu* world map.　外界 *gaikai*
external world.　自然界 *shizenkai* world of nature.

#288 球	11 strokes	丁 王 王 珪 玪 球

kun *tama* ball, bulb
球 *tama* ball, bulb.

ON **KYŪ** ball, bulb

地球 *chikyū* the earth, globe.　地球上 *chikyūjō* on the earth.　半球 *hankyū* hemisphere.　野球 *yakyū* baseball.

#289 **東** | 8 strokes | 一　𠃜　𠃜　車　東　東

kun *higashi* east

東 *higashi* east.　東アジア *Higashi Ajia* East Asia.

ON **TŌ** east

東洋 *Tōyō* Orient.　中東 *Chūtō* Middle East.　東部海岸 *tōbu kaigan* east coast.　東方 *tōhō* east, eastward.

#290 **西** | 6 strokes | 一　𠃌　𠃌　西　西　西

kun *nishi* west

西 *nishi* west.　西日本 *Nishi Nihon* Western Japan.

ON **SEI, SAI** west

大西洋 *Taiseiyō* Atlantic Ocean.　西洋 *seiyō* Occident.　西部 *seibu* western part.　東西 *tōzai* east and west.

#291 **南** | 9 strokes | 十　广　冇　南　南　南

kun *minami* south

南 *minami* south.　南太平洋 *Minami Taiheiyō* South Pacific.　南半球 *minami hankyū* southern hemisphere.

ON **NAN** south

南米 *Nanbei* South America.　東南アジア *Tōnan Ajia* Southeast Asia.　南西 *nansei* southwest.　南下 ⟨v⟩ *nanka* going south.

#292 **北** | 5 strokes | 一　十　土　北　北

kun *kita* north

北 *kita* north.　北半球 *kita hankyū* northern hemisphere.

ON **HOKU** north

南北 *nanboku* north and south.　北部 *hokubu* northern part.　北方 *hoppō* north, northward.　北上 ⟨v⟩ *hokujō* going north.

#293 極	12 strokes	木	杧	柯	極	極	極

kun *kiwa(meru)* reach its end; *kiwa(mi)* height, limit

極める *kiwameru* reach its end. 見極める *mikiwameru* ascertain.

極み *kiwami* height, limit.

ON KYOKU end, pole; GOKU extreme

北極 *Hokkyoku* North Pole. 南極 *Nankyoku* South Pole. 極東 *Kyokutō* Far East. 極度 *kyokudo* highest degree. 極上の *goku-jō no* top-quality (goods).

#294 位	7 strokes	ノ	イ	冇	仁	位	位

kun *kurai* position, rank

位 *kurai* position, rank. 位する *kurai suru* be located, be ranked.

千の位 *sen no kurai* thousands digit.

ON I position, rank

地位 *chii* rank, status. 第五位 *daigoi* 5th place. 上位 *jōi* higher rank. 方位 *hōi* compass direction.

#295 置	13 strokes	冖	罒	罒	罘	罟	置

kun *o(ku)* put, place

置く *oku* put, place. 置物 *okimono* ornament. 物置 *monooki* storeroom. 一日置きに *ichinichi oki ni* every other day.

ON CHI put, place

位置 ⟨v⟩ *ichi* location.

#296 陸	11 strokes	⁊	孑	阝‡	陜	陸	陸

ON RIKU land

陸 *riku* land. 大陸 *tairiku* continent. 上陸 ⟨v⟩ *jōriku* landing. 着陸地 *chakurikuchi* landing ground.

#297 島	10 strokes	亻	戶	自	鸟	鳥	島

kun *shima* island

島 *shima* island. 島々 *shimajima* islands. 小島 *kojima* small

island.

ON   TŌ island
半島 *hantō* peninsula.   群島 *guntō* group of islands.

#298 列	6 strokes	一 フ 歹 歹 列 列

ON   RETSU raw, line
列 *retsu* raw, line.   列島 *rettō* archipelago.   行列 ‹v› *gyōretsu* procession, parade.   前列 *zenretsu* front row.

#299 国	8 strokes	丨 冂 冂 国 国 国

kun   *kuni* country, nation
国 *kuni* country, nation.   島国 *shimaguni* island country.

ON   KOKU country, nation
国家 *kokka* nation.   中国 *Chūgoku* China.   外国 *gaikoku* foreign country.   万国 *bankoku* all nations.   帰国 ‹v› *kikoku* returning to one's own country.

#300 州	6 strokes	丶 ﾉ 小 州 州 州

kun   *su* sandbank
州 *su* sandbank.   中州 *nakasu* sands in the river.

ON   SHŪ province, state
本州 *Honshū* Main Island (of Japan).   九州 *Kyūshū* Kyushu Island.   ワシントン州 *Washinton-shū* Washington State.

#301 道	12 strokes	` ⺀ 并 首 首 道 道

kun   *michi* street, way, path
道 *michi* street, way, path.   近道 *chikamichi* short cut.   散歩道 *sanpomichi* promenade.

ON   DŌ, [TŌ] street, way, path
北海道 *Hokkaidō* Hokkaido Island.   赤道 *sekidō* equator.   国道 *kokudō* national road.   茶道 *sadō* tea ceremony.   神道 #756 *Shintō* Shintoism.

#302 央	5 strokes	ノ 口 口 央 央

ON Ō center

中央 *chūō* center.   中央アメリカ *Chūō Amerika* Central America.
中央広場 *chūō hiroba* central plaza.

#303 多	6 strokes	ノ ク タ タ 多 多

kun *ō(i)* many, much

多い *ōi* many, much.   数多くの *kazu ōku no* many, numerous.

ON TA many, much

多数の *tasū no* many, numerous.   多勢 *tazei* great numbers.   多少
tashō more or less.   多分 *tabun* probably.

#304 約	9 strokes	㇑ 幺 糸 糸 約 約

ON YAKU approximately; promise

約 *yaku* approximately.   約半分 *yaku hanbun* about half.   先約
senyaku previous   engagement.   節約 ⟨v⟩ *setsuyaku* saving, economy.

#305 全	6 strokes	ノ 入 스 슦 全 全

kun *matta(ku)* all, whole

全く *mattaku* quite, entirely.

ON ZEN all, whole

全国 *zenkoku* whole country.   全部 *zenbu* all, whole.   全然 *zen-
zen* wholly, entirely.   万全の *banzen no* prudent (measure).

#306 各	6 strokes	ノ ク 久 冬 各 各

kun *onoono* each, every; various

各·各々 *onoono* each, everyone.

ON KAKU each, every; various

各地 *kakuchi* each area, many places.   世界各国 *sekai kakkoku*
many countries around the world.   各方面 *kakuhōmen* every direction.   各種の *kakushu no* all sorts of.   各自 *kakuji* each person.

#307 境	14 strokes	十 圹 圷 培 塴 境

kun *sakai* border, boundary

境 *sakai* border, boundary.

ON KYŌ, [KEI] border, boundary

国境 *kokkyō* border. 境界 *kyōkai* border, boundary. 境内 *keidai* precinct (of a temple/shrine).

#308 領	14 strokes	𠆢 令 领 領 領 領

ON RYŌ govern, control

領土 *ryōdo* territory. 領地 *ryōchi* territory. 領海 *ryōkai* territorial waters. 領主 *ryōshu* feudal lord.

#309 帯	10 strokes	一 卅 芇 芇 帯 帯

kun *obi* belt, sash; *o(biru)* wear; be tinged

帯 *obi* sash for kimono. 帯びる *obiru* wear (a sword); be tinged (with red).

ON TAI belt, zone

地帯 *chitai* zone, region. 森林地帯 *shinrin chitai* forest region. 火山帯 *kazantai* volcanic zone. 世帯 *setai* household.

#310 熱	15 strokes	土 去 刲 埶 熱 熱

kun *atsu(i)* hot

熱い *atsui* hot (coffee).

ON NETSU heat, fever, zeal

熱 *netsu* heat, fever, zeal. 熱帯 *nettai* tropical zone. 平熱 *heinetsu* normal temperature. 熱中 ‹v›*netchū* being crazy about. 熱のある *netsu no aru* earnest.

#311 域	11 strokes	十 圹 圻 垣 域 域

ON IKI area, region

地域 *chiiki* area, region. 流域 *ryūiki* catchment area. 領域 *ryōiki* territory. 海域 *kaiiki* sea area.

地理	*chiri*	geography
地図	*chizu*	map
地勢図	*chiseizu*	topographic map
世界	*sekai*	world
地球	*chikyū*	the earth, globe
北半球	*kita hankyū*	northern hemisphere
北極	*Hokkyoku*	North Pole
南太平洋	*Minami Taiheiyō*	South Pacific
南米	*Nanbei*	South America
東アジア	*Higashi Ajia*	East Asia
東洋	*Tōyō*	Orient
西日本	*Nishi Nihon*	Western Japan
大西洋	*Taiseiyō*	Atlantic Ocean
中央アメリカ	*Chūō Amerika*	Central America
熱帯	*nettai*	tropical zone
大陸	*tairiku*	continent
島	*shima*	island
列島	*rettō*	archipelago
国	*kuni*	country, nation
国境	*kokkyō*	border
全国	*zenkoku*	whole country
各地	*kakuchi*	each area, many places
地域	*chiiki*	area, region
道	*michi*	street, way, path
北海道	*Hokkaidō*	Hokkaido Island
本州	*Honshū*	Main Island (of Japan)
領土	*ryōdo*	territory
位置‹v›	*ichi*	location
約半分	*yaku hanbun*	about half
数多くの	*kazu ōku no*	many, numerous
多数の	*tasū no*	many, numerous

Read and translate the following.

1. **地理**の本に**世界**の主な**国**の**地図**が出ている。
2. **地勢図**で日本**全国**の土地や山の様子を見る。
3. **地球上**には七つの**大陸**がある。
4. 日本は**北半球**に、オーストラリアは**南半球**に**位**する。
5. **北極**と**南極**の海に**各種**の魚や動物が居る。
6. **南太平洋**に**数多**くの**島**が散在する。
7. **熱帯**の**島々**には**多数**のめずらしい植物が生えている。
8. 日本**列島**にはいくつかの火山脈が走っている。
9. 広い川が二つの**州**の**境**になっている。
10. この**道**はカナダの**国境**までつづく。
11. 日本は**本州**、**九州**、**北海道**、**四国**と、その他の小さい**島**から成っている。
12. その地方の**約半分**は**森林地帯**である。
13. **中央**アメリカはメキシコとコロンビアの間のせまい**地域**である。
14. **中国**はアジア**大陸**に**位置**し、**東洋**で一番広大な**領土**をもっている。
15. 春には**全国各地**から、**大勢**の人がこの**半島**に遊びに来る。

Cities and Prefectures

■ I. Reference ■

#312 市	5 strokes	丶　亠　广　宁　市

kun *ichi* market
市 *ichi* market.　市場 *ichiba* marketplace.　見本市 *mihonichi* trade fair.

ON SHI city
市 *shi* city.　千葉市 *Chiba-shi* Chiba City.　市長 *shichō* mayor. 市場 *shijō* market.　外国市場 *gaikoku shijō* foreign market.　市立 の *shiritsu no* municipal.

#313 町	7 strokes	丨　冂　冂　田　田　町

kun *machi* town, city
町 *machi* town, city.　下町 *shitamachi* downtown area.

ON CHŌ town, city
中野町 *Nakano-chō* Nakano Town.　町長 *chōchō* town headman. 町人 *chōnin* townfolk.

#314 区	4 strokes	一　フ　又　区

ON KU ward, section
区 *ku* ward.　中央区 *Chūō-ku* Chuo Ward.　地区 *chiku* district, zone.　区切る *kugiru* punctuate, divide.

#315 村	7 strokes	十　才　木　朩　村　村

kun *mura* village
村 *mura* village.　村人 *murabito* villager.　キャンプ村 *kyanpu-mura* camping village.

ON SON village
山村 *sanson* mountain village.　村長 *sonchō* village headman. 市町村 *shi-chō-son* cities, towns and villages.

#316 役	7 strokes	ノ　彳　彳　彳　役　役

ON　YAKU office; service, use; EKI service
役場 *yakuba* public office.　村役場 *murayakuba* village office.
役人 *yakunin* official.　役者 *yakusha* actor.　役目 *yakume* duty.
役に立つ *yaku ni tatsu* useful.　現役 *gen'eki* active service.

#317 所	8 strokes	ヲ　戸　戸　戸　所　所　所

kun　*tokoro* place
所 *tokoro* place, one's place/address.

ON　SHO place
役所 *yakusho* public office.　区役所 *kuyakusho* ward office.　住所 *jūsho* address.　名所 *meisho* noted place.　近所 *kinjo* neighborhood.　長所 *chōsho* merit.　短所 *tansho* demerit.

#318 公	4 strokes	ノ　八　公　公

kun　*ōyake* public, official
公の *ōyake no* public, official.　公にする *ōyake ni suru* make public.

ON　KŌ public, official
公立の *kōritsu no* public.　公園 *kōen* park.　国立公園 *kokuritsu kōen* national park.　公平な *kōhei na* fair, impartial.

#319 京	8 strokes	亠　亠　古　古　亨　京

ON　KYŌ, KEI
東京 *Tōkyō* Tokyo.　上京 *jōkyō* coming up to Tokyo.　帰京 *kikyō* returning to Tokyo.　京浜 *keihin* Tokyo and Yokohama.

#320 都	11 strokes	土　耂　者　者　都　都

kun　*miyako* capital, metropolis
都 *miyako* capital, metropolis.

ON　TO, TSU capital, metropolis
東京都 *Tōkyō-to* Tokyo Metropolis.　都内 *tonai* within Tokyo.

京都 *Kyōto* Kyoto.　都市 *toshi* city.　姉妹都市 *shimai toshi* sister city.　都合 *tsugō* convenience, circumstances.　都合する *tsugō suru* arrange.

#321 会　6 strokes　ノ　入　스　仝　会　会

kun　*a(u)* meet
会う *au* meet.

ON　KAI, E meeting, society
会 *kai* meeting, society.　都会 *tokai* city.　国会 *Kokkai* Diet.　機会 *kikai* opportunity, occasion.　会得 ⟨v⟩ #500 *etoku* comprehension.

#322 府　8 strokes　亠　广　疒　庐　府　府

ON　FU urban prefecture; government office
京都府 *Kyōto-fu* Kyoto Prefecture.　府立水族館 *furitsu suizokukan* prefectural aquarium.

#323 県　9 strokes　冂　目　旦　卑　県　県

ON　KEN prefecture
青森県 *Aomori-ken* Aomori Prefecture.　県立の *kenritsu no* prefectural.　都道府県 *to-dō-fu-ken* urban and rural prefectures.

#324 郡　10 strokes　ヨ　尹　君　君⁷　君⁷　郡

ON　GUN county, district
郡 *gun* county.　郡部 *gunbu* rural district.　郡内 *gunnai* within the county.

#325 郷　11 strokes　〈　糸　纟ヨ　鄉　鄉⁷　郷

ON　KYŌ village, native place; GŌ rural area, county
郷土 *kyōdo* native province.　帰郷 ⟨v⟩ *kikyō* homecoming.　近郷 *kingō* neighboring districts.

#326 事	8 strokes	一 丆 亏 写 写 事

kun   *koto* thing, affair
物事 *monogoto* things, matters.   出来事 *dekigoto* incident.   見事な *migoto na* splendid.

ON   JI, [ZU] thing, affair
知事 *chiji* governor.   都知事 *tochiji* governor of Tokyo Metropolis.   県知事 *kenchiji* governor of a prefecture.   事実 *jijitsu* fact.   火事 *kaji* fire.   家事 *kaji* domestic affairs.

#327 庁	5 strokes	' 亠 广 庐 庁

ON   CHŌ government office
都庁 *Tochō* Metropolitan Government Office.   府庁 *fuchō* prefectural office.   県庁 *kenchō* prefectural office.   登庁 *tōchō* attendance at office.

#328 心	4 strokes	丶 心 心 心

kun   *kokoro* heart, mind Ir. *koko(chi)**
心 *kokoro* heart, mind.   心地 *kokochi** feeling.   居心地がいい *igokochi ga ii* comfortable, feel at home.

ON   SHIN heart, mind; core
中心 *chūshin* center, middle.   中心地 *chūshinchi* center.   心理 *shinri* psychology.   心境 *shinkyō* mental state.   熱心な *nesshin na* enthusiastic.

#329 局	7 strokes	⁻ 尸 尸 尸 局 局

ON   KYOKU bureau, office, department
テレビ局 *terebi-kyoku* TV station.   局長 *kyokuchō* bureau chief.   局外者 *kyokugaisha* outsider.   局面 *kyokumen* aspect, situation.

#330 便	9 strokes	イ 仁 仟 仴 伊 便

kun   *tayo(ri)* news; letter
便り *tayori* news; letter.

ON   BEN convenience; excrement; BIN mail
便 *ben* facilities.   バスの便 *basu no ben* bus service.   便所 *benjo* lavatory.   小便 *shōben* urine.   次の便で *tsugi no bin de* by next mail.

#331 郵	11 strokes	二 乒 垂 垂 垂 郵

ON   YŪ mail
郵便 *yūbin* mail.   郵便局 *yūbinkyoku* post office.   郵便ポスト *yūbin-posuto* mailbox.

#332 口	3 strokes	l ⊓ 口

kun   *kuchi* mouth, outlet; lot
口 *kuchi* mouth.   入り口 *iriguchi* entrance.   出口 *deguchi* exist. 東口 *higashiguchi* east gate.   小口 *koguchi* samll lot.

ON   KŌ, KU mouth, outlet; lot
人口 *jinkō* population.   河口 *kakō* estuary.   火口 *kakō* crater. 口実 *kōjitsu* excuse.   口調 #431 *kuchō* tone, intonation.

#333 民	5 strokes	⌐ ⊐ ⼫ ⺋ 民

kun   *tami* people, populace
民 *tami* people, populace.

ON   MIN people, populace
国民 *kokumin* people, nation.   市民 *shimin* citizen.   住民 *jūmin* inhabitants.   公民館 *kōminkan* citizen's hall.   民族 *minzoku* race. 植民地 *shokuminchi* colony.   民間の *minkan no* private (enterprise).

| 総 | 14 strokes | 幺 糸 糸ノ 紒 総 総 |

ON   SŌ general, overall

総人口 *sōjinkō* total population.   総面積 *sōmenseki* total area.
総会 *sōkai* general meeting.   総長 *sōchō* university president.
総理 *sōri* prime minister.   総計 ⟨v⟩ *sōkei* total.

■ II. Vocabulary ■

市	*shi*	city
町	*machi*	town, city
中野町	*Nakano-chō*	Nakano Town
区	*ku*	ward
村	*mura*	village
山村	*sanson*	mountain village
役場・役所	*yakuba/yakusho*	public office
都	*miyako*	capital, metropolis
都会	*tokai*	city
東京都	*Tōkyō-to*	Tokyo Metropolis
京都府	*Kyōto-fu*	Kyoto Prefecture
青森県	*Aomori-ken*	Aomori Prefecture
都道府県	*to-dō-fu-ken*	urban and rural prefectures
郡	*gun*	county
近郷	*kingō*	neighboring districts
郷土	*kyōdo*	native province
中心地	*chūshinchi*	center
都庁	*Tochō*	Metropolitan Government Office
知事	*chiji*	governor
国民	*kokumin*	people, nation
公民館	*kōminkan*	citizen's hall
郵便局	*yūbinkyoku*	post office
人口	*jinkō*	population
総人口	*sōjinkō*	total population

Read and translate the following.

1. **市**はいくつかの**区**に**区切**られている。
2. **区役所**の**近所**に**郵便局**がある。
3. **村**の**公民館**までバスの**便**がある。
4. 昨夜、**山村**の**役場**で火事が起こった。
5. 近年、その**町**の**近郷**では戸数が二倍になった。
6. **郡内**を広い川が東西に流れている。
7. **東京**は日本で一番大きい**都会**である。
8. **東京都**には一千万以上の人が住んでいる。
9. **京都**は日本の古い**都**であり、**名所**が多く、見物人が大勢来る。
10. **都庁**や**府庁**や**県庁**などの役所は**町**の**中心地**にある。
11. **都道府県**の**知事**は**国民**によってえらばれる。
12. 日本の**総人口**は約一億二千万人である。

9

✶✶✶✶✶✶✶✶✶✶✶✶✶✶✶✶✶✶✶✶

Weather and Universe

Weather

■ I. Reference ■

#335 天	4 strokes	一 二 チ 天

kun	*ame*, [*ama*] heaven, sky

天地 *ametsuchi* heaven and earth. 天の川 *Ama no gawa* Milky Way. 天下る *amakudaru* descend from heaven; come from above.

ON	TEN heaven, sky

天地 *tenchi* heaven and earth. 青天 *seiten* blue sky. 天国 *tengo-ku* heaven, pradise. 天然水 *tennensui* natural water.

#336 気	6 strokes	′ ⁻ ⁼ 气 気 気

ON	KI, KE spirit, mind, mood Ir. *(i)ku(ji)** #369

天気 *tenki* weather. 気象庁 *kishōchō* Meteorological Agency. 気流 *kiryū* air current. 気分 *kibun* feeling. 短気 *tanki* short temper. 気配 #517 *kehai* sign, indication.

#337 候	10 strokes	亻 亻′ 亻″ 亻‴ 亻⁗ 候

kun	*sōrō* (classical verb suffix)

行き候 *yukisōrō* go. 居候 *isōrō* freeloader.

ON	KŌ season, weather

天候 *tenkō* weather. 気候 *kikō* climate. 時候 *jikō* season. 兆候 *chōkō* sign, symptom.

#338 良	7 strokes	⁷ ⁼ ⁼ 𦣝 𦣝 良

kun	*yo(i)* good Ir. *(no)ra**

良い *yoi* good. 野良 *nora** fields. 野良犬 *norainu* stray dog.

ON　　RYŌ good

良心 *ryōshin* conscience.　良友 *ryōyū* good friend.　良家 *ryōke* good family.

#339　悪　| 11 strokes　　一　口　亜　亜　悪　悪

kun　　*waru(i)* bad, evil

悪い *warui* bad, evil.　気分が悪い *kibun ga warui* feel sick.

ON　　AKU, O bad, evil

悪天候 *akutenkō* bad weather.　悪友 *akuyū* bad friend.　悪事 *aku-ji* evil deed.　悪性の *akusei no* malignant.　悪寒 #363 *okan* chill.

#340　雨　| 8 strokes　　一　冂　冂　币　雨　雨

kun　　*ame, [ama]* rain Ir. *(ko)same**; *(sami)dare**; *(shi)gure**; *(tsu)yu**

雨 *ame* rain.　大雨 *ōame* heavy rain.　雨だれ *amadare* raindrops.　小雨 *kosame** drizzle.　五月雨 *samidare** early summer rain.　時雨 *shigure** autumnal shower.　梅雨 *tsuyu** spring rainy season.

ON　　U rain

雨天 *uten* rainy weather.　雨季・雨期 *uki* rainy season.

#341　降　| 10 strokes　　フ　阝　阝　阝　降　降

kun　　*fu(ru)* fall, rain; *o(riru)* get off, descend; *o(rosu)* let off

降る *furu* fall, rain.　降りる *oriru* get off (a bus).　降ろす *orosu* unload, drop off (a passenger).

ON　　KŌ fall, descend

降雨 *kōu* rainfall.　降下 ‹v› *kōka* fall, drop.　降参 ‹v› *kōsan* surrender.　以降 *ikō* after, since.

#342　量　| 12 strokes　　冂　旦　旱　昌　量　量

kun　　*haka(ru)* measure, weigh

量る *hakaru* measure (amount/weight).

ON　　RYŌ quantity

降雨量 *kōuryō* amount of rainfall.　分量 *bunryō* amount.　多量 *taryō* large amount.　少量 *shōryō* small amount.

#343 雪	11 strokes	一 干 雨 雪 雪 雪

kun *yuki* snow

雪 *yuki* snow. 初雪 *hatsuyuki* first snow of the season.

ON SETSU snow

降雪 *kōsetsu* snowfall. 新雪 *shinsetsu* fresh snow. 積雪 *sekisetsu* pile of snow.

#344 残	10 strokes	丆 歹 歹 歼 残 残

kun *noko(ru)* remain; *noko(su)* leave behind, save; *noko(ri)* remainder Ir. *(na)gori**

残る *nokoru* remain. 残す *nokosu* leave behind, save. 残り *nokori* remainder. 名残 *nagori** traces, remains.

ON ZAN remain

残雪 *zansetsu* remaining snow. 残金 *zankin* remainder, balance.

#345 晴	12 strokes	几 日 日 晴 晴 晴

kun *ha(reru)* clear up; *ha(rasu)* dispel

晴れる *hareru* clear up. 晴れ *hare* fine weather. 秋晴れ *akibare* clear autumn weather. 晴らす *harasu* dispel (gloom). 見晴らし *miharashi* view.

ON SEI clear

晴天 *seiten* fine weather. 晴雨計 *seiukei* barometer.

#346 空	8 strokes	丶 宀 空 空 空 空

kun *sora* sky; *a(ku)* become vacant; *a(keru)* vacate; *kara* empty

空 *sora* sky. 青空 *aozora* blue sky. 空く *aku* become vacant. 空ける *akeru* vacate (a room). 空の *kara no* empty (bottle).

ON KŪ sky, air

空気 *kūki* air. 空中 *kūchū* in the air. 空間 *kūkan* space. 空白 *kūhaku* blank.

#347 雲	12 strokes	一 二 雨 雨 雲 雲

kun   *kumo* cloud

雲 *kumo* cloud. 雨雲 *amagumo* rain cloud. 雲間 *kumoma* between clouds. 雲行き *kumoyuki* cloud movement; turn of affairs.

ON   UN cloud

白雲 *hakuun* white cloud. 黒雲 *kokuun* black cloud.

#348 暗	13 strokes	冂 日 日 日 暗 暗

kun   *kura(i)* dark

暗い *kurai* dark. 暗がり *kuragari* darkness, dark place.

ON   AN dark

暗雲 *an'un* dark cloud. 明暗 *meian* light and darkness. 暗夜 *an'ya* dark night. 暗黒時代 *Ankoku Jidai* Dark Age.

#349 照	13 strokes	冂 日 日 昭 昭 照

kun   *te(ru)* shine; *te(rasu)* shine on; compare with

照る *teru* shine. 照らす *terasu* shine on (the sea). 日照り *hideri* drought. 照らし合わせる *terashiawaseru* compare (a thing) with.

ON   SHŌ shine; compare with

残照 *zanshō* afterglow. 照明 *shōmei* lighting. 照合 ⟨v⟩ *shōgō* collation, comparison. 参照 ⟨v⟩ *sanshō* reference, comparison.

#350 風	9 strokes	丿 几 凡 凨 風 風

kun   *kaze*, [*kaza*] wind

風 *kaze* wind. 北風 *kitakaze* north wind. 風上 *kazakami* windward.

ON   FŪ, [FU] wind; style; appearance

風雨 *fūu* wind and rain. 風雪 *fūsetsu* wind and snow. 台風 *taifū* typhoon. 日本風 *Nihonfū* Japanese style. 古風な *kofū na* old-fashioned. 風情 #690 *fuzei* appearance; elegance.

#351 強 | 11 strokes コ 弓 弘 弘 弴 強

kun　*tsuyo(i)* strong; *tsuyo(maru)* become strong; *tsuyo(meru)* strengthen; *shi(iru)* force

強い *tsuyoi* strong.　強さ *tsuyosa* strength.　強まる *tsuyomaru* become strong.　強める *tsuyomeru* strengthen.　強いる *shiiru* force.

ON　KYŌ, GŌ strong

強風 *kyōfū* strong wind.　強行〳*kyōkō* enforcement.　5キロ強 *go-kiro kyō* a little over 5 kirograms.　強引に #386 *gōin ni* by force.

#352 弱 | 10 strokes コ 弓 弓 弜 弱 弱

kun　*yowa(i)* weak; *yowa(ru)*, *yowa(maru)* become weak; *yowa(meru)* weaken

弱い *yowai* weak.　弱さ *yowasa* weakness.　弱る・弱まる *yowaru/ yowamaru* become weak.　弱める *yowameru* weaken.

ON　JAKU weak

強弱 *kyōjaku* strength.　1メートル弱 *ichi-mētoru jaku* a little less than 1 meter.

#353 暴 | 15 strokes 日 早 昇 暴 暴 暴

kun　*aba(ku)* disclose, expose; *aba(reru)* act violently

暴く *abaku* disclose, expose.　暴れる *abareru* act violently.

ON　BŌ violent; [BAKU] disclose, expose

暴風 *bōfū* storm.　暴風雨 *bōfūu* violent storm.　暴行〳*bōkō* violence.　暴走〳*bōsō* reckless driving.　暴落〳*bōraku* sudden fall.　暴露〳*bakuro* exposure.

#354 波 | 8 strokes ⺡ ⺡ 汀 沪 波 波

kun　*nami* wave

波 *nami* wave.　大波 *ōnami* great wave.　小波 *konami* ripple.

ON　HA wave

風波 *fūha* wind and waves.　波長 *hachō* wavelength.　短波 *tanpa* shortwave.　波止場 *hatoba** warf, pier.

#355 害	10 strokes	﹀　宀　宀　宭　害　害

ON　　GAI injury, harm, damage

公害 *kōgai* environmental pollution.　水害 *suigai* flood damage.
干害 *kangai* drought disaster.　害虫 *gaichū* harmful insect.

#356 圧	5 strokes	一　厂　厂　圧　圧

ON　　ATSU pressure

気圧 *kiatsu* atmospheric pressure.　気圧の谷 *kiatsu no tani* low
pressure trough.　水圧 *suiatsu* water pressure.　圧巻 *akkan* best
work, masterpiece.　圧死 ⟨v⟩ *asshi* death from pressure.

#357 高	10 strokes	亠　亠　宁　高　高　高

kun　　*taka(i)* high; expensive; *taka* amount; *taka(maru)* rise; *taka(meru)*
raise

高い *takai* high; expensive.　高波 *takanami* high wave.　金高 *kindaka* amount of money.　残高 *zandaka* balance.　高まる *takamaru* rise.　高める *takameru* raise (the position).

ON　　KŌ high; expensive

高気圧 *kōkiatsu* high atmospheric pressure.　高度 *kōdo* altitude;
high degree.　高原 *kōgen* highland.　高価な #497 *kōka na* expensive.

#358 低	7 strokes	亻　亻　仁　低　低　低

kun　　*hiku(i)* low; *hiku(meru)* lower; *hiku(maru)* become lower

低い *hikui* low.　低める *hikumeru* lower (one's voice).　低まる
hikumaru become lower.

ON　　TEI low

低気圧 *teikiatsu* low atmospheric pressure.　高低 *kōtei* height; undulations; pitch.　低下 ⟨v⟩ *teika* decline.

#359 温	12 strokes	氵 沪 沪 泪 温 温

kun   *atata(kai)* warm; *atata(meru)* warm up
温かい *atatakai* warm. 心の温かい *kokoro no atatakai* warm-hearted. 温める *atatameru* warm up (coffee).

ON   ON warm
温度 *ondo* temperature. 気温 *kion* atmospheric temperature. 水温 *suion* water temperature. 温泉 *onsen* hot spring.

#360 最	12 strokes	冃 旱 昮 昮 最 最

kun   *motto(mo)* most, extremely Ir. *mo(yori)** #1016
最も *mottomo* most, extremely. 最も大きい *mottomo ōkii* biggest.

ON   SAI most, extremely
最大の *saidai no* biggest. 最高の *saikō no* highest, best. 最低気温 *saitei kion* lowest temperature. 最初 *saisho* start, first. 最後 *saigo* end, last. 最近 *saikin* lately.

#361 均	7 strokes	十 扌 圹 均 均 均

ON   KIN equal, even
平均 *heikin* average. 平均気温 *heikin kion* average temperature. 千円均一 *sen'en kinitsu* uniform price of 1,000. 均分 ⟨い⟩ *kinbun* dividing equally.

#362 差	10 strokes	丷 丷 羊 差 差 差

kun   *sa(su)* shine upon; hold (an umbrella); wear (a sword)
差す *sasu* shine upon; hold (an umbrella); wear (a sword). 日差し *hizashi* sunlight. 差し出す *sashidasu* hold out; submit.

ON   SA difference
差 *sa* difference. 時差 *jisa* time difference. 大差 *taisa* big difference. 個人差 *kojinsa* individual difference.

#363 寒	12 strokes	宀 宀 宀 宲 寒 寒

kun *samu(i)* cold
寒い *samui* cold.　寒さ *samusa* coldness.　寒気 *samuke* chill.

ON KAN cold
寒気 *kanki* coldness.　寒波 *kanpa* cold wave.　寒流 *kanryū* cold current.　悪寒 *okan* chill.　寒村 *kanson* remote village.

#364 暑	12 strokes	口 日 早 昇 暑 暑

kun *atsu(i)* hot
暑い *atsui* hot.　暑さ *atsusa* heat.　蒸し暑い #429 *mushiatsui* sultry.

ON SHO hot
寒暑 *kansho* heat and cold.　残暑 *zansho* late summer heat.　暑中 *shochū* summer season.

#365 暖	13 strokes	日 日 日 暖 暖 暖

kun *atata(kai)* warm; *atata(meru)* warm up
暖かい *atatakai* warm.　暖める *atatameru* warm up (a room).

ON DAN warm
温暖な *ondan na* warm, mild.　暖冬 *dantō* mild winter.　暖流 *danryū* warm current.　寒暖計 *kandankei* thermometer.

#366 冷	7 strokes	冫 冫 冷 冷 冷 冷

kun *tsume(tai)* cold; *hi(eru)* get cold; *sa(meru)* cool off; *hi(yasu)* cool, chill
冷たい *tsumetai* cold.　冷える *hieru* get cold.　冷める *sameru* cool off.　冷やす *hiyasu* cool, chill (wine).

ON REI cold
冷水 *reisui* cold water.　冷気 *reiki* cold, chill.　冷夏 *reika* cold summer.　冷害 *reigai* cold-weather damage.

#367 氷	5 strokes	丿 丶丿 引 氷 氷

kun   *kōri, hi* ice
     氷 *kōri* ice.   氷雨 *hisame* chill rain.

ON   HYŌ ice
     氷山 *hyōzan* iceberg.   氷河 *hyōga* glacier.   流氷 *ryūhyō* floating ice.

#368 注	8 strokes	氵 氵 汀 汁 汁 注

kun   *soso(gu)* pour, flow
     注ぐ *sosogu* pour, flow.

ON   CHŪ pour, flow; note, comment
     注水 ⟨v⟩ *chūsui* pouring water.   注入 ⟨v⟩ *chūnyū* pouring into.   注目 ⟨v⟩ *chūmoku* attention.   注をつける *chū o tsukeru* annotate.

#369 意	13 strokes	亠 产 音 音 意 意

ON   I will, mind; meaning
     注意 ⟨v⟩ *chūi* attention, caution, warning.   意見 *iken* opinion.   意図 *ito* intention.   意外な *igai na* unexpected.   大意 *taii* gist.

#370 報	12 strokes	土 查 幸 幸卩 報 報

kun   *muku(iru)* reward
     報いる *mukuiru* reward.   報い *mukui* reward.

ON   HŌ news, report
     注意報 *chūihō* warning.   暴風注意報 *bōfū chūihō* storm warning.   報道 ⟨v⟩ *hōdō* news, report.   公報 *kōhō* official report.   時報 *jihō* time signal.   報知機 *hōchiki* alarm.

#371 予	4 strokes	了 マ 予 予

ON   YO previously
     天気予報 *tenki yohō* weather forecast.   予期 ⟨v⟩ *yoki* expectation.   予約 ⟨v⟩ *yoyaku* reservation.

#372 警	19 strokes	⺿ 芍 苟 敬 警 警

ON KEI warn, watch

警報 *keihō* alarm, warning. 大雨警報 *ōame keihō* heavy-rain warning. 夜警⟨ﾍ⟩ *yakei* night watch. 婦警 *fukei* policewoman.

■ II. Vocabulary

良い天気	*yoi tenki*	good weather
悪天候	*akutenkō*	bad weather
晴れ	*hare*	fine weather
晴天	*seiten*	fine weather
雨	*ame*	rain
降雨量	*kōuryō*	amount of rainfall
雪	*yuki*	snow
残雪	*zansetsu*	remaining snow
空	*sora*	sky
空気	*kūki*	air
雲	*kumo*	cloud
暗雲	*an'un*	dark cloud
日照り	*hideri*	drought
残照	*zanshō*	afterglow
弱い風	*yowai kaze*	gentle wind
強風	*kyōfū*	strong wind
暴風	*bōfū*	storm
高波	*takanami*	high wave
風波	*fūha*	wind and waves
高気圧	*kōkiatsu*	high atomospheric pressure
公害	*kōgai*	environmental pollution
最低気温	*saitei kion*	lowest temperature
平均気温	*heikin kion*	average temperature
寒い	*samui*	cold
暑い	*atsui*	hot
寒暑の差	*kansho no sa*	difference in cold and heat
暖かい	*atatakai*	warm
温暖な	*ondan na*	warm, mild

冷たい	*tsumetai*	cold
冷気	*reiki*	cold, chill
氷	*kōri*	ice
氷山	*hyōzan*	iceberg
気象庁	*Kishōchō*	Meteorological Agency
天気予報	*tenki yohō*	weather forcast
注意報	*chūihō*	warning
警報	*keihō*	alarm, warning

■III. Reading Exercises 20 ■

Read and translate the following.

1. 空に暗い雲が広がっている。
2. 今日は天気は良いが、空気は冷たい。
3. この半島は気候が温暖で、冬でも暖かい。
4. 悪天候のため、山道で土砂くずれがあった。
5. 午前中は雨が降ったが、午後は晴れた。
6. 日本で最も降雨量の多い月は六月である。
7. 今年の東京の最低気温は平年より五度も高い。
8. 九州の二月の平均気温は去年より数度低かった。
9. 高気圧のため、晴天がつづいている。
10. 天気予報によると、明日、京都府北部に雪が降るそうだ。
11. 日本海沿岸地方では、毎年、多量の降雪がある。
12. 寒い季節には、大勢の人が暑いハワイに出かける。
13. その都市は大陸の中央部に位置し、寒暑の差が大きい。
14. 北極の海から氷山が流れてくる。
15. 弱い風が強風に変わった。
16. その土地の住民は日照りや公害になやんでいる。
17. 気象庁は高波注意報や暴風警報などを出す。

Universe

■ I. Reference ■

#373 宇 | 6 strokes | ' 宀 宀 宀 宇 宇

ON　U heaven
宇内 *udai* whole world.　気宇広大な *kiukōdai na* magnanimous.

#374 宙 | 8 strokes | ' 宀 宀 宀 宙 宙

ON　CHŪ midair, space
宇宙 *uchū* universe.　宇宙人 *uchūjin* spaceman.　宇宙飛行 *uchū hikō* space flight.　宙ぶらりんの *chūburarin no* pending (project).

#375 士 | 3 strokes | 一 十 士

ON　SHI specialist Ir. *(haka)se**#668
飛行士 *hikōshi* aviator.　宇宙飛行士 *uchū hikōshi* astronaut.　計理士 *keirishi* public accountant.　名士 *meishi* celebrity.

#376 体 | 7 strokes | 亻 亻 什 休 休 体

kun　*karada* body
体 *karada* body.

ON　TAI, TEI body
天体 *tentai* heavenly body.　天体図 *tentaizu* celestial map.　気体 *kitai* vapor.　体積 *taiseki* cubic volume.　大体 *daitai* generally.　世間体 *sekentei* appearance.

#377 陽 | 12 strokes | 阝 阝 阝 阝 陽 陽

ON　YŌ sunshine; positive
太陽 *taiyō* sun.　陽気 *yōki* weather.　陽気な *yōki na* cheerful.　陽性の *yōsei no* positive.　陽極 *yōkyoku* anode.

#378 系	7 strokes	一 ㄥ 乞 玄 糸 糸 系

ON   KEI system; lineage

太陽系 *taiyōkei* solar system. 系列 *keiretsu* system, a series. 体系 *taikei* system. 家系 *kakei* family line. 日系アメリカ人 *Nikkei Amerika-jin* Japanese American. 父系 *fukei* paternal line.

#379 光	6 strokes	丨 丷 丷 屮 屵 光

kun   *hika(ru)* shine; *hikari* light, ray

光る *hikaru* shine. 光 *hikari* light, ray.

ON   KŌ light, ray

日光 *nikkō* sunshine. 陽光 *yōkō* sunshine. 月光 *gekkō* moonlight. 光明 *kōmyō* light. 風光 *fūkō* scenery.

#380 線	15 strokes	幺 糸 紵 紵 緽 線

ON   SEN line

線 *sen* line. 光線 *kōsen* light. 地平線 *chiheisen* horizon. 下線 *kasen* underline. 内線 *naisen* extension (of a telephone).

#381 星	9 strokes	冂 日 尸 旦 早 星

kun   *hoshi* star

星 *hoshi* star. 流れ星 *nagareboshi* shooting star. 星空 *hoshizora* starry sky. 目星 *meboshi* aim, mark.

ON   SEI, [SHŌ] star

流星 *ryūsei* shooting star. 火星 *Kasei* Mars. 木星 *Mokusei* Jupiter. 金星 *Kinsei* Venus. 明星 *Myōjō* Venus.

#382 座	10 strokes	亠 广 庀 库 座 座

kun   *suwa(ru)* sit down

座る *suwaru* sit down.

ON　ZA seat; theater
星座 *seiza* constellation.　中座 ⟨v⟩ *chūza* leaving in the middle of (a meeting).　正座 ⟨v⟩ *seiza* sitting straight　南座 *Minami-za* Minami-za Theater.　口座 *kōza* bank account.

#383　衛　16 strokes　彳　彳ㅗ　徨　徫　徫　衛

ON　EI defend, protest
衛星 *eisei* satellite.　気象衛星 *kishō eisei* weather satellite.　衛星都市 *eisei toshi* satellite city.　自衛 *jiei* self-defense.　前衛 *zen'ei* forward (in volleyball).　衛生 *eisei* hygiene.

#384　工　3 strokes　一　丁　工

ON　KŌ, KU artisan; construction
人工 *jinkō* human work.　人工衛生 *jinkō eisei* man-made satellite.　工場 *kōba/kōjō* factory.　工事 ⟨v⟩ *kōji* construction.　大工 *daiku* carpenter.　工夫 ⟨v⟩ *kufū* device.

#385　力　2 strokes　フ　力

kun　*chikara* power, strength
力 *chikara* power, strength.　力強い *chikarazuyoi* powerful.

ON　RYOKU, RIKI power, strength
圧力 *atsuryoku* pressure.　動力 *dōryoku* motor power.　原子力 *genshiryoku* nuclear energy.　暴力 *bōryoku* violence.　全力で *zenryoku de* with all one's might.　力士 *rikishi* sumo wrestler.

#386　引　4 strokes　フ　コ　弓　引

kun　*hi(ku)* pull, draw
引く *hiku* pull, draw.　引き潮 *hikishio* ebb tide.　引き出し *hikidashi* drawer.　引き分け *hikiwake* drawn game, tie.

ON　IN pull, draw
引力 *inryoku* gravitation.　地球引力 *chikyū inryoku* terrestrial gravitation.　引火 ⟨v⟩ *inka* ignition.　強引に *gōin ni* by force.

#387 文	4 strokes	丶　一　ナ　文

kun *fumi* letter, book Ir. *mo(ji)**#606
文 *fumi* letter, book

ON BUN, MON letter, sentence
天文 *tenmon* astronomy.　天文台 *tenmondai* astronomical observation.　作文 *sakubun* composition.　文明 *bunmei* civilization.　注文 ‹v› *chūmon* order (for goods).

#388 望	11 strokes	亠　亡丿　亡月　望　望　望

kun *nozo(mu)* desire, hope; view; *nozo(mi)* hope
望む *nozomu* desire, hope; view (a mountain).　望み *nozomi* hope.

ON BŌ, MŌ desire; view
遠望 *enbō* distant view.　望見 ‹v› *bōken* watching from afar.　野望 *yabō* ambition.　人望 *jinbō* popularity.　本望 *honmō* long-cherished desire.

#389 鏡	19 strokes	牟　金　鈩　鏱　鏱　鏡

kun *kagami* mirror Ir. *(me)gane**#744
鏡 *kagami* mirror.

ON KYO mirror
望遠鏡 *bōenkyō* telescopc.　鏡台 *kyōdai* dresser.

#390 測	12 strokes	氵　沪　汨　浿　測　測

kun *haka(ru)* measure
測る *hakaru* measure.

ON SOKU measure
測量 ‹v› *sokuryō* measurement, survey.　予測 ‹v› *yosoku* estimate, forecast.　実測 ‹v› *jissoku* actual survcy.　目測 ‹v› *mokusoku* eye measurement.

#391	
観	18 strokes 

ON　KAN view, appearance

観測 ‹v› *kansoku* observation. 人生観 *jinseikan* one's view of life. 主観 *shukan* subjective view. 外観 *gaikan* appearance. 観光 ‹v› *kankō* sightseeing.

#392	
転	11 strokes 

kun　*koro(bu)* fall down; *koro(garu)* roll over; *koro(gasu)* roll

転ぶ *korobu* fall down. 転がる *korogaru* roll over. 転がす *korogasu* roll (a ball).

ON　TEN fall down, roll over

回転 ‹v› *kaiten* rotation. 自転 ‹v› *jiten* turning round (on its own axis). 空転 ‹v› *kūten* running idle. 転落 ‹v› *tenraku* fall.

#393	
周	8 strokes 

kun　*mawa(ri)* circumference; surroundings

周り *mawari* circumference (of a pond); surroundings, neighborhood.

ON　SHŪ circumference; surroundings

円周 *enshū* circumference. 周期 *shūki* cycle. 五周年 *goshūnen* 5th anniversary. 一周 ‹v› *isshū* going around once.

#394	
囲	7 strokes 

kun　*kako(mu)*, *kako(u)* surround, enclose

囲む・囲う *kakomu/kakou* surround, enclose. 囲い *kakoi* enclosure.

ON　I surround, enclose

周囲 *shūi* circumference. 周囲の *shūi no* surrounding (hills).

■ II. Vocabulary

宇宙	*uchū*	universe
宇宙飛行士	*uchū hikōshi*	astronaut

天体	*tentai*	heavenly body
太陽	*taiyō*	sun
太陽系	*taiyōkei*	solar system
光	*hikari*	light
光線	*kōsen*	light
星	*hoshi*	star
火星	*Kasei*	Mars
星座	*seiza*	constellation
衛星	*eisei*	satallite
人工衛星	*jinkō eisei*	man-made satellite
引力	*inryoku*	gravitation
回転‹v›	*kaiten*	rotation
天文台	*tenmondai*	astronomical observatory
観測‹v›	*kansoku*	observation
測量‹v›	*sokuryō*	measurement
鏡	*kagami*	mirror
望遠鏡	*bōenkyō*	telescope
周り	*mawari*	circumference; surroundings
周囲	*shūi*	circumference; surroundings

■ III. Reading Exercises 21 ■

Read and translate the following.

1. 夜空に数千の**星**がきらきら**光**っている。
2. **鏡**のような月が湖面にうつっている。
3. 晴れた晩、**望遠鏡**で**星座**を見た。
4. **太陽**の**光線**が公園の木々に差している。
5. **太陽系**は**太陽**や、地球や、その他多くの**星**から成っている。
6. **人工衛星**が地球の**周り**を回っている。
7. 地球は約三百六十五日で**太陽**の**周囲**を**回転**する。
8. **天文台**で**天体**の**観測**を行なう。
9. 月の**引力**で干潮や満潮が起こる。
10. **宇宙飛行士**が**火星**へ飛ぶ日はあまり遠くないだろう。

10

✼✼✼✼✼✼✼✼✼✼✼✼✼✼✼✼✼✼

Food, Drink, Cooking

Food

■ I. Reference ■

#395 食	9 strokes	𠆢 今 仒 仴 食 食

kun *ta(beru), ku(u)* eat
食べる・食う *taberu/kuu* eat.　食べ物 *tabemono* food.

ON SHOKU, [JIKI] food, eating
食物 *shokumotsu* food.　食事 *shokuji* meal.　朝食 *chōshoku* breakfast.　昼食 *chūshoku* lunch.　洋食 *yōshoku* Western food.　節食 ⟨v⟩ *sesshoku* eating less.　二食 *nijiki* 2 meals a day.

#396 和	8 strokes	二 千 禾 利 和 和

kun *yawa(ragu), nago(mu)* soften, calm down; *nago(yaka)* mild, gentle
Ir. *(hi)yori**; *(yama)to**
和らぐ・和む *yawaragu/nagomu* soften, calm down.　和やかな *nagoyaka na* mild, gentle.　日和り *hiyori** fine weather.　大和 *Yamato** Japan (classical name).

ON WA, O peace, harmony; Japanese
和食 *washoku* Japanese food.　和風 *wafū* Japanese style.　平和 *heiwa* peace.　温和な *onwa na* mild (climate), gentle (person).

#397 定	8 strokes	⟁ 宀 宁 宁 定 定

kun *sada(meru)* decide, fix; *sada(maru)* be decided, fixed
定める *sadameru* fix (the date).　定まる *sadamaru* be decided, fixed.

ON TEI, JŌ decide, fix
定食 *teishoku* set meal.　予定 ⟨v⟩ *yotei* plan, schedule.　定休日

teikyūbi regular day off. 定年 *teinen* retirement age. 未定の *mitei no* undecided. 定石 *jōseki* tactics, formula.

#398 軽	12 strokes	亍 亘 軒 軒 軽 軽

kun   *karu(i), karo(yaka)* light
軽い *karui* light (meal). 軽やかな *karoyaka na* light (steps). 気軽に *kigaru ni* easily, without reserve.

ON   KEI light
軽食 *keishoku* light meal. 軽量 *keiryō* light weight. 軽便な *keiben na* convenient, handy.

#399 飯	12 strokes	宀 今 食 飦 飯 飯

kun   *meshi* cooked rice; meal
飯 *meshi* cooked rice; meal. 夕飯 *yūmeshi* supper.

ON   HAN cooked rice; meal
ご飯 *gohan* cooked rice; meal. 昼ご飯 *hirugohan* lunch. 夕飯 *yūhan* supper. 赤飯 *sekihan* festive red rice. 残飯 *zanpan* leftovers.

#400 堂	11 strokes	` `` 𭥵 峃 堂 堂

ON   DŌ hall
食堂 *shokudō* dining room, restaurant. 公会堂 *kōkaidō* public hall. 本堂 *hondō* main hall of a temple. 堂々と *dōdō to* with great degnity.

#401 固	8 strokes	冂 冂 冃 冏 固 固

kun   *kata(i)* hard; *kata(maru)* become hard; *kata(meru)* harden, tighten
固い *katai* hard (nut). 固まる *katamaru* become hard. 固める *katameru* harden, tighten.

ON   KO hard
固体 *kotai* solid substance. 固定の *kotei no* fixed, stationary. 固有の *koyū no* peculiar, inherent. 強固な *kyōko na* firm.

#402 形	7 strokes	二　子　开　开　形　形

kun *kata, katachi* form, shape
形 *kata/katachi* form, shape. 三日月形の *mikazukigata no* crescent-shaped. 形見 *katami* keepsake.

ON KEI, [GYŌ] form, shape
固形食 *kokeishoku* solid food. 円形 *enkei* round shape. 正方形 *seihōkei* square. 形成 ⟨v⟩ *keisei* formation. 人形 *ningyō* doll.

#403 栄	9 strokes	ヽ　ヽヽ　ﾉﾉ　ﾂﾜ　ﾂヅ　栄　栄

kun *saka(eru)* prosper; *saka(e)* prosperity; *ha(e)* glory
栄える *sakaeru* prosper. 栄え *sakae* prosperity. 栄えある *hae aru* glorious (victory).

ON EI prosperity
栄養 *eiyō* nutrition. 栄養食 *eiyōshoku* nourishing meal. 栄養士 *eiyōshi* dietitian. 栄光 *eikō* glory. 光栄 *kōei* honor.

#404 富	12 strokes	宀　宁　宁　宁　宮　富

kun *to(mu)* be rich; *tomi* wealth Ir. *fuk(ki)**#971
富む *tomu* be rich (with nutrition). 富 *tomi* wealth.

ON FU, [FŪ] wealth
富力 *furyoku* wealth. 富強 *fukyō* wealth and power. 富士山 *Fuji-san* Mr. Fuji. 富貴 #971 *fūki* wealth and honor.

#405 不	4 strokes	一　フ　不　不

ON FU, BU (prefix) not, un-
不足 ⟨v⟩ *fusoku* shortage. 栄養不足 *eiyō busoku* undernourishment. 不便な *fuben na* inconvenient. 不十分な *fujūbun na* insufficient. 不正な *fusei na* unjust. 行方不明 *yukue fumei* whereabouts unknown. 不細工な #732 *busaiku na* clumsy.

| #406 肉 | 6 strokes | 一 冂 内 内 肉 肉 |

ON NIKU meat, flesh
肉 *niku* meat, flesh. 牛肉 *gyūniku* beef. 羊肉 *yōniku* lam. 肉体 *nikutai* body. 肉親 *nikushin* blood relation.

| #407 菜 | 11 strokes | 艹 艹 荢 苙 芷 菜 |

kun *na* greens, vegetable
菜 *na* greens, vegetable. 青菜 *aona* greens.

ON SAI greens, vegetable
野菜 *yasai* vegetable. 山菜 *sansai* edible wild plant. 前菜 *zensai* hors d'oeuvre. 菜園 *saien* vegetable garden.

| #408 卵 | 7 strokes | ' ﾉ 仁 白 白 卯 卵 |

kun *tamago* egg
卵 *tamago* egg. 生卵 *namatamago* raw egg.

ON RAN egg
卵黄 *ran'ō* yolk. 卵白 *ranpaku* white of an egg. 魚卵 *gyoran* spawn. 卵生動物 *ransei dōbutsu* egg-laying animal.

| #409 玉 | 5 strokes | 一 丁 干 王 玉 |

kun *tama* gem, jewel; ball
玉子 *tamago* egg. 目玉 *medama* eyeball. 百円玉 *hyakuendama* 100-yen coin.

ON GYOKU gem, jewel
玉石 *gyokuseki* gems and stones. 玉座 *gyokuza* throne.

| #410 豆 | 7 strokes | 一 厂 厅 豆 豆 豆 |

kun *mame* bean, pea; (prefix for miniature) Ir. *(a)zuki**
豆 *mane* beans, peas. 小豆 *azuki** azuki bean. 豆本 *mamehon* miniature book. 豆台風 *mametaifū* midget typhoon.

ON TŌ, [ZU] bean, pea
豆腐 *tōfu* bean curd. 大豆 *daizu* soybean.

#411 果	8 strokes	冂 日 旦 甲 早 果

kun   *hata(su)* fulfil; *ha(teru)* come to an end; *ha(te)* end, limit
     Ir. *kuda(mono)**
     果たす *hatasu* fulfil.   果てる *hateru* come to an end, die.   地の果て *chi no hate* end of the land.   果物 *kudamono** fruit.

ON   KA fruit; result
     果実 *kajitsu* fruit.   青果 *seika* vegetables and fruits.   果樹園 *kajuen* orchard.   成果 *seika* result.

#412 幸	8 strokes	十 土 圭 圭 圭 幸

kun   *saiwa(i), sachi, shiawa(se)* happiness, blessing
     幸いに *saiwai ni* fortunately.   海の幸 *umi no sachi* sea products.   山の幸 *yama no sachi* land products.   幸せ *shiawase* happiness.

ON   KŌ happiness, blessing
     多幸 *takō* a lot of luck.   不幸 *fukō* unhappiness.

■ II. Vocabulary ■

食べ物	*tabemono*	food
食物	*shokumotsu*	food
食事	*shokuji*	meal
和食	*washoku*	Japanese food
定食	*teishoku*	set meal
軽い朝食	*karui chōshoku*	light breakfast
軽食	*keishoku*	light meal
食堂	*shokudō*	dining room, restaurant
ご飯	*gohan*	cooked rice, meal
夕飯	*yūhan/yūmeshi*	supper
固形食	*kokeishoku*	solid food
栄養	*eiyō*	nutrition
栄養不足	*eiyō busoku*	undernourishment
栄養に富む	*eiyō ni tomu*	be rich with nutrition
固い肉	*katai niku*	tough meat
牛肉	*gyūniku*	beef

青菜	*aona*	greens
野菜	*yasai*	vegetable
卵・玉子	*tamago*	egg
卵黄	*ran'ō*	yolk
豆	*mame*	beans, peas
果物	*kudamono*	fruit
果実	*kajitsu*	fruit
海の幸	*umi no sachi*	sea products

■ III. Reading Exercises 22 ■

Read and translate the following.

1. 毎朝、八時に朝ご**飯**を**食**べる。
2. 今朝、**朝食**に**卵**を二個、トーストを二枚、りんごを一つ**食**べた。
3. **夕飯**は**和食**にするか**洋食**にするかまだ**未定**だ。
4. 「**大和**」という**食堂**で、**定食**を注文した。
5. 家で早目に**軽い食事**をして出かけた。
6. 最近、朝と昼は**軽食**にしている。
7. この**牛肉**は**固**くて**食**べられない。
8. 赤ちゃんの**食**べ物が**固形食**に変わった。
9. **豆**や**野菜**や魚などの**栄養**に**富**む**食物**をとることが大切だ。
10. ある国では、**栄養不足**で多数の幼児が死亡している。
11. 秋は**果実**の季節だけあって、色々の種類の**果物**がある。
12. 二か月**節食**してみたが、あまり良い**成果**は上がらなかった。
13. その沿岸地方は海の幸にも山の幸にもめぐまれている。

Drink

■ I. Reference ■

#413

飲 12 strokes 　〆　　今　　食　　飲ク　　飲ク　　飲

kun　　*no(mu)* drink
飲む *nomu* drink.　飲み物 *nomimono* drink, beverage.　飲み水 *nomimizu* drinking water.

ON　　IN drink
飲食〈い〉*inshoku* eating and drinking.　飲食物 *inshokubutsu* food and drink.　暴飲〈い〉*bōin* heavy drinking.　暴飲暴食〈い〉*bōin bōshoku* eating and drinking immoderately.

#414

吸 6 strokes 　丨　　口　　口　　叮　　吸　　吸

kun　　*su(u)* suck in, inhale; smoke
吸う *suu* inhale (air); smoke (a cigarette).　吸い物 *suimono* soup.

ON　　KYŪ suck in, inhale; smoke
吸入〈い〉*kyūnyū* inhalation.　吸引力 *kyūinryoku* sucking force.

#415

乳 8 strokes 　〈　　冖　　乭　　孚　　孚　　乳

kun　　*chichi, chi* milk Ir. *u(ba)**
乳 *chichi* milk.　乳飲み子 *chinomigo* suckling.　乳母 *uba** wet-nurse.

ON　　NYŪ milk
牛乳 *gyūnyū* cow's milk.　母乳 *bonyū* mother's milk.　豆乳 *tōnyū* soybean milk.　乳牛 *nyūgyū* milking cow.

#416

粉 10 strokes 　丶　　半　　米　　粉ヽ　　粉　　粉

kun　　*ko, kona* flour, powder
粉 *kona* flour, powder.　粉ミルク *kona-miruku* powder milk.　小麦粉 *komugiko* wheat flour.　パン粉 *panko* bread crumbs.

ON FUN flour, powder
粉乳 *funnyū* powdered milk.　粉食 *funshoku* powdered food.
粉末 *funmatsu* powder.　花粉 *kafun* pollen.

#417 酒	10 strokes	氵 氵 沔 沔 洒 酒

kun *sake*, [*saka*] liquor, sake Ir. *(omi)ki** #756
酒 *sake* liquor, sake.　酒飲み *sakenomi* drinker.　酒場 *sakaba*
bar, tavern.
ON SHU liquor, sake
洋酒 *yōshu* foreign liquor.　日本酒 *Nihonshu* Japanese sake.　飲酒
ᴠ *inshu* drinking.

#418 湯	12 strokes	氵 沪 涓 渭 渇 湯

kun *yu* hot water
湯 *yu* hot water.　湯気 *yuge* steam.　湯飲み *yunomi* teacup.　茶の
湯 *cha no yu* tea ceremony.
ON TŌ hot water
熱湯 *nettō* boiling water.

#419 好	6 strokes	く 夕 女 女′ 奵 好

kun *kono(mu), su(ku)* like
好む・好く *konomu/suku* like.好み *konomi* taste, preference.好きな
suki na favorite.　好き好き *sukizuki* a matter of taste.
ON KŌ like
好物 *kōbutsu* favorite food.　好機 *kōki* good opportunity.　好意
kōi good will, kindness.　好都合の *kōtsugō no* convenient.

#420 欲	11 strokes	八 公 谷 谷 谷′ 欲

kun *hos(suru)* desire, want; *ho(shii)* want
欲する *hossuru* desire, want.　欲しい *hoshii* want.　欲しい物 *hoshii*
mono a thing wanted.
ON YOKU greed, desire
食欲 *shokuyoku* appetite.　欲望 *yokubō* desire.　私欲 *shiyoku*
self-desire.　強欲な *gōyoku na* greedy.

■ II. Vocabulary

飲み物	nomimono	drink, beverage
飲食物	inshokubutsu	food and drink
吸い物	suimono	soup
乳	chichi	milk
牛乳	gyūnyū	cow's milk
豆乳	tōnyū	soybean milk
粉ミルク	kona-miruku	powdered milk
粉乳	funnyū	powdered milk
酒	sake	liquor, sake
酒場	sakaba	bar, tavern
洋酒	yōshu	foreign liquor
湯	yu	hot water
茶の湯	cha no yu	tea ceremomy
熱湯	nettō	boiling water
好きな	suki na	favorite
好物	kōbutsu	favorite food
欲しい	hoshii	want
食欲	shokuyoku	appetite

■ III. Reading Exercises 23

Read and translate the following.

1. コーヒーに**粉ミルク**を入れて**飲**んだ。
2. 知らない土地では**飲食物**に注意した方がいい。
3. **牛乳**の代わりに**豆乳**を**飲**むことがある。
4. あなたの**好きな飲み物**は何ですか。
5. ある外人は**洋酒**より日本の**酒**を好むようだ。
6. この島の名物の干物は私の**好物**だ。
7. この**吸い物**には玉子と青菜が入っている。
8. インスタントスープは**熱湯**を注ぐだけで出来る。
9. 寒い朝は、**熱**いコーヒーか紅茶が**欲**しい。
10. 暑い季節には、だれでも多少、**食欲**が低下する。

Cooking

■ I. Reference ■

#421 料

10 strokes   丶 丷 半 米 米 米 料 料

ON RYŌ material; fee

料理 ‹v› *ryōri* cooking; cuisine.　日本料理 *Nihon ryōri* Japanese cuisine.　食料 *shokuryō* foodstuff.　飲料水 *inryōsui* drinking water.　原料 *genryō* raw material.　料金 *ryōkin* fee, charge.

#422 味

8 strokes   口 口一 口二 咡 咔 味

kun *aji* taste, flavor; *aji(wau)* taste, relish.

味 *aji* taste, flavor.　味わう *ajiwau* relish (the best liquor).

ON MI taste, flavor

風味 *fūmi* flavor.　正味 *shōmi* net weight.　意味 *imi* meaning.　味方 *mikata* friend, ally.　三味線 *shamisen** shamisen (Japanese musical instrument).

#423 付

5 strokes   ノ 亻 仁 付 付

kun *tsu(ku)* be attached, stick to; *tsu(keru)* attach, put on

付く *tsuku* be attacherd, stick to.　付ける *tsukeru* attach (a thing to), put (a button) on.　味付け ‹v› *ajitsuke* seasoning.　気付く *kizuku* notice.　付き合う *tsukiau* associate with.

ON FU attach, stick

付着 ‹v› *fuchaku* adhesion.　付近 *fukin* vicinity.

#424 塩

13 strokes   土 圹 圹 塩 塩 塩

kun *shio* salt

塩 *shio* salt.　塩水 *shiomizu* salt water.

ON EN salt

食塩 *shokuen* table salt.　塩分 *enbun* salt content.　塩田 *enden* salt farm.

#425 糖	16 strokes	⼍ 粩 粌 糖 糖 糖

ON TŌ sugar

砂糖 *satō* sugar. 糖分 *tōbun* sugar content. 果糖 *katō* fruit sugar. 乳糖 *nyūtō* milk sugar. 麦芽糖 *bakugatō* malt sugar.

#426 加	5 strokes	フ カ か 加 加

kun *kuwa(eru)* add, include; *kuwa(waru)* join, enter

加える *kuwaeru* add (salt). 加わる *kuwawaru* join (a club).

ON KA add, include; join, enter

加工 ‹v› *kakō* processing. 加熱 ‹v› *kanetsu* heating. 参加 ‹v› *sanka* participation. 加入 ‹v› *kanyū* joining.

#427 混	11 strokes	⺡ 氵 泪 泪 混 混

kun *ma(zeru)* mix; *ma(jiru), ma(zaru)* be mixed

混ぜる *mazeru* mix. 混じる·混ざる *majiru/mazaru* be mixed. 混ぜ物 *mazemono* admixture.

ON KON mix

混合 ‹v› *kongō* mixing. 混合酒 *kongōshu* blended liquor. 混入 ‹v› *konnyū* mixing.

#428 焼	12 strokes	⺌ ⽕ 炻 焃 焼 焼

kun *ya(ku)* burn; broil, roast, bake; *ya(keru)* burn; be broiled, roasted, baked; *-yaki* grill; pottery

焼く *yaku* broil, roast (meat), bake (bread). 焼ける *yakeru* be broiled, roasted, baked. 塩焼き ‹v› *shioyaki* broil with salt. 焼き鳥 *yakitori* grilled chicken. 九谷焼き *Kutaniyaki* Kutani pottery. 夕焼け *yūyake* evening glow. 日焼け ‹v› *hiyake* sunburn.

ON SHŌ burn

全焼 ‹v› *zenshō* being burned down. 焼死 ‹v› *shōshi* death by fire.

#429 蒸	13 strokes	艹　芋　芽　茏　蒸　蒸

kun *mu(su)* steam

蒸す *musu* steam.　蒸し焼き ⟨v⟩ *mushiyaki* baking in a casserole.
蒸し暑い *mushiatsui* sultry.

ON JŌ steam

蒸気 *jōki* steam.　水蒸気 *suijōki* water vapor.

#430 材	7 strokes	一　十　木　术　村　材

ON ZAI material; timber; talent

材料 *zairyō* material.　材木 *zaimoku* timber.　木材 *mokuzai*
wood.　人材 *jinzai* talent, human resources.

#431 調	15 strokes	言　言　訂　訶　調　調

kun *shira(beru)* investigate, study; *shira(be)* investigation; tone;
totono(eru) prepare, arrange; *totono(u)* be prepared.

調べる *shiraberu* investigate, study.　調べ *shirabe* investigation.
うつくしい調べ *utsukushii shirabe* sweet tone.　調える *totonoeru*
prepare (supper).　調う *totonou* be prepared.

ON CHŌ investigate; arrange; tone

調味料 *chōmiryō* seasoning.　調節 ⟨v⟩ *chōsetsu* adjustment.　調子
chōshi condition.　調和 ⟨v⟩ *chōwa* harmony.　口調 *kuchō* tone, intonation.　長調 *chōchō* major key.

#432 器	15 strokes	口　吅　哭　哭　哭　器

kun *utsuwa* container; capacity, ability

器 *utsuwa* container.　器が大きい *utsuwa ga ōkii* be a man of great
capacity.

ON KI container; capacity, ability

食器 *shokki* tableware.　茶器 *chaki* tea-things.　才器 *saiki* ability.
大器晩成 *taiki bansei* Great talents mature late.

#433 具	8 strokes	丨 冂 月 目 且 具 具

ON　GU tool

器具 *kigu* utensil.　道具 *dōgu* tool.　家具 *kagu* furniture.　具合 *guai* condition, order.

#434 用	5 strokes	丿 冂 月 月 用

kun　*mochi(iru)* use

用いる *mochiiru* use.　用い方 *mochiikata* usage.

ON　YŌ use; business

家庭用 *kateiyō* for home use.　実用 *jitsuyō* practical use.　用意 ⟨v⟩ *yōi* preparation.　用事 *yōji* business, errand.　公用 *kōyō* official business.　器用な *kiyō na* skillful.

#435 使	8 strokes	丿 亻 仁 伊 伊 使

kun　*tsuka(u)* use

使う *tsukau* use.　使い方 *tsukaikata* usage.

ON　SHI use; messenger

使用 ⟨v⟩ *shiyō* use.　使用者 *shiyōsha* user.　使者 *shisha* messenger.　大使 *taishi* ambassador.　使命 *shimei* mission.

#436 蔵	15 strokes	艹 广 芹 芦 莐 蔵

kun　*kura* storehouse, repository

蔵 *kura* storehouse.　酒蔵 *sakagura* wine cellar.　米蔵 *komegura* rice granary.

ON　ZŌ storehouse, repository

冷蔵 ⟨v⟩ *reizō* refrigeration.　貯蔵 ⟨v⟩ *chozō* preservation.

#437 庫	10 strokes	亠 广 庐 庐 庫

ON　KO, [KU] storehouse

冷蔵庫 *reizōko* refrigerator.　金庫 *kinko* safe.　国庫 *Kokko* National Treasury.　在庫 *zaiko* goods in stock, inventory.

#438 皿	5 strokes	丨 冂 冂 冊 皿

kun *sara* plate, dish, saucer

皿 *sara* plate, dish, saucer. 小皿 *kozara* small plate. 大皿 *ōzara* platter. 深皿 *fukazara* dish.

#439 洗	9 strokes	丶 氵 汢 泮 泮 洗

kun *ara(u)* wash

洗う *arau* wash. 皿洗い *saraarai* dishwashing.

ON SEN wash

洗面器 *senmenki* washbasin. 洗面所 *senmenjo* washroom. 水洗トイレ *suisen toire* flush toilet.

#440 手	4 strokes	一 二 三 手

kun *te*, [*ta*] hand Ir. *(jō)zu**

手 *te* hand. 手料理 *teryōri* home cooking. 手間 *tema* time, labor, effort. 上手な *jōzu* na* skillfull. 下手な *heta* na* unskillfull. 切手 *kitte* postage stamp. 手入れ *teire* care.

ON SHU hand

入手 ⟨v⟩ *nyūshu* acquisition. 着手 ⟨v⟩ *chakushu* undertaking.

#441 招	8 strokes	一 十 扌 扫 招 招

kun *mane(ku)* invite, beckon

招く *maneku* invite. 招き *maneki* invitation. 手招き ⟨v⟩ *temaneki* beckoning.

ON SHŌ invite

招来 ⟨v⟩ *shōrai* bringing about (a war).

#442 待	9 strokes	彳 彳 彳 往 徔 待

kun *ma(tsu)* wait

待つ *matsu* wait. 待ち合わせる *machiawaseru* meet (a person) by appointment. 待合所 *machiaijo* waiting room.

ON	TAI wait	

招待 ‹v› *shōtai* invitation.　期待 ‹v› *kitai* expectation.　待機 ‹v› *taiki* standing by.　待望の *taibō no* long-awaited.

#443 束	7 strokes	厂　冖　冃　市　束　束

kun	*taba* bundle	

束 *taba* bundle.　花束 *hanataba* bouquet.　束ねる *tabaneru* tie in a bundle.

ON	SOKU bundle	

約束 ‹v› *yakusoku* promise, engagement.　二束三文の *nisoku sanmon no* dog-cheap.

■ II. Vocabulary ■

料理 ‹v›	*ryōri*	cooking; cuisine
日本料理	*Nihon ryōri*	Japanese cuisine
味	*aji*	taste, flavor
味付け ‹v›	*ajitsuke*	seasoning
風味	*fūmi*	flavor
調味料	*chōmiryō*	seasoning
塩	*shio*	salt
食塩	*shokuen*	table salt
砂糖	*satō*	sugar
材料	*zairyō*	material
塩焼き ‹v›	*shioyaki*	broiling with salt
蒸し焼き ‹v›	*mushiyaki*	baking in a casserole
加工 ‹v›	*kakō*	prosessing
混ぜ物	*mazemono*	admixture
混合 ‹v›	*kongō*	mixing
器	*utsuwa*	container
食器	*shokki*	tableware
器具	*kigu*	utensil
皿	*sara*	plate, dish, saucer
皿洗い	*saraarai*	dishwashing
洗面器	*senmenki*	washbasin
酒蔵	*sakagura*	wine cellar

冷蔵庫	reizōko	refrigerator
使用‹v›	shiyō	use
家庭用	kateiyō	for home use
用意‹v›	yōi	preparation
招き	maneki	invitation
招待‹v›	shōtai	invitation
花束	hanataba	bouguet
約束‹v›	yakusoku	promise, engagement
手料理	teryōri	home cooking
上手な	jōzu na	skillfull
下手な	heta na	unskillful

■ III. Reading Exercises 24 ■

Read and translate the following.

1. この**料理**は**味付**けが悪いですね。
2. 魚にレモンを**加**えると、**風味**が良くなる。
3. **加工**した物は出来るだけ**使**わないようにしている。
4. 果物がガラスの**器**に入れてある。
5. 多くの主婦は台所で新しい**器具**を**使用**している。
6. 明日のパーティーに**使**う**食器**を**調**べて下さい。
7. **材料**が良くても、**調味料**が悪いとだめだ。
8. 小麦粉に玉子と**砂糖**を**混**ぜる。
9. 毎朝、色々の野菜を**混合**したジュースを飲む。
10. 広い**酒蔵**に各種の酒がある。
11. **冷蔵庫**の中に食べ物や飲み物が入っている。
12. この魚は**塩焼**きにしたり、**蒸し焼**きにしたりする。
13. 今晩六時に昔の友達と食事の**約束**がある。
14. 母が夕飯の**用意**をし、私が**皿洗**いをした。
15. **料理**の**上手**な姉はよく自分の作った**手料理**に知人を**招待**する。

11

****

Stores, Goods, Business

Stores

■ I. Reference ■

#444 店	8 strokes	一 广 广 广 店 店 店

kun   *mise* shop, store
店 *mise* shop, store.   夜店 *yomise* night stall.   店番 *miseban* shop tender.

ON   TEN shop, store
カメラ店 *kamera-ten* camera shop.   飲食店 *inshokuten* eating house.   代理店 *dairiten* agency.   本店 *honten* main store/office. 店長 *tenchō* store manager.

#445 貨	11 strokes	亻 化 貨 貨 貨 貨

ON   KA goods, money; freight
百貨店 *hyakkaten* department store.   金貨 *kinka* gold coin.   外貨 *gaika* foreign currency.   貨物 *kamotsu* freight, cargo.

#446 員	10 strokes	口 尸 見 貝 員 員

ON   IN member, personnel
店員 *ten'in* store clerk.   会員 *kaiin* member (of a club).   人員 *jin'in* number of persons.   全員 *zen'in* all members.   定員 *teiin* capacity, quota.   満員 *man'in* full capacity.

#447 書	10 strokes	フ ユ ヨ 聿 書 書

kun   *ka(ku)* write
書く *kaku* write.   前書き ⟨v⟩ *maegaki* preface.

ON   SHO write

書店 *shoten* bookstore. 書物 *shomotsu* book. 書類 *shorui* document. 書道 *shodō* calligraphy. 書名 *shomei* title of a book. 図書 *tosho* books. 図書館 *toshokan* library.

#448 屋	9 strokes	⌐ ⊐ 尸 层 屋 屋

kun   *ya* shop, dealer; roof, house

本屋 *hon'ya* bookstore. 果物屋 *kudamono'ya* fruit shop. 八百屋 *yaoya** vegetable store. 部屋 *heya** room. 母屋 *omoya** main building of a house. 屋根 *yane* roof.

ON   OKU roof, house

屋上 *okujō* roof (of a building). 屋上庭園 *okujō teien* roof garden. 家屋 *kaoku* house. 屋内 *okunai* indoors.

#449 服	8 strokes	) 月 月 肟 服 服

ON   FUKU clothes, dress; dose; obey

服屋 *fukuya* clothing shop, tailor. 洋服 *yōfuku* Western clothes. 和服 *wafuku* Japanese clothes. 服用 ⟨v⟩ *fukuyō* taking medicine. 服役 ⟨v⟩ *fukueki* servitude; military service.

#450 電	13 strokes	宀 雨 雫 雫 雷 電

ON   DEN electricity

電気 *denki* electricity, electric light. 電気屋 *denkiya* electric appliances store. 電気器具 *denki kigu* electric appliances. 電池 *denchi* battery. 電球 *denkyū* electric bulb. 電圧 *den'atsu* voltage.

#451 灯	6 strokes	' ' 少 火 灯 灯

kun   *hi* light, lamp

灯 *hi* light, lamp. ろうそくの灯 *rōsoku no hi* candlelight.

ON   TŌ light, lamp

電灯 *dentō* electric light. 灯火 *tōka* lamplight. 走馬灯 *sōmatō* revolving lantern. 灯台 *tōdai* lighthouse.

| #452 消 | 10 strokes | ゛ ゛ ゛゛ ゛゛ 消 消 |

kun *ke(su)* switch off, extinguish, erase; *ki(eru)* vanish, go out
消す *kesu* switch off (the light), extinguish (the fire), erase. 消し
ゴム *keshi-gomu* eraser. 消える *kieru* vanish, go out.

ON SHŌ switch off, extinguish, erase
消灯 ‹v› *shōtō* putting out lights. 消火 ‹v› *shōka* extinguishing the
fire. 消散 ‹v› *shōsan* dispersion.

| #453 薬 | 16 strokes | 艹 艹 苗 莲 葦 薬 |

kun *kusuri* medicine, drug
薬 *kusuri* medicine, drug. 薬屋 *kusuriya* drugstore, pharmacy.
目薬 *megusuri* eye lotion. 粉薬 *konagusuri* powdered medicine.

ON YAKU medicine, drug
薬局 *yakkyoku* drugstore, pharmacy. 薬用の *yakuyō no* medical.
薬草 *yakusō* herb. 薬味 *yakumi* spice.

| #454 開 | 12 strokes | 冂 冂 門 門 開 開 |

kun *hira(ku), a(keru)* open; *a(ku)* open, become empty; *hira(keru)* become developed
開く・開ける *hiraku/akeru* open (a store). 店開き ‹v› *misebiraki*
opening a store. 開く *aku* open, become empty. 開ける *hirakeru*
become developed.

ON KAI open
開店 ‹v› *kaiten* opening a store. 開会 ‹v› *kaikai* opening a meeting.
公開 ‹v› *kōkai* opening to the public. 未開の *mikai no* uncivilized.

| #455 閉 | 11 strokes | 冂 冂 門 門 閉 閉 |

kun *shi(meru), to(jiru)* close; *shi(maru)* be closed
閉める *shimeru* close (the door). 閉じる *tojiru* close (one's eyes).
閉まる *shimaru* be closed.

ON HEI close
閉店 ‹v› *heiten* closing a store. 閉会 ‹v› *heikai* closing a meeting.
開閉 ‹v› *kaihei* opening and closing.

#456 商	11 strokes	一 广 产 产 商 商

kun   *akina(u)* sell, trade

商う *akinau* sell (tea).   商い *akinai* business, dealing.

ON   SHŌ sell, trade

商店 *shōten* store.   商人 *shōnin* merchant.   行商 ⟨v⟩ *gyōshō* peddling.

#457 街	12 strokes	彳 彳 徍 徍 街 街

kun   *machi* street; town, city

街 *machi* street.   京都の街 *Kyōto no machi* City of Kyoto.

ON   GAI, [KAI] street; town, city

商店街 *shōtengai* shopping street.   地下街 *chikagai* underground shopping mall.   街灯 *gaitō* street light.   街道 *kaidō* highway.

#458 並	8 strokes	` ` 丷 丷 並 並

kun   *nami* ordinary, average; *nara(bu)* be lined up; *nara(beru)* line (things) up; *nara(bi ni)* and, as well as

並の *nami no* ordinary (store).   並木 *namiki* roadside trees.   並ぶ *narabu* be lined up.   並べる *naraberu* line (things) up.   並びに *narabi ni* and, as well as.   並びない *narabi nai* unequaled.

ON   HEI be lined up

平行線 *heikōsen* parallel lines.   並列 ⟨v⟩ *heiretsu* standing in a row.

#459 路	13 strokes	口 足 足 跕 路 路

kun   *ji* street, way

家路 *ieji* one's way home.   大路 *ōji* main street.

ON   RO street, way

道路 *dōro* street, road.   並木路 *namikiro* tree-lined street.   路地 *roji* alley.   路面 *romen* road surface.   線路 *senro* railroad track.

#460 角	7 strokes	丶　宀　勹　角　角　角

kun　*kado* corner, angle; *tsuno* horn
角 *kado* corner.　街角 *machikado* street corner.　四つ角 *yotsuka-do* street corner.　羊の角 *hitsuji no tsuno* sheep's horn.

ON　KAKU corner, angle
三角 *sankaku* triangle.　四角 *shikaku* square.　角度 *kakudo* angle.
方角 *hōgaku* direction.　死角 *shikaku* dead angle.

#461 右	5 strokes	ノ　ナ　ナ　右　右

kun　*migi* right
右 *migi* right.　右手 *migite* right hand/arm.　右手の店 *migite no mise* store on the right.

ON　U, YŪ right
右岸 *ugan* right-hand shore.　右折 ⟨v⟩*usetsu* turning to the right.

#462 左	5 strokes	一　ナ　た　た　左

kun　*hidari* left
左 *hidari* left.　左手 *hidarite* left hand/arm.　左手の店 *hidarite no mise* store on the left.

ON　SA left
左右 *sayū* right and left.　左右する *sayū suru* control, affect.　左折 ⟨v⟩*sasetsu* turning to the left.

#463 側	11 strokes	亻　仴　但　俱　側　側

kun　*kawa* side
右側 *migigawa* right side.　外側 *sotogawa* outside.　内側 *uchigawa* inside.　両側 *ryōgawa* both sides.

ON　SOKU side
側面 *sokumen* side.　側面図 *sokumenzu* side view.　側近 *sokkin* close associate.

| #464 | 通 | 10 strokes | マ 予 予 涌 通 通 |

kun   *tō(ru)* pass, go through; *tō(su)* let through; *kayo(u)* commute
通る *tōru* pass, go through.   通り *tōri* street.   通す *tōsu* let through.   通う *kayou* commute (by bus).

ON   TSŪ, [TSU] pass, go through
通路 *tsūro* passage.   一方通行 *ippō tsūkō* one-way traffic.   通行人 *tsūkōnin* passer-by.   開通 ⟨v⟩ *kaitsū* opening to traffic.   通知 ⟨v⟩ *tsūchi* notification.   通夜 *tsuya* wake.

| #465 | 集 | 12 strokes | イ 什 隹 隹 隼 集 |

kun   *atsu(maru), atsu(meru)* gather, collect; *tsudo(u)* gather, meet
集まる *atsumaru* gather, get together.   集まり *atsumari* gathering. 集める *atsumeru* collect(stamps).   集う *tsudou* gather, meet. 集い *tsudoi* gathering.

ON   SHŪ gather, collect
集合 ⟨v⟩ *shūgō* gathering, meeting.   集金 ⟨v⟩ *shūkin* collecting money.   群集 *gunshū* throng.   文集 *bunshū* anthology.

■ II. Vocabulary ■

店	*mise*	store, shop
書店	*shoten*	bookstore
百貨店	*hyakkaten*	department store
店員	*ten'in*	store clerk
服屋	*fukuya*	clothing shop, tailor
屋上	*okujō*	roof (of a building)
電気屋	*denkiya*	electric appliances store
灯	*hi*	light
電灯	*dentō*	electric light
消灯 ⟨v⟩	*shōtō*	putting out lights
薬屋	*kusuriya*	drugstore, pharmacy
薬局	*yakkyoku*	drugstore, pharmacy
店開き ⟨v⟩	*misebiraki*	opening a store

開店‹v›	*kaiten*	opening a store
閉店‹v›	*heiten*	closing a store
商い	*akinai*	business, dealing
商店	*shōten*	store
街角	*machikado*	street corner
商店街	*shōtengai*	shopping street
道路	*dōro*	street, road
並木路	*namikiro*	tree-lined street
通り	*tōri*	street
通路	*tsūro*	passage
右側	*migigawa*	right side
側面	*sokumen*	side
左手の店	*hidarite no mise*	store on the left
左右	*sayū*	left and right
集まり	*atsumari*	gathering
集合‹v›	*shūgō*	gathering, meeting

■III. Reading Exercises 25 ■

Read and translate the following.

1. 服屋でスーツを一着注文した。
2. あの店の店員は若くて親切だ。
3. 電気屋に新しい器具が色々出ている。
4. 時計店のショーウインドーの灯がついたり消えたりしている。
5. この通りは街灯が一晩中ついていて明るい。
6. あの通路はせまくて、バスは通れない。
7. 酒屋の前の道路は今工事をしている。
8. 百貨店の十階には各種の飲食店が並んでいる。
9. ビルの屋上から並木路を散歩する人々が見える。
10. 家具屋の右側に薬局があり、左側にカメラ屋がある。
11. あの四つ角を左折すると、右手に本屋がある。
12. その書店の左右にレストランがある。
13. 地下街の店は朝十時に開いて、夜八時に閉まる。

14. あの**果物屋**は先月**開店**したばかりだ。
15. **閉店**までにまだ三十分ほどある。
16. **街**には様々な**商店**が**集**まっている。
17. 数名の主婦が**商店街**の入り口で**集合**した。

Goods

#466 品	9 strokes	冂	口	品	品	品	品

kun *shina* goods; quality

品 *shina* goods, article. 品物 *shinamono* goods, article. 品切れ *shinagire* out of stock. 品不足 *shinabusoku* shortage of goods. 品が良い *shina ga yoi* be of good quality.

ON HIN goods; refinement

商品 *shōhin* merchandise. 日用品 *nichiyōhin* daily necessities. 台所用品 *daidokoro yōhin* kitchen utensils. 薬品 *yakuhin* medicine. 上品な *jōhin na* refined. 下品な *gehin na* vulgar.

#467 質	15 strokes	广	斤	斦	斦	皙	質

ON SHITSU quality, nature; SHICHI, [CHI] hostage; pawn

品質 *hinshitsu* quality of goods. 悪質 *akushitsu* bad quality. 実質 *jisshitsu* substance. 性質 *seishitsu* nature. 質屋 *shichiya* pawn-shop. 人質 *hitojichi* hostage. 言質 #566 *genchi/genshitsu* pledge.

#468 級	9 strokes	乡	幺	糸	幻	級	級

ON KYŪ rank, grade

高級品 *kōkyūhin* high-quality goods. 高級店 *kōkyūten* high-quality store. 低級な *teikyū na* low-class (restaurant). 中流階級 *chūryū kaikyū* middle class. 上級生 *jōkyūsei* senior student.

#469 安	6 strokes	ノ	⺊	宀	灾	安	安

kun *yasu(i)* cheap, inexpensive

安い *yasui* cheap, inexpensive. 安物 *yasumono* cheap goods.

ON AN peace, safe

安全 *anzen* safety. 不安 *fuan* anxiety. 安心 (v)*anshin* relief. 安定 (v)*antei* stability. 平安朝 *Heianchō* Heian Dynasty/period.

#470 似	7 strokes	イ 亻 仏 仏 似 似

kun   *ni(ru)* resemble
似る *niru* resemble.   似合う *niau* match well.

ON   JI resemble
類似 ‹v› *ruiji* resemblance.   類似品 *ruijihin* similar goods; imitations.

#471 常	11 strokes	⅋ 𫞩 常 常 常 常

kun   *tsune* normal, usual; *toko-* ever-, always
常に *tsune ni* always.   常々 *tsunezune* always.   常夏の国 *tokonatsu no kuni* land of everlasting summer.

ON   JŌ normal, usual
常用 ‹v› *jōyō* habitual use.   日常 *nichijō* daily.   平常の通り *heijō no tōri* as usual.   正常な *seijō na* normal.

#472 非	8 strokes	丿 丬 非 非 非 非

ON   HI (prefix for non-, un-); mistake
非常用 *hijōyō* for emergency use.   非常口 *hijōguchi* emergency exit.   非公開の *hikōkai no* not open, private.   非常に *hijō ni* extremely.   非合理な *higōri na* irrational.   非行 *hikō* misdeed.

#473 衣	6 strokes	` 亠 ナ 衣 衣 衣

kun   *koromo* garment, clothes Ir. *(yuka)ta** #774
衣 *koromo* garment, clothes.   衣替え ‹v› *koromogae* changing clothes.   羽衣 *hagoromo* robe of feathers.

ON   I garment, clothes
衣類 *irui* clothing.   衣服 *ifuku* clothes.   衣料品 *iryōhin* clothing.   衣食住 *ishokujū* food, clothing and shelter.

#474 装	12 strokes	丬 壯 壯 斗 裝 裝

kun   *yosoo(u)* wear; pretend, disguise
装う *yosoou* wear (a dress); pretend (illness), disguise (as a man).

春の装い *haru no yosooi* spring attire.

ON　SŌ, SHŌ wear; pretend, disguise

服装 *fukusō* dress, costume.　洋装店 *yōsōten* dress-making shop.
変装 ⟨v⟩ *hensō* disguise.　装置 *sōchi* equipment, device.　衣装 *ishō*
costume.　民族衣装 *minzoku ishō* folk costume.

#475 宝	8 strokes	丶　宀　宀　宇　宝　宝

kun　*takara* treasure
宝 *takara* treasure.　宝物 *takaramono* treasure.

ON　HŌ treasure
宝石 *hōseki* precious stone, gem.　宝石店 *hōsekiten* jeweler's.　宝
物 *hōmotsu* treasure.　国宝 *kokuhō* national treasure.

#476 箱	15 strokes	⺮　竺　筦　箱　箱　箱

kun　*hako* box
箱 *hako* box.　宝石箱 *hōsekibako* jewel box.　本箱 *honbako*
bookcase.　貯金箱 *chokinbako* savings box.

#477 指	9 strokes	扌　扩　扞　指　指　指

kun　*yubi* finger; *sa(su)* point at
指 *yubi* finger.　親指 *oyayubi* thumb, big toe.　指す *sasu* point at.
目指す *mezasu* aim at.　指図 ⟨v⟩ *sashizu* instruction.

ON　SHI finger; point at
指名 ⟨v⟩ *shimei* nomination.　指定 ⟨v⟩ *shitei* designation.　指針 *shishin*
compass needle; guideline.　指数 *shisū* index number.

#478 輪	15 strokes	冂　車　軯　輪　輪　輪

kun　*wa* ring, circle, wheel
指輪 *yubiwa* ring.　花輪 *hanawa* wreath.　輪を作る *wa o tsukuru*
make a circle.　輪を付ける *wa o tsukeru* fix a wheel.

ON　RIN ring, circle, wheel; (counter for flowers)
年輪 *nenrin* annual ring (of a tree).　輪転機 *rintenki* rotary press.
一輪の花 *ichirin no hana* a flower.

#479 銀	14 strokes	𠂉 金 鈩 鈩 銀 銀

ON GIN silver
銀 *gin* silver.　銀貨 *ginka* silver coin.　金銀 *kingin* gold and silver.　水銀 *suigin* mercury.　銀行 *ginkō* bank. 日銀 *Nichigin* Bank of Japan.　銀座通り *Ginza-dōri* Ginza Street.

#480 磁	14 strokes	厂 矿 矿 磁 磁 磁

ON JI porcelain; magnet
磁器 *jiki* porcelain.　青磁 *seiji* celadon porcelain.　磁気 *jiki* magnetism.　磁石 *jishaku* magnet.　磁針 *jishin* magnetic needle.

#481 製	14 strokes	𠂉 𠂢 制 制 製 製

ON SEI manufacture
製品 *seihin* product.　日本製 *Nihonsei* made in Japan.　自家製 *jikasei* homemade.　制作 ⟨v⟩ *seisaku* manufacture.　製薬 ⟨v⟩ *seiyaku* medicine manufacture.　製本 ⟨v⟩ *seihon* bookbinding.

#482 皮	5 strokes	ノ 厂 广 皮 皮

kun *kawa* skin, leather, bark
皮 *kawa* skin, leather, bark.　皮製品 *kawaseihin* leather product.　わに皮 *wanigawa* crocodile skin.　皮切り *kawakiri* initiation.

ON HI skin, leather, bark
牛皮 *gyūhi* oxhide.　樹皮 *juhi* bark.　皮肉 *hiniku* irony; sarcasm.

#483 毛	4 strokes	一 二 三 毛

kun *ke* hair, fur, wool
毛 *ke* hair.　毛皮 *kegawa* fur.　毛のシャツ *ke no shatsu* woolen shirt.

ON MŌ hair, fur, wool
羊毛 *yōmō* wool.　羽毛 *umō* feathers, down.　不毛の *fumō no* unproductive, barren (land).

11　Stores, Goods, Business　*Goods* —— *159*

#484

布

5 strokes 

kun — *nuno* cloth

布 *nuno* cloth.　布地 *nunoji* cloth.　布目 *nunome* texture.

ON — FU cloth; spread

毛布 *mōfu* blanket.　分布 ‹v› *bunpu* distribution.　公布 ‹v› *kōfu* official announcement.　散布 ‹v› *sanpu* sprinkling.　流布 ‹v› *rufu* circulation, spreading.

#485

糸

6 strokes 

kun — *ito* thread

糸 *ito* thread.　毛糸 *keito* woolen yarn.　生糸 *kiito* raw silk.　糸口 *itoguchi* end of a thread; clue.

ON — SHI thread

製糸 *seishi* silk manufacture.　製糸場 *seishijō* silk manufactory.

#486

綿

14 strokes 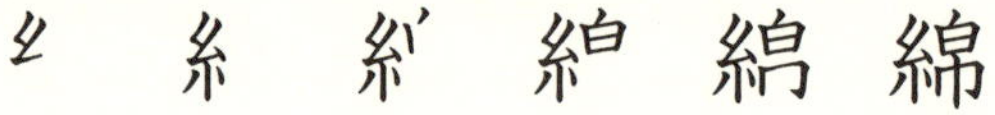

kun — *wata* cotton

綿 *wata* cotton.　綿毛 *watage* down.

ON — MEN cotton

綿糸 *menshi* cotton thread.　綿製品 *menseihin* cotton goods.　綿花 *menka* raw cotton.　木綿 *momen** cotton.

#487

絹

13 strokes 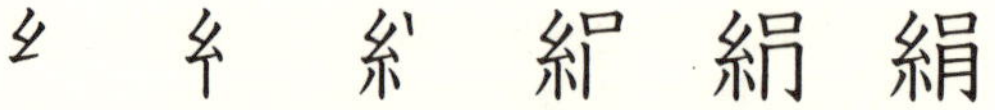

kun — *kinu* silk

絹 *kinu* silk.　絹糸 *kinuito* silk thread.　絹地 *kinuji* silk stuff.

ON — KEN silk

絹糸 *kenshi* silk thread.　人絹 *jinken* artificial silk.

#488

芸

7 strokes 

ON — GEI art, craft

民芸品 *mingeihin* folk-art article.　工芸品 *kōgeihin* object of industrial art.　手芸品 *shugeihin* handicraft article.　園芸 *engei* gardening.　文芸作品 *bungei sakuhin* literary work.

包	5 strokes	ノ ク ク 勺 包

kun   *tsutsu(mu)* wrap up
包む *tsutsumu* wrap up.   包み *tsutsumi* package.   小包 *kozutsumi* parcel.

ON   HŌ wrap up
包装 ⟨v⟩ *hōsō* packing, wrapping.   包帯 *hōtai* bandage.   包丁 *hōchō* kitchen knife.   包囲 ⟨v⟩ *hōi* encirclement.

紙	10 strokes	幺 糸 糸 紀 紙 紙

kun   *kami* paper
紙 *kami* paper.   包み紙 *tsutsumigami* wrapping paper.   紙製品 *kamiseihin* paper product.   手紙 *tegami* letter.

ON   SHI paper
包装紙 *hōsōshi* wrapping paper.   用紙 *yōshi* form.   和紙 *washi* Japanese paper.   白紙 *hakushi* blank paper.

■ II. Vocabulary

品	*shina*	goods, article
商品	*shōhin*	merchandise
品質	*hinshitsu*	quality of goods
高級品	*kōkyūhin*	high-quality goods
安物	*yasumono*	cheap goods
類似品	*ruijihin*	similar goods; imitations
常用 ⟨v⟩	*jōyō*	habitual use
非常用	*hijōyō*	for emergency use
衣	*koromo*	garment, clothes
衣類	*irui*	clothing
春の装い	*haru no yosooi*	spring attire
服装	*fukusō*	dress, costume
衣装	*ishō*	costume
宝物	*takaramono/hōmotsu*	treasure
宝石箱	*hōsekibako*	jewel box
指輪	*yubiwa*	ring

金銀	*kingin*	gold and silver
磁器	*jiki*	porcelain
製品	*seihin*	product
皮製品	*kawaseihin*	leather product
毛皮	*kegawa*	fur
毛布	*mōfu*	blanket
布地	*nunoji*	cloth
毛糸	*keito*	woolen yarn
綿	*wata*	cotton
綿糸	*menshi*	cotton thread
絹	*kinu*	silk
絹糸	*kinuito/kenshi*	silk thread
民芸品	*mingeihin*	folk-art article
包み紙	*tsutsumigami*	wrapping paper
包装紙	*hōsōshi*	wrapping paper

■ III. Reading Exercises 26

Read and translate the following.

1. この品は安くて品質が良い。
2. この二つはよく似ているが、こちらは高級品でそちらは安物だ。
3. 悪質の商品や類似品に注意して下さい。
4. ある薬品は常用しない方がいい。
5. 非常用の食料があの箱に入っている。
6. 洋装店のマネキンが春の装いに衣替えした。
7. 外国で、数々の民族衣装や民芸品を見て回った。
8. あの店は洋服の布地や毛糸などを置いている。
9. 台所用品はこの百貨店の五階に、毛布は八階にある。
10. 今年は暖冬で毛皮のコートを着る機会がなかった。
11. 地下街に皮製品の高級店が開店した。
12. 宝石箱に金銀の指輪やブローチが入れてある。
13. 夏の季節には絹より綿製品が好まれる。
14. ガラスのケースの中に、高級な磁器が並んでいる。
15. 店員が人形を箱に入れて、黄色の包装紙で包んでくれた。

Business

■ I. Reference

#491 買 | 12 strokes | 丶 冖 罒 罒 買 買

kun　*ka(u)* buy
買う *kau* buy.　買い物 ⟨v⟩ *kaimono* shopping.　買い手 *kaite* buyer.

ON　BAI buy
買収 ⟨v⟩ #508 *baishū* buying; bribe.

#492 売 | 7 strokes | 十 士 声 声 声 売

kun　*u(ru)* sell; *u(reru)* be sold
売る *uru* sell.　売れる *ureru* sell (well).　安売り ⟨v⟩ *yasuuri* bargain sale.　前売り ⟨v⟩ *maeuri* advance sale.　売り上げ *uriage* proceeds.　売れ行き *ureyuki* sales.

ON　BAI sell
売買 ⟨v⟩ *baibai* purchase and sale.　商売 ⟨v⟩ *shōbai* business, trade.　売店 *baiten* stand, booth.　売名 *baimei* self-advertisement.

#493 客 | 9 strokes | 丶 宀 宀 宊 客 客

ON　KYAKU, KAKU guest, customer
客 *kyaku* guest, customer.　買物客 *kaimonokyaku* shopper.　常客 *jōkyaku* regular customer.　観光客 *kankōkyaku* tourist.　観客 *kankyaku* audience.　客死 ⟨v⟩ *kakushi* death in a strange land.

#494 取 | 8 strokes | 一 厂 耳 耳 取 取

kun　*to(ru)* take
取る *toru* take.　取り引き ⟨v⟩ *torihiki* dealings, transactions.　取り上げる *toriageru* take up.　取り入れる *toriireru* take in.　書き取り *kakitori* dictation.

ON　SHU take
取材 ⟨v⟩ *shuzai* collecting news material.

#495 値

10 strokes 　イ　仁　仵　佔　値　値

kun *ne, atai* price, value
安値 *yasune* low price.　高値 *takane* high price.　小売値 *kourine* retail price.　値上げ *neage* price increase.

ON CHI price, value
数値 *sūchi* numerical value.　平均値 *heikinchi* mean value.

#496 段

9 strokes 　イ　手　身　殳　段　段

ON DAN step; stairs; rank
値段 *nedan* price.　階段 *kaidan* stairs.　段階 *dankai* stage (in a project).　手段 *shudan* measure.　二段 *nidan* 2nd grade (in karate).

#497 価

8 strokes 　イ　仁　仃　価　価　価

kun *atai* price, value
価 *atai* price, value

ON KA price, value
価値 *kachi* value.　物価 *bukka* prices.　定価 *teika* list price.　原価 *genka* cost.　高価な *kōka na* expensive.

#498 単

9 strokes 　丶　丷　当　当　単　単

ON TAN single
単価 *tanka* unit price.　単位 *tan'i* unit; credit (in education).　単数 *tansū* singular number.　単調な *tanchō na* monotonous.

#499 格

10 strokes 　十　才　杉　杦　格　格

ON KAKU, [KŌ] status, rank; standard; case
価格 *kakaku* price.　格安品 *kakuyasuhin* low-priced goods.　合格 *gōkaku* success (in an examination).　性格 *seikaku* personality.　主格 *shukaku* nominative case.　格子 *kōshi* lattice.

#500 得	11 strokes	ク イ 行 冴 徂 得

kun   *e(ru), u(ru)* gain, obtain; *-e(ru), -u(ru)* be able to

得る *eru/uru* gain, obtain. なし得る *nashieru/nashiuru* be able to do. 心得る *kokoroeru* understand.

ON   TOKU gain, profit

得 *toku* gain, profit. 得意 *tokui* strong point; customer. 取得 ‹v› *shutoku* acquisition. 拾得物 *shūtokubutsu* a find. 会得 ‹v› *etoku* comprehension.

#501 損	13 strokes	扌 扌 护 捐 揖 損

kun   *soko(nau), soko(neru)* damage; *-soko(nau), -soko(neru)* fail to do

損なう・損ねる *sokonau/sokoneru* damage (a plate). 買い損なう *kai-sokonau* fail to buy. 見損ねる *misokoneru* fail to see.

ON   SON loss, damage

損 *son* loss. 損得 *sontoku* gain and loss. 損害 *songai* damage.

#502 利	7 strokes	ノ ニ 千 禾 利 利

kun   *ki(ku)* take effect

利く *kiku* take effect. 左利き *hidarikiki* left-handed.

ON   RI advantage; interest

利子 *rishi* interest (at 5%). 利害 *rigai* advantages and dis-advantages. 利用 ‹v› *riyō* utilization. 便利な *benri na* convenient. 砂利 *jari** gravel.

#503 益	10 strokes	一 ゛ 兴 咅 益 益

ON   EKI, [YAKU] benefit

利益 *rieki* profit. 損益 *son'eki* profit and loss. 公益 *kōeki* public interest. 有益な *yūeki na* useful. ご利益 *goriyaku* devine favor.

#504 額	18 strokes	宀 灾 客 額 額 額

kun *hitai* forehead
額 *hitai* forehead.

ON GAKU amount; framed picture
額 *gaku* amount of money; framed picture.　金額 *kingaku* amount of money.　全額 *zengaku* total amount.　半額 *hangaku* half amount.　差額 *sagaku* difference.　額面 *gakumen* face value.

#505 割	12 strokes	宀 宀 宝 害 害 割

kun *wa(ru)* divide; *wa(reru)* be broken; *sa(ku)* spare; *wari* proportion
割る *waru* divide (in 2).　割れる *wareru* be broken.　割く *saku* spare (time/money).　割引 ⟨v⟩ *waribiki* discount.　二割引き *niwari-biki* 20% discount.　割合 *wariai* proportion.

ON KATSU devide
分割 ⟨v⟩ *bunkatsu* division.　分割払い ⟨v⟩ *bunkatsu barai* payment in installments.

#506 福	13 strokes	⻊ ネ ⻈ ⻈ 福 福

ON FUKU fortune
福引き *fukubiki* lottery.　幸福 *kōfuku* happiness.　祝福 ⟨v⟩ *shukufuku* blessing.

#507 告	7 strokes	ノ ⺊ 牛 生 告 告

kun *tsu(geru)* tell, inform
告げる *tsugeru* tell, inform.　告げ口 ⟨v⟩ *tsugeguchi* taletelling.

ON KOKU tell, inform
広告 ⟨v⟩ *kōkoku* advertisement.　報告 ⟨v⟩ *hōkoku* report.　警告 ⟨v⟩ *keikoku* warning.　予告 ⟨v⟩ *yokoku* advance notice.　告白 ⟨v⟩ *kokuhaku* confession.

#508 収	4 strokes	丿 丩 収 収

kun   *osa(meru)* obtain; *osa(maru)* settle down

収める *osameru* obtain (profit).   収まる *osamaru* settle down.

ON   SHŪ obtain

収入 *shūnyū* income.   収益 *shūeki* earnings.   領収書 *ryōshūsho* receipt.   買収 ‹v› *baishū* buying; bride.

#509 支	4 strokes	一 十 ナ 支

kun   *sasa(eru)* support Ir. *tsuka(eru)**

支える *sasaeru* support (one's family).   差し支える *sashitsukaeru** be hindered (from doing).

ON   SHI pay; branch; support

支出 ‹v› *shishutsu* expenditure.   収支 *shūshi* income and outgo. 支店 *shiten* branch shop/office.   支度 ‹v› *shitaku* preparation.   支持 ‹v› #551 *shiji* support.

#510 算	14 strokes	⺮ 竹 竻 笛 算 算

ON   SAN calculation

計算 ‹v› *keisan* calculation.   暗算 ‹v› *anzan* mental calculation. 算数 *sansū* arithmatic.   予算 *yosan* budget.

#511 決	7 strokes	丶 氵 汀 沪 決 決

kun   *ki(meru)* decide; *ki(maru)* be decided

決める *kimeru* decide.   決め手 *kimete* decisive factor.   決まる *kimaru* be decided.

ON   KETSU decide

決算 ‹v› *kessan* settlement of accounts.   決心 ‹v› *kesshin* resolution. 決定 ‹v› *kettei* decision, settlement.   決して *kesshite* never.

#512 納

10 strokes　く　タ　彡　糸　糿　納

kun　*osa(meru)* pay; supply; accept; *osa(maru)* be paid, supplied
納める *osameru* pay (tax); supply/accept (goods).　収まる *osamaru* be paid, supplied.

ON　NŌ, [TŌ], [NA], [NA'], [NAN] pay; supply; accept
納入 ⟨v⟩ *nōnyū* payment (of tax); supply (of goods).　分納 ⟨n⟩ *bunnō* installment payment.　出納 *suitō* receipts and disbursements.　納屋 *naya* barn.　納得 ⟨v⟩ *nattoku* consent.　納戸 *nando* storeroom.

#513 倉

10 strokes　ㅅ　今　今　倉　倉　倉

kun　*kura* warehouse
倉 *kura* warehouse.　米倉 *komegura* rice granary.

ON　SŌ warehouse
倉庫 *sōko* warehouse.　穀倉 *kokusō* granary.

#514 話

13 strokes　言　言　計　計　話

kun　*hana(su)* speak, talk; *hanashi* story, conversation
話す *hanasu* speak, talk.　話し合う *hanashiau* discuss.　話の種 *hanashi no tane* topic of conversation.

ON　WA story, conversation
電話 ⟨v⟩ *denwa* telephone.　会話 ⟨v⟩ *kaiwa* conversation.　民話 *min-wa* folktale.　実話 *jitsuwa* true story.　世話 ⟨v⟩ *sewa* care, help.

#515 受

8 strokes　く　爫　爫　𤣥　受　受

kun　*u(keru)* receive
受ける *ukeru* receive (orders).　受け取る *uketoru* receive, accept.　受取 *uketori* receipt.　受付 *uketsuke* reception desk; acceptance.

ON　JU receive
受注 ⟨v⟩ *juchū* receiving orders.　受理 ⟨v⟩ *juri* acceptance (of a report).　受話器 *juwaki* receiver.

#516						
札	5 strokes	一	十	才	木	札

kun   *fuda* tag, label
札 *fuda* tag, label.   名札 *nafuda* name tag.

ON   SATSU paper money, card
千円札 *sen'ensatsu* 1,000-yen bill.   札束 *satsutaba* roll of bills.
入札 ‹v› *nyūsatsu* bid.   落札 ‹v› *rakusatsu* successful bid.

#517						
配	10 strokes	厂	冂	酉	酉ꞈ	酉ꞈ 配

kun   *kuba(ru)* deliver, distribute
配る *kubaru* deliver (mail), distribute (handbills).

ON   HAI deliver, distribute
配達 ‹v› *haitatsu* delivery.   分配 ‹v› *bunpai* distribution.   配置 ‹v›
haichi arrangement.   心配 ‹v› *shinpai* worry.   配役 *haiyaku* cast (of
a play).   気配 *kehai* sign, indication.

#518						
発	9 strokes	ヲ	ヺ	癶	癶	癶 発

ON   HATSU, HOTSU start, depart; emit
発売 ‹v› *hatsubai* sale, putting on market.   出発 ‹v› *shuppatsu* departure.   発行 ‹v› *hakkō* publication.   発見 ‹v› *hakken* discovery.   発明
‹v› *hatsumei* invention.   発達 ‹v› *hattatsu* development.   発散 ‹v›
hassan emission.   発足 ‹v› *hossoku/hassoku* start.

#519						
送	9 strokes	ʼʼ	丷	关	关	送 送

kun   *oku(ru)* send
送る *okuru* send.   送り先 *okurisaki* destination.   送り主 *okuri-
nushi* sender.   見送る *miokuru* see someone off.

ON   SŌ send
発送 ‹v› *hassō* sending out.   郵送 ‹v› *yūsō* sending by mail.   送金 ‹v›
sōkin remittance.   送料 *sōryō* postage.

#520 運	12 strokes	冖　冐　冒　軍　運　運

kun　*hako(bu)* carry, transport
運ぶ *hakobu* carry, transport.　運び *hakobi* progress, arrangement.

ON　UN carry, transport
運送‹v› *unsō* trnsport.　運転‹v› *unten* driving, operation.　運動‹v› *undō* movement; physical exercise.　運命 *unmei* fate.　幸運 *kōun* good luck.

#521 賃	13 strokes	亻　任　侜　侜　賃　賃

ON　CHIN wages, fee, fare, rent
運賃 *unchin* fare.　賃金 *chingin* wages.　手間賃 *temachin* wages for labor.　家賃 *yachin* rent.　賃上げ‹v› *chin'age* wage hike.

#522 荷	10 strokes	一　艹　茫　苻　荷　荷

kun　*ni* load, cargo, baggage
荷物 *nimotsu* load, baggage.　積み荷 *tsumini* load, cargo.　荷札 *nifuda* tag, label.

ON　KA load, cargo, baggage
出荷‹v› *shukka* shipment of goods.　入荷‹v› *nyūka* arrival/receipt of goods

■ II. Vocabulary

買い物‹v›	*kaimono*	shopping
買物客	*kaimonokyaku*	shopper
安売り‹v›	*yasuuri*	bargain sale
売買‹v›	*baibai*	purchase and sale
取り引き‹v›	*torihiki*	dealings, transactions
値段	*nedan*	price
価値	*kachi*	value
価格	*kakaku*	price
単価	*tanka*	unit price

損得	*sontoku*	loss and gain
利益	*rieki*	profit
金額	*kingaku*	amount of money
割引‹v›	*waribiki*	discount
分割払い‹v›	*bunkatsubarai*	payment in installments
福引き	*fukubiki*	lottery
広告‹v›	*kōkoku*	advertisement
収入	*shūnyū*	income
支出‹v›	*shishutsu*	expenditure
決算‹v›	*kessan*	settlement of accounts
納入‹v›	*nōnyū*	payment; supply
受取	*uketori*	receipt
受注‹v›	*juchū*	receiving orders
電話‹v›	*denwa*	telephone
倉庫	*sōko*	warehouse
配達‹v›	*haitatsu*	delivery
発送‹v›	*hassō*	sending out
運賃	*unchin*	fare
荷物	*nimotsu*	load, baggage
出荷‹v›	*shukka*	shipment of goods
荷札	*nifuda*	tag, label
入札‹v›	*nyūsatsu*	bid

■ III. Reading Exercises 27 ■

Read and translate the following.

1. 商店の**安売り**や**福引**きに大勢の**買物客**が集まった。
2. 私の友人は土地や家屋の**売買**をしている。
3. この品は品質は良いが、**値段**が高過ぎる。
4. ある郵便切手は一万円の**価値**がある。
5. 今年の電気製品に高い**価格**が付いている。
6. この器具は**単価**二千円で三万台売れた。
7. 銀座の宝石店で、**高価**な指輪を**半額**で買った。
8. 父は材木の**商売**で大きな**利益**を**得**た。
9. 毎月、月末に取り引きの**損得**を**計算**する。

10. 注文を**受け**次第、品物を**発送**する。
11. ある店は週に七日、**電話**で**受注**している。
12. 店員が**入荷**した商品を**倉庫**に運んでいる。
13. 野菜や果物をトラックで町へ**出荷**する。
14. この**運賃**には二割の**割引**がある。
15. **分割**払いで冷蔵庫を買った。
16. 兄は付近の役所に品物を**納入**している。
17. 日曜日と祭日には郵便の**配達**はない。
18. 来年度の**予算**が**決**まった。
19. 我々は一年に二度、**収入**と支出の**決算**をする。
20. 数日前から道路工事の**入札広告**が出ている。

12

****
Education

Schools

■ **I. Reference** ━━━━━━━━━━━━━━━━━

#523

学 | 8 strokes | 〝　　〟　　`⺍`　　学　　学　　学

kun | *mana(bu)* learn, study
学ぶ *manabu* learn, study.

ON | GAKU learn, study.
大学 *daigaku* college, university. 学生 *gakusei* student. 学者 *gakusha* scholar. 学長 *gakuchō* university president. 数学 *sūgaku* mathematics. 文学部 *bungakubu* department of literature. 学期 *gakki* school term. 入学 ‹v› *nyūgaku* entering a school.

#524

共 | 6 strokes | 一　　十,　　卄　　卅　　共　　共

kun | *tomo* together, both, all
共に *tomo ni* together. 送料共 *sōryō tomo* including shipping.

ON | KYŌ together, both, all
共学 *kyōgaku* coeducation. 共通の *kyōtsū no* common, mutual. 公共の *kōkyō no* public (interest). 共存 ‹v› *kyōzon* coexistence. 共鳴 ‹v› *kyōmei* resonance; sympathy.

#525

校 | 10 strokes | 十　　木　　朮゛　　栌　　栌　　校

ON | KŌ school; correction; officer
学校 *gakkō* school. 小学校 *shōgakkō* elementary school. 高校 *kōkō* high school. 校長 *kōchō* principal. 登校 ‹v› *tōkō* attending school. 校正 ‹v› *kōsei* proofreading. 将校 *shōkō* officer.

#526 等	12 strokes ⺌ ⺮ 竺 竺 等 等

kun *hito(shii)* equal
等しい *hitoshii* equal. 等しくする *hitoshiku suru* equalize.

ON TŌ equality; rank, grade
高等学校 *kōtō gakkō* high school. 等級 *tōkyū* rank. 一等 *ittō* 1st rank. 平等 *byōdō* equality. 上等の *jōtō no* superior.

#527 保	9 strokes イ 亻 仴 伴 保 保

kun *tamo(tsu)* keep, preserve
保つ *tamotsu* keep (safety), preserve (life).

ON HO keep, preserve
保育園 *hoikuen* nursery school. 保母 *hobo* kindergarten teacher. 保安 *hoan* maintenance of security. 保存 ⟨v⟩ *hozon* preservation.

#528 院	10 strokes ⁊ ㇌ ㇌ 阝 陀 陀 院

ON IN institution
大学院 *daigakuin* graduate school. 院長 *inchō* president of an academy; director of a hospital. 入院 ⟨v⟩ *nyūin* entering hospital.

#529 備	12 strokes イ 伊 伊 俏 備 備

kun *sona(eru)* furnish; prepare; *sona(waru)* be furnished
備える *sonaeru* furnish (a room with furniture); prepare (for a test). 備わる *sonawaru* be furnished with.

ON BI furnish; prepare
予備校 *yobikō* preparatory school. 備品 *bihin* fixtures. 装備 ⟨v⟩ *sōbi* equipment. 警備 ⟨v⟩ *keibi* defense, guarding.

#530 徒	10 strokes ㇒ 彳 彳 徍 徍 徒

ON TO companion; on foot; useless
生徒 *seito* pupil. 徒弟 *totei* apprentice. 暴徒 *bōto* riotors. 徒歩で *toho de* on foot. 徒食 ⟨v⟩ *toshoku* living in idleness.

#531 留	10 strokes	㇑ ㄥ 幻 邜 留 留

kun   *to(meru)* fasten, detain; *to(maru)* be fastened
留める *tomeru* fasten (a button). 引き留める *hikitomeru* detain (a person). 留まる *tomaru* be fastened.

ON   RYŪ, [RU] fasten, detain
留学 ‹v› *ryūgaku* studying abroad. 留学生 *ryūgakusei* foreign student. 留置 ‹v› *ryūchi* detention. 保留 ‹v› *horyū* reservation.
留守 #936 *rusu* being away from home.

#532 童	12 strokes	亠 产 音 竜 童 童

kun   *warabe* child
童 *warabe* child. 童歌 #670 *warabeuta* children's song.

ON   DŌ child
児童 *jidō* child. 学童 *gakudō* schoolchild. 童話 *dōwa* children's story. 童心 *dōshin* child's mind.

#533 舎	8 strokes	人 仒 全 全 舎 舎

kun   Ir. *(i)naka**
田舎 *inaka** country, countryside.

ON   SHA house, shelter
校舎 *kōsha* school building. 牛舎 *gyūsha* cowhouse.

#534 建	9 strokes	㇇ � 聿 津 建 建

kun   *ta(teru)* build; *ta(tsu)* be built; *-date* -stories
建てる *tateru* build. 建物 *tatemono* building. 建つ *tatsu* be built. 二階建て *nikaidate* 2-story (house).

ON   KEN, [KON] build
建国 ‹v› *kenkoku* founding of a country. 建立 ‹v› *konryū* constructing (of a Buddhist temple).

#535 門	8 strokes	丨 冂 冂 冃 門 門 門

kun   *kado* gate

門口 *kadoguchi* entrance.   門松 *kadomatsu* New Year's decoration pines.   門出 〈v〉 *kadode* setting out.

ON   MON gate

校門 *kōmon* school gate.   正門 *seimon* front gate.   名門校 *meimonkō* prestigious school.   入門書 *nyūmonsho* introductory book.

#536 始	8 strokes	く 女 妗 妗 始 始

kun   *haji(meru)*, *haji(maru)* begin, start

始める *hajimeru* start (the meeting).   始まる *hajimaru* (Schools) begin.   書き始める *kakihajimeru* start to write.   始まり *hajimari* beginning.

ON   SHI begin, start

開始 〈v〉 *kaishi* start.   年始 *nenshi* New Year's call.   始発 *shihatsu* 1st train/bus of the day.

#537 終	11 strokes	幺 幺 糹 紒 終 終

kun   *o(waru)* end; *o(eru)* finish

終わる *owaru* end, be completed.   終える *oeru* finish (a test).

ON   SHŪ end; all through

始終 *shijū* all the time.   終日 *shūjitsu* all day long.   終夜 *shūya* all night long.   最終回 *saishūkai* last round, last inning.

#538 教	11 strokes	土 耂 考 孝 孝 教

kun   *oshi(eru)* teach; *oso(waru)* be taught

教える *oshieru* teach.   教え *oshie* teaching.   教え方 *oshiekata* teaching method.   教わる *osowaru* be taught (by a teacher).

ON   KYŌ teach; religion

教育 〈v〉 *kyōiku* education.   教材 *kyōzai* teaching materials.   教員 *kyōin* teaching staff.   教会 *kyōkai* church.   キリスト教 *Kirisuto-kyō* Christianity.

#539 室	9 strokes	` ´ 宀 宏 宏 宰 室

kun   *muro* celler
室 *muro* celler.   氷室 *himuro* ice room.

ON   SHITSU room
教室 *kyōshitsu* classroom.   教員室 *kyōinshitsu* teachers' room.
待合室 *machiaishitsu* waiting room.   和室 *washitsu* Japanese-style
room.   温室 *onshitsu* greenhouse.   室内 *shitsunai* indoor.

#540 板	8 strokes	十 木 杧 扳 板 板

kun   *ita* board
板 *ita* board.   板前 *itamae* chef of Japanese cuisine.

ON   HAN, BAN board
黒板 *kokuban* blackboard.   合板 *gōhan* plywood.

#541 机	6 strokes	一 十 オ 木 朾 机

kun   *tsukue* desk
机 *tsukue* desk.   書き物机 *kakimonozukue* writing desk.

ON   KI desk
机上 *kijō* on the desk.   机上の計画 #656 *kijō no keikaku* desk plan.

#542 筆	12 strokes	⺮ 竹 竺 竺 筆 筆

kun   *fude* writing brush, pen
筆 *fude* writing brush.   筆がたつ *fude ga tatsu* be a good writer.

ON   HITSU writing brush, pen
万年筆 *mannenhitsu* fountain pen.   毛筆 *mōhitsu* writing brush.
自筆 *jihitsu* one's own hand writing.   筆者 *hissha* author.

#543 科	9 strokes	´ 千 禾 禾 科 科

ON   KA branch, division; penalty
教科書 *kyōkasho* textbook.   学科 *gakka* subject of study.   科目
kamoku subject.   科学 *kagaku* science.   内科 *naika* internal
medicine.   前科 *zenka* previous conviction.

# 544 考	6 strokes	一　十　土　耂　考　考

kun   *kanga(eru)* think, consider
考える *kangaeru* think, consider.   考え *kangae* idea, thought.
考え深い *kangaebukai* thoughtful.

ON   KŌ think, consider
参考書 *sankōsho* reference book.   思考力 *shikōryoku* thinking power.   考古学 *kōkogaku* archaeology.

# 545 辞	13 strokes	二　千　舌ﾉ　舌ﾉﾉ　辞　辞

kun   *ya(meru)* resign, quit
辞める *yameru* resign, quit.

ON   JI word; resignation
辞書 *jisho* dictionary.   祝辞 *shukuji* congratulatory address.
辞令 *jirei* written appointment.   辞去 ⟨ﾘ⟩ *jikyo* taking one's leave.

# 546 典	8 strokes	丨　冂　冊　曲　曲　典

ON   TEN classical book; ceremony
辞典 *jiten* dictionary.   百科事典 *hyakka jiten* encyclopedia.   古典 *koten* classics.   教典 *kyōten* Buddhist scripture.   祭典 *saiten* festival.   祝典 *shukuten* celebration.

# 547 容	10 strokes	丶　宀　空　突　容　容

ON   YŌ content; form, appearance
内容 *naiyō* content.   容器 *yōki* container.   容量 *yōryō* capacity, volume.   形容 ⟨ﾘ⟩ *keiyō* modification; figure of speech.
容色 *yōshoku* personal appearance.

# 548 組	11 strokes	く　乡　糸　糸　紅　組

kun   *ku(mu)* assemble; *kumi* class, group, set
組む *kumu* construct (a raft).   組み立てる *kumitateru* assemble.   組み合わせ *kumiawase* combination.   赤組 *akagumi* red team.   組合 *kumiai* union.   番組 *bangumi* program.   一組 *hitokumi* a set.

ON   SO assemble
組成 ‹v› *sosei* formation, composition.

#549 | 同 | 6 strokes | 丨 冂 冂 冂 同 同

kun   *ona(ji)* same
同じ *onaji* same.   同じ組 *onaji kumi* same class.
ON   DŌ same
同級生 *dōkyūsei* classmate.   一同 *ichidō* all the persons.   同時に *dōji ni* at the same time.   同意 ‹v› *dōi* agreement.

#550 | 窓 | 11 strokes | 丶 宀 空 空 空 窓 窓

kun   *mado* window
窓 *mado* window.   窓口 *madoguchi* ticket window.
ON   SŌ window
同窓会 *dōsōkai* alumni meeting/society.   同窓生 *dōsōsei* schoolmate, alumnus.

#551 | 持 | 9 strokes | 一 十 扌 扩 扞 持

kun   *mo(tsu)* have, hold
持つ *motsu* have, hold.   持ち物 *mochimono* one's belongings.   持ち主 *mochinushi* owner.   受け持つ *ukemotsu* take charge of.   受け持ちの先生 *ukemochi no sensei* homeroom teacher.   気持ち *kimochi* feeling.
ON   JI have, hold
支持 ‹v› *shiji* support.   持参 ‹v› *jisan* bringing/taking.

■ II. Vocabulary

学校	*gakkō*	school
高等学校	*kōtōgakkō*	high school
大学	*daigaku*	college, university
大学院	*daigakuin*	graduate school
予備校	*yobikō*	preparatory school
保育園	*hoikuen*	nursery school

共学	*kyōgaku*	coeducation
留学 ‹v›	*ryūgaku*	studying abroad
生徒	*seito*	pupil
児童	*jidō*	children
校舎	*kōsha*	school building
校門	*kōmon*	school gate
建物	*tatemono*	building
教え	*oshie*	teaching
教育 ‹v›	*kyōiku*	education
教室	*kyōshitsu*	classroom
黒板	*kokuban*	blackboard
机	*tsukue*	desk
万年筆	*mannenhitsu*	fountain pen
教科書	*kyōkasho*	textbook
参考書	*sankōsho*	reference book
辞書	*jisho*	dictionary
百科辞典	*hyakka jiten*	encyclopedia
内容	*naiyō*	content
同じ組	*onaji kumi*	same class
同窓会	*dōsōkai*	alumni meeting/society
受け持ちの先生	*ukemochi no sensei*	homeroom teacher
始終	*shijū*	all the time

■ III. Reading Exercises 28 ■

Read and translate the following.

1. 小学校は午前八時に始まって、午後三時半に終わる。
2. 私達の受け持ちの先生は田中先生です。
3. 長女も次女も共学の大学で学んだ。
4. 兄の知人は有名な学者で、現在京大の大学院で教えている。
5. 長男は日本で教育を受けたが、次男は今パリに留学している。
6. ある高等学校は大学の予備校だと考えられている。
7. 妹は保育園で幼い子供達の世話をしている。
8. ある地域では、学校を辞める児童や生徒の数が多くなった。
9. 机の上に辞書が三冊と万年筆が二本置いてある。

10. **参考書**や**百科辞典**で色々な事を調べる。

11. **教室**の**黒板**に北海道の地図がかいてある。

12. 山田先生は**始終**新しい**教材**を使い、**教え**方も上手だ。

13. この**教科書**は**内容**が少し古いですね。

14. **校舎**の後ろに大きい図書館が**建**った。

15. **校門**を入ると、右手に三階**建**ての**建物**が見える。

16. 暑いから、**窓**を開けて下さい。

17. 私と春子さんは**高校**で同じ**組**だった。

18. 毎年五月の**同窓会**には、昔の**同級生**が二十人以上集まる。

Learning

#552
課 15 strokes   亠 訂 訶 訷 評 課

ON   KA lesson; section
学課 *gakka* lesson, school work.   第一課 *daiikka* Lesson 1.   日課
nikka daily task.   課外の *kagai no* extracurricular.   人事課 *jinjika*
personnel section.   課長 *kachō* section chief.

#553
程 12 strokes   ニ 利 和 秤 秬 程

kun   *hodo* degree, extent
程 *hodo* degree, extent.   五千円程 *gosen'en hodo* about 5,000 yen.
先程 *sakihodo* a while ago.   後程 *nochihodo* later.

ON   TEI degree, extent
課程 *katei* course.   過程 *katei* process.   程度 *teido* degree.
道程 *dōtei* distance; journey.   日程 *nittei* day's schedule.

#554
授 11 strokes   扌 扩 扩 护 捋 授

kun   *sazu(keru)* grant, teach; *sazu(karu)* be granted, taught.
授ける *sazukeru* grant (degrees), teach (lessons).   授かる *sazukaru*
be granted (degrees), be taught (lessons).

ON   JU grant, teach
教授⟨v⟩ *kyōju* instruction.   大学教授 *daigaku kyōju* college professor.   天授 *tenju* natural gifts.   授受⟨v⟩ *juju* giving and receiving;
transfer.

#555
業 13 strokes   〃 〃〃 〃〃 业 丵 業

kun   *waza* work, skill
業 *waza* work, skill.   早業 *hayawaza* quick trick.

ON GYŌ occupation, business; GŌ karma

授業 ‹v› *jugyō* instruction, class work. 事業 *jigyō* business.
開業 ‹v› *kaigyō* opening business. 商業 *shōgyō* commerce. 業績
gyōseki achievements. 悪業 *akugō* sinful deed.

#556 講	17 strokes	言	計	請	講	講	講

ON KŌ lecture

講堂 *kōdō* lecture hall. 講座 *kōza* chair; course. 受講 ‹v› *jukō*
attending lectures. 休講 ‹v› *kyūkō* cancelation of a lecture.

#557 義	13 strokes	丷	羊	羊	美	義	義

ON GI meaning; justice; in-laws; artificial

講義 ‹v› *kōgi* lecture. 意義 *igi* meaning. 定義 ‹v› *teigi* definition.
正義 *seigi* justice. 義父 *gifu* father-in-law. 義足 *gisoku* artificial
leg.

#558 師	10 strokes	亻	阝	𠂤	𠂤	師	師

ON SHI teacher, expert; army

講師 *kōshi* lecturer. 教師 *kyōshi* teacher. 牧師 *bokushi* pastor.
師団 #676 *shidan* army division. 師走 *shiwasu** December.

#559 助	7 strokes	丨	冂	月	且	助	助

kun *tasu(keru)* help, rescue; *tasu(karu)* be helped, rescued; *suke* assistance

助ける *tasukeru* help, rescue. 助け合う *tasukeau* help each other.
助かる *tasukaru* be helped, rescued. 助太刀 #941 *sukedachi* assistance (in fight).

ON JO help, rescue

助教授 *jokyōju* assistant professor. 助手 *joshu* assistant. 助役
joyaku assistant official. 助力 ‹v› *joryoku* help.

#560 席	10 strokes	亠 广 庐 庐 庐 席 席

ON   SEKI seat Ir. *(yo)se** #1016

席 *seki* seat.   出席 ‹v› *shusseki* attendance.   席次 *sekiji* seating order; class standing.   座席 *zaseki* seat.   指定席 *shiteiseki* reserved seat.   末席 *basseki/masseki* lowest seat; bottom.

#561 欠	4 strokes	ノ 𠂉 ケ 欠

kun   *ka(keru)* be lacking; *ka(ku)* lack

欠ける *kakeru* be lacking.   欠く *kaku* lack (intelligence).

ON   KETSU lack

欠席 ‹v› *kesseki* nonattendance.   出欠 *shukketsu* attendance or absence.   欠員 *ketsuin* vacancy (in the staff).

#562 届	8 strokes	⁊ ⊐ 尸 戸 届 届

kun   *todo(keru)* send, report; *todo(ku)* arrive, reach, be delivered

届ける *todokeru* send (an article), report (to the police).   届け *todoke* notice.   欠席届 *kesseki todoke* notice of absence.   届く *todoku* arrive, reach, be delivered.

#563 勉	10 strokes	⁊ 夕 免 免 免 勉

ON   BEN effort, hard work

勉強 ‹v› *benkyō* study.   勉強家 *benkyōka* studious person.   勉学 ‹v› *bengaku* study.

#564 習	11 strokes	コ 习 羽 羽 習 習

kun   *nara(u)* learn

習う *narau* learn.   見習う *minarau* follow a person's example.

ON   SHŪ learn

予習 ‹v› *yoshū* preparation of lessons.   自習 ‹v› *jishū* study by oneself.   学習 ‹v› *gakushū* learning, study.   風習 *fūshū* customs.

#565 復	12 strokes	ク 彳 行 復 復 復

ON FUKU return, be restored

復習 ‹v› *fukushū* review.   回復 ‹v› *kaifuku* recovery.   復帰 ‹v› *fukki* comeback, return.   復古 ‹v› *fukko* restoration.

#566 言	7 strokes	丶 二 言 言 言 言

Kun *i(u)* say; *koto* word

言う *iu* say.   言い分 *iibun* one's say.   言葉 *kotoba* word, language.   一言 *hitokoto* single word.

ON GEN, GON word

方言 *hōgen* dialect.   発言 ‹v› *hatsugen* speech.   言質 *genchi*/*genshitsu* pledge.   祝言 *shūgen* wedding.   他言 ‹v› *tagon* telling others.

#567 読	14 strokes	言 言 言 詿 詩 読

kun *yo(mu)* read Ir. *do(kyō)**#822

読む *yomu* read.   読み書き *yomikaki* reading and writing.   読み方 *yomikata* reading, how to read.

ON DOKU, TOKU, [TO] read

読本 *tokuhon* reader.   読書 ‹v› *dokusho* reading.   読者 *dokusha* reader.   読点 #581 *tōten* (Japanese) comma.

#568 聞	14 strokes	厂 戶 門 門 聞 聞

kun *ki(ku)* hear, listen; ask; *ki(koeru)* be heard, audible

聞く *kiku* hear (a sound), listen (to a tape); ask (the teacher).   聞こえる *kikoeru* be heard, audible.

ON BUN, MON hear, listen

新聞 *shinbun* newspaper.   外聞 *gaibun* reputation.   見聞が広い *kenbun ga hiroi* be well-informed.   前代未聞の *zendaimimon no* unprecedented.

#569 問	11 strokes	ﾌ ﾌﾞ 門 門 問 問

kun　*to(i)*, [*ton*] question; *to(u)* ask, inquire
問い *toi* question.　問い合せる *toiawaseru* make inquiries.　問う
tou ask, inquire.　問屋 *ton'ya* wholesaler.

ON　MON question
質問 ⟨v⟩ *shitsumon* question.　学問 ⟨v⟩ *gakumon* learning, study.

#570 答	12 strokes	ﾟ ﾟﾟ 竹 竻 笤 答

kun　*kota(e)* answer; *kota(eru)* answer
答え *kotae* answer.　口答え ⟨v⟩ *kuchigotae* talking back.　答える
kotaeru answer (a question).

ON　TŌ answer
回答 ⟨v⟩ *kaitō* answer.　問答 ⟨v⟩ *mondō* questions and answers.

#571 案	10 strokes	ﾟ ﾞ 宀 安 安 宰 案

ON　AN plan, idea, proposal
案 *an* plan, idea, proposal.　答案 *tōan* examination paper.　名案
meian good idea.　原案 *gen'an* original plan.　具体案 *gutaian* concrete proposal.　案内 ⟨v⟩ *annai* showing around; information.
案外 *angai* unexpectedly.　案の定 *annojō* as expected.

#572 題	18 strokes	日 早 昰 題 題 題

ON　DAI title; subject, topic
題 *dai* title (of a book).　問題 *mondai* question, problem.　主題
shudai subject matter.　話題 *wadai* topic of conversation.　出題 ⟨v⟩
shutsudai making questions.　外題 *gedai* title of a play.

#573 宿	11 strokes	ﾟ 宀 疒 疒 宿 宿

kun　*yado* lodging; *yado(ru)* lodge
宿 *yado* lodging.　宿屋 *yadoya* inn.　宿る *yadoru* lodge (at an
inn).

ON SHUKU lodging
宿題 *shukudai* homework.　下宿 ‹v› *geshuku* boarding, lodging (at a person's).　宿舎 *shukusha* lodgings.　宿命 *shukumei* fate.

#574 提	12 strokes	扌　扩　扪　捍　捍　捍　提

kun *sa(geru)* carry in hand
提げる *sageru* carry (a thing) in one's hand.
ON TEI present
提出 ‹v› *teishutsu* presentation.　提案 ‹v› *teian* proposal.　提供 ‹v› *teikyō* offer.　前提 *zentei* presupposition.

#575 忘	7 strokes	丶　亠　亡　亡　忘　忘

kun *wasu(reru)* forget
忘れる *wasureru* forget.　忘れ物 *wasuremono* forgotten item.
ON BŌ forget
忘年会 *bōnenkai* year-end party.　忘我 *bōga* self-oblivion.

#576 解	13 strokes	广　角　觖　觖　解　解

kun *to(ku)* solve; *to(keru)* be solved
解く *toku* solve (a problem).　解ける *tokeru* be solved.
ON KAI, GE solve
解答 ‹v› *kaitō* answer, solution.　理解 ‹v› *rikai* understanding.　解決 ‹v› *kaiketsu* solution.　解熱 ‹v› *genetsu* reduction of fever.

#577 練	14 strokes	纟　纟　糺　糾　紳　練

kun *ne(ru)* knead; train; polish
練る *neru* knead (flour); train (one's body); polish (one's style).
ON REN knead; train; polish
練習 ‹v› *renshū* practice.　熟練 ‹v› *jukuren* skill, mastery.　洗練 ‹v› *senren* refinement.　老練家 *rōrenka* expert.

#578 試	13 strokes	三 言 計 訂 訂 試 試

kun **kokoro(miru), tame(su)** test, try
試みる *kokoromiru* try (to do). 試す *tamesu* test (one's strength).

ON **SHI** test, try
試練 *shiren* ordial, trial. 試合 *shiai* match, game. 試運転 ⟨v⟩
shiunten trial run. 試食 ⟨v⟩ *shishoku* sampling (the cake).

#579 験	18 strokes	厂 厈 馬 駖 駖 験

ON **KEN** effect; testing; [GEN] omen; beneficial effect
試験 ⟨v⟩ *shiken* examination. 実験 ⟨v⟩ *jikken* experiment. 体験
taiken actual experience. 受験 ⟨v⟩ *juken* undergoing examinations.
験 *gen* omen; beneficial effect (of the medicine).

#580 応	7 strokes	' 亠 广 广 応 応

ON **Ō** respond, react Ir. *(han)nō* #927
応用 ⟨v⟩ *ōyō* application, adaptation. 応用問題 *ōyō mondai* applied
question. 応答 ⟨v⟩ *ōtō* response.

#581 点	9 strokes	' ト 占 占 占 点

ON **TEN** point, mark
点 *ten* point, mark. 満点 *manten* perfect score. 出発点 *shuppatsu-ten* starting point. 欠点 *ketten* flaw. 読点 *tōten* (Japanese)
comma. 合点 ⟨v⟩ *gaten** understanding.

#582 採	11 strokes	扌 扩 扩 抨 抨 採

kun **to(ru)** take, adopt; collect
採る *toru* take, adopt (a measure); collect (insects).

ON **SAI** take, adopt; collect
採点 ⟨v⟩ *saiten* marking. 採用 ⟨v⟩ *saiyō* adoption; employment.
採集 ⟨v⟩ *saishū* collecting for specimens. 採決 ⟨v⟩ *saiketsu*
ballot taking.

#583 績	17 strokes	幺 糸 糸一 綪 綪 績

ON **SEKI** achievement; spinning
成績 *seiseki* achievement, score.　実績 *jisseki* actual results.　業績 *gyōseki* achievements.　紡績 *bōseki* spinning.

#584 論	15 strokes	三 言 訟 論 論 論

ON **RON** discussion, argument
論じる *ronjiru* discuss.　理論 *riron* theory.　論理 *ronri* logic.
論文 *ronbun* thesis.　世論 *seron/yoron* public opinion.

#585 専	9 strokes	厂 戸 百 甫 亩 専

kun *moppa(ra)* exclusively
専ら *moppara* exclusively.

ON **SEN** exclusively
専門 *senmon* one's speciality.　専用 ⟨v⟩*senyō* exclusive use.
専売 ⟨v⟩*senbai* monopoly.　専有 ⟨v⟩*senyū* exclusive possession.

#586 識	19 strokes	三 言 許 諳 識 識

ON **SHIKI** knowledge, recognition
知識 *chishiki* knowledge.　常識 *jōshiki* common sense.　学識 *gakushiki* scholarship.　面識 *menshiki* acquaintance.

#587 願	19 strokes	厂 厉 原 原一 願 願

kun *nega(u)* wish, request, pray
願う *negau* wish, request, pray.　願い *negai* wish, request.

ON **GAN** wish, request, pray
願書 *gansho* application form.　出願 ⟨v⟩*shutsugan* making an application.　願望 ⟨v⟩*ganbō* wish.　宿願 *shukugan* long-cherished desire.

#588 修	10 strokes	イ 亻 俢 俢 修 修

kun *osa(meru)* study, master
修める *osameru* study, master (the course of).

ON SHŪ, [SHU] study, master; amend
修業 ‹v›*shūgyō* study, pursuit.　修得 ‹v›*shūtoku* learning, acquirement.　修行 ‹v›*shugyō* training, ascetic practices.　修正 ‹v›*shūsei* amendment.　修理 ‹v›*shūri* repair.

#589 研	9 strokes	一 厂 石 石 研 研

kun *to(gu)* polish, sharpen
研ぐ *togu* sharpen (a knife).

ON KEN polish, sharpen
研修 ‹v›*kenshū* study and training.　研修生 *kenshūsei* trainee.

#590 究	7 strokes	` ` 宀 空 空 究

kun *kiwa(meru)* investigate thoroughly
究める *kiwameru* investigate thoroughly.

ON KYŪ investigate thoroughly
研究 ‹v›*kenkyū* study, research.　究明 ‹v›*kyūmei* investigation, clarification.　究極 *kyūkyoku* ultimate, extreme.

#591 想	13 strokes	十 机 相 相 想 想

ON SŌ, [SO] idea, thought
思想 *shisō* thought, idea.　理想 *risō* ideal.　予想 ‹v›*yosō* expectation.　空想 ‹v›*kūsō* fancy.　回想 ‹v›*kaisō* recollection.

#592 探	11 strokes	十 才 扩 挃 挀 探

kun *sagu(ru)* search; *saga(su)* look for
探る *saguru* search (one's pocket).　探す *sagasu* look for (a pen).

ON TAN search, look for
探究 ‹v›*tankyū* search.　探知 ‹v›*tanchi* detection.

#593 求	7 strokes	一　十　十　才　求　求

kun   *moto(meru)* request, seek; buy
求める *motomeru* request (a reply), seek (happiness); buy (a book).

ON   KYŪ request, seek
探求 ⟨v⟩ *tankyū* search.   求人 ⟨v⟩ *kyūjin* help wanted.   欲求 *yokkyū* desire.   求道 ⟨v⟩ *kyūdō* seeking after truth.

#594 率	11 strokes	亠　亠　玄　泫　浕　率

kun   *hiki(iru)* lead, command
率いる *hikiiru* lead (students).

ON   SOTSU lead, command; RITSU rate
引率 ⟨v⟩ *insotsu* leading, commanding.   率先 ⟨v⟩ *sossen* taking the initiative.   利率 *riritsu* interest rate.   高率 *kōritsu* high rate.

#595 卒	8 strokes	亠　广　六　卆　卆　卒

ON   SOTSU graduate; sudden finish; soldier
卒業 ⟨v⟩ *sotsugyō* graduation.   卒業生 *sotsugyōsei* graduate, alumni.
卒中 *sotchū* apoplexy.   兵卒 #932 *heisotsu* private soldier.

#596 式	6 strokes	一　二　二　弋　式　式

ON   SHIKI ceremony; style, method; formula
式 *shiki* ceremony.   卒業式 *sotsugyōshiki* graduation ceremony.
形式 *keishiki* form.   日本式 *Nihonshiki* Japanese method.   公式の *kōshiki no* official.   方程式 *hōteishiki* equation.

■ II. Vocabulary

学課	*gakka*	lesson, school work
課程	*katei*	course
授業 ⟨v⟩	*jugyō*	instruction, class work
講義 ⟨v⟩	*kōgi*	lecture

講師	*kōshi*	lecturer
助教授	*jokyōju*	assistant professor
出席‹v›	*shusseki*	attendance
欠席届	*kesseki todoke*	notice of absence
勉強‹v›	*benkyō*	study
予習‹v›	*yoshū*	preparation of lessons
復習‹v›	*fukushū*	review
練習‹v›	*renshū*	practice
言葉	*kotoba*	word, language
方言	*hōgen*	dialect
読み書き	*yomikaki*	reading and writing
読書‹v›	*dokusho*	reading
新聞	*shinbun*	newspaper
問い	*toi*	question
質問‹v›	*shitsumon*	question
宿題	*shukudai*	homework
提出‹v›	*teishutsu*	presentation
忘れ物	*wasuremono*	forgotten item
答え	*kotae*	answer
答案	*tōan*	examination paper
試験‹v›	*shiken*	examination
成績	*seiseki*	achievement, score
応用‹v›	*ōyō*	application, adaptation
採点‹v›	*saiten*	marking
解答‹v›	*kaitō*	answer, solution
理論	*riron*	theory
思想	*shisō*	thought, idea
知識	*chishiki*	knowledge
専門	*senmon*	one's speciality
修業‹v›	*shūgyō*	study, pursuit
願書	*gansho*	application
研究‹v›	*kenkyū*	study, research
探求‹v›	*tankyū*	search
引率‹v›	*insotsu*	leading, commanding
卒業式	*sotsugyōshiki*	graduation ceremony

Read and translate the following.
1. 毎晩家で、**学課**の**予習**や**復習**をします。
2. 私の受け持ちの生徒は先月、高校の**課程**を**修業**した。
3. **授業**が**休講**になったので、ジムで運動をした。
4. 三木**助教授**の**講義**には学生が大勢集まってくる。
5. あのアメリカ人の**講師**は日本文学の**研究**でよく知られている。
6. **試験**に備えてよく**勉強**したので、**成績**が上がった。
7. 分かりません。もう一度**言**ってください。
8. テープを**聞**きながら、外国の**言葉**を**練習**します。
9. **新聞**で**求人**の広告を見て、**願書**を**提出**した。
10. あの留学生は日本人のように話せるが、**読み書き**は下手だ。
11. **読書**や**体験**を通じて、人生の**意義**を**探求**する。
12. この**問**いの**答**えは教科書の後ろに付いている。
13. 数学は私の**専門**ではないから、その**質問**には**解答**出来ません。
14. **答案**を**採点**したところ、**満点**を取った学生は一人もいなかった。
15. **宿題**を**忘**れて、先生に注意された。
16. **理論**は単に知っているだけでなく、**応用**することが大切だ。
17. この本は面白いですが、**思想**は浅いです。
18. あの人は**知識**は広いが、**常識**が**欠**けている。
19. 児童は先生に**引率**されて遠足に行った。
20. **卒業式**に土地の名士、並びに大勢の父兄が**出席**した。

Languages

■ I. Reference ■

#597 語	14 strokes	言 言 訂 訝 語 語

kun   *kata(ru)* talk
語る *kataru* talk.   物語 *monogatari* story.

ON   GO word, language
日本語 *Nihongo/Nippongo* Japanese language.   外国語 *gaikokugo* foreign language.   語学 *gogaku* language study.   言語学 *gengogaku* linguistics.

#598 英	8 strokes	艹 艹 节 苎 英 英

ON   EI England; brilliant, talented
英語 *eigo* English language.   英会話 *eikaiwa* English conversation. 英国 *Eikoku* England.   英才 *eisai* brilliant intellect, genius.

#599 法	8 strokes	丶 氵 汁 泔 法 法

ON   HŌ, [HA'], [HO'] law; method
文法 *bunpō* grammar.   方法 *hōhō* method.   法学 *hōgaku* study of law.   法案 *hōan* bill.   法度 *hatto* law; ban.

#600 章	11 strokes	亠 立 产 音 音 章

ON   SHŌ chapter; badge
文章 *bunshō* sentence, composition.   第二章 *dainishō* 2nd chapter. 校章 *kōshō* school badge.   会員章 *kaiinshō* membership badge.

#601 音	9 strokes	亠 ナ 立 产 音 音

kun   *oto, ne* sound
音 *oto* sound.   足音 *ashioto* footsteps.   本音 *honne* real intention.

ON   ON, IN sound

発音 ⟨v⟩ *hatsuon* pronunciation.　母音 *boin* vowel.　子音 *shiin* consonant.　福音 *fukuin* gospel.

#602

句　5 strokes　ノ　勹　勹　句　句

ON　KU phrase, sentence, verse
語句 *goku* words and phrases.　文句 *monku* phrase; complain.
名句 *meiku* famous phrase.　句読点 *kutōten* punctuation mark.

#603

詞　12 strokes　言　言　訂　訂　詞　詞

ON　SHI word; part of speech Ir. *(nori)to**
名詞 *meishi* noun.　動詞 *dōshi* verb.　形容詞 *keiyōshi* adjective.
品詞 *hinshi* part of speech.　祝詞 *norito** Shinto prayer.

#604

副　11 strokes　厂　戸　畐　畐　副　副

ON　FUKU assistant, supplement; sub-, vice-
副詞 *fukushi* adverb.　副読本 *fukudokuhon* supplementary reader.
副校長 *fukukōchō* vice-principal.　副作用 *fukusayō* side effects.

#605

例　8 strokes　亻　亻　伢　伢　例　例

kun　*tato(e)* example; *tato(eru)* liken
例え *tatoe* example.　例えば *tatoeba* for example.　例える *tatoeru* liken (life to a journey).

ON　REI example; regular, usual
例 *rei* example.　例文 *reibun* example sentence.　例外 *reigai* exception.　例会 *reikai* regular meeting.　例年 *reinen* average year.

#606

字　6 strokes　宀　宀　宀　宀　字　字

kun　*aza* village section
字 *aza* village section.

ON　JI letter, character
字 *ji* letter, character.　文字 *monji/moji** letter.　字引 *jibiki* dictionary.　数字 *sūji* numeral.　名字 *myōji* surname.

#607 漢	13 strokes	氵 汀 汧 淮 漢 漢

ON　KAN China; guy
漢字 *kanji* Chinese character.　漢文 *kanbun* Chinese classics.　悪漢 *akkan* rascal.　門外漢 *mongaikan* outsider.

#608 仮	6 strokes	ノ イ 仁 仄 仮 仮

kun　*kari* temporary, supposing; pretended
仮の *kari no* temporary.　仮住居 *karizumai* temporary residence.
ON　KA, [KE] temporary, supposing; pretended
仮名 *kana* Japanese syllabic letter.　平仮名 *hiragana* hiragana.
仮定 ⟨v⟩ *katei* supposition.　仮病 #758 *kebyō* faked illness.

#609 片	4 strokes	ノ 丿 ト 片

kun　*kata* one(of two); piece; remote
片仮名 *katakana* katakana.　片手 *katate* one hand/arm.　片道 *kata-michi* one-way (ticket).　片田舎 *katainaka* remote village.
ON　HEN part, piece
紙片 *shihen* scrap of paper.　木片 *mokuhen* chip of wood.

#610 順	12 strokes	川 川厂 川厂 順厂 順頁 順

ON　JUN order, turn
順番 *junban* order, turn.　筆順 *hitsujun* stroke order.　道順 *michi-jun* route.　順調な *junchō na* favorable, satisfactory.

#611 序	7 strokes	亠 广 庁 庁 庁 序

ON　JO order; preface
順序 *junjo* order.　序列 *joretsu* ranking.　序論 *joron* introductory remark.　序文 *jobun* preface.　序の口 *jo no kuchi* beginning.

#612 難	18 strokes	サ 苫 菓 莫 蛑 難

kun *muzuka(shii)*, *mutsuka(shii)*, *gata(i)* difficult

難しい *muzukashii/mutsukashii* difficult.　得難い *egatai* difficult to get.　有り難い *arigatai* thankful.

ON NAN difficult

難問 *nanmon* difficult problem.　難解な *nankai na* difficult (to understand).　非難〈v〉 *hinan* reproach.　難民 *nanmin* refugee.

#613 困	7 strokes	丨 冂 冃 囲 困 困

kun *koma(ru)* be in trouble

困る *komaru* be in trouble.　困り切る *komarikiru* be greatly troubled.

ON KON trouble

困難 *konnan* difficulty.

#614 誤	14 strokes	言 言 訂 訳 誤 誤

kun *ayama(ru)* make a mistake; *ayama(ri)* mistake

誤る *ayamaru* make a mistake.　誤り *ayamari* mistake.

ON GO mistake

誤解〈v〉 *gokai* misunderstanding.　誤読〈v〉 *godoku* misreading.　誤字 *goji* wrong word.　誤報〈v〉 *gohō* false report.

#615 直	8 strokes	一 十 古 肖 直 直

kun *nao(su)* correct; *nao(ru)* be corrected; *tada(chi ni)* immediately

直す *naosu* correct (mistakes).　見直す *minaosu* reconsider.　直る *naoru* be corrected.　直ちに *tadachi ni* immediately.

ON CHOKU, JIKI direct, honest

直通〈v〉 *chokutsū* direct communication.　直前 *chokuzen* immediately before.　正直な *shōjiki na* honest.　直に *jiki ni* immediately.

#616 覚	12 strokes	⺍ 亠 严 覚 覚 覚

kun *obo(eru)* learn, remember; feel; *sa(masu)*, *sa(meru)* wake up, awake

覚える *oboeru* learn (words); feel (cold).　覚え書き *oboegaki* memorandum.　目を覚ます *me o samasu* wake up.　目が覚める *me ga sameru* awake.

ON KAKU learn, remember; feel

自覚 ‹v› *jikaku* self-consciousness.　知覚 ‹v› *chikaku* perception.　発覚 ‹v› *hakkaku* disclosure.　味覚 *mikaku* (sense of) taste.

#617 能	10 strokes	⺄ 亻 台 台 能 能

ON NŌ ability; Noh drama

能力 *nōryoku* ability.　語学の才能 *gogaku no sainō* linguistic talent.　知能 *chinō* intelligence.　機能 *kinō* function.　能率 *nōritsu* efficiency.　能 *nō* Noh drama.　能面 *nōmen* Noh mask.

#618 努	7 strokes	く 夕 如 奴 努 努

kun *tsuto(meru)* make efforts

努める *tsutomeru* make efforts.

ON DO make efforts

努力 ‹v› *doryoku* effort.　努力家 *doryokuka* hard worker.

#619 必	5 strokes	ヽ ソ 义 必 必

kun *kanara(zu)* without fail, necessarily

必ず *kanarazu* without fail.　必ずしも *kanarazushimo* not always.

ON HITSU necessity

必修科目 *hisshū kamoku* required subject.　必読書 *hitsudokusho* must book.　必然 *hitsuzen* necessity.　必死に *hisshi ni* desperately.

#620								
要	9 strokes	一	戸	西	要	要	要

kun   *i(ru)* need, be necessary

要る *iru* need.   辞書が要る *jisho ga iru* need a dictionary.

ON   YŌ necessity, main point

必要な *hitsuyō na* necessary.   要求‹v› *yōkyū* demand.   要点 *yōten* main points.   要約‹v› *yōyaku* summary.

■ II. Vocabulary

日本語	*Nihongo/Nippongo*	Japanese language
英会話	*eikaiwa*	English conversation
文法	*bunpō*	grammar
文章	*bunshō*	sentence, compositon
発音‹v›	*hatsuon*	pronunciation
語句	*goku*	words and phrases
名詞	*meishi*	noun
副詞	*fukushi*	adverb
例え	*tatoe*	example
例	*rei*	example
漢字	*kanji*	Chinese character
平仮名	*hiragana*	hiragana
片仮名	*katakana*	katakana
順序	*junjo*	order
筆順	*hitsujun*	stroke order
難しい	*muzukashii/mutsukashii*	difficult
困難	*konnan*	difficulty
誤り	*ayamari*	mistake
誤解‹v›	*gokai*	misunderstanding
覚え書き	*oboegaki*	memorandum
自覚‹v›	*jikaku*	self-consciousness
能力	*nōryoku*	ability
努力‹v›	*doryoku*	effort
必要な	*hitsuyō na*	necessary

Read and translate the following.

1. スミスさんはアメリカの州立大学で**日本語**を学んだ。

2. 若いカナダ人の先生が東京の私立高校で**英会話**を教えている。

3. 毎晩夕飯の後で、テープを聞きながら**発音**の練習をしています。

4. **平仮名**と**片仮名**は読めるが、**漢字**はまだ少ししか読めない。

5. 言葉は**名詞**、**動詞**、**形容詞**、**副詞**など種々の**品詞**に分けられる。

6. 色々の**例え**を引いて教えると、生徒は早く理解します。

7. **文法**には**必ず例外**がある。

8. **漢字**の**筆順**を習うことは**必要**だ。

9. この**文章**は**語句**の**順序**を変えて**句読点**を正しくうつと、読みやすくなる。

10. あの学生は**外国語**を覚える**能力**がないと**自覚**しているようだ。

11. **語学**の**才能**があっても**努力**しなければ、成績は上がらない。

12. 上級生は難しい試験や宿題が多くて**困**っている。

13. 留学した時、言葉が**難**しくて、あらゆる**困難**に会った。

14. この**文章**に**誤り**があったら、**直**して下さい。

15. **外国語**で話していると、度々**誤解**が起こる。

13

∗∗∗∗∗∗∗∗∗∗∗∗∗∗∗∗∗∗∗∗
Sports

■ I. Reference ▬▬▬▬▬▬▬▬▬▬▬▬▬▬

#621 操	16 strokes	扌 扩 护 揁 捰 操

kun   *ayatsu(ru)* handle, manipulate; *misao* chastity
操る *ayatsuru* handle, manipulate.   操り人形 *ayatsuriningyō* puppet.   操 *misao* chastity.

ON   SŌ handle, manipulate; chastity
体操 *taisō* gymnastics.   操作 ‹v›*sōsa* operation, manipulation.   操業 ‹v›*sōgyō* operation.   節操 *sessō* fidelity, integrity.

#622 競	20 strokes	宀 咅 竞 竞 竞 競

kun   *kiso(u)* compete; *se(ru)* bid for; *se(ri)* auction
競う *kisou* compete.   競る *seru* bid for (10,000 yen).   競り *seri* auction.

ON   KYŌ, KEI compete
競走 ‹v›*kyōsō* running race.   競泳 ‹v›*kyōei* swimming race.   競買 ‹v›*kyōbai* auction.   競馬 *keiba* horse race.

#623 技	7 strokes	扌 扌 扩 扩 找 技

kun   *waza* art, skill
技 *waza* art, skill

ON   GI art, skill
競技 *kyōgi* game, sports.   陸上競技 *rikujō kyōgi* field and track events.   技能 *ginō* skill.   技師 *gishi* engineer.

#624 争	6 strokes	ノ ク ク 刍 刍 争

kun   *araso(u)* dispute, quarrel, compete

争う *arasou* dispute, quarrel, compete.   言い争う *iiarasou* quarrel.
争い *arasoi* dispute, quarrel.

ON   SŌ dispute, quarrel, compete

競争 ‹v› *kyōso* competition.   論争 ‹v› *ronsō* dispute.   争点 *sōten*
point of dispute.

#625 勝	12 strokes	刀 月ˋ 胪 朕 胜 勝

kun   *ka(tsu)* win; *masa(ru)* be superior

勝つ *katsu* win (a game).   勝る *masaru* be superior (to others).

ON   SHŌ win; be superior

勝利 *shōri* victory.   連勝 ‹v› *renshō* consecutive victories.   決勝線
kesshōsen goal line.   名勝 *meishō* scenic spot.

#626 負	9 strokes	ノ ク 冇 角 負 負

kun   *ma(keru)* lose, be defeated; give a discount; *ma(kasu)* beat; *o(u)*
carry; owe; suffer

負ける *makeru* lose (a game); give a (10%) discount.   勝ち負け
kachimake victory and defeat.   負かす *makasu* beat (one's rival).
負う *ou* carry (a pack) on one's back; owe (to one's parents); suffer (an injury).

ON   FU lose, be defeated

勝負 ‹v› *shōbu* victory or defeat, contest.   勝負師 *shōbushi* crack
player; gambler.   自負 ‹v› *jifu* self-conceit.

#627 敗	11 strokes	冂 目 貝ˋ 貯ˋ 敗 敗

kun   *yabu(reru)* lose, be defeated

敗れる *yabureru* lose (a game).

ON   HAI lose, be defeated

勝敗 *shōhai* victory or defeat.   敗北 ‹v› *haiboku* defeat.   連敗 ‹v›
renpai consecutive defeats.   一勝三敗 *isshō sanpai* 1 win and 3 defeats.

#628 失　5 strokes　ノ　ノ　ニ　チ　失

kun　　*ushina(u)* lose
　　　　失う *ushinau* lose (one's hope).　見失う *miushinau* lose sight of.
ON　　SHITSU lose
　　　　失敗 ‹v› *shippai* failure, blunder.　過失 *kashitsu* fault.　失望 ‹v›
　　　　shitsubō disappointment.　失業 ‹v› *shitsugyō* unemployment.

#629 優　17 strokes　亻　伵　傊　傷　傷　優

kun　　*sugu(reru)* be superior; *yasa(shii)* gentle, tender
　　　　優れる *sugureru* be superior.　優しい *yasashii* gentle, tender.
ON　　YŪ superior; actor
　　　　優勝 ‹v› *yūshō* victory; championship.　優勢 *yūsei* superiority.　優等
　　　　生 *yūtōsei* honor student.　女優 *joyū* actress.

#630 戦　13 strokes　ヅ　ツ　当　単　戦　戦

kun　　*tataka(u)* fight; *ikusa* war, battle
　　　　戦う *tatakau* fight.　堂々と戦う *dōdō to tatakau* play a game with
　　　　dignity.　戦い *tatakai* battle; match, game.　戦 *ikusa* war, battle.
ON　　SEN war, battle; match
　　　　決勝戦 *kesshōsen* final match.　熱戦 *nessen* hot contest.　戦争 *sen-
　　　　sō* war, battle.　合戦 *kassen* battle.　戦場 *senjō* battlefield.

#631 延　8 strokes　亻　千　正　延　延　延

kun　　*no(basu)* postpone, extend; *no(biru)* be postponed, extend
　　　　延ばす *nobasu* postpone, extend.　延びる *nobiru* be postponed,
　　　　extend.　延べ *nobe* total (number of hours).
ON　　EN postpone, extend
　　　　延長 ‹v› *enchō* extension.　延長戦 *enchōsen* extended game.　延期 ‹v›
　　　　enki postponement.　延着 ‹v› *enchaku* delayed arrival.

#632 投	7 strokes	十 扌 扌 扩 抄 投

kun   *na(geru)* throw; give up
投げる *nageru* throw (a ball); give up (the game).

ON   TŌ throw
投球 ⟨v⟩ *tōkyū* pitching.   投手 *tōshu* pitcher.   暴投 ⟨v⟩ *bōtō* wild pitch.   投書 ⟨v⟩ *tōsho* letter to an editor; anonymous notice.

#633 打	5 strokes	一 十 扌 扩 打

kun   *u(tsu)* strike, hit
打つ *utsu* hit (a home run).   打ち消す *uchikesu* deny.

ON   DA strike, hit
打者 *dasha* batter.   打率 *daritsu* batting average.   打順 *dajun* batting order.   打開 ⟨v⟩ *dakai* breaking (of a deadlock).

#634 相	9 strokes	十 木 机 机 相 相

kun   *ai-* mutual, each other
相手 *aite* opponent, partner.   相変わらず *aikawarazu* as usual.

ON   SŌ aspect, appearance; SHŌ government minister
世相 *sesō* aspects of life.   人相 *ninsō* looks.   外相 *gaishō* minister of foreign affairs.   文相 *bunshō* minister of education.

#635 選	15 strokes	己 己 弫 巽 巽 選

kun   *era(bu)* choose, select
選ぶ *erabu* choose, select.

ON   SEN choose, select
選手 *senshu* player.   予選 ⟨v⟩ *yosen* preliminary contest.   選定 ⟨v⟩ *sentei* selection.   入選 ⟨v⟩ *nyūsen* being selected.

#636 補	12 strokes	ア　ネ　ネ　初　袻　補

kun   *ogina(u)* compensate, supply
補う *oginau* compensate, supply

ON HO compensate, supply
補欠 *hoketsu* substitute (player).　補助 ⟨v⟩ *hojo* assistance; aid.
補習 ⟨v⟩ *hoshū* supplementary lesson.　補正予算 *hosei yosan* supplementary budget.　警部補 *keibuho* assistant police inspector.

#637 表	8 strokes	十　圭　声　声　表　表

kun *omote* surface, front; *arawa(su)* express; *arawa(reru)* be expressed
表 *omote* surface, front.　二回の表 *nikai no omote* 1st half of the
2nd inning.　表す *arawasu* express (in words).　表れる *arawareru*
be expressed.
ON HYŌ table, chart; expression; surface
表 *hyō* table, chart.　得点表 *tokutenhyō* points table.　発表 ⟨v⟩
happyō announcement.　表現 ⟨v⟩ *hyōgen* expression.　表面 *hyōmen*
surface.　代表 ⟨v⟩ *daihyō* representative.

#638 裏	13 strokes	亠　审　軍　裏　裏　裏

kun *ura* reverse side, back
裏 *ura* reverse side, back.　五回の裏 *gokai no ura* 2nd half of the
5th inning.　裏表 *uraomote* both sides.　裏切る *uragiru* betray.
ON RI reverse side, back
表裏 *hyōri* both sides.　裏面 *rimen* reverse side.

#639 対	7 strokes	亠　ナ　文　文　対　対

ON TAI against; TSUI pair
三対一 *san tai ichi* 3 to 1.　対戦 ⟨v⟩ *taisen* playing a match against.
対立 ⟨v⟩ *tairitsu* opposition.　対等の *taitō no* equal.　一対 *ittsui* a
pair.　対句 *tsuiku* couplet.

#640 弓	3 strokes	⁻　コ　弓

kun *yumi* bow, archery
弓 *yumi* bow, archery.　弓形窓 *yumigata mado* arched window.
ON KYŪ bow, archery
弓道 *kyūdō* Japanese archery.　洋弓 *yōkyū* Western archery.

#641 矢	5 strokes	ノ ヒ ヒ 午 矢

kun *ya* arrow

矢 *ya* arrow.　弓矢 *yumiya* bow and arrow.　矢印 #724 *yajirushi* arrow mark.

ON SHI arrow

一矢を報いる *isshi o mukuiru* take a fling, shoot back.

#642 射	10 strokes	⼻ ⼺ 身 身 身 射

kun *i(ru)* shoot

射る *iru* shoot (an arrow).

ON SHA shoot

射程 *shatei* shooting range.　発射 ⟨v⟩ *hassha* discharge, firing.　注射 ⟨v⟩ *chūsha* injection.　日射 *nissha* solar radiation.

#643 的	8 strokes	⼻ ⼷ 白 白 的 的

kun *mato* target

的 *mato* target.　的はずれの *matohazure no* off the point.

ON TEKI target; (adjectival suffix)

射的 *shateki* shooting.　的中 ⟨v⟩ *tekichū* good hit.　目的 *mokuteki* purpose.　実用的 *jitsuyōteki* practical.　理想的 *risōteki* ideal.　知的 *chiteki* intellectual.　民主的 *minshuteki* democratic.

#644 武	8 strokes	二 ⼀ ⼀ ⼀ 正 武

ON BU, MU military

武道 *budō* martial arts.　武士 *bushi* warrior.　武器 *buki* arms.　武装 ⟨v⟩ *busō* armament.　武者 *musha* warrior.

#645 俵	10 strokes	⼻ ⼶ 俳 俵 俵 俵

kun *tawara* straw bag

俵 *tawara* straw bag.　米俵 *komedawara* straw rice bag.

ON HYŌ straw bag

土俵 *dohyō* sumo ring.　一俵の米 *ippyō no kome* a bag of rice.

#646

奮 16 strokes 木 奔 奞 奮 奮 奮

kun *furu(u)* stir up; display
奮う *furuu* stir up (the morale); display (one's ability). 奮い立つ *furuitatsu* be inspired.

ON FUN stir up; display
奮戦 ‹v›*funsen* desperate fight. 奮起 ‹v›*funki* stirring up. 奮発 ‹v› *funpatsu* strenuous efforts. 奮然として *funzen to shite* resolutely.

#647

興 16 strokes ｆ 臼 佀7 與 興 興

kun *oko(ru)* rise; prosper; *oko(su)* restore
興る *okoru* rise; prosper. 興す *okosu* restore (a ruined family).

ON KŌ, KYŌ prosperity; interest
興奮 ‹v›*kōfun* excitement. 復興 ‹v›*fukkō* revival. 興亡 ‹v›*kōbō* rise and fall. 興味 *kyōmi* interest.

#648

声 7 strokes 十 士 吉 吉 吉 声

kun *koe*, [*kowa-*] voice
声 *koe* voice. 声色 *kowairo* tone of voice; assumed voice.

ON SEI, [SHO] voice
音声 *onsei* voice, sound. 声帯 *seitai* vocal cords. 声明 *seimei* statement. 大音声 *daionjō* loud voice.

#649

歓 15 strokes 亠 卆 弇 雈 雈 歓

ON KAN joy, pleasure
歓声 *kansei* shout of joy. 歓待 ‹v›*kantai* cordial reception. 歓送 ‹v› *kansō* sending off. 歓送会 *kansōkai* farewell party.

#650 旗	14 strokes	亠 宀 扩 抃 旌 旗

kun *hata* flag, banner
旗 *hata* flag, banner.　白旗 *shirahata* white flag.

ON KI flag, banner
国旗 *kokki* national flag.　校旗 *kōki* school banner.　優勝旗 *yūshōki* champion flag.　旗手 *kishu* standard-bearer.

#651 丸	3 strokes	ノ 九 丸

kun *maru* circle; entire; (suffix for ship name); *maru(i)* round; *maru(meru)* make round
丸 *maru* circle.　日の丸 *hi no maru* Rising Sun Flag.　丸二年 *maru ninen* whole 2 years.　日本丸 *Nihon-maru* the ship Nihon.　丸い *marui* round (shape).　丸める *marumeru* make round.　丸太 *maruta* log.

ON GAN round
丸薬 *ganyaku* pill.　一丸となって *ichigan to natte* in union.

#652 念	8 strokes	ノ 人 今 今 念 念

ON NEN sense, feeling; attention; desire
残念な *zannen na* regrettable.　念入りの *nen'iri no* careful.　専念 ‹v› *sennen* devotion.　念願 *nengan* one's heart's desire.

■ II. Vocabulary

体操	*taisō*	gymnastics
競技	*kyōgi*	game, sports
競走‹v›	*kyōsō*	running race
競争‹v›	*kyōsō*	competition
勝ち負け	*kachimake*	victory and defeat
勝負‹v›	*shōbu*	victory or defeat, contest
失敗‹v›	*shippai*	failure, blunder
優勝‹v›	*yūshō*	victory, championship
戦い	*tatakai*	battle; match, game

決勝戦	*kesshōsen*	final match
延長戦	*enchōsen*	extended game
投球‹v›	*tōkyū*	pitching
投手	*tōshu*	pitcher
打者	*dasha*	batter
相手	*aite*	opponent, partner
選手	*senshu*	player
補欠	*hoketsu*	substitute (player)
二回の表	*nikai no omote*	1st half of the 2nd inning
得点表	*tokutenhyō*	points table
五回の裏	*gokai no ura*	2nd half of the 5th inning
三対一	*san tai ichi*	3 to 1
弓矢	*yumiya*	bow and arrow
弓道	*kyūdō*	archery
的	*mato*	target
射的	*shateki*	shooting
武道	*budō*	martial arts
土俵	*dohyō*	sumo ring
興奮‹v›	*kōfun*	excitement
興味	*kyōmi*	interest
歓声	*kansei*	shout of joy
旗	*hata*	flag, banner
国旗	*kokki*	national flag
日の丸	*hi no maru*	Rising Sun Flag
残念な	*zannen na*	regrettable

■ III. Reading Exercises 31 ■

Read and translate the following.

1. 毎日、朝と昼にラジオ**体操**をしています。
2. 毎年、ボストンのマラソン**競走**に大勢の人が参加する。
3. 冬季オリンピックでドイツ人やアメリカ人の**選手**が各種の**競技**で勝った。
4. 水泳の**競争**で本田君と一位を**争**ったが、二人とも三位以下になった。
5. ここは「野球の町」として**復興**し、商業も**興**った。
6. 観客は**熱戦**に大いに**興奮**した。
7. 五番**打者**の山下がバッターボックスに立つと、どっと**歓声**が起った。

8. 多くの外国人が日本の**武道**に**興味**を持っているようだ。

9. **補欠**の選手の**失敗**で**相手**に三点も取られた。

10. 左利きの**投手**が**決勝戦**で**優**れた**技能**を見せた。

11. **優勝**出来なくて**残念**だったが、全員最後まで堂々と**戦**った。

12. 強いチームとの**対戦**に三対五の得点で負けた。

13. 両チームともよく**奮戦**したが、九回の裏のホームランで**勝負**が決まった。

14. 試合は**延長戦**となり、十回の**表**でピンチヒッターの名前が**発表**された。

15. 前日**敗**れた力士が足に包帯をして**土俵**に現われた。

16. **弓道**を始めたばかりでまだ下手です。

17. その**武者**は弓の名人で必ず**的**を**射**ったそうだ。

18. ここは**射的**の練習に**理想的**な場所だ。

19. スタジアムに各国の**国旗**—— アメリカの**旗**も日の丸も立っている。

14

****

Arts

Fine Arts

■ I. Reference ■

#653 術	11 strokes	ケ 彳 彳 彴 秫 秫 術

ON JUTSU art, skill, tactics
芸術 *geijutsu* art. 技術 *gijutsu* technique. 手術 *shujutsu* surgery.
術語 *jutsugo* technical term. 戦術 *senjutsu* tactics.

#654 美	9 strokes	丶 ソ 丷 羊 羊 美 美

kun *utsuku(shii)* beautiful
美しい *utsukushii* beautiful.

ON BI beauty
美術 *bijutsu* fine arts. 美術館 *bijutsukan* art museum. 自然美
shizenbi natural beauty. 美人 *bijin* beauty. 優美な *yūbi na* refined, elegant.

#655 絵	12 strokes	乡 糸 糸 糸 絵 絵

ON KAI, E picture
絵 *e* drawing, painting. 絵本 *ehon* picture book. 絵葉書 *ehagaki*
picture postcard. 絵の具 *enogu* paints, colors.

#656 画	8 strokes	一 冂 币 而 画 画

ON GA picture, drawing; KAKU stroke (of Chinese characters)
絵画 *kaiga* drawing, painting. 画家 *gaka* painter. 洋画 *yōga*
Western painting; foreign film. 計画 ⟨ᵛ⟩ *keikaku* plan. 画数 *kaku-
sū* number of strokes. 五画 *gokaku* 5 strokes.

#657 油	8 strokes	丶 氵 汩 油 油 油

kun *abura* oil
油 *abura* oil.　油絵 *aburae* oil painting.　食用油 *shokuyō abura* cooking oil.

ON YU oil
石油 *sekiyu* petroleum.　原油 *genyu* crude oil.　油田 *yuden* oil field.　灯油 *tōyu* kerosene.

#658 版	8 strokes	丿 ゲ 片 片 版 版

ON HAN printing block; edition
版画 *hanga* woodblock print.　出版 ⟨v⟩ *shuppan* publication.　初版 *shohan* 1st edition.　日曜版 *nichiyōban* Sunday edition.

#659 静	14 strokes	十 圭 青 靑 静 静

kun *shizu(ka)* quiet, still; *shizu(maru)* become quiet; *shizu(meru)* calm
静かな *shizuka na* quiet.　静けさ *shizukesa* stillness, calm.　静まる *shizumaru* become quiet.　静める *shizumeru* calm (oneself).

ON SEI, [JŌ] quiet, still
静物画 *seibutsuga* painting of a still life.　平静 *heisei* composure.　冷静な *reisei na* calm.　静脈 *jōmyaku* vein.

#660 景	12 strokes	冂 旦 旱 昙 景 景

ON KEI, [KE] view, scene
風景画 *fūkeiga* landscape.　光景 *kōkei* scene.　夜景 *yakei* night view.　景色 *keshiki* scenery.　景気 *keiki* business conditions.

#661 写	5 strokes	丶 冖 冖 写 写

kun *utsu(su)* copy; photograph; *utsu(ru)* be photographed
写す *utsusu* copy (from a book); photograph (a scenery).　写る *utsuru* be photographed (in a snapshot).

ON SHA copy; photograph
写生 ⟨v⟩ *shasei* sketching.　試写会 *shishakai* preview showing.

| #662 真 | 10 strokes | 一 | 市 | 直 | 直 | 真 | 真 |

kun   *ma* true, pure; exactly
真っ赤な *makka* na* deep-red.   真っ青な *massao* na* deep-blue.
真心 *magokoro* sincerity.   真上 *maue* exactly above.

ON   SHIN truth, reality
写真 *shashin* photograph.   真理 *shinri* truth.   真実 *shinjitsu* truth.
真価 *shinka* real value.   真紅 *shinku* crimson.

| #663 映 | 9 strokes | 刀 | 日' | 日⁻ | 旷 | 映 | 映 |

kun   *utsu(su)* reflect, project; *utsu(ru)* be reflected, projected; *ha(eru)*
shine, glow
映す *utsusu* project (slides), reflect (oneself in a mirror).   映る
utsuru be reflected (on the water).   映える *haeru* shine (in the
evening sun).   夕映え *yūbae* evening glow.

ON   EI reflect, project
映画 *eiga* movie.   映写機 *eishaki* movie projector.   上映 ‹v› *jōei*
showing (a movie).

| #664 像 | 14 strokes | 伫 | 伊 | 俨 | 傍 | 像 | 像 |

ON   ZŌ image, statue
映像 *eizō* projected image.   現像 ‹v› *genzō* developement (of film).
画像 *gazō* portrait.   石像 *sekizō* stone statue.   想像 ‹v› *sōzō* im-
agination.

| #665 展 | 10 strokes | 一 | 尸 | 屏 | 展 | 展 | 展 |

ON   TEN exhibit, expand
美術展 *bijutsuten* art exhibition.   写真展 *shashinten* photograph exhibition.   発展 ‹v› *hatten* development.   展望 ‹v› *tenbō* view.

#666 示	5 strokes	一　二　〒　示　示

kun　*shime(su)* show
示す *shimesu* show (one's ability).

ON　JI, SHI show
展示 ‹v›*tenji* display.　展示会 *tenjikai* exhibition.　指示 ‹v›*shiji* instructions.　暗示 ‹v›*anji* hint, suggestion.

#667 覧	17 strokes	厂　戶　臣'　臤'　臤見　覧

ON　RAN see, look at
展覧会 *tenrankai* exhibition.　一覧表 *ichiranhyō* list.　遊覧 ‹v›*yūran* sight-seeing.　回覧 ‹v›*kairan* circulation (of documents).

#668 博	12 strokes	十　忄戶　忄甫　忄甫　博　博

ON　HAKU, [BAKU] extensive; gamble Ir. *haka(se)**
博物館 *hakubutsukan* museum.　博覧会 *hakurankai* exposition.　万国博 *bankokuhaku* world fair.　博士 *hakushi/hakase** doctor.　博徒 *bakuto* professional gambler.

■ II. Vocabulary ■

芸術	*geijutsu*	art
美術館	*bijutsukan*	art museum
絵	*e*	drawing, painting
油絵	*aburae*	oil painting
絵画	*kaiga*	drawing, painting
静物画	*seibutsuga*	painting of a still life
風景画	*fūkeiga*	landscape
景色	*keshiki*	scenery
版画	*hanga*	woodblock print
写生 ‹v›	*shasei*	sketching
写真	*shashin*	photograph
美術展	*bijutsuten*	art exhibition
展示 ‹v›	*tenji*	display

展覧会	tenrankai	exhibition
博物館	hakubutsukan	museum
博覧会	hakurankai	exposition
万国博	bankokuhaku	world fair
映像	eizō	projected image
現像‹v›	genzō	development (of film)
夕映え	yūbae	evening glow
映画	eiga	movie
映写機	eishaki	movie projector

■ III. Reading Exercises 32 ■

Read and translate the following.

1. スミス教授は東洋の**芸術**に深い興味を持っている。
2. 明日から町の**美術館**で**絵画**の展覧会が開かれる。
3. 姉は最近**油絵**に熱中している。
4. あの**画家**は**静物画**より**風景画**の方が得意だ。
5. 暖かい日に、海岸の**景色**を**写生**した。
6. 昨日の美術展で古い日本の**版画**が**展示**されていた。
7. **万国博**で各国のパビリオンを見て回った。
8. 静かな湖の水面に円い月が**映**っている。
9. 美しい**夕映え**を**写**して、**写真**を**現像**した。
10. **博物館**の前の広場に白い**石像**が立っている。
11. 午後三時から講堂で**映画**の**試写会**が行なわれる。
12. 受け持ちの先生に**映写機**の使い方を教わった。

Music

#669

楽　　13 strokes　　亻　白　冶′　泊　楽　楽

kun　　*tano(shii)* pleasant, joyful; *tano(shimu)* enjoy Ir. *(kagu)ra** #756
　　　　楽しい *tanoshii* pleasant, joyful.　楽しむ *tanoshimu* enjoy (sports).
　　　　楽しみにする *tanoshimi ni suru* look forward to.

ON　　GAKU music; RAKU pleasure, comfort
　　　　音楽 *ongaku* music.　楽器 *gakki* musical instrument.　楽園 *rakuen*
　　　　paradise.　楽観的 *rakkanteki* optimistic.

#670

歌　　14 strokes　　ロ　ロ　哥　哥　歌　歌

kun　　*uta* song; *uta(u)* sing
　　　　歌 *uta* song.　童歌 *warabeuta* children's song.　歌声 *utagoe* sing-
　　　　ing voice.

ON　　KA song
　　　　国歌 *kokka* national anthem.　和歌 *waka* 31-syllable Japanese
　　　　poem.　流行歌 *ryūkōka* popular song.　歌手 *kashu* singer.

#671

唱　　11 strokes　　口　叩　唱　呷　唱　唱

kun　　*tona(eru)* chant, recite; advocate
　　　　唱える *tonaeru* chant (the name of Buddha), advocate (a new
　　　　theory).

ON　　SHŌ chant, recite; advocate
　　　　唱歌 *shōka* singing.　合唱 ⟨v⟩ *gasshō* chorus.　暗唱 ⟨v⟩ *anshō* recita-
　　　　tion.　提唱 ⟨v⟩ *teishō* advocacy.

#672

独　　9 strokes　　ノ　犭　犭　犯　独　独

kun　　*hito(ri)* alone
　　　　独り *hitori* alone.　独り立ち ⟨v⟩ *hitoridachi* being independent.

ON DOKU alone; Germany

独唱 ⟨v⟩ *dokushō* vocal solo.　独学 ⟨v⟩ *dokugaku* self-education.
独立 ⟨v⟩ *dokuritsu* independence.　日独の *Nichi-Doku no* Germano-Japanese.

#673　奏　9 strokes　三　声　夫　秦　奏　奏

kun　*kana(deru)* play music
奏でる *kanaderu* play (a string instrument).

ON　SŌ play music
独奏 ⟨v⟩ *dokusō* playing solo.　独奏会 *dokusōkai* recital.　合奏 ⟨v⟩
gassō concert.　三部合奏 *sanbu gassō* trio.

#674　曲　6 strokes　丨　冂　巾　曲　曲　曲

kun　*ma(geru)* bend; *ma(garu)* bend, turn
曲げる *mageru* bend (a wire).　曲がる *magaru* (trees) bend, turn
(to the right).

ON　KYOKU tune, musical composition; curve
曲 *kyoku* music, tune.　前奏曲 *zensōkyoku* overture.　名曲
meikyoku famous work of music.　作曲 ⟨v⟩ *sakkyoku* musical composition.　曲線 *kyokusen* curve.

#675　協　8 strokes　十　忄　忄　拶　協　協

ON　KYŌ cooperation
協奏曲 *kyōsōkyoku* concerto.　協力 ⟨v⟩ *kyōryoku* cooperation.
協定 ⟨v⟩ *kyōtei* agreement.　協会 *kyōkai* association.

#676　団　6 strokes　丨　冂　冂　冃　冃　団

ON　DAN, [TON] group
楽団 *gakudan* band, orchestra.　合唱団 *gasshōdan* choir.　団体
dantai group (of tourists).　師団 *shidan* army division.　団地 *dan-
chi* housing complex.　布団 *futon* futon, quilted bedmat.

#677 揮	12 strokes	十 扌 扩 捛 揎 揮

ON   KI command, display; scatter

指揮 ⟨v⟩ *shiki* command, conduct.   指揮者 *shikisha* conductor, leader.   発揮 ⟨v⟩ *hakki* display (of one's ability).   揮発油 *kihatsuyu* volatile oils.

#678 管	14 strokes	⺮ ⺮ ⺮ 笒 笡 管

kun   *kuda* pipe, tube

管 *kuda* pipe, tube.

ON   KAN pipe; wind instrument; control

管楽器 *kangakki* wind instrument.   水道管 *suidōkan* water pipe. 管理 ⟨v⟩ *kanri* management.   管区 *kanku* district, jurisdiction.

#679 尺	4 strokes	⁃ ⁃ 尸 尺

ON   SHAKU (old unit of length); measure

尺八 *shakuhachi* Japanese bamboo flute.   尺度 *shakudo* measure. 巻き尺 *makijaku* tape measure.

#680 笛	11 strokes	⺮ ⺮ 笁 笛 笛 笛

kun   *fue* flute, whistle

笛 *fue* flute.   口笛 *kuchibue* whistle.   角笛 *tsunobue* bugle.

ON   TEKI flute, whistle

警笛 *keiteki* alarm whistle.

■ II. Vocabulary ■

音楽	*ongaku*	music
歌	*uta*	song
国歌	*kokka*	national anthem
歌手	*kashu*	singer
唱歌	*shōka*	singing
合唱 ⟨v⟩	*gasshō*	chorus

独唱⟨v⟩	*dokushō*	vocal solo
独奏会	*dokusōkai*	recital
曲	*kyoku*	music, tune
作曲⟨v⟩	*sakkyoku*	musical composition
前奏曲	*zensōkyoku*	overture
協奏曲	*kyōsōkyoku*	concerto
楽団	*gakudan*	band, orchestra
指揮者	*shikisha*	conductor, leader
管楽器	*kangakki*	wind instrument
尺八	*shakuhachi*	Japanese bamboo flute
笛	*fue*	flute
警笛	*keiteki*	alarm whistle

■ III. Reading Exercises 33 ■

Read and translate the following.

1. 高校で若い女の先生に**音楽**を習った。
2. **唱歌**教室から子供達の**楽**しそうな**歌声**が聞こえてくる。
3. 全員起立して力強く**国歌**を**歌**った。
4. 学校のパーティーで、児童がクリスマスカロルを**合唱**した。
5. 昨夜のコンサートで、黒人の**歌手**が数々の**名曲**を**独唱**した。
6. ラジオから優美なピアノ**協奏曲**が流れてくる。
7. 十三才の少女がバイオリンの**独奏会**で優れた才能を**発揮**した。
8. 場内の電灯が消えて、**指揮者**のタクトの下に静かな**前奏曲**が流れ出した。
9. **楽団**にはフルートやオーボエなどの**管楽器**も必要だ。
10. 少年が**口笛**をふきながら林の中を歩いている。
11. パトカーが**警笛**を鳴らしながら走り去った。

Theater

■ **I. Reference** ■

#681 劇	15 strokes	广 卢 虍 虏 虑 劇

ON GEKI drama, play; intense, severe
劇 *geki* drama, play. 劇場 *gekijō* theater. 劇作家 *gekisakka* playwrite. 劇的な *gekiteki na* dramatic. 劇薬 *gekiyaku* powerful medicine.

#682 演	14 strokes	氵 氵 沪 沪 沛 演 演

ON EN performance, play
演劇 *engeki* drama, play. 主役を演じる *shuyaku o enjiru* perform a leading role. 出演 ⟨ヽ⟩ *shutsuen* appearance (in a movie/play). 上演 ⟨ヽ⟩ *jōen* staging (of a play). 演技 *engi* acting. 演習 *enshū* seminar.

#683 喜	12 strokes	士 吉 吉 吉 喜 喜

kun *yoroko(bi)* joy, delight; *yoroko(bu)* rejoice
喜び *yorokobi* joy, delight. 大喜び *ōyorokobi* great joy. 喜ぶ *yorokobu* rejoice.

ON KI joy, pleasure
喜劇 *kigeki* comedy. 歓喜 ⟨ヽ⟩ *kanki* joy, delight.

#684 悲	12 strokes	ｺ ｺl 非 非 悲 悲

kun *kana(shii)* sad; *kana(shimu)* be sad
悲しい *kanashii* sad. 悲しい場面 *kanashii bamen* sad scene. 悲しむ *kanashimu* be sad. 悲しみ *kanashimi* sorrow.

ON HI sad
悲劇 *higeki* tragedy. 悲観 ⟨ヽ⟩ *hikan* pessimism. 悲報 *hihō* sad news. 悲鳴 *himei* scream.

#685 笑	10 strokes	᾿ ᾿ᶜᵗ ᾿ᵗ᾿ ᵗ᾿ ᾿ᵗ᾿ ᵗᵗᵗ 笑

kun *wara(u)* laugh, smile; *e(mu)* smile
笑う *warau* laugh, smile.　笑い話 *waraibanashi* funny story.　ほほ
笑む *hohoemu* smile.　笑みをうかべる *emi o ukaberu* have a smile.

ON SHŌ laugh, smile
笑劇 *shōgeki* farce.　失笑 ⟨v⟩ *shisshō* breaking into laughter.

#686 泣	8 strokes	᾿ ᾿ ᾿ ᾿ ᾿ 泣

kun *na(ku)* cry, weep
泣く *naku* cry, weep.　泣き笑い ⟨v⟩ *nakiwarai* tearful smile.

ON KYŪ cry, weep
感泣 ⟨v⟩ #688 *kankyū* being moved to tears.

#687 幕	13 strokes	᾿᾿ ᾿ 茸 莫 莫 幕 幕

ON MAKU curtain; act (of a play); BAKU Shogunate
幕 *maku* curtain.　開幕 ⟨v⟩ *kaimaku* curtain-rising.　幕切れ *maku-gire* fall of the curtain.　第二幕第三場 *dainimaku daisanba* Act 2, Scene 3.　幕府 *bakufu* Shogunate.

#688 感	13 strokes	ノ 厂 咸 咸 感 感

ON KAN feeling, sensation
感じる *kanjiru* feel, sense. 感想 *kansō* one's thoughts.　感心 ⟨v⟩ *kanshin* being impressed.　感泣 ⟨v⟩ *kankyū* being moved to tears. 感動 ⟨v⟩ *kandō* being moved.　感受性 *kanjusei* sensitivity.

#689 愛	13 strokes	᾿᾿ ᾿ 冊 愛 愛 愛

ON AI love
愛 *ai* love.　愛する *aisuru* love (art).　愛好 ⟨v⟩ *aikō* love.　演劇愛好
者 *engeki aikōsha* theater lover.　人類愛 *jinruiai* humanism.　愛国
心 *aikokushin* patriotism.

#690 情	11 strokes	⺖ 忄 忄 忭 情 情

kun **nasa(ke)** feeling, sympathy
情け *nasake* feeling, sympathy. 情け深い *nasakebukai* compassionate.

ON **JŌ, [SEI]** feeling, sympathy; circumstances
愛情 *aijō* love. 感情 *kanjō* feeling, emotion. 情熱 *jōnetsu* passion. 同情 ‹v› *dōjō* sympathy. 風情 *fuzei* appearance; elegance.

#691 激	16 strokes	氵 沪 泻 澎 激 激

kun **hage(shii)** violent, fierce
激しい *hageshii* violent (emotion), fierce (battle).

ON **GEKI** violent, fierce
感激 ‹v› *kangeki* deep emotion. 激戦 *gekisen* fierce battle. 激論 ‹v› *gekiron* heated argument. 過激な *kageki na* extreme, radical.

#692 夢	13 strokes	一 芦 芦 莩 夢 夢

kun **yume** dream
夢 *yume* dream. 夢見る *yumemiru* dream of (success).

ON **MU** dream
悪夢 *akumu* nightmare. 夢中になる *muchū ni naru* be absorbed in.

#693 再	6 strokes	一 冂 冂 币 再 再

kun **futata(bi)** again
再び *futatabi* again.

ON **SAI, [SA]** again
再演 ‹v› *saien* repeat performance. 再開 ‹v› *saikai* reopening. 再会 ‹v› *saikai* meeting again. 再来週 *saraishū* week after next.

#694 活	9 strokes	氵 氵 氵 汗 活 活

ON **KATSU** life, activity
生活 ‹v› *seikatsu* life. 活動 ‹v› *katsudō* activity. 復活 ‹v› *fukkatsu* revival. 活発な *kappatsu na* lively.

俳 | 10 strokes ⺅ ⺅ 付 俳 俳 俳

ON **HAI** actor, humor
俳優 *haiyū* actor.　性格俳優 *seikaku haiyū* character actor.　俳句 *haiku* haiku poem.　俳人 *haijin* haiku poet.

俗 | 9 strokes ⺅ ⺅ 俗 俗 俗 俗

ON **ZOKU** customs; the world; vulgar
風俗 *fūzoku* customs, manners.　俗世間 *zokuseken* this world.
通俗的な *tsūzokuteki na* popular.　低俗な *teizoku na* vulgar.

慣 | 14 strokes ⺁ 忄 忄 慣 慣 慣

kun **na(reru)** get used to; **nara(su)** make used to
慣れる *nareru* get used to.　見慣れた *minareta* familiar.　慣らす *narasu* make (oneself) used to (cold).

ON **KAN** accustom
習慣 *shūkan* habit, custom.　風俗習慣 *fūzoku shūkan* manners and customs.　慣例 *kanrei* custom, usage.　慣用語 *kanyōgo* idiom.

功 | 5 strokes ⼀ 丁 工 功 功

ON **KŌ, [KU]** merit, success
成功 *seikō* success.　功績 *kōseki* merit, great services.　功名 *kōmyō* glorious deed.　功徳 #1009 *kudoku* charity.

■ II. Vocabulary ■

劇	*geki*	drama, play
演劇	*engeki*	drama, play
劇作家	*gekisakka*	playwrite
喜び	*yorokobi*	joy, delight
喜劇	*kigeki*	comedy
悲しみ	*kanashimi*	sorrow
悲劇	*higeki*	tragedy

笑い話	*waraibanashi*	funny story
笑劇	*shōgeki*	farce
泣き笑い‹v›	*nakiwarai*	tearful smile
開幕‹v›	*kaimaku*	curtain-rising
第二幕第三場	*dainimaku daisanba*	Act 2, Scene 3
激しい感情	*hageshii kanjō*	violent emotion
感激‹v›	*kangeki*	deep emotion
愛	*ai*	love
演劇愛好者	*engeki aikōsha*	theater lover
夢	*yume*	dream
悪夢	*akumu*	nightmare
再演‹v›	*saien*	repeat performance
俳優	*haiyū*	actor
生活‹v›	*seikatsu*	life
風俗	*fūzoku*	customs, manners
習慣	*shūkan*	habit, custom
成功‹v›	*seikō*	success

■ III. Reading Exercises 34 ■

Read and translate the following.

1. 劇場に着いたら、開幕の五分前だった。
2. 第三幕の幕切れは実に劇的だった。
3. 悲しい場面に女性の観客が泣いていた。
4. あの人は笑い話を聞いても、笑劇を見ても、笑ったことがない。
5. これは家族連れで見られる軽い喜劇です。
6. 有名な性格俳優がシェークスピアの悲劇の主役を演じている。
7. 私は演劇の世界に入ったばかりで、まだその習慣に慣れません。
8. この劇は現代の若者の生活や風俗をよく表している。
9. あの女優は激しい感情の表現が優れている。
10. 老練な俳優のすばらしい演技に感激した。
11. 月に一度、演劇愛好者が集まって、情報を提供し合っている。
12. 木村さんは学生時代に演劇に夢中になり、劇作家を夢見ていたそうだ。
13. 初めて上演されたその劇は成功に終わり、近い将来再演が予定されている。

Literature

■ I. Reference ■

#699 詩	13 strokes	言 言 計 詿 詩 詩

ON   SHI poetry, poem Ir. *shī(ka)**
詩 *shi* poetry, poem.   詩集 *shishū* collection of poems.   漢詩 *kanshi* Chinese poetry.   詩人 *shijin* poet.   詩歌 *shika/shīka** poetry.

#700 朗	10 strokes	ㄱ ㅋ 自 郎 朗 朗

kun   *hoga(raka)* clear, bright, cheerful
朗らかな *hogaraka na* bright (day), cheerful (person).

ON   RŌ clear, bright, cheerful
朗読 ‹v› *rōdoku* reading aloud.   朗報 *rōhō* good news.   明朗な *meirōna* bright, cheerful.   朗々と *rōrō to* sonorously.

#701 記	10 strokes	言 言 言 訂 記 記

kun   *shiru(su)* write down, inscribe
記す *shirusu* write down (one's name).

ON   KI write down, inscribe
日記 *nikki* diary.   記事 *kiji* article (of newspaper/magazine).   記者 *kisha* journalist.   記念 ‹v› *kinen* commemoration.

#702 伝	6 strokes	ノ イ 仁 仁 伝 伝

kun   *tsuta(eru)* report, transmit; *tsuta(waru)* be reported, transmitted Ir. *(te)tsuda(u)**; *ten(masen)** #820
伝える *tsutaeru* report (news), transmit (sound).   伝わる *tsutawaru* be reported, transmitted.   手伝う *tetsudau** help, assist.

ON   DEN report, transmit
伝記 *denki* biography.   伝言 ‹v› *dengon* message.   伝言板 *dengonban* message board.   伝来 ‹v› *denrai* transmission, being introduced.

#703 旅	10 strokes	亠 宀 方 扩 斻 旅

kun *tabi* trip, travel

旅 *tabi* trip, travel.　旅人 *tabibito* traveler.

ON RYO trip, travel

旅行 ⟨v⟩ *ryokō* travel.　旅行記 *ryokōki* travel book.　旅行者 *ryokōsha* traveler.　旅館 *ryokan* Japanese inn.

#704 録	16 strokes	牟 釒 釤 釨 鈩 録

ON ROKU record

記録 ⟨v⟩ *kiroku* record.　回想録 *kaisōroku* memoirs.　録音 ⟨v⟩ *rokuon* audiotape recording.　登録 ⟨v⟩ *tōroku* registration.

#705 誌	14 strokes	言 言 訂 計 誌 誌

ON SHI record, chronicle; magazine

日誌 *nisshi* daily record.　書誌 *shoshi* bibliography.

#706 雑	14 strokes	丿 九 杂 糸 雑 雑

ON ZATSU, ZŌ rough, miscellaneous Ir. *za(ko)**

雑誌 *zasshi* magazine.　文芸雑誌 *bungei zasshi* literary magazine.　雑音 *zatsuon* noise.　雑木林 *zōkibayashi* coppice.　雑魚 *zako** small fish.

#707 刊	5 strokes	一 二 干 刊 刊

ON KAN publish

刊行 ⟨v⟩ *kankō* publication.　週刊誌 *shūkanshi* weekly magazine.　月刊誌 *gekkanshi* monthly.　季刊誌 *kikanshi* quarterly.　新刊書 *shinkansho* new book.　朝刊 *chōkan* morning paper.

#708 説	14 strokes	言 言 訃 訰 訰 説

kun *to(ku)* explain; persuade

説く *toku* explain (main points), persuade (a person to do).

ON   SETSU explain; persuade; ZEI persuade
      小説 *shōsetsu* novel, fiction.   伝説 *densetsu* legend.   説明 ⟨v⟩
      setsumei explanation.   演説 ⟨v⟩ *enzetsu* speech.   遊説 ⟨v⟩ *yūzei* can-
      vassing (for votes).

#709

編	15 strokes	幺　糸　紅　紀　絹　編

kun   *a(mu)* knit
      編む *amu* knit (a sweater).   編み物 *amimono* knitting.
ON   HEN compile, edit
      編集 ⟨v⟩ *henshū* editing.   編集長 *henshūchō* chief editor.   短編 *tan-
      pen* short story.   編成 ⟨v⟩ *hensei* formation, organization.

#710

推	11 strokes	一　扌　扞　扩　扗　推

kun   *o(su)* infer, deduce; recommend
      推す *osu* infer (from the report); recommend (a person for the
      job).
ON   SUI infer, deduce; recommend
      推理 ⟨v⟩ *suiri* inference.   推理小説 *suiri shōsetsu* detective story.
      推定 ⟨v⟩ *suitei* presumption.   推論 ⟨v⟩ *suiron* reasoning.

#711

史	5 strokes	丿　冂　口　史　史

ON   SHI history, chronicle
      日本史 *Nihonshi* Japanese history.   世界史 *sekaishi* world history.
      文学史 *bungakushi* history of literature.   史実 *shijitsu* historical
      fact.   史上 *shijō* in history.

#712

歴	14 strokes	一　厂　厤　厤　歴　歴

ON   REKI continuation
      歴史 *rekishi* history.   歴史小説 *rekishi shōsetsu* historical novel.
      歴史家 *rekishika* historian.   学歴 *gakureki* academic background.

#713 筋	12 strokes	⺦ 竹 笁 笁 筋 筋

kun **suji** line; plot; vein; logic; source
筋 *suji* line.　話の筋 *hanashi no suji* story's plot.　青筋 *aosuji* blue veins.　筋の通った *suji no tōtta* logical.　その筋 *sono suji* authorities.

ON **KIN** muscle
筋肉 *kinniku* muscle.　筋力 *kinryoku* muscular power.

#714 著	11 strokes	一 艹 芏 茅 著 著

kun **arawa(su)** write; **ichijiru(shii)** remarkable
著す *arawasu* write (a book).　著しい *ichijirushii* remarkable.

ON **CHO** write; remarkable
著者 *chosha* author.　著書 *chosho* book.　共著 *kyōcho* joint authorship.　著名な *chomei na* well-known (writer).

#715 訳	11 strokes	言 言 訂 訂 訳 訳

kun **wake** meaning; reason; circumstances
訳 *wake* meaning (of a word); reason.　言い訳 *iiwake* excuse.　内訳 *uchiwake* itemization.

ON **YAKU** translation
訳 *yaku* translation.　訳す *yakusu* translate.　和訳〈v〉*wayaku* translation into Japanese.　訳者 *yakusha* translator.

#716 純	10 strokes	⼂ 糸 糺 紅 紀 純

ON **JUN** pure
純文学 *junbungaku* pure literature.　純金 *junkin* pure gold.　純益 *jun'eki* net profit.　単純な *tanjun na* simple.

#717 賞	15 strokes	⼂ ⺌ 尚 常 賞 賞

ON **SHŌ** prize, praise
賞 *shō* prize.　ノーベル賞 *Nōberu Shō* Nobel Prize.　受賞者 *jushōsha* prize winner.　観賞〈v〉*kanshō* admiration.

#718 評	12 strokes	言 言 言 訂 評 評

ON HYŌ criticism, comment
評論 ‹v› *hyōron* criticism, review. 評論家 *hyōronka* critic. 評価 ‹v› *hyōka* evaluation. 書評 *shohyō* book review.

#719 批	7 strokes	一 扌 扌 批 批 批

ON HI critique
批評 ‹v› *hihyō* critique, comment. 文芸批評 *bungei hihyō* literary criticism. 批評家 *hihyōka* critic. 批難 ‹v› *hinan* reproach.

#720 寸	3 strokes	一 寸 寸

ON SUN brief; (unit of length)
寸評 *sunpyō* brief comment. 寸劇 *sungeki* skit. 寸前 *sunzen* just before. 寸法 *sunpō* measurement. 一寸 *issun* 1 sun (3.03 cm).

#721 釈	11 strokes	平 采 采 釈 釈 釈

ON SHAKU explanation
解釈 ‹v› *kaishaku* interpretation. 注釈 ‹v› *chūshaku* annotation. 釈明 ‹v› *shakumei* explanation. 保釈 ‹v› *hoshaku* bailment.

#722 完	7 strokes	丶 宀 宀 宀 宀 完

ON KAN completion
完成 ‹v› *kansei* completion. 未完の作 *mikan no saku* unfinished work. 完全な *kanzen na* complete (success). 完備 ‹v› *kanbi* being full-equipped. 完勝 ‹v› *kanshō* sweeping triumph.

#723 化	4 strokes	ノ イ 亻 化

kun *ba(keru)* change itself; *ba(kasu)* bewitch
化ける *bakeru* disguise oneself (as a man). 化かす *bakasu* bewitch.

KA, KE change itself
文化 *bunka* culture, civilization.　文化祭 *bunkasai* cultural festival.
映画化 ‹v›*eigaka* cinematization.　変化 ‹v›*henka* change.　化学
kagaku chemistry.　化身 #728 *keshin* incarnation.

#724 印	6 strokes	′ イ Ƒ Ɛ 臼 印

kun　*shirushi* sign, mark
印 *shirushi* sign, mark.　矢印 *yajirushi* arrow mark.

ON　IN seal, stamp
印 *in* seal, stamp.　印象 *inshō* impression.　調印 ‹v›*chōin* signing
(a treaty).　消印 *keshiin* postmark.

#725 刷	8 strokes	㇇ ㇕ 尸 尸 刷 刷

kun　*su(ru)* print
刷る *suru* print.　校正刷り *kōseizuri* proof.

ON　SATSU print
印刷 ‹v›*insatsu* printing.　刷新 ‹v›*sasshin* reform, innovation.

#726 希	7 strokes	′ ㇒ 产 产 希 希

ON　KI hope, desire; scarcity
希望 ‹v›*kibō* hope.　希少価値 *kishō kachi* scarcity value.　希代の
kidai no remarkable, rare; notorious (villan).

#727 志	7 strokes	一 十 士 志 志 志

kun　*kokoroza(su)* intend, aspire; *kokorozashi* will, aspiration
志す *kokorozasu* intend (to be a writer).　志 *kokorozashi* will,
aspiration.

ON　SHI will, aspiration
志望 ‹v›*shibō* aspiration.　作家志望 *sakka shibō* desire of being a
writer.　意志 *ishi* will.　志願 ‹v›*shigan* aspiration, aplication.

詩	*shi*	poetry, poem
朗読‹v›	*rōdoku*	reading aloud
日記	*nikki*	diary
伝記	*denki*	biography
旅行記	*ryokōki*	travel book
回想録	*kaisōroku*	memoirs
雑誌	*zasshi*	magazine
刊行‹v›	*kankō*	publication
編集‹v›	*henshū*	editing
小説	*shōsetsu*	novel, fiction
短編	*tanpen*	short story
推理小説	*suiri shōsetsu*	detective story
歴史小説	*rekishi shōsetsu*	historical novel
話の筋	*hanashi no suji*	story's plot
著者	*chosha*	author
訳	*wake*	meaning; reason
訳	*yaku*	translation
純文学	*junbungaku*	pure literature
ノーベル賞	*Nōberu Shō*	Nobel Prize
評論‹v›	*hyōron*	criticism, review
文芸批評	*bungei hihyō*	literary criticism
寸評	*sunpyō*	brief comment
解釈‹v›	*kaishaku*	interpretation
完成‹v›	*kansei*	completion
映画化‹v›	*eigaka*	cinematization
校正刷り	*kōseizuri*	proof
印刷‹v›	*insatsu*	printing
希少価値	*kishō kachi*	scarcity value
作家志望	*sakka shibō*	desire of being a writer

Read and translate the following.

1. 詩人が自分の詩を朗読した。
2. その少女の日記は百万部以上も売れた。
3. モーツアルトの伝記を読んで感動した。
4. このアメリカ旅行記は面白いばかりでなく、とても役に立つ。
5. この回想録には著者の深い人類愛がにじみ出ている。
6. 山田さんは新聞記者を辞めて雑誌の編集をしている。
7. その作家の短編はいつも話の筋が単純だ。
8. 歴史小説の中には史実と全くちがったものもある。
9. ノーベル賞を受賞した作品は色々の言葉に訳されて、世界各国で刊行されている。
10. 小説の映画化が純文学を通俗なものにしたと言われている。
11. この季刊誌に新刊書の文芸批評が出ている。
12. 評論家によって文章の解釈がちがうことは度々ある。
13. この校正刷りには誤字や句読点の誤りが多い。
14. その推理小説は初版が一万部印刷された。
15. ある作品は希少価値で注目を集めている。
16. 作家志望の田中さんは最初の小説を完成したばかりだ。

15

Body and Health

Body

▪ I. Reference

#728 身	7 strokes	´ 丶 勹 自 身 身

kun   *mi* body, self, flesh

身も心も *mi mo kokoro mo* soul and body.   身分 *mibun* one's status.   中身 *nakami* content.   赤身 *akami* lean meat.   身の代金 *minoshiro-kin* ransom.

ON   SHIN body, self

身体 *shintai* body.   身長 *shinchō* height.   心身 *shinshin* mind and body.   出身地 *shusshinchi* one's native place.   出身校 *shusshinkō* one's alma mater.   化身 *keshin* incarnation.

#729 重	9 strokes	一 亠 旨 盲 重 重

kun   *omo(i)* heavy, serious, important; *kasa(neru)* pile up; *kasa(naru)* be piled up; -*e* -fold

重い *omoi* heavy (box), serious (illness), important (position). 重ねる *kasaneru* pile up (books).   重なる *kasanaru* be piled up. 二重 *futae* 2 fold.

ON   JŪ, CHŌ heavy, serious, important

体重 *taijū* weight.   重体 *jūtai* serious condition.   重点 *jūten* important point.   重大な *jūdai na* important, serious.   貴重品 #971 *kichōhin* valuables.

#730 耳	6 strokes	一 丆 下 下 耳 耳

kun   *mimi* ear

耳 *mimi* ear.   耳が遠い *mimi ga tōi* be hard of hearing.   耳鳴りがする *miminari ga suru* have a ringing in one's ears.

ON   JI ear
中耳 *chūji* middle ear.   内耳 *naiji* internal ear.   耳目を引く *jimoku o hiku* attract a person's attention.

#731 首	9 strokes	` 亠 产 节 首 首

kun   *kubi* neck, head
首 *kubi* neck, head.   手首 *tekubi* wrist.   足首 *ashikubi* ankle.
乳首 *chikubi* nipple.   首切り *kubikiri* dismissal.

ON   SHU neck, head
首席 *shuseki* top rank.   首位 *shui* top place.   首都 *shuto* capital.
首相 *shushō* prime minister.   自首 ⟨v⟩ *jishu* self-surrender (to the police).

#732 細	11 strokes	乡 糸 糸 紲 細 細

kun   *hoso(i)* thin, slender; *koma(kai)* small, detailed
細い *hosoi* thin (voice), slender (neck).   細かい *komakai* small (money), detailed (instructions).

ON   SAI narrow, small, fine
細工 ⟨v⟩ *saiku* craftsmanship, work.   細部 *saibu* details.   明細書 *meisaisho* detailed statement.   不細工な *busaiku na* clumsy.

#733 顔	18 strokes	立 产 彦 顔 顔 顔

kun   *kao* face
顔 *kao* face.   顔色 *kaoiro* complexion; look.   笑顔 *egao* smiling face.   赤ら顔 *akaragao* ruddy face.

ON   GAN face
顔色 *ganshoku* complexion; look.   顔面 *ganmen* face.   紅顔 *kōgan* rosy face.   洗顔 ⟨v⟩ *sengan* washing one's face.

#734 頭	16 strokes	冂 豆 豇 頭 頭 頭

kun   *atama, kashira* head, leader, top
頭 *atama* head.   頭金 *atamakin* down payment.   頭 *kashira* head; chief.   頭文字 *kashiramoji* initial letter; capital letter.

ON   TŌ, [TO], ZU head, leader, top

頭取 *tōdori* bank president. 先頭 *sentō* the lead. 店頭 *tentō* shop front. 頭上に *zujō ni* overhead. 音頭 *ondo* Japanese folk song. 音頭取り *ondotori* chorus leader; leader.

#735 鼻	14 strokes	宀 自 鼻 鼻 鼻 鼻

kun   *hana* nose

鼻 *hana* nose. 鼻声 *hanagoe* nasal voice.

ON   BI nose

耳鼻科 *jibika* otorhinology. 鼻音 *bion* nasal sound. 鼻音化 ⟨v⟩ *bionka* nasalization.

#736 舌	6 strokes	ノ 二 千 舌 舌 舌

kun   *shita* tongue

舌 *shita* tongue. 舌打ち ⟨v⟩*shitauchi* clicking one's tongue. 二枚舌 *nimaijita* forked tongue.

ON   ZETSU tongue

舌がん *zetsugan* cancer of the tongue. 舌戦 *zessen* wordy war.

#737 歯	12 strokes	卜 止 歨 歨 齒 歯

kun   *ha* tooth

歯 *ha* tooth. 虫歯 *mushiba* decayed tooth. 歯ブラシ *ha-burashi* toothbrush.

ON   SHI tooth

乳歯 *nyūshi* milk tooth. 歯科 *shika* dentistry.

#738 痛	12 strokes	亠 广 疒 疖 痈 痛

kun   *ita(i)* painful; *ita(mu)* feel a pain; *ita(meru)* hurt

痛い *itai* painful. 痛み *itami* pain. 痛む *itamu* feel a pain (in the eye). 痛める *itameru* get hurt (in the leg).

ON   TSŪ pain

歯痛 *shitsū* toothache. 頭痛 *zutsū* headache. 激痛 *gekitsū* acute pain. 痛感する *tsūkan suru* feel keenly.

#739 苦

8 strokes ー 丷 芒 苎 苦 苦

kun *kuru(shimu)* suffer; *kuru(shimeru)* torment; *kuru(shii)* painful; *niga(i)* bitter

苦しむ *kurushimu* suffer. 苦しみ *kurushimi* pain, distress. 苦しめる *kurushimeru* torment. 苦しい *kurushii* painful, difficult. 苦い *nigai* bitter (pill). 苦味 *nigami* bitter taste.

ON KU suffering, pain

苦痛 *kutsū* pain. 苦心 ⟨v⟩ *kushin* efforts, hard work. 苦戦 ⟨v⟩ *kusen* hard fight; close match.

#740 胸

10 strokes 刀 肎 肎 胸 胸 胸

kun *mune*, [*muna*] chest, bosom

胸 *mune* chest. 胸焼け *muneyake* heartburn. 胸毛 *munage* chest hair. 胸苦しい *munagurushii* feel oppressed in the chest.

ON KYŌ chest, bosom

胸囲 *kyōi* girth of the chest. 胸部 *kyōbu* breast, chest. 胸中 *kyōchū* one's bosom/mind/heart. 度胸 *dokyō* courage, boldness.

#741 腹

13 strokes 刀 扩 肋 肋 脂 腹

kun *hara* abdomen; mind, heart

腹 *hara* abdomen. 腹の大きい *hara no ōkii* large-minded. 腹が立つ *hara ga tatsu* get angry. 腹を決める *hara o kimeru* make up one's mind.

ON FUKU abdomen; mind, heart

腹痛 *fukutsū* stomachache. 空腹な *kūfuku na* hungry. 満腹 ⟨v⟩ *manpuku* full stomach. 腹心の友 *fukushin no tomo* confidant.

#742 背

9 strokes ー ⼗ ⼟ 北 背 背

kun *se* back; height; *sei* height; *somu(ku)* act against; *somu(keru)* avert

背 *se* back. 背が高い *se/sei ga takai* tall. 背中 *senaka* back. 背筋 *sesuji* spinal column. 背広 *sebiro* man's suit. 背く *somuku* break (one's word). 背ける *somukeru* avert (one's face).

ON　　HAI back
背景 *haikei* background.　背後 *haigo* back, rear.

#743 比　　4 strokes　　`一　比　比´　比`

kun　　*kura(beru)* compare
比べる *kuraberu* compare.　背比べ *seikurabe* comparison of heights.　見比べる *mikuraberu* compare visually.

ON　　HI compare
比例 ‹v› *hirei* proportion.　比率 *hiritsu* ratio.　比重 *hijū* specific gravity.　対比 ‹v› *taihi* contrast.　比類のない *hirui no nai* matchless.

#744 眼　　11 strokes　　`冂　目ヿ　目ヨ　眃　眼´　眼`

kun　　*manako* eye Ir. *me(gane)**
心の眼 *kokoro no manako* mind's eye.　眼鏡 *megane** eyeglasses.

ON　　GAN, [GEN] eye
近眼 *kingan* nearsightedness.　眼科 *ganka* ophthalmology.　主眼 *shugan* primary object.　開眼 *kaigan* gaining eyesight.　開眼 ‹v› *kaigen* enlightment.

#745 視　　11 strokes　　`丶　ラ　ネ　礻刀　祖　視`

ON　　SHI seeing, regarding as
視力 *shiryoku* eyesight.　近視 *kinshi* nearshightedness.　視野 *shiya* visual field, scope.　視界 *shikai* visibility.　重視 ‹v› *jūshi* attaching importance to.　軽視 ‹v› *keishi* making light of.

#746 姿　　9 strokes　　`冫　氵　次　姿　姿　姿`

kun　　*sugata* figure, appearance
姿 *sugata* figure, appearance.　後ろ姿 *ushirosugata* one's appearance from behind.　立ち姿 *tachisugata* one's standing posture.

ON　　SHI figure, appearance
姿勢 *shisei* posture; attitude.　容姿 *yōshi* one's face and figure.

#747 臓	19 strokes	肙 肶 腜 腤 臓 臓

ON   ZŌ internal organs
心臓 *shinzō* heart.   心臓発作 *shinzō hossa* heart attack.   内蔵 *naizō* internal organs.   臓器 *zōki* internal organs.

#748 肺	9 strokes	几 月 肀 肀 肺 肺

ON   HAI lung
肺 *hai* lung.   肺臓 *haizō* lungs.   肺活量 *haikatsuryō* lung capacity.

#749 胃	9 strokes	丶 口 田 甲 胃 胃

ON   I stomach
胃 *i* stomach.   胃痛 *itsū* stomachache.   胃弱 *ijaku* dyspepsia.

#750 腸	13 strokes	几 月 朋 腭 腸 腸

ON   CHŌ intestines
腸 *chō* intestines.   胃腸 *ichō* stomach and intestines.   大腸 *daichō* large intestine.   小腸 *shōchō* small intestine.

#751 脳	11 strokes	几 月 肜 脃 脳 脳

ON   NŌ brain
脳 *nō* brain.   脳卒中 *nōsotchū* cerebral apoplexy.   洗脳 ‹v› *sennō* brainwashing.   首脳 *shunō* leader.

#752 骨	10 strokes	冂 冋 咼 咼 骨 骨

kun   *hone* bone
骨 *hone* bone.   背骨 *sebone* spine.   骨組み *honegumi* body frame; framework.

ON   KOTSU bone
骨折 ‹v› *kossetsu* bone fracture.   胸骨 *kyōkotsu* breastbone.   骨格 *kokkaku* build, physique.   骨肉 *kotsuniku* one's own flesh and blood.   骨肉の争い *kotsuniku no arasoi* domestic discord.

#753 血	6 strokes	ノ イ ⼕ 竹 血 血

kun   *chi* blood
血 *chi* blood.   鼻血 *hanaji* nosebleed.

ON   KETSU blood
出血 ‹v›*shukketsu* bleeding.   止血 ‹v›*shiketsu* stop bleeding.   血圧 *ketsuatsu* blood pressure.   採血 ‹v›*saiketsu* drawing blood.

#754 液	11 strokes	氵 氵 氵 氵 液 液

ON   EKI liquid, fluid, juice
血液 *ketsueki* blood.   液体 *ekitai* liquid.   胃液 *ieki* gastric juice.   乳液 *nyūeki* milky lotion.   液化 ‹v›*ekika* liquefaction.

#755 精	14 strokes	ヽ ⼿ ⽶ 精 精 精

ON   SEI, [SHŌ] spirit, energy, vitality; refine, fine
水の精 *mizu no sei* nymph.   精力 *seiryoku* vitality.   精力的な *seiryokuteki na* energetic.   精糖 *seitō* refined sugar.   精読 ‹v›*seidoku* attentive reading.   不精 *bushō* laziness.

#756 神	9 strokes	ゥ ネ ネ 初 袒 神

kun   *kami*, [*kan*], [*kō*] god, divine Ir. *(o)mi(ki)**; *kagu(ra)**
神 *kami* god.   神業 *kamiwaza* devine work.   神主 *kannushi* Shinto priest.   神々しい *kōgōshii* divine.   お神酒 *o-miki** votive sake. 神楽 *kagura** Shinto music and dance.

ON   SHIN, JIN god, divine
精神 *seishin* soul, spirit, mind.   精神衛生 *seishin eisei* mental hygine.   神道 *shintō* Shintoism.   神話 *shinwa* myth.   神父 *shinpu* Catholic priest.   山田神父 *Yamada-shinpu* Frather Yamada.

■ II. Vocabulary ■

身体	*shintai*	body
重い	*omoi*	heavy, serious, important

体重	*taijū*	weight
耳	*mimi*	ear
中耳	*chūji*	middle ear
首	*kubi*	neck, head
細い	*hosoi*	thin, slender
顔	*kao*	face
顔色	*kaoiro/ganshoku*	complexion; look
頭	*atama*	head
頭痛	*zutsū*	headache
鼻	*hana*	nose
耳鼻科	*jibika*	otorhinology
舌	*shita*	tongue
舌がん	*zetsugan*	cancer of the tongue
歯	*ha*	tooth
乳歯	*nyūshi*	milk tooth
痛み	*itami*	pain
苦痛	*kutsū*	pain
胸	*mune*	chest
胸囲	*kyōi*	girth of the chest
腹	*hara*	abdomen
腹痛	*fukutsū*	stomachache
背中	*senaka*	back
背比べ	*seikurabe*	comparison of heights
比例‹v›	*hirei*	proportion
眼鏡	*megane*	eyeglasses
近眼	*kingan*	nearsightedness
視力	*shiryoku*	eyesight
姿	*sugata*	figure, appearance
姿勢	*shisei*	posture; attitude
心臓	*shinzō*	heart
肺	*hai*	lung
胃	*i*	stomach
胃腸	*ichō*	stomach and intestines
脳	*nō*	brain
骨	*hone*	bone
骨折‹v›	*kossetsu*	bone fracture
血	*chi*	blood
血液	*ketsueki*	blood
精神	*seishin*	soul, spirit, mind

Read and translate the following.

1. あの学生は**身**も心も勉強に打ちこんでいる。
2. 子供は**身体**も**精神**も強い人間に育てたい。
3. 祖父は最近、**耳**が遠くなったようだ。
4. 祖母は**歯**が悪いので、固い物は食べられない。
5. 幼児は生まれてから半年ぐらいで**乳歯**が生え始める。
6. 兄の息子は**胃腸**が弱いから、常に**顔色**が良くない。
7. 転んだ時、**鼻**を打って**鼻血**が出た。
8. ブラウン夫人は**首**が細くて**姿勢**が良く、実に**容姿**が美しい。
9. 主人は**肺**や**心臓**を強くするため、毎日軽い運動をしている。
10. 家内の父親は去年**脳卒中**で死亡した。
11. 私達の先生はひどい**近眼**で、あつい**眼鏡**をかけている。
12. その老人は目の手術を受けて、**視力**を回復した。
13. かぜのため熱があり、**頭**が**痛**く**舌**もあれている。
14. 昨夜のパーティーで飲み過ぎて、今朝から**頭痛**がする。
15. 重い物を運んだ後で、**胸**と**背中**に**痛**みを感じた。
16. 昨日は一日中**腹痛**で**苦**しんだが、今日はもう**苦痛**はない。
17. **背**が同じぐらいの長男と次男はよく**背比**べをしている。
18. このグラフは**身長**と**体重**の**比例**を示している。
19. その選手は足の**骨折**のため、試合に出られなかった。
20. クリニックで**血圧**を測ったり、**血液**を調べたりしてもらった。

Health

#757 元	4 strokes	一　二　テ　元

kun　*moto* source, root, origin
火の元 *hi no moto* origin of a fire.　根元 *nemoto* root.　元手 *motode* capital.　元学長 *moto gakuchō* former university president.

ON　GEN, GAN source, root, origin
元気な *genki na* healthy.　次元 *jigen* dimension, aspect.　元日 *ganjitsu* New Year's Day.　元金 *gankin* principal.

#758 病	10 strokes	一　广　疒　疔　病　病

kun　*ya(mu)* fall ill; *yamai* illness
病む *yamu* fall ill.　病 *yamai* illness.

ON　BYŌ, [HEI] illness.
病気 *byōki* illness.　心臓病 *shinzōbyō* heart disease.　病人 *byōnin* sick person.　病院 *byōin* hospital.　仮病 *kebyō* faked illness.　疾病 *shippei* disease.

#759 医	7 strokes	一　ア　三　歹　歨　医

ON　I medicine, healing
医者 *isha* doctor.　歯医者 *haisha* dentist.　外科医 *gekai* surgeon.　医学 *igaku* medicine.　医院 *iin* doctor's office.

#760 健	11 strokes	亻　亻ㄱ　亻ㅋ　亻彐　健　健

kun　*suko(yaka)* healthy, sound
健やかな *sukoyaka na* healthy (body), sound (mind).

ON　KEN healthy, sound
健全な *kenzen na* sound.　強健な *kyōken na* robust.　健在 *kenzai* being in good health.　健児 *kenji* vigorous boy.

#761 康	11 strokes	亠 广 庐 序 序 康

ON KŌ ease, peace
健康 *kenkō* health.   不健康な *fukenkō na* unhealthy.   小康 *shōkō* lull.

#762 属	12 strokes	一 尸 戸 屈 属 属

ON ZOKU belong to
付属 ‹v›*fuzoku* being attached to.   付属病院 *fuzoku byōin* hospital attached to (a university).   所属 ‹v›*shozoku* belonging to.   金属 *kinzoku* metal.   属性 *zokusei* attribute.

#763 看	9 strokes	一 三 手 看 看 看

ON KAN look, watch
看病 ‹v›*kanbyō* nursing.   看板 *kanban* signboard.   看取 ‹v›*kanshu* seeing through, detection.   看過 ‹v›*kanka* overlooking (a fault).

#764 護	20 strokes	言 訂 評 評 護 護

ON GO protect, defend
看護 ‹v›*kango* nursing.   看護婦 *kangofu* nurse.   保護 ‹v›*hogo* protection.   護衛 ‹v›*goei* gaurd, escort.

#765 当	6 strokes	丨 丷 丷 尚 当 当

kun *a(taru)* hit; *a(teru)* hit, strike; put
当たる *ataru* (stones) hit (a person on the head).   当てる *ateru* hit (a target); put (one's hand on the face).   手当 ‹v›*teate* medical treatment.   当たり前 *atarimae* natural, proper.

ON TŌ concerned, in question
当人 *tōnin* person involved.   当日 *tōjitsu* day in question.   当局 *tōkyoku* authorities.   当地 *tōchi* this place.   正当な *seitō na* proper.   本当の *hontō no* true.

#766 傷

13 strokes　イ　仃　仴　俏　傝　傷

kun　*kizu* wound, injury; *ita(mu)* have a pain, be damaged; *ita(meru)* injure, damage

傷 *kizu* wound, injury.　傷口 *kizuguchi* wound.　傷む *itamu* have a pain (in the stomach), (oranges) be damaged.　傷める *itameru* injure (one's foot).

ON　SHŌ wound, injury

軽傷 *keishō* slight injury.　重傷 *jūshō* serious injury.　死傷者 *shishōsha* casualties.　負傷 ⟨v⟩ *fushō* injury.　中傷 ⟨v⟩ *chūshō* slander.

#767 毒

8 strokes　一　十　圭　青　青　毒

ON　DOKU poison

毒 *doku* poison.　消毒 ⟨v⟩ *shōdoku* disinfection.　中毒 ⟨v⟩ *chūdoku* poisoning.　毒物 *dokubutsu* toxic substance.　有毒な *yūdoku na* poisonous.

#768 酸

14 strokes　冂　酉　酌　酌　酸　酸

kun　*su(i)* acid, sour

酸い *sui* sour.　酸っぱい *suppai* sour (lemon).

ON　SAN acid, sour

酸性の *sansei no* acid.　酸味 *sanmi* sour taste.　酸化 ⟨v⟩ *sanka* oxidation.　乳酸 *nyūsan* lactic acid.

#769 素

10 strokes　一　十　圭　青　素　素

kun　Ir. *shirō(to)**

素人 *shirōto** amateur.

ON　SO element; original; SU simple, plain

酸素 *sanso* oxygen.　酸素吸入 *sanso kyūnyū* oxygen inhalation.　水素 *suiso* hydrogen.　素材 *sozai* material.　素晴らしい *subarashii* splendid.　素直な *sunao na* obedient; gentle.

#770 **呼**	8 strokes 

kun *yo(bu)* call, send for

呼ぶ *yobu* call (a person by name), send for (a doctor). 呼びかける *yobikakeru* address, hail. 呼び声 *yobigoe* call, shout.

ON KO call; exhale

呼吸‹v› *kokyū* breathing. 呼吸困難 *kokyū konnan* difficulty in breathing. 歓呼‹v› *kanko* cheering. 点呼 *tenko* roll call.

#771 **効**	8 strokes 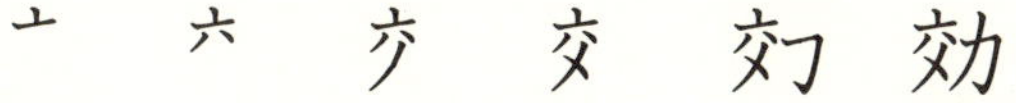

kun *ki(ku)* be effective

効く *kiku* be effective. 効き目 *kikime* effect (of a medicine).

ON KŌ effect

効果 *kōka* effect. 効力 *kōryoku* effectiveness. 効率 *kōritsu* efficiency. 有効な *yūkō na* effective, valid.

#772 **清**	11 strokes 

kun *kiyo(i)* clean, pure; *kiyo(meru)* cleanse; *kiyo(maru)* be cleansed Ir. *shi(mizu)**

清い *kiyoi* clean (water). 清める *kiyomeru* cleanse (one's hands). 清まる *kiyomaru* be cleansed. 清水 *shimizu** spring water.

ON SEI, [SHŌ] clean, pure

血清 *kessei* scrum. 血清注射 *kessei chūsha* scrum injection. 清書‹v› *seisho* fair copy. 清算‹v› *seisan* liquidation.

#773 **潔**	15 strokes 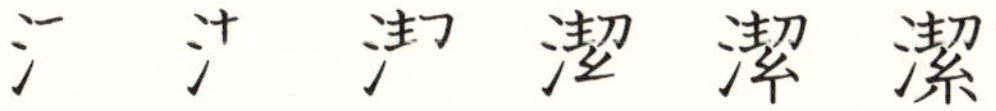

kun *isagiyo(i)* brave, manly

潔い *isagiyoi* brave, manly. 潔く負ける *isagiyoku makeru* be a good loser.

ON KETSU pure, clean

清潔な *seiketsu na* clean. 不潔な *fuketsu na* dirty, unclean. 潔白 *keppaku* innocence.

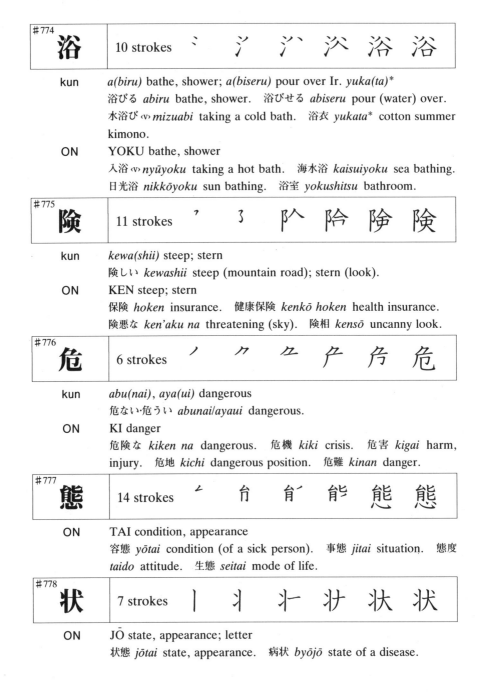

#774 浴 10 strokes ﾆ ｼ ｼ 汐 浴 浴

kun *a(biru)* bathe, shower; *a(biseru)* pour over Ir. *yuka(ta)**
浴びる *abiru* bathe, shower. 浴びせる *abiseru* pour (water) over.
水浴び ‹v› *mizuabi* taking a cold bath. 浴衣 *yukata** cotton summer
kimono.

ON YOKU bathe, shower
入浴 ‹v› *nyūyoku* taking a hot bath. 海水浴 *kaisuiyoku* sea bathing.
日光浴 *nikkōyoku* sun bathing. 浴室 *yokushitsu* bathroom.

#775 険 11 strokes ﾉ ３ 阝 阶 险 険

kun *kewa(shii)* steep; stern
険しい *kewashii* steep (mountain road); stern (look).

ON KEN steep; stern
保険 *hoken* insurance. 健康保険 *kenkō hoken* health insurance.
険悪な *ken'aku na* threatening (sky). 険相 *kensō* uncanny look.

#776 危 6 strokes ﾉ ﾌ ｸ 产 产 危

kun *abu(nai)*, *aya(ui)* dangerous
危ない・危うい *abunai/ayaui* dangerous.

ON KI danger
危険な *kiken na* dangerous. 危機 *kiki* crisis. 危害 *kigai* harm,
injury. 危地 *kichi* dangerous position. 危難 *kinan* danger.

#777 態 14 strokes ﾑ 台 台ﾞ 能ﾞ 態 態

ON TAI condition, appearance
容態 *yōtai* condition (of a sick person). 事態 *jitai* situation. 態度
taido attitude. 生態 *seitai* mode of life.

#778 状 7 strokes ｜ ﾖ 丬 丬ﾞ 状 状

ON JŌ state, appearance; letter
状態 *jōtai* state, appearance. 病状 *byōjō* state of a disease.

現状 *genjō* present condition.　書状 *shojō* letter.　招待状 *shōtaijō* invitation card/letter.

| #779 因 | 6 strokes | 丨 | 冂 | 日 | 用 | 因 | 因 |

kun　*yo(ru)* depend on, be due to
因る *yoru* depend on (circumstances), be due to (carelessness).

ON　IN cause
原因 ⟨v⟩ *gen'in* cause.　死因 *shiin* cause of a person's death.　要因 *yōin* main cause.　因習 *inshū* long-established custom.

| #780 結 | 12 strokes | 乡 | 糸 | 紅 | 結 | 結 | 結 |

kun　*musu(bu)* tie; conclude; *yu(u)* dress the hair
結ぶ *musubu* tie (a shoestring); conclude (a treaty).　結う *yuu* dress one's hair (in Japanese style).

ON　KETSU tie; conclude
結果 *kekka* result.　結論 *ketsuron* conclusion.　結局 *kekkyoku* after all.　結末 *ketsumatsu* end.　結合 ⟨v⟩ *ketsugō* combination.

| #781 検 | 12 strokes | 十 | 朴 | 朳 | 枱 | 梌 | 検 |

ON　KEN investigate, inspect
検温 ⟨v⟩ *ken'on* taking one's temperature.　検眼 ⟨v⟩ *kengan* eye examination.　検定 ⟨v⟩ *kentei* official approval.　点検 ⟨v⟩ *tenken* inspection.　検事 *kenji* public prosecutor.

| #782 査 | 9 strokes | 一 | 才 | 木 | 杏 | 杳 | 査 |

ON　SA investigate
検査 *kensa* inspection, test.　身体検査 *shintai kensa* physical examination.　調査 ⟨v⟩ *chōsa* investigation.　査定 ⟨v⟩ *satei* assessment.

| #783 快 | 7 strokes | ハ | 忄 | 忙 | 忙 | 快 | 快 |

kun　*kokoroyo(i)* pleasant
快い *kokoroyoi* pleasant (feeling/autumn day).

ON   KAI pleasant
快復 ‹v› *kaifuku* recovery.   全快 ‹v› *zenkai* complete recovery.   快晴
kaisei fine weather.   不快な *fukai na* unpleasant.

#784 退	9 strokes	ヲ 尸 尸 艮 退 退

kun   *shirizo(ku)* retreat; *shirizo(keru)* drive away Ir. *(tachi)no(ku)**
退く *shirizoku* retreat.   退ける *shirizokeru* drive away.   立ち退く
tachinoku* move out, evacuate.
ON   TAI retreat
退院 ‹v› *taiin* leaving the hospital.   退学 ‹v› *taigaku* leaving school.
引退 ‹v› *intai* retirement.   辞退 ‹v› *jitai* declination.

#785 費	12 strokes	一 二 弓 弗 昔 費

kun   *tsui(yasu)* spend
費やす *tsuiyasu* spend (money).
ON   HI expense
費用 *hiyō* expense.   入院費 *nyūinhi* hospital expenses.   生活費
seikatsuhi living expenses.   食費 *shokuhi* food expenses.   旅費
ryohi traveling expenses.

■ II. Vocabulary ■

元気な	*genki na*	healthy
病	*yamai*	illness
病気	*byōki*	illness
健やかな	*sukoyaka na*	healthy, sound
健康	*kenkō*	health
付属病院	*fuzoku byōin*	hospital attached to (a university)
医者	*isha*	doctor
看護婦	*kangofu*	nurse
手当 ‹v›	*teate*	medical treatment
傷	*kizu*	wound, injury
軽傷	*keishō*	slight wound
消毒 ‹v›	*shōdoku*	disinfection
酸素	*sanso*	oxygen

呼吸‹v›	*kokyū*	breathing
効果	*kōka*	effect
清潔な	*seiketsu na*	clean
水浴び‹v›	*mizuabi*	taking a cold bath
入浴‹v›	*nyūyoku*	taking a hot bath
危ない	*abunai*	dangerous
危険な	*kiken na*	dangerous
状態	*jōtai*	state, appearance
原因‹v›	*gen'in*	cause
結果	*kekka*	result
身体検査	*shintai kensa*	physical examination
快復‹v›	*kaifuku*	recovery
退院‹v›	*taiin*	leaving the hospital
費用	*hiyō*	expense
健康保険	*kenkō hoken*	health insurance

■ III. Reading Exercises 37 ■

Read and translate the following.

1. 母は相変わらず**元気**ですが、父は今年の四月以来**病気**です。
2. 木村さんのお父さんは**心臓病**で入院している。
3. 秋子さんのお姉さんは大学の**付属病院**の**看護婦**です。
4. あの兄弟は二人共アメリカで**医学**を学んで**医者**になった。
5. 石が額に**当たって傷**を負ったので、近くの**医院**で**手当**を受けた。
6. **外科医**は**傷口**を**消毒**して五つ針ぬった。
7. 昨日の土砂くずれで数人の**死傷者**が出た。
8. **医者**は**呼吸困難**の**病人**に**酸素吸入**を行なった。
9. **入浴**する時間のない時は、代わりにシャワーを**浴**びます。
10. 知人の息子さんは**病気**が**快復**して、一週間前に**退院**した。
11. この薬は**効果**が早い。
12. 何度も**検査**を行なったが、**病気**の**原因**はまだ不明である。
13. 先週**身体検査**を受けて、今その**結果**を待っています。
14. 体を**清潔**に保つことが**健康**への第一歩である。
15. 昨夜まで**危険**な**状態**にあった**病人**は今朝から**小康**を得た。
16. **医者**や**病院**の**費用**がかさんだが、幸い**健康保険**がほとんどカバーした。

16
✷✷✷✷✷✷✷✷✷✷✷✷✷✷✷✷✷✷
Transportation

Vehicles and Roads

■ I. Reference ■

#786

車   7 strokes   一   厂   盲   亘   車

kun   *kuruma* vehicle; wheel Ir. *(da)shi**
車 *kuruma* car.   乳母車 *ubaguruma* baby carriage.   車いす *kurumaisu* wheel chair.   山車 *dashi** float, festival car.

ON   SHA vehicle; wheel
自動車 *jidōsha* automobile.   自転車 *jitensha* bicycle.   電車 *densha* train.   列車 *ressha* train.   発車 ⟨v⟩ *hassha* departure(of a train/car). 車輪 *sharin* wheel.

#787

乗   9 strokes   二   丘   乒   乖   乗   乗

kun   *no(ru)* ride, get on, take (a train); *no(seru)* let ride, load
乗る *noru* ride (a bicycle), get on/take (a train).   乗り場 *noriba* car stop, platform.   乗せる *noseru* let (a child) ride (in a car). 乗り出す *noridasu* start out (in business).   乗組員 *norikumiin* crew.

ON   JŌ ride, get on, take (a train)
乗車 ⟨v⟩ *jōsha* taking a train/car, getting on.   乗客 *jōkyaku* passenger.   乗用車 *jōyōsha* passenger car.

#788

向   6 strokes   ′   亻   冂   向   向   向

kun   *mu(kau)* go toward; *mu(ku)*, *mu(keru)* turn; *mu(kō)* opposite side
向かう *mukau* go toward (the south).   向く *muku* turn (to the left).   向ける *mukeru* turn (one's face to).   向こう側 *mukōgawa* opposite side.   向き *muki* direction.

ON   KŌ direction

方向 *hōkō* direction.　向上 ⟨v⟩ *kōjō* improvement.　意向 *ikō* intention.　回向 *ekō* Buddhist memorial service.

#789

交	6 strokes	丶 亠 六 六 亣 交

kun   *ma(jiru)* get mixed; *maji(waru)* associate with; cross; *kawa(su)* exchange

交じる *majiru* (colors) get mixed.　交わる *majiwaru* associate with (foreigners); (roads) cross.　交わす *kawasu* exchange (one's views).

ON   KŌ exchange, cross

交通 *kōtsū* traffic, transportation.　交差点 *kōsaten* crossing.　交代 ⟨v⟩ *kōtai* taking turns.　外交 *gaikō* foreign affairs.　国交 *kokkō* diplomatic relations.　交流 ⟨v⟩ *kōryū* interchange.

#790

故	9 strokes	一 十 古 古 故 故

kun   *yue* reason

故あって *yue atte* for a certain reason.　故に *yue ni* consequently.

ON   KO obstacle; deceased: old and dear

事故 *jiko* accident.　交通事故 *kōtsū jiko* traffic accident.　故人 *kojin* the deceased.　故三木氏 *ko Miki-shi* the late Mr. Miki.　故国 *kokoku* one's homeland.　故郷 *kokyō* one's native place.

#791

障	14 strokes	⁷ 阝 阝 陪 陪 障

kun   *sawa(ru)* hinder; harm

障る *sawaru* hinder (a person from doing); harm (one's health).

ON   SHŌ obstacle

故障 ⟨v⟩ *koshō* trouble, breakdown.　障害 *shōgai* obstacle.　支障 *shishō* hinderance.　保障 ⟨v⟩ *hoshō* guarantee.

#792

速	10 strokes	一 申 束 束 速 速

kun   *haya(i)*, *sumi(yaka)* fast, speedy

速い *hayai* fast, speedy.　速やかな *sumiyaka na* prompt (answer).

ON SOKU fast, speedy

速度 *sokudo* speed.　時速 *jisoku* speed per hour.　高速道路 *kōsoku dōro* expressway.　速達 *sokutatsu* special delivery.　早速 *sassoku* right away.

#793 坂	7 strokes	一 十 打 圹 坂 坂

kun *saka* slope, hill

坂 *saka* slope, hill.　坂道 *sakamichi* slope.　上り坂 *noborizaka* upward slope.　下り坂 *kudarizaka* downward slope; decline.

ON HAN slope, hill

登坂 ‹v› *tōhan* climbing up a slope.

#794 迷	9 strokes	丶 丷 半 米 米 迷 迷

kun *mayo(u)* stray Ir. *mai(go)**

道に迷う *michi ni mayou* lose one's way.　迷子 *maigo** stray child.

ON MEI stray

迷路 *meiro* maze.　低迷 ‹v› *teimei* hanging low; being sluggish.

#795 横	15 strokes	十 村 棤 槠 横 横

kun *yoko* side, width; perverse

横 *yoko* side, width.　横道 *yokomichi* byroad.　横顔 *yokogao* profile.　横切る *yokogiru* cross.　横車 *yokoguruma* persersity.

ON Ō side, width; perverse

横転 ‹v› *ōten* rolling sideways.　横行 ‹v› *ōkō* swagger.　横暴な *ōbō na* tyrannical.　横領 ‹v› *ōryō* usurpation.

#796 縦	16 strokes	幺 糸 糸 絲 縱 縦

kun *tate* length, height, vertical

縦 *tate* length, height.　縦の *tate no* vertical.　縦横 *tateyoko* length and width.　縦線 *tatesen* vertical line.

ON JŪ length, height, vertical

縦横 *jūō* length and width.　縦横に *jūō ni* vertically and horizontally, in all directions.　操縦 ‹v› *sōjū* steering.　縦走 ‹v› *jūsō* mountain-range traversing.

#797 断	11 strokes	丷 米 迷 断 断 断

kun *ta(tsu)* cut off; *kotowa(ru)* decline, refuse
断つ *tatsu* cut off (communications). 断る *kotowaru* decline (an invitation).

ON DAN cut off; decision, judgment
横断 ‹v› *ōdan* crossing. 横断歩道 *ōdan hodō* pedestrian crossing. 切断 ‹v› *setsudan* cutting. 決断 ‹v› *ketsudan* decision. 断念 ‹v› *dannen* abandonment. 断行 ‹v› *dankō* decisive action.

#798 垂	8 strokes	二 三 丘 乒 垂 垂

kun *ta(reru)*, *ta(rasu)* hang down, suspend, drip
垂れる *tareru* hang (one's head). 垂らす *tarasu* suspend (a curtain). 雨垂れ *amadare* raindrops.

ON SUI hang down, suspend
垂直の *suichoku no* perpendicular. 垂直に交わる *suichoku ni majiwaru* cross at right angles. 垂線 *suisen* perpendicular line.

#799 号	5 strokes	丶 口 口 号 号

ON GŌ number, issue; sign; naming
番号 *bangō* number. 電話番号 *denwa bangō* telephone number. 三月号 *sangatsugō* March issue (of a magazine). 記号 *kigō* sign. 暗号 *angō* secret code. ひかり号 *Hikari-gō* Hikari (of the Shinkansen).

#800 信	9 strokes	亻 亻 信 信 信 信

ON SHIN message; trust, believe
信号 *shingō* traffic light. 通信 ‹v› *tsūshin* communication, correspondence. 信じる *shinjiru* believe. 信者 *shinja* believer (of a religion). 信用 ‹v› *shinyō* trust, credit. 自信 *jishin* confidence.

#801

橋　16 strokes 　十　栌　栴　橋　橋　橋

kun　*hashi* bridge
橋 *hashi* bridge.　石橋 *ishibashi* stone bridge.

ON　KYŌ bridge
陸橋 *rikkyō* bridge over a road.　歩道橋 *hodōkyō* pedestrian bridge.

#802

停　11 strokes 　亻　广　停　停　停　停

ON　TEI stop
停留所 *teiryūjo* stopping place.　バス停 *basu-tei* bus stop.　停止 ‹v› *teishi* stop.　停車 ‹v› *teisha* stop (of a car/train).　停電 ‹v› *teiden* blackout.　停戦 ‹v› *teisen* cease-fire.

#803

標　15 strokes 　栌　栌　栖　標　標　標

ON　HYŌ mark, sign
標識 *hyōshiki* mark, sign.　道路標識 *dōro hyōshiki* traffic sign.　標語 *hyōgo* motto.　標本 *hyōhon* specimen.　目標 *mokuhyō* goal.

#804

里　7 strokes 　丶　冂　日　甲　甲　里

kun　*sato* village; one's parents' home
里 *sato* village; one's parents' home.　里親 *satooya* foster parent.　里心 *satogokoro* homesickness.　村里 *murazato* village.

ON　RI (old unit of length)
千里 *senri* 1,000 ri (4,000 km); a great distance.　海里 *kairi* sea mile.　里程 *ritei* mileage, distance.

#805

至　6 strokes 　一　厶　云　圣　至　至

kun　*ita(ru)* lead to, arrive
至る *itaru* lead to (Chiba).　至る所 *itaru tokoro* everywhere.

ON　SHI to; extreme
自東京至千葉 *ji Tōkyō shi Chiba* from Tokyo to Chiba.　自一時至三時 *ji ichiji shi sanji* 1:00 — 3:00.　至難 *shinan* extreme difficulty.

必至の *hisshi no* inevitable.　夏至 *geshi* summer solstice.　冬至 *tōji* winter solstice.

#806 辺	5 strokes	フ　刀　ﾞ刀　辺　辺　辺

kun　*ata(ri)*, *-be* vicinity
　　この辺り *kono atari* this vicinity.　海辺 *umibe* seashore.　水辺 *mizube* water's edge.

ON　HEN vicinity
　　この辺 *kono hen* this vicinity.　近辺 *kinpen* neighborhood.　京都周辺 *Kyōto shūhen* environs of Kyoto.　底辺 *teihen* vase, bottom.

■ II. Vocabulary ■

車	*kuruma*	car
自動車	*jidōsha*	automobile
乗り場	*noriba*	car stop, platform
乗客	*jōkyaku*	passenger
向こう側	*mukōgawa*	opposite side
向き	*muki*	direction
方向	*hōkō*	direction
交通	*kōtsū*	traffic, transportation
事故	*jiko*	accident
故障‹v›	*koshō*	trouble, breakdown
速度	*sokudo*	speed
高速道路	*kōsoku dōro*	expressway
坂道	*sakamichi*	slope
登坂‹v›	*tōhan*	climbing up a slope
道に迷う	*michi ni mayou*	lose one's way
迷路	*meiro*	maze
縦横	*tateyoko/jūō*	length and width
横断歩道	*ōdan hodō*	pedestrian crossing
垂直の	*suichoku no*	perpendicular
信号	*shingō*	traffic light
橋	*hashi*	bridge
陸橋	*rikkyō*	bridge over a road
停留所	*teiryūjo*	stopping place

道路標識	*dōro hyōshiki*	traffic sign
千里	*senri*	1,000 ri; great distance
至る所	*itaru tokoro*	everywhere
自東京至千葉	*ji Tōkyō shi Chiba*	from Tokyo to Chiba
この辺り	*kono atari*	this vicinity
京都周辺	*Kyōto shūhen*	environs of kyoto

■ III. Reading Exercises 38

Read and translate the following.

1. ある学生は**車**で学校に通っている。
2. 古い**自動車**がゆっくりと**坂道**を上がっていく。
3. 新宿で**乗客**の過半数が**電車**を降りた。
4. 雨の降る日には、タクシー**乗り場**に人が長い列を作っている。
5. 北の**方向**に向かって50マイル程**車**を運転した。
6. **信号**が青に変わってから、通りを**向**こう側へ**横切**った。
7. 児童の一群が**横断歩道**をわたっている。
8. この町の中心には道路が**縦横**に走っている。
9. 知らない土地で道に**迷**って大変困った。
10. 暗い**迷路**を通りぬけると、街灯で明るい大通りに出た。
11. この道は少し先で、街道と**垂直**に交わっている。
12. **交通**が激しい**交差点**でよく**事故**が起こる。
13. 赤いスポーツカーが**時速**80マイルで**高速道路**を飛ばしている。
14. **橋**の上で遊覧バスが**故障**した。
15. **陸橋**は現在工事しているので、遠回りしなければならない。
16. **交通**安全のため、**道路標識**に注意すべきだ。
17. **千里**の道も一歩より始まる。
18. ガイドブックにこのバスは「**自東京至千葉**」と出ている。
19. 以前はこの**辺**りにバスの**停留所**があったと思う。
20. **京都周辺**は今でも緑の木々が多い。

Trains and Ships

■ I. Reference ■

#807 鉄	13 strokes	ノ 仁 全 釒 鈇 鉄

ON TETSU iron
鉄 *tetsu* iron. 鉄道 *tetsudō* railway. 地下鉄 *chikatetsu* subway.
私鉄 *shitetsu* private railway. 鉄橋 *tekkyō* railway bridge. 鉄筋
tekkin steel reinforcing rod.

#808 汽	7 strokes	` 氵 汙 汽 汽

ON KI steam
汽車 *kisha* steam train. 夜汽車 *yogisha* night train. 汽笛 *kiteki*
steam whistle.

#809 急	9 strokes	ノ ク 刍 刍 急 急

kun *iso(gu)* hurry
急ぐ *isogu* hurry. 急いで *isoide* in a hurry.

ON KYŪ sudden, steep
急に *kyū ni* suddenly. 急な *kyū na* steep (slope). 急行(列車)
kyūkō (ressha) express (train). 急用 *kyūyō* urgent business.
早急に *sōkyū/sakkyū ni* in a hurry.

#810 準	13 strokes	氵 汁 汁 淮 準 準

ON JUN semi-; level; correspond to
準急 *junkyū* semi-express. 準決勝 *junkesshō* semifinal. 水準
suijun standard. 標準語 *hyōjungo* standard language. 準備 ‹v›
junbi preparation. 準じる *junjiru* correspond to.

#811 特	10 strokes 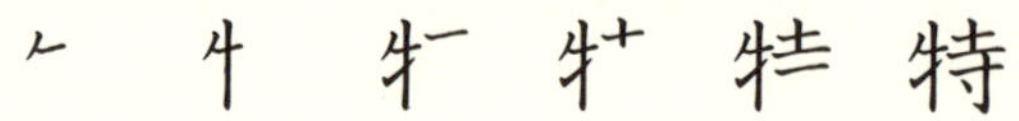

ON TOKU special

特急 *tokkyū* super express. 特色 *tokushoku* specific character. 特技 *tokugi* special talent. 特売‹v› *tokubai* bargain sale. 特に *toku ni* specially. 独特の *dokutoku no* peculiar.

#812 別	7 strokes 

kun *waka(reru)* part

別れる *wakareru* part (from a friend). 別れ *wakare* farewell.

ON BETSU separate; different; another, special

特別急行 *tokubetsu kyūkō* super express. 別館 *bekkan* annex. 別便 *betsubin* separate mail. 差別‹v› *sabetsu* discrimination. 別の *betsu no* another (train). 特別な *tokubetsu na* special.

#813 臨	18 strokes 

kun *nozo(mu)* face, confront; attend

臨む *nozomu* face (the sea/a crisis); attend (a ceremony).

ON RIN face, confront; attend

臨時の *rinji no* temporary. 臨時列車 *rinji ressha* special train. 臨席‹v› *rinseki* attendance. 臨終 *rinjū* one's last moments.

#814 駅	14 strokes 

ON EKI station

駅 *eki* station. 東京駅 *Tōkyō-eki* Tokyo Station. 駅長 *ekichō* station master. 各駅停車 *kakueki teisha* slow train (which stops at every station). 始発駅 *shihatsueki* starting station. 終着駅 *shūchakueki* terminal station.

#815 改	7 strokes 

kun *arata(meru)* renew, reform; *arata(maru)* be renewed, reformed

改める *aratameru* renew (a timetable). 改まる *aratamaru* be renewed, reformed. 改めて *aratamete* newly, formally.

ON   KAI renew, reform
改札口 *kaisatsuguchi* station wicket.   改正 ‹v› *kaisei* revision.
改良 ‹v› *kairyō* improvement.   改定 ‹v› *kaitei* reformation.

#816
刻   8 strokes   一　ﾅ　亥　亥　刻　刻

kun   *kiza(mu)* carve, chop
刻む *kizamu* carve (one's name on a tree), chop (a radish).   時を
刻む *toki o kizamu* tick away the time.
ON   KOKU carve; time
時刻 *jikoku* time.   時刻表 *jikokuhyō* timetable.   定刻 *teikoku*
appointed hour.   先刻 *senkoku* a while ago.   深刻な *shinkoku na*
serious (problem).

#817
券   8 strokes   ﾉ　ﾞ　ﾂ　半　关　券　券

ON   KEN ticket, certificate
乗車券 *jōshaken* passenger ticket.   特急券 *tokkyūken* super express
ticket.   前売券 *maeuriken* advance ticket.   入場券 *nyūjōken*
admission ticket.   券売機 *kenbaiki* ticket vending machine.

#818
往   8 strokes   ﾉ　彳　彳　行　彳　往

ON   Ō go away
往復 ‹v› *ōfuku* going and returning.   往復乗車券 *ōfuku jōshaken*
round-trip ticket.   往来 *ōrai* traffice; street.   立ち往生 ‹v› *tachiōjō*
coming to a standstill.   右往左往 ‹v› *uōsaō* going this way and that,
running about in confusion.

#819
港   12 strokes   氵　氵　浐　洪　港　港

kun   *minato* harbor, port
港 *minato* harbor, port.   港町 *minatomachi* port town.
ON   KŌ harbor, port
東京港 *Tōkyō-kō* Tokyo Harbor.   空港 *kūkō* airport.   入港 ‹v›
nyūkō entry into port.   出港 ‹v› *shukkō* departure from a port.

#820 船	11 strokes	丿 丹 舟 舟ヽ 船ヽ 船

kun *fune*, [*funa*] ship, boat

船 *fune* ship, boat.　船便 *funabin* seamail.　船旅 *funatabi* sea trip.
船乗り *funanori* sailor.

ON SEN ship, boat

汽船 *kisen* steamship.　客船 *kyakusen* passenger ship.　貨物船 *kamotsusen* cargo ship.　宇宙船 *uchūsen* spaceship.　伝馬船 *tenmasen** lighter, jolly boat.

#821 航	10 strokes	丿 丹 舟 舟゛ 舟゛ 航

ON KŌ navigation, sailing

航海 ‹v› *kōkai* voyage.　出航 ‹v› *shukkō* sailing off.　航路 *kōro* sea route.　欠航 ‹v› *kekkō* suspension of sailing.　航空券 *kōkūken* airplane ticket.

■ II. Vocabulary ■

鉄道	*tetsudō*	railway
汽車	*kisha*	steam train
急行(列車)	*kyūkō (ressha)*	express (train)
準急	*junkyū*	semi-express
特急	*tokkyū*	super express
特別急行	*tokubetsu kyūkō*	super express
臨時列車	*rinji ressha*	special train
駅	*eki*	station
各駅停車	*kakueki teisha*	slow train
改札口	*kaisatsuguchi*	station wicket
時刻表	*jikokuhyō*	timetable
乗車券	*jōshaken*	passenger ticket
特急券	*tokkyūken*	super express ticket
往復乗車券	*ōfuku jōshaken*	round-trip ticket
港	*minato*	harbor, port
東京港	*Tōkyō-kō*	Tokyo Harbor
船	*fune*	ship, boat

船便	*funabin*	seamail
汽船	*kisen*	steamship
航海‹v›	*kōkai*	voyage
出航‹v›	*shukkō*	sailing off

■ III. Reading Exercises 39 ■

Read and translate the following.

1. 日本中、至る所に**鉄道**が通じている。
2. 三時の列車に間に合うように**急**いで**駅**へ行った。
3. 京都**駅**で**急行**を降りて、**準急**に乗りかえた。
4. **特急**は二番ホームから、**各駅停車**は五番ホームから発車します。
5. 窓口で**特急券**と**乗車券**を求めた。
6. この**券売機**では**往復乗車券**は買えません。
7. **汽車**が長いトンネルを出ると、左手に真っ青な海が広がった。
8. 海岸に**臨**んだホテルから美しい夜景を楽しんだ。
9. スキーの季節には**臨時列車**が何本も出る。
10. 最近、その**私鉄**の運賃が**改**まった。**時刻表**も**改正**された。
11. **改札口**を通って**駅**のホームに上がるやいなや、電車のドアが閉まった。
12. ある晴れた日に、白い大きな**船**が**港**に入った。
13. アメリカの友達に**船便**で本を送った。
14. 気象庁の警告で**汽船**の**出航**が延期になった。
15. 素晴らしい**客船**で太平洋を**航海**した。

17

✻✻✻✻✻✻✻✻✻✻✻✻✻✻✻✻✻✻✻
Economy

Industry

■ I. Reference ■

#822 経	11 strokes ㄠ 糸 紀 経 経 経

kun *he(ru)* elapse, go through

経る *heru* (years) elapse, go through (difficulties). ハワイを経て *Hawai o hete* via Hawaii.

ON KEI passage of time; longitude; KYŌ sutra

経過 ⟨v⟩ *keika* lapse; progress. 経験 ⟨v⟩ *keiken* experience. 経費 *keihi* expense. 経路 *keiro* route. 経度 *keido* longitude. 経文 *kyōmon* sutra. 読経 ⟨v⟩ *dokyō** sutra-chanting.

#823 済	11 strokes 氵 汸 汸 済 済 済

kun *su(mu)* end, be settled; *su(masu)* finish, settle

済む *sumu* end, be settled. 済ます *sumasu* finish (a report), settle (the accounts). 検査済み *kensazumi* inspection passed.

ON SAI finish, settle

経済 *keizai* economy. 決済 ⟨v⟩ *kessai* settlement of accounts. 未済注文 *misai chūmon* unfilled order. 共済事業 *kyōsai jigyō* mutual aid project.

#824 財	10 strokes 丨 月 貝 貝 財 財

ON ZAI, [SAI] money, wealth, property

財界 *zaikai* financial world. 財力 *zairyoku* financial power. 財団 *zaidan* foundation. 消費財 *shōhizai* consumer goods. 財布 *saifu* wallet.

#825 資	13 strokes	冫 冫 次 汄 沓 資

ON SHI fund, capital; fundamental
資本 *shihon* capital. 資金 *shikin* fund. 資料 *shiryō* material,
data. 投資 ⟨v⟩ *tōshi* investment. 資格 *shikaku* qualification.

#826 源	13 strokes	冫 冫 沪 沪 源 源

kun *minamoto* origin, source
源 *minamoto* origin, source.

ON GEN origin, source
資源 *shigen* resources. 天然資源 *tennen shigen* natural resources.
財源 *zaigen* financial resources. 起源 *kigen* origin.

#827 産	11 strokes	亠 立 产 产 斉 産

kun *u(mu)* produce, give birth; *u(mareru)* be born; *ubu* birth
産む *umu* give birth (to a boy). 産まれる *umareru* be born. 産湯
ubuyu baby's 1st bath. 土産 *miyage** gift, souvenir.

ON SAN production; property; childbirth
生産 ⟨v⟩ *seisan* production. 産業 *sangyō* industry. 産物 *sanbutsu*
product. 産地 *sanchi* producing area. 財産 *zaisan* fortune. 出産
⟨v⟩ *shussan* childbirth.

#828 革	9 strokes	一 艹 芦 苫 苹 革

kun *kawa* leather
革 *kawa* leather. 革細工 *kawazaiku* leatherwork.

ON KAKU reform, leather
革命 *kakumei* revolution. 産業革命 *sangyō kakumei* industrial revolution. 改革 ⟨v⟩ *kaikaku* reform. 変革 ⟨v⟩ *henkaku* reform,
change. 皮革製品 *hikaku seihin* leather goods.

#829 需	14 strokes	宀 雨 雨 雫 需 需

ON   JU demand, request

需要 *juyō* demand.   必需品 *hitsujuhin* necessaries.   特需 *tokuju* special procurements.   民需産業 *minju sangyō* civilian industry.

#830 給	12 strokes	幺 糸 糸 給 給 給

ON   KYŪ supply

供給 ‹v› *kyōkyū* supply.   需給 *jukyū* supply and demand.   配給 ‹v› *haikyū* distribution, rationing.   自給 ‹v› *jikyū* self-supply.   給食 ‹v› *kyūshoku* provision of meals.   給料 *kyūryō* salary, pay.

#831 進	11 strokes	亻 忄 忄 隹 隹 進

kun   *susu(mu)* advance, progress; *susu(meru)* advance, carry forward

進む *susumu* advance, progress.   進める *susumeru* advance (a clock by 1 hour), carry forward (a scheme).

ON   SHIN advance, progress

進歩 ‹v› *shinpo* advance, progress.   進展 ‹v› *shinten* development.   進出 ‹v› *shinshutsu* marching out.   行進 ‹v› *kōshin* march.

#832 増	14 strokes	土 圤 圸 増 増 増

kun   *ma(su)*, *fue(ru)* increase; *fu(yasu)* increase

増す・増える *masu/fueru* (orders) increase.   増やす *fuyasu* increase (production).   五割増し *gowarimashi* 50% added.

ON   ZŌ increase

増加 ‹v› *zōka* increase.   増産 ‹v› *zōsan* increase in production.   増資 ‹v› *zōshi* increase of capital.   増員 ‹v› *zōin* increase of the staff.   増強 ‹v› *zōkyō* reinforcement.

#833 減	12 strokes	冫 氵 沪 沪 減 減

kun   *he(ru)* decrease; *he(rasu)* reduce, cut down

減る *heru* decrease.   減らす *herasu* cut down (the staff).

ON   GEN decrease

減少 ‹v› *genshō* decrease.   増減 ‹v› *zōgen* increase and decrease. 減産 ‹v› *gensan* reduction in production.   一割減 *ichiwarigen* 10% less.   減退 ‹v› *gentai* decline.

#834 拡	8 strokes	一 才 扩 扩 拡 拡

ON   KAKU expand, extend

拡大 ‹v› *kakudai* expansion, magnification.   拡大鏡 *kakudaikyō* magnifying glass.   拡声器 *kakuseiki* loudspeaker.   拡散 ‹v› *kakusan* diffusion.

#835 張	11 strokes	⊐ 引 弭 張 張 張

kun   *ha(ru)* stretch, spread

張る *haru* stretch (a tent).   見張る *miharu* keep watch.

ON   CHŌ stretch, spread

拡張 ‹v› *kakuchō* extension, expansion.   拡張工事 *kakuchō kōji* extension work.   出張 ‹v› *shutchō* business trip.   主張 ‹v› *shuchō* assertion.

#836 縮	17 strokes	纟 糸 紵 縃 縮 縮

kun   *chiji(mu)* shrink; *chiji(meru)* shorten

縮む *chijimu* shrink.   縮める *chijimeru* shorten (the term).

ON   SHUKU shrink

縮小 ‹v› *shukushō* reduction.   短縮 ‹v› *tanshuku* shortening.   縮図 *shukuzu* reduced drawing.   縮写 ‹v› *shukusha* reduced copy.

#837 従	10 strokes	彳 彳 徉 徉 徉 従

kun   *shitaga(u)* follow, obey

従う *shitagau* follow (the instructions), obey (the law).   従って *shitagatte* consequently; as, in proportion to.

ON   JŪ, [SHŌ], [JU] follow, obey

従事 ‹v› *jūji* being engaged.   従業員 *jūgyōin* employee.   服従 ‹v› *fukujū* obedience.   従容として *shōyō to shite* calmly.

#838 農	13 strokes	冂　曲　曲　農　農　農

ON　NŌ agriculture

農業 *nōgyō* agriculture.　農産物 *nōsanbutsu* agricultural product.
農村 *nōson* farm village.　農家 *nōka* farmhouse, farming family.
農民 *nōmin* farmer.　農地 *nōchi* agricultural land.

#839 肥	8 strokes	丿　刀　月ㄱ　月ㄲ　肝ㄗ　肥

kun　*koe, ko(yashi)* manure; *ko(yasu)* fertilize; *ko(eru)* grow fat; grow
fertile

肥・肥やし *koe/koyashi* manure.　肥やす *koyasu* fertilize (the land).
肥える *koeru* grow fat; grow fertile.

ON　HI fertile, fat

肥料 *hiryō* fertilizer.　化学肥料 *kagaku hiryō* chemical fertilizer.
魚肥 *gyohi* fish fertilizer.　肥満〈v〉*himan* obesity.

#840 灰	6 strokes	一　厂　厃　厈　灰　灰

kun　*hai* ash

灰 *hai* ash.　灰皿 *haizara* ashtray.　火山灰 *kazanbai* volcanic ash.

ON　KAI ash

石灰 *sekkai* lime.　石灰水 *sekkaisui* limewater.

#841 盛	11 strokes	厂　厃　成　咸　盛　盛

kun　*saka(n)* prosperous, energetic; *mo(ru)* pile up

盛んな *sakan na* prosperous, energetic.　盛り *sakari* peak, prime.
盛り場 *sakariba* amusement quarters.　盛る *moru* pile up (fruits).

ON　SEI, [JŌ] prosperous, energetic

盛大な *seidai na* grand, magnificent.　盛会 *seikai* successful meeting.　全盛 *zensei* height of prosperity.　盛夏 *seika* midsummer.

#842 漁	14 strokes	氵　沪　沿　漁　漁　漁

ON　GYO, RYŌ fishing

漁業 *gyogyō* fishing industry.　漁船 *gyosen* fishing boat.　漁港

gyokō fishing port.　漁場 *gyojō* fishing ground.　大漁 *tairyō* large catch.　漁師 *ryōshi* fisherman.

#843 鉱	13 strokes	ハ　　ケ　　金　　金'　　鉱　　鉱

ON　　KŌ ore

鉱業 *kōgyō* mining industry.　鉱山 *kōzan* mine.　鉱物 *kōbutsu* mineral.　金鉱 *kinkō* gold mine.　採鉱 *saikō* mining.

#844 炭	9 strokes	'　　山　　凵　　炭　　炭　　炭

kun　　*sumi* charcoal

炭 *sumi* charcoal.　炭火 *sumibi* charcoal fire.

ON　　TAN charcoal

石炭 *sekitan* coal.　炭鉱 *tankō* coal mine.　炭素 *tanso* carbon.
炭酸水 *tansansui* carbonated water.

#845 銅	14 strokes	ハ　　ケ　　釒　　釘　　銅　　銅

ON　　DŌ copper

銅 *dō* copper.　銅山 *dōzan* copper mine.　赤銅 *shakudō* alloy of copper and gold.　赤銅色 *shakudōiro* brown.　銅像 *dōzō* bronze statue.

#846 鋼	16 strokes	ケ　　釘　　鈿　　鋼　　鋼　　鋼

kun　　*hagane* steel

鋼 *hagane* steel.　鋼色 *haganeiro* steel blue.

ON　　KŌ steel

鉄鋼業 *tekkōgyō* iron and steel industry.　鋼鉄 *kōtetsu* steel.　鋼管 *kōkan* steel tube.　鋼材 *kōzai* steel materials.

#847 造	10 strokes	广　　屮　　告　　告　　造　　造

kun　　*tsuku(ru)* build, construct

造る *tsukuru* build (a ship).

ON   ZŌ build, construct

造船業 *zōsengyō* shipbuilding industry.   製造 ‹v› *seizō* manufacture.   改造 ‹v› *kaizō* reconstruction.   木造家屋 *mokuzō kaoku*
wooden house.   造花 *zōka* artificial flower.

#848 築	16 strokes	⺮	⺮	筑	筑	筞	築

kun   *kizu(ku)* build, construct Ir. *tsuki(yama)**

築く *kizuku* build (a school building).   築山 *tsukiyama** mound.

ON   CHIKU build, construct

建築 ‹v› *kenchiku* architecutre, building.   増築 ‹v› *zōchiku* extending
a building.   改築 ‹v› *kaichiku* rebuilding.   築港工事 *chikkō kōji* harbor works.   新築の *shinchiku no* newly-constructed.

#849 設	11 strokes	二	言	訁	訳	設	設

kun   *mō(keru)* establish, set up

設ける *mōkeru* establish (a branch office).

ON   SETSU establish, set up

建設業 *kensetsugyō* construction industry.   設立 ‹v› *setsuritsu* establishment.   設計 ‹v› *sekkei* plan, design.   設備 ‹v› *setsubi* equipment,
facilities.   増設 ‹v› *zōsetsu* establishing more (halls).

#850 械	11 strokes	十	木	杚	枅	械	械

ON   KAI machine

機械 *kikai* machine.   機械産業 *kikai sangyō* machinery industry.
機械化 ‹v› *kikaika* mechanization.   通信機械 *tsūshin kikai* communication equipment.   機械技師 *kikai gishi* mechanical engineer.

#851 密	11 strokes	宀	宀	空	宓	密	密

ON   MITSU minute, fine; close, dense; secret

精密機械 *seimitsu kikai* precision machinery.   密度 *mitsudo* density.
密林 *mitsurin* jungle.   機密書類 *kimitsu shorui* secret documents.

#852 織	18 strokes	乡　糸　紀　紵　織　織

kun   *o(ru)* weave
織る *oru* weave. 織物 *orimono* textiles. 絹織物 *kinuorimono* silk fabric. 織物工業 *orimono kōgyō* textile industry.

ON   SHOKU, SHIKI weave
織工 *shokkō* weaver. 組織 ⟨v⟩ *soshiki* organization.

#853 染	9 strokes	ヽ　氵　氿　染　染　染

kun   *so(meru)* dye; *so(maru)* be dyed; *shi(miru)* soak into; *shi(mi)* stain. 染める *someru* dye (the cloth red). 染まる *somaru* be dyed (black). 染みる *shimiru* soak into (the soil). 染み *shimi* stain.

ON   SEN dye, stain
染料 *senryō* dyes. 染色工場 *senshoku kōjō* dye works. 感染 ⟨v⟩ *kansen* infection. 伝染病 *densenbyō* communicable disease.

#854 燃	16 strokes	' 火 灯 炒 燃 燃

kun   *mo(eru)* burn; *mo(yasu)* burn
燃える *moeru* burn. 燃やす *moyasu* burn (fallen leaves).

ON   NEN burn
燃料 *nenryō* fuel. 燃焼 ⟨v⟩ *nenshō* combustion. 再燃 ⟨v⟩ *sainen* reignition. 不燃性の *funensei no* nonflammable.

#855 豊	13 strokes	冂　曲　曲　曹　曹　豊

kun   *yuta(ka)* abundant
豊かな *yutaka na* abundant (crops).

ON   HŌ abundant
豊富な *hōfu na* abundant. 豊漁 *hōryō* good catch of fish. 豊年 *hōnen* year of abundance. 豊作 *hōsaku* good harvest.

経済	keizai	economy
財界	zaikai	financial world
資本	shihon	capital
資源	shigen	resources
生産‹v›	seisan	production
産業革命	sangyō kakumei	industrial revolution
需要	juyō	demand
供給‹v›	kyōkyū	supply
進歩‹v›	shinpo	advance, progress
増加‹v›	zōka	increase
減少‹v›	genshō	decrease
拡張‹v›	kakuchō	extention, expansion
縮小‹v›	shukushō	reduction
従事‹v›	jūji	being engaged
農業	nōgyō	agriculture
肥・肥やし	koe/koyashi	manure
化学肥料	kagaku hiryō	chemical fertilizer
灰	hai	ash
石灰	sekkai	lime
盛んな	sakan na	prosperous, energetic
盛大な	seidai na	grand, magnificent
漁業	gyogyō	fishing industry
鉱業	kōgyō	mining industry
炭	sumi	charcoal
石炭	sekitan	coal
銅	dō	copper
鋼	hagane	steel
鉄鋼業	tekkōgyō	iron and steel industry
造船業	zōsengyō	shipbuilding industry
建築‹v›	kenchiku	architecture, building
建設業	kensetsugyō	construction industry
機械産業	kikai sangyō	machinery industry
精密機械	seimitsu kikai	precision machinery
織物工業	orimono kōgyō	textile industry
織工	shokkō	weaver
染色工場	senshoku kōjō	dye works

燃料	*nenryō*	fuel
豊かな	*yutaka na*	abundant
豊富な	*hōfu na*	abundant

■ III. Reading Exercises 40 ■

Read and translate the following.

1. 近年、中国の**経済**は著しく**進歩**した。
2. ニューヨークは**財界**の中心である。
3. かれは危険な事業に多くの**資本を投資**した。
4. この国は**天然資源**が豊かである。
5. 石油の**豊富**な国家が世界各国に**燃料を供給**している。
6. 人口が**増**えて、住宅の**需要**が**増加**した。
7. 工場は品物の**需要**が**減**ったので、**生産を減少**した。
8. 市はやっと道路の**拡張工事**に乗り出した。
9. 商業が進むに**従**って、市民の**生活水準**が向上した。
10. **造船業**が下り坂になり、**従業員**の**縮小**が行われた。
11. この村の住民は**農業**か**漁業**に**従事**している。
12. **農産物**の成長を助けるために、**化学肥料**や**石灰**や**漁肥**などが使われる。
13. **鉱業**が**盛**んなその地方は鉄や**銅**や**石炭**などの**産地**として知られている。
14. この町は**鉄鋼業**が**盛**んであり、工場はすべて近代的**設備**を備えている。
15. **建設業**は五十年代の日本の復興に大切な役目を果たした。
16. 日本製の**精密機械**は外国市場で**需要**が高い。
17. 当地の主な**産業**は**織物工業**で、特に**絹織物**は有名である。
18. **染色工場**の背後に大きい倉庫を**建築**している。
19. **築港工事**が終わって、**盛大**な祝典を行った。
20. 優れた技術や新しい**機械**の発明が**産業革命**をもたらした。

Trade

■ I. Reference ■

#856 易	8 strokes	丿 冂 日 尸 匂 易

kun   *yasa(shii)* easy
易しい *yasashii* easy (problem).

ON   EKI exchange; divination; I easy
交易 ⟨v⟩ *kōeki* trade.   易者 *ekisha* fortuneteller.   安易な *an'i na* easy (life).   容易に *yōi ni* easily.

#857 貿	12 strokes	⺋ ⺌ ⺈ 卯 留 貿

ON   BŌ trade, exchange
貿易 ⟨v⟩ *bōeki* trade.   貿易港 *bōekikō* trade port.   保護貿易 *hogo-bōeki* protective trade.   貿易協定 *bōeki kyōtei* trade agreement. 貿易黒字 *bōeki kuroji* trade surplus.

#858 由	5 strokes	丨 冂 巾 庘 由

kun   *yoshi* reason
病気の由 *byōki no yoshi* due to illness.   知る由もない *shiru yoshi mo nai* no way of knowing.

ON   YU, YŪ, [YUI] reason, means
自由 *jiyū* freedom.   自由貿易 *jiyū bōeki* free trade.   理由 *riyū* reason.   経由 ⟨v⟩ *keiyu* going by way (of).   ハワイ経由で *Hawai keiyu de* via Hawaii.   由来 ⟨v⟩ *yurai* origin, source.

#859 輸	16 strokes	冂 亘 軒 軡 輪 輸

ON   YU transport
輸入 ⟨v⟩ *yunyū* import.   輸出 ⟨v⟩ *yushutsu* export.   輸入品 *yunyūhin* imports.   密輸入品 *mitsuyunyūhin* smuggled goods.   輸送 ⟨v⟩ *yusō* transport.   空輸 ⟨v⟩ *kūyu* air transport.

#860 径	8 strokes ⁄ 彳 徉 径 径 径

ON KEI path; diameter
径路 *keiro* route, channel.　情報径路 *jōhō keiro* channel of information.　直径 *chokkei* diameter.　半径 *hankei* radius.

#861 制	8 strokes ⁄ 㐃 缶 缶 制 制

ON SEI system; regulations
制度 *seido* system.　会員制 *kaiinsei* membership system.　制作 ‹v› *seisaku* production (in arts).　制定 ‹v› *seitei* establishment (of rules).

#862 限	9 strokes ⁊ 阝 阝ㄱ 阻 限 限

kun *kagi(ru)* limit
限る *kagiru* limit.　先着50人限り *senchaku gojūnin kagiri* limited to the 1st 50 customers.

ON GEN limit
制限 ‹v› *seigen* restriction.　輸入制限 *yunyū seigen* import restriction.　限度 *gendo* limit.　期限 *kigen* term.

#863 税	12 strokes ⼆ 千 禾 禾′ 秒 税

ON ZEI tax
税金 *zeikin* tax.　輸出税 *yushutsuzei* export duty.　物品税 *buppinzei* excise tax.　所得税 *shotokuzei* income tax.　課税 ‹v› *kazei* taxation.

#864 関	14 strokes 冂 冂ⁱ 門 門 閂 関

kun *seki* barrier
関所 *sekisho* barrier, check point.

ON KAN barrier; relate
関税 *kanzei* tariff.　関税制度 *kanzei seido* tariff system.　税関 *zeikan* customs.　機関 *kikan* engine; organ; organization.　関心 *kanshin* interest.　関する *kansuru* relate to.

#865 申	5 strokes	丨 冂 冃 日 申

kun *mō(su)* call, appeal

申す *mōsu* call, appeal　申し訳 *mōshiwake* apology, excuse.　申し立て *mōshitate* allegation.

ON SHIN call, appeal

申告 ⟨v⟩ *shinkoku* report (to the authorities).　税関申告書 *zeikan shinkokusho* customs declaration.　申告納税 *shinkoku nōzei* payment by self-assessment.　答申書 *tōshinsho* report of an inquiry.

#866 続	13 strokes	纟 糸 紵 紵 続 続

kun *tsuzu(ku)* continue; *tsuzu(keru)* continue

続く *tsuzuku* continue.　続ける *tsuzukeru* continue (the work).　手続き *tetsuzuki* procedure.　入国手続き *nyūkoku tetsuzuki* formalities for entry.

ON ZOKU continue

続出 ⟨v⟩ *zokushutsu* successive occurrence.　続行 ⟨v⟩ *zokkō* continuation.　相続税 *sōzokuzei* inheritance tax.　続編 *zokuhen* sequel.

#867 接	11 strokes	扌 扩 护 接 接 接

kun *tsu(gu)* join together

接ぐ *tsugu* join (A to B).　骨を接ぐ *hone o tsugu* set a broken bone.

ON SETSU touch, contact

直接税 *chokusetsuzei* direct tax.　間接税 *kansetsuzei* indirect tax.　接近 ⟨v⟩ *sekkin* approach.　接続 ⟨v⟩ *setsuzoku* connection.　面接 ⟨v⟩ *mensetsu* interview.　接収 ⟨v⟩ *sesshū* confiscation.

#868 無	12 strokes	𠂉 𠂊 無 無 無 無

kun *na(i)* not be

無い *nai* not exist, not have

ON   MU, BU (prefix) un-, without, -less

無税品 *muzeihin* duty-free goods.   無料の *muryō no* free of charge.   無視 ‹v› *mushi* neglect.   有無 *umu* existence; yes or no. 無事に *buji ni* safely.   不器用な *bukiyō na* awkward, clumsy.

■ II. Vocabulary

貿易	*bōeki*	trade
自由貿易	*jiyū bōeki*	free trade
保護貿易	*hogo bōeki*	protective trade
貿易協定	*bōeki kyōtei*	trade agreement
輸入 ‹v›	*yunyū*	import
輸出 ‹v›	*yushutsu*	export
密輸入品	*mitsuyunyūhin*	smuggled goods
径路	*keiro*	route, channel
制度	*seido*	system
制限 ‹v›	*seigen*	restriction
税金	*zeikin*	tax
直接税	*chokusetsuzei*	direct tax
間接税	*kansetsuzei*	indirect tax
関税	*kanzei*	tariff
税関	*zeikan*	customs
申告 ‹v›	*shinkoku*	report (to the authorities)
手続き	*tetsuzuki*	procedure
入国手続き	*nyūkoku tetsuzuki*	formalities for entry
続出 ‹v›	*zokushutsu*	successive occurrence
無税品	*muzeihin*	duty-free goods

■ III. Reading Exercises 41

Read and translate the following.

1. 日本は世界の多くの国と**貿易**を行っている。
2. 資源や原料を外国から**輸入**して、製品や技術などを海外へ**輸出**する。
3. この町は**貿易港**で知られ、**輸入品**の高級店が多い。

4. **密輸入品**が不正な**径路**を経て、安値で市場に出回っている。

5. 材木を積んだ貨物船がハワイ**経由**で今朝入港した。

6. **税金**には**直接税**と**間接税**がある。

7. **関税**は外国から**輸入**される品物に対して国家が**課税**する。

8. **関税制度**の改革を望む声が高まっている。

9. **税関**で**入国手続**きを済ませてから、荷物の検査がある。

10. 以前、悪質な**輸入品**が続出したことがある。

11. **税関**で外国で買った商品を**申告**した。

12. 空港の店で**無税品**を売っている。

13. 世界経済を発展させるため、**自由貿易**は必要である。

14. **輸入**を**制限**したり、特別な**関税**をかけるのは**保護貿易**である。

15. 二国間で市場を自由に開くための**貿易協定**が発足した。

Company and Bank

| #869 社 | 7 strokes | ` ゥ ラ ネ ネ 社 社 |

kun *yashiro* Shinto shrine
社 *yashiro* Shinto shrine.

ON SHA company; Shinto shrine
会社 *kaisha* company. 新聞社 *shinbunsha* newspaper company.
社長 *shachō* company president. 社員 *shain* employee. 本社
honsha head office. 支社 *shisha* branch office. 社会 *shakai* society. 神社 *jinja* Shinto shrine.

| #870 営 | 12 strokes | ` ` ` ` ` ` 営 営 営 営 |

kun *itona(mu)* run, operate
営む *itonamu* run (a hotel).

ON EI run, operate
経営 ⟨v⟩ *keiei* management. 経営者側 *keieishagawa* management (of
a company). 営業 ⟨v⟩ *eigyō* business. 国営 *kokuei* government
management. 民営 *minei* private management.

| #871 務 | 11 strokes | マ 予 矛 矛 務 務 |

kun *tsuto(meru)* work, serve
務める *tsutomeru* work, serve (as a guide).

ON MU work, serve
事務 *jimu* clerical work. 事務所 *jimusho* office. 義務 *gimu* duty.
公務員 *kōmuin* civil servant.

| #872 勤 | 12 strokes | 艹 苎 节 堇 勤 勤 |

kun *tsuto(meru)* be employed
勤める *tsutomeru* be employed (in a bank). 勤め先 *tsutomesaki*
one's workplace. 勤め人 *tsutomenin* salaried man.

ON   KIN, [GON] be employed
勤務 ‹v› *kinmu* being employed.   勤務時間 *kinmu jikan* office hours.
出勤 ‹v› *shukkin* attending at one's office.   欠勤 ‹v› *kekkin* absence
from office.   勤行 ‹v› *gongyō* Buddhist service.

#873 仕	5 strokes	ノ イ 仁 什 仕

kun   *tsuka(eru)* serve
仕える *tsukaeru* serve (a person).

ON   SHI, [JI] serve, do
仕事 *shigoto* work, job.   仕方 *shikata* way, means.   仕組み *shiku-mi* device.   仕上げる *shiageru* finish.   給仕 ‹v› *kyūji* waiting on;
page.

#874 職	18 strokes	丁 王 耳 耶 職 職

ON   SHOKU occupation, job
職 *shoku* job.   職業 *shokugyō* occupation.   職員 *shokuin* staff.
職場 *shokuba* workplace.   職務 *shokumu* duty.   辞職 ‹v› *jishoku*
resignation.   公職 *kōshoku* public office.

#875 就	12 strokes	亠 亨 京 京 尌 就

kun   *tsu(ku)* take up, engage
就く *tsuku* take up (a job).

ON   SHŪ, [JU] take up, engage
就職 ‹v› *shūshoku* finding employment.   就学 ‹v› *shūgaku* entering/
attending school.   成就 ‹v› *jōju* accomplishment (of one's purpose).

#876 係	9 strokes	イ 仁 伫 侟 係 係

kun   *kaka(ru)* related to; *kakari* in charge
係る *kakaru* (a problem) related to (safety).   係り *kakari* person
in charge.   係員 *kakariin* person in charge.

ON   KEI related to; in charge

関係 ⟨v⟩ *kankei* relation.   関係者 *kankeisha* persons concerned. 利害関係 *rigai kankei* interst, concern. 友好関係 *yūkō kankei* friendly relations.

#877

担   8 strokes   一　 寸　 扌　 扣　 扣　 担

kun   *katsu(gu), nina(u)* carry on the shoulder; bear

担ぐ *katsugu* carry (a load) on one's shoulder. 担う *ninau* carry (a load) on one's shoulder; bear (responsibility).

ON   TAN bear

担当 ⟨v⟩ *tantō* being in charge. 担当者 *tantōsha* person in charge. 負担 ⟨v⟩ *futan* burden, charge. 担保 *tanpo* mortgage, collateral.

#878

秘   10 strokes   二　 千　 禾　 秒　 秘　 秘

kun   *hi(meru)* keep secret

秘める *himeru* keep (a thing) secret.

ON   HI secret

秘書 *hisho* secretary. 秘密 *himitsu* secret. 極秘 *gokuhi* top secret. 神秘な *shinpi na* mysterious.

#879

整   16 strokes   𠚍　 申　 敕　 敕　 整　 整

kun   *totono(eru)* arrange, adjust; *totono(u)* be arranged, adjusted

整える *totonoeru* arrange (one's room), adjust (one's dress). 整う *totonou* be arranged, adjusted.

ON   SEI arrange, adjust

整理 ⟨v⟩ *seiri* arrangement, adjustment. 調整 ⟨v⟩ *chōsei* adjustment. 整列 ⟨v⟩ *seiretsu* standing in a row.

#880

処   5 strokes   ノ　 ク　 久　 処　 処

ON   SHO manage, deal with

処理 ⟨v⟩ *shori* management, disposition. 処分 ⟨v⟩ *shobun* disposition. 処置 ⟨v⟩ *shochi* treatment, measures. 処方 ⟨v⟩ *shohō* prescription.

#881	
労	7 strokes 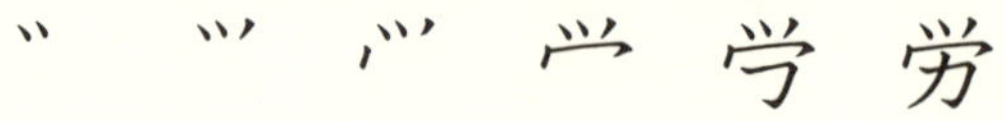

ON RŌ labor, toil

労力 *rōryoku* labor; effort. 苦労‹v› *kurō* hardship. 心労 *shinrō* worry, concern. 過労‹v› *karō* overwork.

#882	
働	13 strokes 

kun *hatara(ku)* work

働く *hataraku* work. 働き手 *hatarakite* worker.

ON DŌ work

労働‹v› *rōdō* work, labor. 労働組合 *rōdō kumiai* labor union. 労働者 *rōdōsha* worker, laborer. 労働力 *rōdōryoku* manpower.

#883	
創	12 strokes 

ON SŌ creation

創立‹v› *sōritsu* foundation. 創立記念日 *sōritsu kinenbi* anniversary of the founding. 創業‹v› *sōgyō* inauguration (of an enterprise). 創始者 *sōshisha* founder. 独創的な *dokusōteki na* creative.

#884	
旧	5 strokes 

ON KYŪ old, former

旧式の *kyūshiki no* old-fashioned. 旧制度 *kyūseido* old system. 復旧工事 *fukkyū kōji* repair work. 旧友 *kyūyū* old friend.

#885	
型	9 strokes 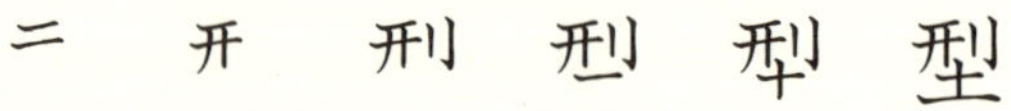

kun *kata* type, model

型 *kata* type, model. 大型 *ōgata* large size. 旧型 *kyūgata* old model. 標準型 *hyōjungata* standard type.

ON KEI type, model

原型 *genkei* prototype. 典型的な *tenkeiteki na* typical.

| #886 模 | 14 strokes | 十　朾　栌　楼　模　模 |

ON　MO, BO model, copy, imitate
模型 *mokei* model.　模造品 *mozōhin* imitation.　模様 *moyō* design, pattern; appearance.　規模 #973 *kibo* scale.

| #887 預 | 13 strokes | マ　予　予　预　預　預 |

kun　*azu(keru)* deposit, entrust; *azu(karu)* receive for safekeeping
預ける *azukeru* deposit (money in a bank).　預かる *azukaru* receive (goods) for safekeeping.

ON　YO deposit, entrust
預金 ⟨v⟩ *yokin* bank deposit.　定期預金 *teiki yokin* time deposit.
預金口座 *yokin kōza* bank account.

| #888 帳 | 11 strokes | 冂　忛　帳　帳　帳　帳 |

ON　CHŌ notebook
通帳 *tsūchō* passbook, bankbook.　手帳 *techō* memobook.　電話帳 *denwachō* telephone book.　帳消し *chōkeshi* cancellation of a debt.

| #889 借 | 10 strokes | 亻　仁　伷　供　借　借 |

kun　*ka(riru)* borrow, rent
借りる *kariru* borrow, rent.　借り *kari* debt, loan.

ON　SHAKU borrow, rent
借金 ⟨v⟩ *shakkin* bebt, loan.　借用 ⟨v⟩ *shakuyō* borrowing.　前借 ⟨v⟩ *zenshaku* borrowing in advace.　借家 *shakuya* rented house.

| #890 貸 | 12 strokes | 仁　代　代　伐　侪　貸 |

kun　*ka(su)* lend, rent out
貸す *kasu* lend, rent out.　貸し借り *kashikari* lending and borrowing.　貸家 *kashiya* house for rent.

ON　　TAI lend, rent out

貸借 ‹v› *taishaku* lending and borrowing; debit and credit.　貸借期間 *taishaku kikan* term of a loan.　賃貸 ‹v› *chintai* lease, renting.

#891　返　　7 strokes　　一　厂　万　仮　返　返

kun　　*kae(su)*, *kae(ru)* return

返す *kaesu* return (one's debt).　送り返す *okurikaesu* send back.
返る *kaeru* return (to one's old job).

ON　　HEN return

返済 ‹v› *hensai* repayment, reimbursement.　返事 ‹v› *henji* reply.
返答 ‹v› *hentō* answer.　返信 *henshin* reply letter.

#892　複　　14 strokes　　ラ　ネ　衤　衤　衤　複

ON　　FUKU double, duplicate

複利 *fukuri* compound interest.　複写 ‹v› *fukusha* reproduction.
複数の *fukusū no* plural.　複雑な *fukuzatsu na* complicated.

#893　株　　10 strokes　　十　木　杧　杜　株　株

kun　　*kabu* stock; stump

株 *kabu* stock.　株式市場 *kabushiki shijō* stock market.　株主
kabunushi shareholder.　株式会社 *kabushiki-gaisha* joint-stock cor-
poration.　切り株 *kirikabu* stump.

#894　勧　　13 strokes　　ヒ　ケ　乍　隹　勧　勧

kun　　*susu(meru)* advise, recommend

勧める *susumeru* advise (a person to do), recommend (oil stocks).

ON　　KAN advise, recommend

勧告 ‹v› *kankoku* advice, recommendation.　勧業博覧会 *kangyō
hakurankai* industrial exhibition.

#895　銭　　14 strokes　　乍　牟　釒　銈　銭　銭

kun　　*zeni* money

小銭 *kozeni* small changes.　小銭入れ *kozeniire* change purse.

ON   SEN money
金銭 *kinsen* money.   金銭上の *kinsenjō no* monetary.   口銭 *kōsen* commmission.   悪銭 *akusen* ill-gotten money.

#896 穴	5 strokes	` 宀 宀 宀 穴

kun   *ana* hole; deficit
穴 *ana* hole.   穴をあける *ana o akeru* make a hole (in one's capital).   落とし穴 *otoshiana* pitfall, trap.   穴蔵 *anagura* cellar.

ON   KETSU hole
穴居 ‹v› *kekkyo* cave dwelling.   墓穴 #997 *boketsu* grave.

#897 捨	11 strokes	扌 扩 抖 捨 捨 捨

kun   *su(teru)* throw away
捨てる *suteru* throw away.   見捨てる *misuteru* forsake.   捨て値 *sutene* sacrifice price.   捨て金 *sutegane* wasted money.

ON   SHA throw away
四捨五入 ‹v› *shishagonyū* rounding to the nearest whole number.
喜捨 ‹v› *kisha* contribution, donation.

#898 余	7 strokes	ノ 人 合 今 余 余

kun   *ama(ru)* be left over; *ama(su)* leave over, save
余る *amaru* be left over.   余す *amasu* save (money).   余り *amari* remainder.   千円余り *sen'en amari* more than 1,000 yen.

ON   YO surplus
余分な *yobun na* surplus.   千余円 *sen-yo-en* 1,000 odd yen.   余地 *yochi* room, margin.   残余 *zanyo* remainder.   余計な *yokei na* extra.

■ II. Vocabulary ■

会社	*kaisha*	company
新聞社	*shinbunsha*	newspaper company
経営 ‹v›	*keiei*	management
事務所	*jimusho*	office

勤務‹v›	*kinmu*	being employed
仕事	*shigoto*	work, job
職業	*shokugyō*	occupation
就職‹v›	*shūshoku*	finding employment
係員	*kakariin*	person in charge
関係者	*kankeisha*	persons concerned
担当‹v›	*tantō*	being in charge
秘書	*hisho*	secretary
整理‹v›	*seiri*	arrangement, adjustment
処理‹v›	*shori*	management, disposition
労力	*rōryoku*	labor; effort
働き手	*hatarakite*	worker
労働‹v›	*rōdō*	work, labor
創立‹v›	*sōritsu*	foundation
旧式の	*kyūshiki no*	old-fashioned
型	*kata*	type, model
模型	*mokei*	model
預金‹v›	*yokin*	bank deposit
通帳	*tsūchō*	passbook, bankbook
複利	*fukuri*	compound interest
借金‹v›	*shakkin*	debt
貸し借り	*kashikari*	lending and borrowing
貸借‹v›	*taishaku*	lending and borrowing; debit and credit
返済‹v›	*hensai*	repayment, reimbursement
株	*kabu*	stock; stump
勧告‹v›	*kankoku*	advice, rcommendation
小銭	*kozeni*	small changes
金銭	*kinsen*	money
穴	*ana*	hole; deficit
捨て値	*sutene*	sacrifice price
四捨五入‹v›	*shisha gonyū*	rounding to the nearest whole number
余り	*amari*	remainder
余分な	*yobun na*	surplus

Read and translate the following.

1. 長男は銀座で飲食店を**経営**し、次男は九州で**会社**に**勤務**している。

2. あなたはどんな**職業**に**就**きたいのですか。

3. 姉の息子は今年大学を卒業して、**新聞社**に**就職**した。

4. その**事務所**ではまだ**旧式**の器械を使っている。

5. 午前中にこの資料を**整理**して下さい。

6. 社長**秘書**は自分の**仕事**をうまく**処理**している。

7. **係員**の案内で新しい機械の**模型**を見て回った。

8. その事なら、人事課の山田さんが**担当**しています。

9. **労力**が不足して、生産が減少した。

10. **労働組合**は**経営者側**に賃金の値上げを要求した。

11. 会社の**創立**五十周年を祝って、盛大なパーティーが開かれた。

12. あの人はあちこちの銀行に金を**預**けて、**通帳**を何冊も持っている。

13. この**定期預金**は6パーセントの**複利**を生む。

14. 私の知人は銀行から金を**借**りて、商売を始めた。

15. かれは元手に**穴**をあけて、**借金**の**返済**に困っている。

16. 友達の間では**金銭**の貸し借り（**貸借**）をしない方がいい。

17. **余分**な資本があったので、友人の**勧告**に従って**株**に投資した。

18. 品物を**捨**て値で売って大きな損をした。

19. このレポートの数字はすべて**四捨五入**してあります。

18

****

Government

Diet

■ I. Reference ■

#899 政	9 strokes	丁　下　正　正　政　政

kun　*matsurigoto* administration, politics
政 *matsurigoto* state affairs, politics.

ON　SEI, [SHŌ] administration, politics
政府 *seifu* government.　政界 *seikai* political world.　政局 *seikyoku* political situation.　行政 *gyōsei* administration.

#900 治	8 strokes	冫　氵　氵　氵　治　治

kun　*osa(meru)* govern; *osa(maru)* be governed; *nao(su)* cure; *nao(ru)* be cured
治める *osameru* govern (a country).　治まる *osamaru* be governed.
治す *naosu* cure (a disease).　治る *naoru* be cured.

ON　JI, CHI government; peace; healing
政治 *seiji* politics, government.　民主政治 *minshu seiji* democratic government.　政治家 *seijika* statesman.　明治時代 *Meiji jidai* Meiji era.　治安 *chian* public peace.　全治 ⟨v⟩ *zenchi* complete recovery.

#901 王	4 strokes	一　丁　干　王

ON　Ō king
王 *ō* king.　王政 *ōsei* monarchy.　女王 *joō* queen.　法王 *hōō* pope.　発明王 *hatsumeiō* king of inventors.

#902 皇	9 strokes	ノ ſ ⼧ 白 阜 皇

ON   KŌ, Ō emperor Ir. *(ten)nō**
皇居 *kōkyo* Imperial Palace.　皇室 *kōshitsu* Imperial Family.　皇子 *ōji* prince.　天皇 *tennō** emperor.

#903 后	6 strokes	ノ 厂 厂 斤 后 后

ON   KŌ empress
皇后 *kōgō* empress.　皇太后 *kōtaigō* empress dowager.

#904 陛	10 strokes	⼄ ⻖ ⻖ 陛 陛 陛

ON   HEI steps of the throne
陛下 *heika* His/Her Majesty.　天皇陛下 *Tennō-heika* His Majesty the Emperor.　両陛下 *ryōheika* Their Majesties.　今上陛下 *kinjō-heika* reigning emperor.

#905 昭	9 strokes	丨 冂 日⁊ 日刀 昭 昭

ON   SHŌ bright
昭和時代 *Shōwa jidai* Showa era (1926-1989).　昭和元年 *Shōwa gannen* 1st year of the Showa.

#906 統	12 strokes	⼳ ⾱ 紆 紵 紵 統

kun   *su(beru)* control, govern
統べる *suberu* govern (a country).

ON   TŌ control, govern; lineage
大統領 *daitōryō* president (of the U.S.A.).　統一 ⟨v⟩ *tōitsu* unity. 統制 ⟨v⟩ *tōsei* control.　統計 *tōkei* statistics.　伝統 *dentō* tradition. 正統の *seitō no* legitimate; orthodox.

#907 党	10 strokes	⼂ ⺌ ⺌ 兴 党 党

ON   TŌ party
政党 *seitō* political party.　政党政治 *seitō seiji* party politics.

民主党 *Minshutō* Democratic Party.　共和党 *Kyōwatō* Republican Party.　革新党 *kakushintō* reformist party.　野党 *yatō* opposition party.　党首 *tōshu* party leader.　党員 *tōin* party member.

#908 議	20 strokes	言 訂 詳 詳 議 議

ON　GI debate, discussion

議会 *gikai* Diet, Congress, Parliament.　国会議員 *kokkai giin* Diet member.　参議院 *Sangiin* House of Councilors.　議決 ‹v›*giketsu* vote, decision.　会議 *kaigi* conference.　議論 ‹v›*giron* discussion.

#909 衆	12 strokes	宀 血 卆 尜 尜 衆

ON　SHŪ, [SHU] multitude

衆議院 *Shūgiin* House of Representatives.　合衆国 *gasshūkoku* United States (of America).　大衆 *taishū* masses (of people).　群衆 *gunshū* crowd.　衆生 *shujō* living things.

#910 委	8 strokes	二 千 禾 禾 委 委

ON　I entrust

委員 *iin* committee member.　委員会 *iinkai* committee.　委員長 *iinchō* chairman of a committee.　委細 *isai* particulars, details.

#911 票	11 strokes	一 一 西 覀 票 票

ON　HYŌ ballot, vote, slip of paper

投票 ‹v›*tōhyō* voting.　票決 ‹v›*hyōketsu* decision by vote.　開票 ‹v›*kaihyō* counting the votes.　得票数 *tokuhyōsū* number of votes obtained.　伝票 *denpyō* bill, slip.

#912 挙	10 strokes	丶 丷 癶 兴 誉 挙

kun　*a(geru)* raise; perform; arrest

挙げる *ageru* raise (a hand); perform (a ceremony); arrest (a gang)

ON　KYO raise; perform; arrest

選挙 ‹v›*senkyo* election.　挙手 ‹v›*kyoshu* raising one's hand.　挙行 ‹v›*kyokō* performance.　検挙 ‹v›*kenkyo* arrest.

#913 閣	14 strokes	尸 門 門 閉 閉 閣

ON KAKU cabinet; grand building

内閣 *naikaku* cabinet. 閣議 *kakugi* cabinet meeting. 組閣 ‹v›
sokaku organizing a cabinet. 金閣寺 *Kinkakuji* Kinkakuji
Temple.

#914 臣	7 strokes	丨 匚 匚 臣 臣 臣

ON SHIN, JIN subject, retainer

大臣 *daijin* cabinet minister. 総理大臣 *Sōri daijin* Prime Minister.
国務大臣 *kokumu daijin* minister of state. 文部大臣 *monbu daijin*
minister of education. 外務大臣 *gaimu daijin* minister of foreign
affairs. 日本臣民 *Nihon shinmin* Japanese subject.

#915 省	9 strokes	丿 小 少 少 省 省

kun *kaeri(miru)* reflect (on oneself); *habu(ku)* omit

省みる *kaerimiru* reflect on (one's conducts); omit (explanations).

ON SEI reflect (on oneself); SHŌ government ministry

大蔵省 *ōkurashō* Ministry of Finance. 運輸省 *unyushō* Ministry of
Transport. 自省 ‹v› *jisei* self-examination.

#916 官	8 strokes	丶 宀 宀 宀 官 官

ON KAN government, authorities

官庁 *kanchō* government office. 外交官 *gaikōkan* diplomat. 警官
keikan policeman. 教官 *kyōkan* instructor.

#917 権	15 strokes	十 柠 栌 栌 栌 権

ON KEN, [GON] authority, power; right

権利 *kenri* right. 人権 *jinken* human right. 政権 *seiken* political
power. 選挙権 *senkyoken* suffrage. 権化 *gonge* incarnation.

#918 基	11 strokes	一　廿　其　其　基　基

kun   *moto*, *motoi* base, foundation
基 *moto, motoi* foundation.   基づく *motozuku* be based on (the data).

ON   KI base, foundation
基本 *kihon* fundamentals.   基本的人権 *kihonteki jinken* fundamental human right.   基準 *kijun* standard.   基金 *kikin* fund.

#919 策	12 strokes	⺮　竹　笁　笁　第　策

ON   SAKU policy, plan, measure
政策 *seisaku* policy.   対策 *taisaku* countermeasure.   物価対策 *bukka taisaku* price policy.   具体策 *gutaisaku* concrete measure.

#920 任	6 strokes	ノ　イ　仁　仁　仟　任

kun   *maka(seru)*, *maka(su)* entrust
任せる・任す *makaseru/makasu* entrust (a matter to a person).

ON   NIN duty, office, commission
任命 ⟨v⟩ *ninmei* appointment.   任期 *ninki* term of office.   任務 *ninmu* duty.   辞任 ⟨v⟩ *jinin* resignation.   後任 *kōnin* successor.

#921 適	14 strokes	广　商　商　滴　滴　適

ON   TEKI fit, be suitable
適する *tekisuru* be suitable.   適任の *tekinin no* fitted (for).   適任者 *tekininsha* well-qualified person.   適用 ⟨v⟩ *tekiyō* application.   適度な *tekido na* moderate.   適当な *tekitō na* suitable.

#922 兼	10 strokes	丷　䒑　当　兼　兼　兼

kun   *ka(neru)* serve both; *-ka(neru)* cannot
兼ねる *kaneru* hold (an additional post).   待ち兼ねる *machikaneru* cannot wait.

ON   KEN serve both
兼任 ⟨v⟩ *kennin* holding an additional post.   首相兼外相 *shushō-*

ken-gaishō prime minister who is also the foreign minister.　兼業 ‹v› *kengyō* doing dual business.　兼用 ‹v› *kenyō* combined use.

#923 討	10 strokes	二　言　言　言　討　討

kun　*u(tsu)* attack
　　討つ *utsu* attack.　夜討ち *youchi* night attack.

ON　TŌ attack
　　討議 ‹v› *tōgi* discussion, debate.　討論 ‹v› *tōron* discussion, debate.
　　検討 ‹v› *kentō* examination, investigation.

#924 可	5 strokes	一　丁　可　可　可

ON　KA good; possible; approval
　　可決 ‹v› *kaketsu* approval, passing (a bill).　可能な *kanō na* possible.　不可能な *fukanō na* impossible.　可能性 *kanōsei* possibility.

#925 否	7 strokes	一　ア　不　不　否　否

kun　*ina* no, nay
　　否 *ina* no, nay.

ON　HI no, nay
　　否決 ‹v› *hiketsu* rejection (by vote).　可否 *kahi* aye or nay.　否定 ‹v› *hitei* negation.　真否 *shinpi* truth or falsehood.

#926 賛	15 strokes	二　ナ　夫夫　替　替　賛

ON　SAN agreement; praise
　　賛成 ‹v› *sansei* approval.　賛否 *sanpi* approval or disapproval.　賞賛 ‹v› *shōsan* praise.　賛美歌 *sanbika* hymn.

#927 反	4 strokes	一　厂　反　反

kun　*so(ru)*, *so(rasu)* bend
　　反る *soru* (boards) warp.　反らす *sorasu* bend (oneself backward).

ON　HAN, [HON] opposit, anti-; [TAN] (unit of land/cloth measurement)

反対 ‹v› *hantai* objection.　反論 ‹v› *hanron* counterargument.　反応 ‹v› *hannō** reaction.　反戦 *hansen* anti-war.　反物 *tanmono* dry goods.

#928 憲	16 strokes	宀 宀 宔 害 憲 憲

ON　　KEN constitution, law
憲法 *kenpō* constitution.　憲法改正 *kenpō kaisei* revision of the constitution.　立憲政治 *rikken seiji* constitutional government.

■ II. Vocabulary ■

政府	seifu	government
政治	seiji	politics, government
王	ō	king
王政	ōsei	Imperial Rule
天皇	tennō	emperor
皇后	kōgō	empress
陛下	heika	His/Her Majesty
昭和時代	Shōwa jidai	Showa era (1926-1989)
大統領	daitōryō	president
政党	seitō	political party
議会	gikai	Diet, Congress, Parliament
国会議員	kokkai giin	Diet member
衆議院	shūgiin	House of Representatives
参議院	sangiin	House of Councilors
委員会	iinkai	committee
投票 ‹v›	tōhyō	voting
選挙 ‹v›	senkyo	election
内閣	naikaku	cabinet
大臣	daijin	cabinet minister
総理大臣	Sōri daijin	Prime Minister
大蔵省	Ōkurashō	Ministry of Finance
官庁	kanchō	government office
外交官	gaikōkan	diplomat
権利	kenri	right
基本的人権	kihonteki jinken	fundamental human right

政策	*seisaku*	policy
任命‹v›	*ninmei*	appointment
適任者	*tekininsha*	well-qualified person
兼任‹v›	*kennin*	holding an additional post
討議‹v›	*tōgi*	discussion, debate
可決‹v›	*kaketsu*	approval, passing (a bill)
否決‹v›	*hiketsu*	rejection (by vote)
賛成‹v›	*sansei*	approval
反対‹v›	*hantai*	objection
憲法	*kenpō*	constitution

■ III. Reading Exercises 43 ■

Read and translate the following.

1. 国民は**政府**に清潔な**政治**を期待している。
2. 日本の**天皇**は国家のシンボルであり、**政治**には直接に関係しない。
3. 今日、**王政**を行っている国はほとんど無い。
4. **昭和時代**は千九百二十六年に始まり、六十余年も続いた。
5. あなたの支持する**政党**は**革新党**ですか。
6. アメリカ**合衆国**では、四年ごとに**大統領**の**選挙**が行われる。
7. 日本の**議会**は**衆議院**と**参議院**から成り、**国会議員**は国民によって選ばれる。
8. **内閣**は**総理大臣**とその他の**国務大臣**で組織する。
9. 村山氏は**大蔵省**に三十年勤務して去年引退した。
10. この近辺には**官庁**が集まっている。
11. 山中氏は**外交官**として長年の経験がある。
12. 二十才以上の男女全員に**投票**の**権利**がある。
13. **憲法**に**基**づいて、個人の**基本的人権**が保護されている。
14. 元学長の小川博士が**文部大臣**に**任命**された。
15. この仕事にはかれが最高の**適任者**だ。
16. 昨年の五月以来、**総理大臣**が**外務大臣**を**兼任**している。
17. **委員会**で経済**政策**を**討議**している。
18. **委員**の過半数が**物価対策**に反対した。
19. 法案は全員の**賛成**を得て**可決**された。
20. その提案は40対10で**否決**された。

Defense

■ I. Reference ■

#929

防 | 7 strokes | ⁷ 　 ⁷ 　 阝 　 阝⁻ 　 防 　 防

kun　*fuse(gu)* defend, prevent
防ぐ *fusegu* defend (one's country), prevent (pollution).

ON　BŌ defend, prevent
国防 *kokubō* national defense.　防衛 ⟨v⟩ *bōei* defense, protection.
防衛費 *bōeihi* defense expenses.　防止 ⟨v⟩ *bōshi* prevention.　予防 ⟨v⟩
yobō prevention (of diseases).

#930

軍 | 9 strokes | ′ 　 冖 　 冟 　 冒 　 宣 　 軍

ON　GUN army, troops
陸軍 *rikugun* army.　海軍 *kaigun* navy.　空軍 *kūgun* air force.
軍人 *gunjin* soldier.　将軍 *shōgun* general.　国連軍 *kokurengun*
United Nations forces.　軍備 *gunbi* armaments.

#931

隊 | 12 strokes | 阝 　 阝⁻ 　 阝⁻ 　 阝 　 隊 　 隊

ON　TAI troops, group
軍隊 *guntai* army, troops.　自衛隊 *Jieitai* Self-Defense Forces.　隊
員 *taiin* member (of the Force).　部隊 *butai* troops.　隊長 *taichō*
commander, captain.　楽隊 *gakutai* musical band.

#932

兵 | 7 strokes | ′ 　 亻 　 ┍ 　 斤 　 丘 　 兵

ON　HEI, HYŌ
兵隊 *heitai* soldier, airman, sailor.　兵卒 *heisotsu* private soldier.
海兵隊 *kaiheitai* marine corps.　志願兵 *shiganhei* volunteer.　兵器
heiki weapon.　兵力 *heiryoku* military force.

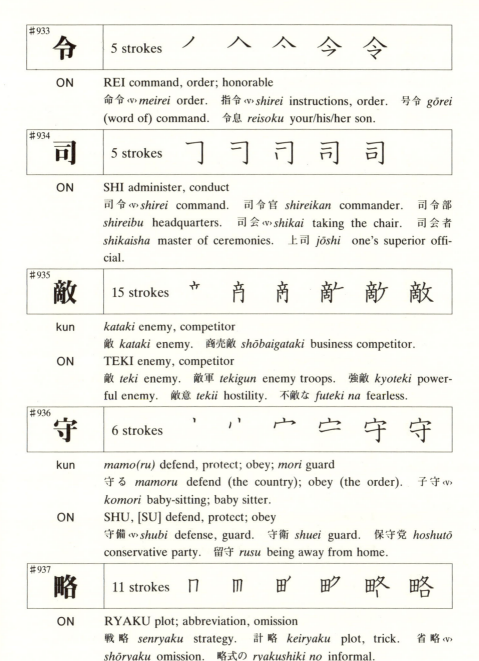

#933 令 5 strokes ノ 入 仒 今 令

ON REI command, order; honorable
命令 ⟨v⟩ *meirei* order.   指令 ⟨v⟩ *shirei* instructions, order.   号令 *gōrei*
(word of) command.   令息 *reisoku* your/his/her son.

#934 司 5 strokes ㇆ ㇆ 司 司 司

ON SHI administer, conduct
司令 ⟨v⟩ *shirei* command.   司令官 *shireikan* commander.   司令部
shireibu headquarters.   司会 ⟨v⟩ *shikai* taking the chair.   司会者
shikaisha master of ceremonies.   上司 *jōshi* one's superior official.

#935 敵 15 strokes 亠 甬 商 啇 敵 敵

kun *kataki* enemy, competitor
敵 *kataki* enemy.   商売敵 *shōbaigataki* business competitor.

ON TEKI enemy, competitor
敵 *teki* enemy.   敵軍 *tekigun* enemy troops.   強敵 *kyoteki* powerful enemy.   敵意 *tekii* hostility.   不敵な *futeki na* fearless.

#936 守 6 strokes ′ ⼧ 宀 宀 守 守

kun *mamo(ru)* defend, protect; obey; *mori* guard
守る *mamoru* defend (the country); obey (the order).   子守 ⟨v⟩
komori baby-sitting; baby sitter.

ON SHU, [SU] defend, protect; obey
守備 ⟨v⟩ *shubi* defense, guard.   守衛 *shuei* guard.   保守党 *hoshutō*
conservative party.   留守 *rusu* being away from home.

#937 略 11 strokes 冂 冊 田′ 田′ 畋 略

ON RYAKU plot; abbreviation, omission
戦略 *senryaku* strategy.   計略 *keiryaku* plot, trick.   省略 ⟨v⟩
shōryaku omission.   略式の *ryakushiki no* informal.

#938 勇	9 strokes	マ 丹 丹 甬 勇 勇

kun　isa(mu) be spirited; isa(mashii) brave
　　　勇む isamu be spirited.　勇ましい isamashii brave (soldier).

ON　YŪ brave
　　　勇士 yūshi brave soldier.　勇気 yūki courage.　勇退 ⟨v⟩ yūtai
　　　voluntary retirement.　勇断 ⟨v⟩ yūdan courageous decision.

#939 忠	8 strokes	丶 口 口 中 忠 忠

ON　CHŪ loyalty
　　　忠義 chūgi loyalty.　忠実な chūjitsu na faithful.　忠告 ⟨v⟩ chūkoku
　　　advice.　忠臣 chūshin loyal retainer.

#940 誠	13 strokes	言 訁 訂 訢 誠 誠

kun　makoto truth; sincerity
　　　誠 makoto truth; sincerity.　誠に makoto ni truly.

ON　SEI truth; sincerity
　　　忠誠 chūsei loyalty.　誠意 seii sincerity.　誠実な seijitsu na sin-
　　　cere.　誠心誠意 seishin seii in all sincerity.

#941 刀	2 strokes	フ 刀

kun　katana sword, blade Ir. (shi)nai*; (ta)chi*
　　　刀 katana sword.　竹刀 shinai* bamboo sword.　太刀 tachi* long
　　　sword.　助太刀 sukedachi assistance (in fight).

ON　TŌ sword, blade
　　　日本刀 Nihontō Japanese sword.　軍刀 guntō military sword.　木刀
　　　bokutō wooden sword.　名刀 meitō noted sword.

#942 乱	7 strokes	二 千 千 舌 舌 乱

kun　mida(reru) be disordered; mida(su) disturb
　　　乱れる midareru be disordered.　乱す midasu disturb (peace).

ON　RAN riot, disorder

内乱 *nairan* rebellion, civil war.　乱暴 ‹v› *ranbō* violence.　乱用 ‹v› *ranyō* abuse.　乱雑な *ranzatsu na* disorderly.

#943 責	11 strokes 一 十 圭 責 責 責

kun　*se(meru)* blame; torture

責める *semeru* blame; torture.　水責め *mizuzeme* torture by water.

ON　SEKI blame, burden

責任 *sekinin* responsibility.　責務 *sekimu* duty.　自責 *jiseki* self-reproach.　引責 ‹v› *inseki* assuming responsibility.

#944 班	10 strokes 一 丁 王 玗 玤 班

ON　HAN squad, group

班 *han* squad, group.　班長 *hanchō* squad/group leader.　取材班 *shuzaihan* reportage team.

■ II. Vocabulary ■

国防	*kokubō*	national defense
防衛費	*bōeihi*	defense expenses
陸軍	*rikugun*	army
海軍	*kaigun*	navy
空軍	*kūgun*	air force
軍隊	*guntai*	army, troops
自衛隊	*Jieitai*	Self-Defense Forces
兵隊	*heitai*	soldier, airman, sailor
志願兵	*shiganhei*	volunteer
命令 ‹v›	*meirei*	order
司令官	*shireikan*	commander
敵軍	*tekigun*	enemy troops
守備 ‹v›	*shubi*	defense, guard
戦略	*senryaku*	strategy
勇ましい	*isamashii*	brave
勇士	*yūshi*	brave soldier

忠誠	*chūsei*	loyalty
刀	*katana*	sword
日本刀	*Nihontō*	Japanese sword
内乱	*nairan*	rebellion, civil war
責任	*sekinin*	responsibility
班	*han*	squad, group
班長	*hanchō*	squad/group leader

■ III. Reading Exercises 44 ■

Read and translate the following.

1. アメリカでは**陸軍**、**海軍**、**空軍**、並びに**海兵隊**が**国防**の役目を果たしている。
2. トムは高校を卒業するとすぐ、**軍隊**に入った。
3. **防衛費**を節約して**軍備**の縮小を行った。
4. **自衛隊**の主な任務は日本の平和と独立を**守り**、公共の治安を保つことである。
5. **自衛隊**には、陸上、海上、航空**自衛隊**があり、**隊員**はすべて**志願兵**である。
6. ある国では少年少女が**兵隊**になって**敵**と戦っている。
7. **司令官**の**命令**に従って**部隊**は行進した。
8. その地域に平和を回復するために、**国連軍**が**守備**についている。
9. **隊長**は**戦略**の失敗に**責任**を感じて辞職した。
10. 冷たい戦争は終わったが、世界の至る所で**内乱**が人々を苦しめている。
11. その**将軍**は陸軍を**勇退**して政界に入った。
12. 我が**部隊**は**敵軍**の**計略**にかかって苦戦したが、最後まで**勇**ましく戦った。
13. その合戦で功績を立てた**軍人**は**勇士**の中の**勇士**であると賞賛された。
14. 大勢の若者が国家に**忠誠**をちかって戦場に臨んだ。
15. **班長**の**号令**で、**兵卒**全員が発射した。
16. **取材班**は海外の危険地帯に向かって出発した。
17. **刀**の展示会で**日本刀**の**名刀**が特に多くの関心を集めていた。

Foreign Affairs

■ I. Reference ■

#945 際	14 strokes	了 阝 阝〃 陘 陘 際

kun *kiwa* edge, side
際 *kiwa* edge (of a cliff). 水際 *mizugiwa* water edge.

ON SAI occasion
国際的な *kokusaiteki na* international. 国際連合 *Kokusai Rengō* United Natiions. 国際関係 *kokusai kankei* international relations. 交際 ⟨v⟩ *kōsai* friendly relations.

#946 構	14 strokes	朴 枆 枻 構 構 構

kun *kama(eru)* build, set up; *kama(u)* care; meddle
構える *kamaeru* set up (a store). 構う *kamau* care (about); meddle (with other's business). 心構え *kokorogamae* mental attitude.

ON KŌ structure, construction
機構 *kikō* organization. 国際機構 *kokusai kikō* international orgnization. 社会機構 *shakai kikō* social structure. 構成 ⟨v⟩ *kōsei* composition. 構想 *kōsō* plan, plot.

#947 条	7 strokes	ノ ク 夂 夂 各 条

ON JŌ article, clause; line
条約 *jōyaku* treaty. 通商条約 *tsūshō jōyaku* commercial treaty. 憲法第一条 *kenpō daiichijō* Article 1 of the Constitution. 条例 *jōrei* regulations. 星条旗 *seijōki* Stars and Strips.

#948 認	14 strokes	言 言 訒 認 認 認

kun *mito(meru)* perceive; recognize; approve of
認める *mitomeru* perceive (a figure); recognize (one's ability); approve of (a measure).

ON   NIN perceive; recognize; approve of
認識 ‹v› *ninshiki* perception.   認定 ‹v› *nintei* recognition.   認可 ‹v›
ninka approval.   否認 ‹v› *hinin* disapproval.

#949 承	8 strokes	｀ 了 手 手 承 承

kun   *uketamawa(ru)* listen to; receive
承る *uketamawaru* listen to (a lecture); receive (a command).
ON   SHŌ listen to; receive
承認 ‹v› *shōnin* approval.   承知 ‹v› *shōchi* consent; knowing.   伝承 ‹v›
denshō transmission, handing down.

#950 談	15 strokes	言 言 言 訲 談 談

ON   DAN talk
会談 ‹v› *kaidan* conversation, conference.   対談 ‹v› *taidan* face-to-
face talk.   談話 ‹v› *danwa* talk.   相談 ‹v› *sōdan* consultation.

#951 是	9 strokes	口 日 早 早 昰 是

ON   ZE right, just
是正 ‹v› *zesei* correction.   是認 ‹v› *zenin* approval.   国是 *kokuze*
national policy.   是非 *zehi* right or wrong; by all means.

#952 述	8 strokes	一 十 木 求 述 述

kun   *no(beru)* state, mention
述べる *noberu* state (one's opinions).
ON   JUTSU state, mention
記述 ‹v› *kijutsu* description.   口述 ‹v› *kōjutsu* oral statement.   著述 ‹v›
chojutsu writing (a book).   供述 ‹v› *kyōjutsu* deposition.

#953 異	11 strokes	口 田 甼 畀 畢 異

kun   *koto(naru)* differ
異なる *kotonaru* (customs) differ.   異なった *kotonatta* different.

ON   I differ

異議 *igi* objection.   異例 *irei* exceptional case.   異国 *ikoku* foreign country.   異常な *ijō na* unusual, abnormal.

#954 除   10 strokes   ⁷ ⁷ 阝 阶 除 除

kun   *nozo(ku)* exclude, remove

除く *nozoku* exclude (a person from), remove (an obstacle).

ON   JO, [JI] exclude, remove

解除 ‹v› *kaijo* cancellation.   除外 ‹v› *jogai* exclusion.   除去 ‹v› *jokyo* removal.   除名 ‹v› *jomei* removing one's name (from a list).

#955 確   15 strokes   石 矿 矿 砟 砟 確

kun   *tashi(ka)* certain; *tashi(kameru)* make sure

確かな *tashika na* certain, sure.   確かめる *tashikameru* make sure.

ON   KAKU certain

確認 ‹v› *kakunin* confirmation.   確立 ‹v› *kakuritsu* establishment.   確信 ‹v› *kakushin* conviction.   正確な *seikaku na* accurate.

#956 永   5 strokes   ˋ 丁 刁 永 永

kun   *naga(i)* long time

永い *nagai* long time.

ON   EI long time

永遠の *eien no* eternal (peace).   永住 ‹v› *eijū* permanent residence.   永世中立国 *eisei chūritsukoku* permanent neutral country.

#957 久   3 strokes   ノ ク 久

kun   *hisa(shii)* long time

久しい *hisashii* long time.   久しぶりに *hisashiburi ni* after a long interval.

ON   KYŪ, [KU] long time

永久に *eikyū ni* permanently.   持久力 *jikyūryoku* sustaining power.   持久戦 *jikyūsen* drawn-out war.   久遠の *kuon no* eternal.

#958

移 11 strokes ニ 千 禾 科 移 移

kun *utsu(ru)* move; *utsu(su)* move, transfer

移る *utsuru* move (into Tokyo).　移す *utsusu* move (the office elsewhere), transfer (a tree).

ON I move, transfer

移住〈v〉*ijū* immigration, emigration.　移民法 *iminhō* immigration law.　移転〈v〉*iten* moving.　移動〈v〉*idō* moving, migration.

#959

許 11 strokes ニ 言 言 言 許 許

kun *yuru(su)* permit; forgive

許す *yurusu* permit (a person to do); forgive (a person).

ON KYO permit; forgive

許可〈v〉*kyoka* permission.　許否〈v〉*kyohi* refusal.　許容〈v〉*kyoyō* permission; pardon.　特許 *tokkyo* patent.

#960

導 15 strokes 首 首 道 道 道 導

kun *michibi(ku)* guide, lead

導く *michibiku* guide, lead.

ON DŌ guide, lead

指導〈v〉*shidō* guidance.　指導者 *shidōsha* leader.　導入〈v〉*dōnyū* introduction, bringing in.　主導権 *shudōken* leadership.

#961

絶 12 strokes 幺 糸 紹 絽 絶 絶

kun *ta(eru)* die out; *ta(tsu)* cut off; *ta(yasu)* let die out

絶える *taeru* die out.　断つ *tatsu* cut off (communications).　絶やす *tayasu* let (harmful insects) die out.

ON ZETSU die out; extremity

断絶〈v〉*danzetsu* severance.　国交断絶 *kokkō danzetsu* severance of diplomatic relations.　絶望〈v〉*zetsubō* despair.　絶対に *zettai ni* absolutely.　絶好の *zekkō no* best (opportunity).

#962 救	11 strokes	十 寸 求 求 救 救

kun   *suku(u)* help, rescue
救う *sukuu* help, rescue

ON   KYŪ help, rescue
救助 ‹v› *kyūjo* rescue.   救済 ‹v› *kyūsai* relief.   救済基金 *kyūsai kikin* relief fund.   救急車 *kyūkyūsha* ambulance.

#963 盟	13 strokes	冂 明 明 明 盟 盟

ON   MEI oath; alliance
同盟 ‹v› *dōmei* alliance.   同盟国 *dōmeikoku* allied nation.   経済同盟 *keizai dōmei* economic alliance.   加盟 ‹v› *kamei* affiliation.   盟約 *meiyaku* pledge; alliance.

#964 厚	9 strokes	一 厂 戸 厚 厚 厚

kun   *atsu(i)* kind, cordial; thick
厚い *atsui* cordial (reception).   厚紙 *atsugami* cardboard.

ON   KŌ kind, cordial; thick
厚生 *kōsei* welfare.   厚生事業 *kōsei jigyō* welfare enterprise.   厚情 *kōjō* kindness.   厚顔の *kōgan no* brazenfaced.

#965 善	12 strokes	丷 䒑 羊 羊 善 善

kun   *yo(i)* good
善い *yoi* good.

ON   ZEN good
親善 *shinzen* goodwill, friendship.   善意 *zen'i* good intention.   改善 ‹v› *kaizen* improvement.   最善の *saizen no* best (measure).

#966 訪	11 strokes	二 言 言 訂 訪 訪

kun   *otozu(reru)*, *tazu(neru)* visit
訪れる・訪ねる *otozureru/tazuneru* visit.   訪れ *otozure* visit.

ON   HŌ visit
訪問 ‹v› *hōmon* visit.   親善訪問 *shinzen hōmon* goodwill visit.   訪日 ‹v› *hōnichi* visit to Japan.   訪米 ‹v› *hōbei* visit to America.

#967 貧	11 strokes	八 分 尒 兮 貧 貧

kun *mazu(shii)* poor
貧しい *mazushii* poor (people).

ON HIN, BIN poor
貧民 *hinmin* the poor.　貧困 *hinkon* poverty.　貧苦 *hinku* hardships of poverty.　貧乏 ⟨v⟩ *binbō* poverty.

#968 柱	9 strokes	一 十 木 杧 杧 柱

kun *hashira* pillar, prop
柱 *hashira* pillar.　一家の柱 *ikka no hashira* prop of a family.

ON CHŪ pillar, prop
支柱 *shichū* support, prop.　柱石 *chūseki* pillar, foundation.　電柱 *denchū* telephone/utility pole.

#969 称	10 strokes	二 千 禾 秆 秆 称

ON SHŌ name, title
称号 *shōgō* title.　愛称 *aishō* nickname.　略称 *ryakushō* abbreviated name.　自称の *jishō no* self-professed.

#970 逆	9 strokes	䒑 并 屰 逆 逆 逆

kun *saka(sa)* reverse; *saka(rau)* oppose, go against
逆さ *sakasa* reverse.　逆らう *sakarau* oppose, go against.

ON GYAKU reverse, opposite; treason
逆境 *gyakkyō* adversity.　逆転 ⟨v⟩ *gyakuten* inversion.　逆説 *gyakusetsu* paradox.　反逆 ⟨v⟩ *hangyaku* treason.

#971 貴	12 strokes	口 中 虫 串 昔 貴

kun *tōto(i)*, *tatto(i)* noble, precious; *tatto(bu)*, *tōto(bu)* value, respect
貴い *tōtoi/tattoi* noble (birth), precious (thing).　貴ぶ *tattobu/tōtobu* value (a thing), respect (a person).

ON KI noble, precious
貴重な *kichō na* valuable.　貴族 *kizoku* nobility.　貴金属 *kikinzoku* precious metals.　富貴 *fūki/fukki** wealth and honor.

■ II. Vocabulary

国際連合	*Kokusai Rengō*	United Nations
機構	*kikō*	organization
条約	*jōyaku*	treaty
承認‹v›	*shōnin*	approval
会談	*kaidan*	conversation, conference
是正‹v›	*zesei*	correction
記述‹v›	*kijutsu*	description
異議	*igi*	objection
解除‹v›	*kaijo*	cancellation
確認‹v›	*kakunin*	confirmation
永遠の	*eien no*	eternal
永久に	*eikyū ni*	permanently
移住‹v›	*ijū*	immigration, emigration
移民法	*iminhō*	immigration law
許可‹v›	*kyoka*	permission
指導‹v›	*shidō*	guidance
国交断絶	*kokkō danzetsu*	severance of diplomatic relations
同盟‹v›	*dōmei*	alliance
救助‹v›	*kyūjo*	rescue
救済基金	*kyūsai kikin*	relief fund
貧民	*hinmin*	the poor
逆境	*gyakkyō*	adversity
親善	*shinzen*	goodwill, friendship
訪問‹v›	*hōmon*	visit
支柱	*shichū*	support, prop
称号	*shōgō*	title
尊い	*tōtoi/tattoi*	noble, precious
貴重な	*kichō na*	valuable

■ III. Reading Exercises 45

Read and translate the following.

1. **国際連合**は1945年、世界平和を保つために組織された。
2. 国連は多数の国が加わって作られた**国際機構**である。
3. 二国間で**通商条約**が結ばれた。
4. 政府は植民地の独立を**承認**した。

5. 大蔵大臣はアメリカ大統領との**会談**で貿易問題を討議した。

6. この**条例**には二、三是正すべき点がある。

7. 日本の国防に関する事は憲法**第九条**に**記述**されている。

8. その国は武装を**解除**して、**永世中立国**になった。

9. 予期されていた外務大臣の辞職が**確認**された。

10. **永遠**の平和は全人類の念願である。

11. 国家の**支柱**と言われた政治家の業績は**永久**に伝えられるだろう。

12. 私が子供の時、山中さんの家族はブラジルへ**移住**した。

13. **移民法**の改正にはだれも**異議**がない。

14. 政府の**許可**なしに入国する外国人の数が毎年増加している。

15. 両国は**国交断絶**を中止して、友好関係を回復し、**経済同盟**を結んだ。

16. 日本はアジアの各地域で技術の**指導**を行っている。

17. **貧民**を**逆境**から**救助**するために、**救済基金**が必要である。

18. 複雑な**社会機構**の中で、**厚生事業**を成功させるのは実に困難である。

19. 天皇、皇后、両陛下は**親善**のためアメリカを**訪問**された。

20. かれは外交問題に関する**貴重**な研究で博士の**称号**を授かった。

19

✽✽✽✽✽✽✽✽✽✽✽✽✽✽✽✽✽✽✽✽

Law and Crime

■ I. Reference ■

#972 律	9 strokes	ノ 彳 彳 彳 彳 律

ON RITSU, [RICHI] law, regulation
法律 *hōritsu* law. 自律 ⟨v⟩ *jiritsu* self-regulation. 調律 ⟨v⟩ *chōritsu* tuning. 律義な *richigi na* honest.

#973 規	11 strokes	二 夫 扣 扣 扣 規

ON KI standard, measure
規律 *kiritsu* discipline. 規準 *kijun* standard. 規定 ⟨v⟩ *kitei* regulation. 規模 *kibo* scale. 定規 *jōgi* ruler.

#974 則	9 strokes	丨 冂 目 貝 則 則

ON SOKU rule, law
規則 *kisoku* rule, regulation. 交通規則 *kōtsū kisoku* traffic regulations. 原則 *gensoku* principle. 反則 ⟨v⟩ *hansoku* violation of rules.
自然の法則 *shizen no hōsoku* natural law.

#975 裁	12 strokes	十 圭 圭 圭 裁 裁

kun *saba(ku)* judge, decide; *ta(tsu)* cut out (cloth)
裁く *sabaku* judge, decide (a case). 裁つ *tatsu* cut out (cloth).

ON SAI judge, decide, tailor
制裁 ⟨v⟩ *seisai* sanction. 裁決 ⟨v⟩ *saiketsu* judgement. 仲裁 ⟨v⟩ *chūsai* arbitration. 独裁者 *dokusaisha* dictator. 総裁 *sōsai* president, general director. 洋裁 *yōsai* Western tailoring.

#976 判	7 strokes	丶 丷 ⺧ 半 半 判

ON HAN judge; seal, stamp; BAN paper size
裁判 ‹v› *saiban* trial.　裁判官 *saibankan* judge.　判事 *hanji* judge.
判決 ‹v› *hanketsu* decisioin, ruling.　判断 ‹v› *handan* judgment.　判
han seal, stamp.　A5判 *Ei-goban* A-5 size (of a book).

#977 件	6 strokes	ノ イ イ 伫 仵 件

ON KEN matter, affair, case
事件 *jiken* incident, affair, case.　民事事件 *minji jiken* civil case.
条件 *jōken* condition.　用件 *yōken* business.

#978 察	14 strokes	宀 宀 宏 察 察 察

ON SATSU surmise, judge
警察 *keisatsu* police.　警察官 *keisatsukan* police officer.　検察庁
kensatsuchō public prosecutors office.　視察 ‹v› *shisatsu* inspection.
観察 ‹v› *kansatsu* observation.　推察 ‹v› *suisatsu* guess.

#979 署	13 strokes	冖 罒 罒 罘 署 署

ON SHO government office; signature
警察署 *keisatsusho* police station.　消防署 *shōbōsho* fire station.
税務署 *zeimusho* tax office.　署名 ‹v› *shomei* signaturc.

#980 破	10 strokes	一 丆 石 矿 破 破

kun *yabu(ru)* tear, break; *yabu(reru)* be torn, broken
破る *yaburu* tear (paper), break (a rule).　破れる *yabureru* be
torn, broken.　見破る *miyaburu* see through (a plot).

ON HA tear, break
破損 ‹v› *hason* damage.　破産 ‹v› *hasan* bankruptcy.　破約 ‹v› *hayaku*
break of contract.　破局 *hakyoku* catastrophe.

#981 禁	13 strokes 一 十 村 埜 埜 禁

ON KIN prohibit
禁じる *kinjiru* prohibit. 禁止 ⟨v⟩ *kinshi* prohibition. 禁酒 ⟨v⟩ *kinshu* abstinence from drinking. 禁固 ⟨v⟩ *kinko* imprisonment.

#982 罪	13 strokes 冂 罒 罒 罘 罪 罪

kun *tsumi* crime, sin
罪 *tsumi* crime, sin. 罪人 *tsumibito* criminal, sinner.

ON ZAI crime, sin
罪人 *zainin* criminal, sinner. 有罪 *yūzai* guilty. 無罪 *muzai* not guilty. 罪悪 *zaiaku* vice, sin.

#983 犯	5 strokes ノ 丿 犭 犭 犯

kun *oka(su)* commit, violate
犯す *okasu* commit (a crime/sin).

ON HAN commit, violate
犯罪 *hanzai* crime. 犯人 *hannin* criminal. 主犯 *shuhan* master criminal. 共犯者 *kyōhansha* accomplice. 犯行 *hankō* crime.

#984 疑	14 strokes ノ 匕 匙 匙 疑 疑

kun *utaga(u)* doubt, suspect
疑う *utagau* doubt, suspect. 疑い *utagai* doubt, suspicion.

ON GI doubt, suspect
疑問 *gimon* question, doubt. 容疑者 *yōgisha* suspect. 疑念 *ginen* doubt. 半信半疑で *hanshin hangi de* half in doubt, doutfully.

#985 弁	5 strokes ㇑ ム 丄 弁 弁

ON BEN speech, dialect; valve; petal
弁護士 *bengoshi* lawyer. 弁解 ⟨v⟩ *benkai* excuse. 弁論 ⟨v⟩ *benron* argument. 関西弁 *kansaiben* Kansai dialect. 安全弁 *anzenben* safety valve. 花弁 *kaben* flower petal.

#986 証	12 strokes	ニ ゠ 訂 訐 証 証

ON SHŌ proof, evidence, certificate
証人 *shōnin* witness. 証言 ‹v› *shōgen* testimony. 証明 ‹v› *shōmei* proof, certification. 保証 ‹v› *hoshō* guarantee. 学生証 *gakuseishō* student's ID card.

#987 放	8 strokes	ユ 方 方 方 放 放

kun *hana(su)*, *hana(tsu)* let go, release
放す *hanasu* let go (a bird). 放つ *hanatsu* let fly (an arrow).
ON HŌ let go, release
放火 *hōka* arson; incendiary fire. 釈放 ‹v› *shakuhō* release (from jail). 解放 ‹v› *kaihō* liberation. 放送 ‹v› *hōsō* broadcasting.

#988 殺	10 strokes	ノ 千 釆 釈 殺 殺

kun *koro(su)* kill
殺す *korosu* kill. 人殺し *hitogoroshi* murder; murderer.
ON SATSU, [SAI], [SETSU] kill
殺人 *satsujin* murder. 殺人事件 *satsujin jiken* murder case. 自殺 ‹v› *jisatsu* suicide. 暗殺 ‹v› *ansatsu* assassination. 相殺 ‹v› *sōsai* offsetting each other. 殺生 ‹v› *sesshō* wanton slaughter.

#989 災	7 strokes	く くく くくく 〵〵〵 〴〵 災

kun *wazawa(i)* disaster, misfortune
災い ‹v› *wazawai* disaster, misfortune.
ON SAI disaster, misfortune
災難 *sainan* disaster, misfortune. 火災 *kasai* fire. 天災 *tensai* natural disaster. 戦災 *sensai* war damage.

#990 追	9 strokes	亻 户 阜 阜 追 追

kun *o(u)* chase, pursue
追う *ou* chase (a criminal), pursue (pleasure).
ON TSUI chase, pursue

追放 ‹v› *tsuihō* purge, banishment.　追求 ‹v› *tsuikyū* pursuit.　追加 ‹v› *tsuika* addition.

#991 簡	18 strokes	⺮ 笁 筲 筲 簡 簡

ON　KAN simple, brief; letter
簡易な *kan'i na* simple.　簡易裁判所 *kan'i saibansho* summary court.　簡単な *kantan na* simple, brief.　書簡 *shokan* letter.

#992 棒	12 strokes	十 杆 桙 桙 棒 棒

ON　BŌ stick, club
棒 *bō* stick, club.　鉄棒 *tetsubō* iron bar.　泥棒 *dorobō* theft; thief.　用心棒 *yōjinbō* bodyguard.

■ II. Vocabulary ■

法律	*hōritsu*	law
規則	*kisoku*	rule, regulation
規律	*kiritsu*	discipline
制裁 ‹v›	*seisai*	sanction
裁判 ‹v›	*saiban*	trial
裁判官	*saibankan*	judge
判決 ‹v›	*hunketsu*	decision, ruling
事件	*jiken*	incident, affair, case
警察署	*keisatsusho*	police station
検察庁	*kensatsuchō*	public prosecutors office
破損 ‹v›	*hason*	damage
禁止 ‹v›	*kinshi*	prohibition
罪	*tsumi*	crime, sin
犯罪	*hanzai*	crime
犯人	*hannin*	criminal
疑い	*utagai*	doubt, suspicion
疑問	*gimon*	question, doubt
容疑者	*yōgisha*	suspect
弁護士	*bengoshi*	lawyer
証人	*shōnin*	witness

証言⟨v⟩	*shōgen*	testimony
放火	*hōka*	arson; incendiary fire
人殺し	*hitogoroshi*	murder; murderer
殺人事件	*satsujin jiken*	murder case
災い⟨v⟩	*wazawai*	disaster, misfortune
災難	*sainan*	disaster, misfortune
追放⟨v⟩	*tsuihō*	purge, banishment
泥棒⟨v⟩	*dorobō*	theft; thief
簡易裁判所	*kan'i saibansho*	summary court

■ III. Reading Exercises 46 ■

Read and translate the following.

1. 社会の治安を保つために、種々の**法律**が制定されている。
2. かれは**法律**を破って**裁判**にかけられた。
3. 子供の投げたボールが当たって、窓ガラスが**破損**した。
4. 青年は**交通規則**を無視して事故を起こした。
5. 少年少女を**規律**のある生活に導くことが最も大切である。
6. 学校当局は不正な活動に参加した学生に**制裁**を加えた。
7. その男は調査のため**警察署**に留置された。
8. **事件**は**警察**から**検察庁**へ回された。
9. 未成年者が酒を飲むことは**法律**で禁止されている。
10. かれは重い**罪**を**犯**して世間から見捨てられた。
11. **簡易裁判所**は軽い**犯罪**を処理する。
12. **裁判官**はその女に**有罪**の**判決**を下した。
13. アリバイが無いため**疑**われてとんだ**災難**を受けた。
14. **律義**なあの先生が教科書**事件**に関係があるかどうか**疑問**だ。
15. **証人**は容疑者の**無罪**を**証言**した。
16. 若い**弁護士**が**殺人事件**を担当した。
17. 昨夜の商店街の**火災**は**放火**だった。
18. **警察官**がオートバイで**犯人**を追っている。
19. その役人は横領の**疑**いで公職から**追放**された。
20. 留守の間に、家に**泥棒**が入って時計や、宝石や、その他色々の物がぬすまれた。

20

Religion and Morality

■ I. Reference ■

#993 宗	8 strokes	丶 宀 宁 宇 宗 宗

ON   SHŪ, SŌ religion, sect; originator

宗教 *shūkyō* religion.   改宗‹ν›*kaishū* conversion (to another religion).   宗家 *sōke* head family (of a Noh school).

#994 派	9 strokes	丶 氵 沪 沠 沠 派

ON   HA faction, sect, school

宗派 *shūha* religious sect.   右派 *uha* right wing.   左派 *saha* left wing.   正統派 *seitōha* orthodox school.   特派員 *tokuhain* special correspondent.   立派な *rippa na* fine, splendid.

#995 寺	6 strokes	一 十 土 圭 寺 寺

kun   *tera* temple

寺 *tera* temple.   山寺 *yamadera* mountain temple.

ON   JI temple

東大寺 *Tōdaiji* Todaiji Temple.   寺院 *jiin* temple, cathedral. 寺院建築 *jiin kenchiku* Buddhist architecture.

#996 宮	10 strokes	丷 宀 宮 宮 宮 宮

kun   *miya* shrine, prince

宮 *miya* Shinto shrine.   宮様 *miya-sama* Imperial prince/princess.

ON   KYŪ, GŪ, [KU] shrine, palace

宮中 *kyūchū* Imperial Court.   明治神宮 *Meiji Jingū* Meiji Shrine. 宮内庁 *Kunaichō* Imperial Household Agency.

#997 墓	13 strokes	艹　芐　苩　莫　莫　墓

kun *haka* grave, tomb
墓 *haka* grave, tomb.　墓参り ⟨v⟩ *hakamairi* visit to a grave.

ON BO grave, tomb
墓地 *bochi* cemetery.　墓穴 *boketsu* grave.

#998 遺	15 strokes	口　虫　貴　貴　遺　遺

ON I, [YUI] leave behind, bequeath
遺産 *isan* inheritance, legacy.　遺骨 *ikotsu* one's ashes.　遺族 *izoku* family of the deceased.　遺言 ⟨v⟩ *yuigon* one's will.

#999 城	9 strokes	十　圠　圹　圻　城　城

kun *shiro* castle
城 *shiro* castle.　根城 *nejiro* base of operations.

ON JŌ castle
宮城 *kyūjō* Imperial Palace.　二条城 *Nijōjō* Nijo Castle.　城下町 *jōkamachi* castle town.　築城 ⟨v⟩ *chikujō* construction of a castle.

#1000 仏	4 strokes	ノ　イ　仏　仏

kun *hotoke* Buddha; the deceased
仏 *hotoke* Buddha; the deceased.　仏になる *hotoke ni naru* die.

ON BUTSU Buddha; France
仏教 *bukkyō* buddhism.　仏像 *butsuzō* image of Buddha.　大仏 *daibutsu* great image of Buddha.　仏領 *Futsuryō* French territory.

#1001 拝	8 strokes	一　十　才　扩　拝　拝

kun *oga(mu)* pray, venerate
拝む *ogamu* pray (to gods and Buddha).

ON HAI pray, venerate
参拝 ⟨v⟩ *sanpai* visiting a temple/shrine.　拝見 ⟨v⟩ *haiken* being allowed to see.　拝借 ⟨v⟩ *haishaku* being allowed to borrow.

#1002 礼	5 strokes	丶 ラ ネ ネ 礼

ON   REI, RAI bow; gratitude; ceremony
礼 *rei* bow; gratitude.　礼拝 ‹v› *reihai/raihai* worship; church service.　祭礼 *sairei* festival.　失礼な *shitsurei na* impolite.

#1003 聖	13 strokes	厂 亡 耶 耵 聖 聖

ON   SEI holy
聖書 *seisho* Bible.　聖人 *seijin* saint.　聖母マリア *Seibo Maria* Virgin Mary.　神聖な *shinsei na* sacred.

#1004 宣	9 strokes	丶 宀 宀 宁 宣 宣

ON   SEN announce
宣教師 *senkyōshi* missionary.　宣言 ‹v› *sengen* declaration.　宣告 ‹v›
senkoku sentence.　宣伝 ‹v› *senden* advertisement, propaganda.

#1005 恩	10 strokes	丨 冂 冈 因 恩 恩

ON   ON kindness; obligation; gratitude
恩 *on* kindness; debt of gratitude.　恩師 *onshi* one's respected
teacher.　恩人 *onjin* benefactor.　恩返し ‹v› *ongaeshi* repayment of
debt of gratitude.　恩知らずな *onshirazu na* ungrateful.

#1006 賀	12 strokes	フ カ 加 智 賀 賀

ON   GA congratulate
年賀状 *nengajō* New Year's card.　祝賀会 *shukugakai* celebration.
参賀 ‹v› *sanga* congraturatory visit to the Imperial Palace.

#1007 訓	10 strokes	二 言 言 訂 訓 訓

ON   KUN teaching; Japanese reading of kanji
教訓 *kyōkun* lesson, teachings.　訓話 *kunwa* moral story.　訓練 ‹v›
kunren training.　訓読み ‹v› *kun-yomi* kun reading.

#1008 謝	17 strokes	言 訁 訂 訃 訐 謝 謝

kun   *ayama(ru)* apologize

謝る *ayamaru* apologize (for one's error).

ON   SHA gratitude; apology

感謝 ⟨v⟩*kansha* gratitude.   謝恩会 *shaonkai* thank-you party.   謝礼 *sharei* honorarium.   謝罪 ⟨v⟩*shazai* apology.

#1009 徳	14 strokes	彳 彳 徊 徊 徳 徳

ON   TOKU virtue; profit

道徳 *dōtoku* morality.   美徳 *bitoku* virtue.   功徳 *kudoku* charity.   徳用の *tokuyō no* economical.   徳用品 *tokuyōhin* economy packet.

#1010 厳	17 strokes	丷 产 产 岸 厳 厳

kun   *kibi(shii)* strict, severe; *ogoso(ka)* solemn

厳しい *kibishii* strict (teacher).   厳かな式 *ogosoka na shiki* solemn ceremony.

ON   GEN, [GON] strict, severe; solemn

厳格な *genkaku na* strict, severe.   厳禁 ⟨v⟩*genkin* strict prohibition.   厳守 ⟨v⟩*genshu* strict observance.

#1011 孝	7 strokes	十 土 耂 考 考 孝

ON   KŌ filial piety

孝行 ⟨v⟩*kōkō* filial piety.   不孝 ⟨v⟩*fukō* filial impiety.   忠孝 *chūkō* loyalty and filial piety.   孝行な *kōkō na* dutiful.

#1012 仁	4 strokes	ノ イ 仁 仁

ON   JIN, [NI] virtue, humanity, benevolence

仁義 *jingi* humaniy and justice.   仁術 *jinjutsu* benevolent act; the healing art.   仁王 *Niō* 2 guardian gods at a Buddhist temple gate.

#1013 存	6 strokes	一　ナ　ナ　ナ　存　存

ON　SON, ZON exist; know, think

存在 ‹v› *sonzai* existence.　存続 ‹v› *sonzoku* continuation.　共存 ‹v›
kyōzon coexistence.　生存者 *seizonsha* survivor.　存じる *zonjiru*
know, think.　ご存じですか *Go-zonji desu ka* Do you know?

#1014 敬	12 strokes	十　产　苟　苟　敬　敬

kun　*uyama(u)* respect, honor

敬う *uyamau* respect (one's teacher).

ON　KEI respect, honor

敬意 *keii* respect.　敬語 *keigo* honorific.　敬称 *keishō* courtesy title.　敬服 ‹v› *keifuku* respect, admiration.

#1015 尊	12 strokes	亠　并　芇　酋　酋　尊

kun　*tatto(bu)*, *tōto(bu)* value, respect; *tatto(i)*, *tōto (i)* valuable, respect-
able

尊ぶ *tattobu/tōtobu* value (the teachings).　尊い *tattoi/tōtoi* valuable (lesson).

ON　SON value, respect

尊敬 ‹v› *sonkei* respect.　尊重 ‹v› *sonchō* esteem.　尊厳 *songen* dignity.　自尊心 *jisonshin* self-respect, pride.

#1016 寄	11 strokes	宀　宇　空　空　害　寄

kun　*yo(ru)* draw near; drop in; *yo(seru)* bring close; collect

寄る *yoru* draw near (to the window); drop in (one's friend's
house).　寄せる *yoseru* bring (a chair) close to (the wall); collect
(money).　最寄りの *moyori* no* nearest.　寄席 *yose** vaudeville
theater.

ON　KI draw near; drop in; collect

寄付 ‹v› *kifu* donation.　寄付金 *kifukin* donation, gift of money.
寄港 ‹v› *kikō* stop at a port.　寄宿舎 *kishukusha* dormitory.

■ II. Vocabulary

宗教	*shūkyō*	religion
宗派	*shūha*	religious sect
仏教	*bukkyō*	Buddhism
寺	*tera*	temple
東大寺	*Tōdaiji*	Todaiji Temple
宮	*miya*	Shinto shrine
明治神宮	*Meiji Jingū*	Meiji Shrine
墓	*haka*	grave
墓地	*bochi*	cemetery
遺産	*isan*	inheritance, legacy
遺言‹v›	*yuigon*	one's will
城	*shiro*	castle
宮城	*kyūjō*	Imperial Palace
礼拝‹v›	*reihai/raihai*	worship; church service
聖書	*seisho*	Bible
宣教師	*senkyōshi*	missionary
恩師	*onshi*	one's respected teacher
年賀状	*nengajō*	New Year's card
教訓	*kyōkun*	lesson, teachings
道徳	*dōtoku*	morality
感謝‹v›	*kansha*	gratitude
厳しい	*kibishii*	strict, severe
厳格な	*genkaku na*	strict, severe
孝行‹v›	*kōkō*	filial piety
仁義	*jingi*	humanity and justice
存在‹v›	*sonzai*	existence
尊い	*tattoi/tōtoi*	valuable, respectable
尊敬‹v›	*sonkei*	respect
寄付‹v›	*kifu*	donation

■ III. Reading Exercises 47

Read and translate the following.

1. 日本の主な**宗教**には神道、**仏教**、キリスト教がある。
2. ある国では今日でも**宗派**の争いが続いている。

3. 古い都の京都には、寺や神社が多く、観光客が絶えない。

4. 元日に家族連れで**明治神宮**に**参拝**した。

5. **東大寺**は日本一の**大仏**で有名である。

6. 私達の祖先の墓は小山の上の広い**墓地**に在る。

7. その兄弟は父親の**遺言**に従って**遺産**を均分した。

8. 全国各地に幕府時代に築かれた**立派**な**城**が残っている。

9. 天皇誕生日に大勢の人が**宮城**に**参賀**した。

10. 留学生のトム君から日本語で書いた**年賀状**が来た。

11. クリスチャンの春子さんは毎日曜日、必ず教会の**礼拝**に出席する。

12. 日曜学校で**聖書**を読んだり、賛美歌を歌ったりした。

13. ブラウン神父は**宣教師**として前世紀に来日し、一生を日本で終えた。

14. 卒業生が**恩師**のために**謝恩会**を開いて、**感謝**の心を表した。

15. 幼い子供には**教訓**のある物語を読ませたい。

16. **道徳**が低下するに従って、犯罪が増加した。

17. かれは厳しい先生だったが、何よりも**仁義**を尊重し学生から**尊敬**されていた。

18. **厳格**な家庭に育った本田さんは親にとても**孝行**だ。

19. 私は神の**存在**を信じた時、**仏教**を捨てて、キリスト教に**改宗**した。

20. 古い木造の教会を改築するために**寄付**を集めている。

ANSWERS

1. *Ringo ga muttsu arimasu.* There are six apples.
2. *Orenji ga yattsu to remon ga mittsu arimasu.* There are eight oranges and three lemons.
3. *Biru to Tomu wa kurasu de ichini o arasotte iru.* Bill and Tom contend for first place in the class.
4. *Asoko made goroku-mairu arimasu.* It's five or six miles (from here) to there.
5. *Kuri o tō bakari hiroimashita.* I picked up about ten chestnuts.
6. *Musume wa kokonotsu de musuko wa nanatsu desu.* My daughter is nine years old and my son is seven years old.
7. *Jūni-pēji ni nisan no misu ga arimasu.* There are two or three mistakes on page 12.
8. *Watashi no ban desu. Anata wa yonbanme desu yo.* It's my turn. You are fourth.
9. *Kore wa futatsume no hanbāgā desu.* This is my second hamburger.
10. *Isu no kazu o kazoete kudasai.* Please count the number of chairs.
11. *hyakugojū* 150, *sanzen roppyaku* 3,600, *goman yonsen* 54,000, *ichioku hassenman* 180 million, *sanchō* 3 trillion, *nijūkyūman* 290,000, *issen nanahyaku* 1,700, *sūhyaku* hundreds (of something)

1. *Marui tēburu ga futatsu to isu ga yattsu arimasu.* There are two round tables and eight chairs.
2. *Hon ga sansatsu to nōto ga shigosatsu arimasu.* There are three books and four or five notebooks.
3. *Ofisu ni kopī-ki ga nidai arimasu.* There are two copy machines in the office.
4. *Todana ni sara ga jūmai to koppu ga rokko to naifu ga jūnihon aru.* There are ten plates, six cups and twelve knives in the cupboard.
5. *Asoko ni Amerika-jin ga futari imasu.* There are two Americans over there.

6. *Sono gurūpu ni Kanada-jin ga sūmei imashita.* There were several Canadians in that group.
7. *Jimu wa jūkyūsai de Sara wa hatachi desu.* Jim is nineteen years old and Sarah is twenty years old.
8. *Kamome ga sanba esa o asatte imasu.* Three seagulls are searching for food.
9. *Kosū ga nibai ni natta.* The number of houses doubled.
10. *Daihon o sanbu moraemasen ka.* Can I get three copies of the script?
11. *Honbu wa ano biru no jūsankai desu.* The head office is on the 13th floor of that building.
12. *Merīgōrando ga yonkai mawatte, sutoppu shita.* The merry-go-round went round four times and stopped.
13. *Kono repōto o mō ichido mawashite kudasai.* Please pass this report round once more.
14. *Ninzū o kazoeru tabi ni hitori tarimasen.* Each time I count the number of people, I find one short.
15. *Jetto-ki ga niki tsuita tokoro desu.* Two jets have just arrived.
16. *Doitsu-jin ga marason de itchaku ni narimashita.* A German finished first in the marathon.
17. *Sono hito wa sūtsu ga rokuchaku to kutsu ga hassoku arimasu.* He has six suits and eight pairs of shoes.
18. *Kono hon no dai-ikkan wa sanzen nihyakuen de, dai-nikan wa nisen gohyakuen desu.* The first volume of this book is 3,200 yen, and the second volume is 2,500 yen.

■ Reading Exercises 3 (p.17) ■

1. *Kyō wa mikka desu.* Today is the 3rd.
2. *Kinō/sakujitsu wa shukujitsu deshita.* Yesterday was a national holiday.
3. *Issakujitsu o-iwai no pātī o shimashita.* We had a celebration party the day before yesterday.
4. *Nanoka/nanuka to hatsuka ni matsuri ga arimasu.* There will be a festival on the 7th and the 20th.
5. *Asu/myōnichi wa saijitsu na node yasumimasu.* Tomorrow is a holiday, so I'll take a day off.
6. *Pari kara no jetto-ki wa ima tsuita tokoro desu.* The jet from Paris has just arrived.

7. *Kondo no yasumi wa jūyokka desu.* The next holiday is the 14th.
8. *Kyūjitsu wa tsure to tenisu o shimasu.* I play tennis with my companions on my days off/holidays.
9. *Nijūkunichi kara itsuka no renkyū desu.* There will be five consecutive holidays starting the 29th.
10. *Hi ga akarui node, renjitsu gorufu o yatte imasu.* Because the sun is bright, I play golf every day.

■ Reading Exercises 4 (p.22) ■

1. *Ichigatsu mikka* January 3, *shigatsu muika* April 6, *shichigatsu yokka* July 4, *hachigatsu yōka* August 8, *jūichigatsu tōka* November 10, *senkyūhyaku hachijūgonen* the year 1985
2. *Kongetsu no sue ni tesuto ga arimasu.* There will be a test at the end of this month.
3. *Nenmatsu made ni ato nisannichi shika nai.* There are only a few days until the end of the year.
4. *Kyonen no rokugatsu ni Kanada e ikimashita.* I went to Canada in June of last year.
5. *Sono ikkō wa kokonoka ni tsuite, yokujitsu sarimashita.* The party arrived on the 9th and left the following day.
6. *Sengetsu no hajime ni Amerika kara kaerimashita.* I returned from America at the beginning of last month.
7. *Sumō no shonichi wa nannichi desu ka.* What is the opening day of the sumo tournament?
8. *Kugatsu ni saijitsu ga futsuka arimasu.* There are two holidays in September.
9. *Kotoshi wa hajimete ikkagetsu no yasumi o torimashita.* I took a month off for the first time this year.
10. *Sakunen wa nido Pari e ikimashita.* I went to Paris twice last year.
11. *Rainen no shōgatsu wa Hawai de iwaimasu.* We will celebrate the next New Year in Hawaii.
12. *Kitaru nigatsu yokka, kono hōru de konsāto ga okonawaremasu.* On the 4th of this coming February, a concert will be held in this hall.
13. *Sumisu-san ga Nihon e kite kara nannen ni narimasu ka.* How many years has it been since Mr. Smith came to Japan?

■ Reading Exercises 5 (p.25) ■■■■■■■■■■■■

1. *Kyō wa nanyōbi desu ka.* What day (of the week) is it today?
2. *Kinō/sakujitsu wa kayōbi deshita.* Yesterday was Tuesday.
3. *Kin'yobi ni pikunikku ga aru.* There will be a picnic on Friday.
4. *Maishū, doyōbi ka nichiyōbi ni tenisu o shimasu.* Every week, I play tennis either on Saturday or Sunday.
5. *Senshū gorufu no konpe ga atta.* There were golf tournaments last week.
6. *Isshūkan ni sando kuizu ga arimasu.* We have quizzes three times a week.
7. *Konshū wa ichido mo jimu e ikanakatta.* I didn't go to the gymnasium even once this week.
8. *Getsu-ka-sui ni joggingu o shimasu.* I jog on Monday, Tuesday and Wednesday.
9. *Depāto wa maigetsuyōbi ni yasumimasu.* The department store closes every Monday.
10. *Shūjitsu wa sūpā e iku ma ga arimasen.* I have no time to go to the supermarket on weekdays.
11. *O-kane ga nai kara, raishūmatsu wa doko e mo ikenai.* Since I have no money, I can't go anyplace next weekend.
12. *Konsāto wa kongetsu no daisan mokuyōbi ni okonawareru.* The concert will be held on the 3rd Thursday of this month.

■ Reading Exercises 6 (p.29) ■■■■■■■■■■■■

1. *Aki wa supōtsu no kisetsu desu.* Autumn is the season for sports.
2. *Nihon niwa shiki — haru, natsu, aki, fuyu ga aru.* Japan has four seasons — spring, summer, autumn and winter.
3. *O-hima no setsu wa kite kudasai.* Please come when you are free.
4. *Haruyasumi wa nanshūkan desu ka.* How many weeks are there for the spring vacation?
5. *Konshū no suiyōbi wa shunbun desu.* This Wednesday is the Vernal Equinox Day.
6. *Buraun-san wa raishun Yōroppa kara kaerimasu.* Miss Brown will return from Europe next spring.
7. *Fuyu ni wa sukī ni ikimasu.* I go skiing in winter.

8. *Kotoshi no rittō wa nannichi desu ka.* What is the first day of winter this year?
9. *Kare wa Tōki Orinpikku de kin-medaru o futatsu moratta.* He won two gold medals in the Winter Olympics.
10. *Mada natsu na noni shoshū no yō desu ne.* Although it's still summer, it still feels as if it were early autumn.
11. *Kyō kara gogatsu. Mō shoka desu ne.* May starts today. It's already early summer, isn't it?
12. *Kyonen no geshi wa hachigatsu no daisan kayōbi deshita.* The summer solstice last year was on the third Tuesday of August.

■ Reading Exercises 7 (p.38) ■

1. *Shichiji/nanaji* 7:00, *sanji juppun/jippun* 3:10, *yoji gofun mae* 5 to 4, *rokuji-han* half past 6, *hachiji chōdo* exactly 8 o'clock, *ippun nijūbyō* 1 minute 20 seconds
2. *Hiruyasumi wa shōgo kara ichiji made desu.* The noon recess is from noon to 1 o'clock.
3. *Senshūmatsu wa ichinichijū gorufu o shita.* Last weekend I played golf all day long.
4. *Tokei no byōshin ga tomatte imasu.* The second hand of the watch has stopped.
5. *Asu/myōnichi no hi no de wa nanji desu ka.* What time is tomorrow's sunrise?
6. *Kugatsu no nakaba ni wa asayu suzushiku naru.* It gets cool in the mornings and evenings during mid-September.
7. *Maiasa hayaku okite, sanjuppun ijō joggingu o shimasu.* I get up early every morning, and go jogging for more than 30 minutes.
8. *Gozenchū wa isogashii kara, sanji igo ni kite kudasai.* I'm busy in the morning, so please come after 3 o'clock.
9. *Konban wa hayame ni ofisu o dete, Shopan no yūbe ni iku tsumori desu.* I intend to leave the office earlier this evening to go to the Chopin Evening.
10. *Depāto wa kayōbi o nozoite wa, gozen jūji-han kara gogo shichiji made desu.* Except for Tuesdays, the department store is open from 10:30 A.M. to 7:00 P.M.
11. *Sakkon, yoru ga nagaku, hiru ga mijikaku natta.* Recently, the nights have become longer and the days shorter.

12. *Ima kara itte mo, niji no basu ni wa ma ni aimasen yo.* Even if you leave now, you won't be in time for the 2 o'clock bus, I'm afraid.

■ Reading Exercises 8 (p.42)

1. *Nagai fuyu ga sari, Afurika ni shinjidai ga yatte kita.* A long winter has gone and a new era has come to Africa.
2. *Watashi no atarashii ofisu wa Roppongi sanchōme ni arimasu.* My new office is at 3-chome in Roppongi.
3. *Chikai shōrai, kare no Kanada kikō ga deru sō desu.* I hear that his book on his Canadian journey will be out in the near future.
4. *Kinnen, zainichi Amerika-jin no kazu ga sanbai ni natta.* In recent years, the number of Americans staying in Japan has trebled.
5. *Marui tsuki ga biru no ue ni arawaremashita.* A round moon appeared above the building.
6. *Gendaijin ni wa sonna furui aidia wa wakaranai.* Modern people don't understand such old ideas.
7. *Kodai no hitobito wa nan de jikan o hakarimashita ka.* How did the ancient people measure time?
8. *Kore wa tōi mukashi, dojin ga kite ita mono desu.* These are the things that native people wore long ago.
9. *Ima no sedai to mae no sedai no aida ni wa kanari no gyappu ga aru.* There is a considerable gap between the present and previous generations.
10. *Ato sūnen de nijūisseiki ni narimasu.* It will be the 21st century in several years.
11. *Kare wa zenseiki no nakaba ni tabitabi rainichi shimashita.* He visited Japan many times in the middle of the previous century.
12. *Tōmawari shita node, soko e iku noni ichijikan ijō kakatta.* Because we made a long detour, it took us more than one hour to get there.
13. *Chūsei no omokage no aru chaperu ni haitte, sunappu o sūmai totta.* I entered the chapel which had traces of the Middle Ages and took several snapshots.

■ Reading Exercises 9 (p.52)

1. *Ki no shita ni otoko no ko to onna no ko ga imasu.* There are a boy and a girl under the tree.

2. *Dansei to josei ga futatsu no chīmu ni wakaremashita.* Men and women are divided into two teams.

3. *Ane no chōjo wa jūgosai desuga, jinan wa mada mittsu desu.* My older sister's oldest daughter is fifteen years old, but her second son is still three years old.

4. *Ani no ofisu wa biru no hachikai ni aru.* My older brother's office is on the 8th floor of the building.

5. *Tomu wa kyōdai ga rokunin arimasu. O-nīsan ga futari to, otōto-san ga sannin to o-nēsan ga hitori desu.* Tom has six siblings. He has two older brothers, three younger brothers and one older sister.

6. *Musuko wa maiban shichiji ni kitaku shimasu.* My son returns home at 7 o'clock every evening.

7. *Shujin ga kaeri shidai, dekakemasu.* As soon as my husband returns, I'll go out.

8. *Sumisu-fusai wa asu no gogo yoji ni tsukimasu.* Mr. and Mrs. Smith will arrive at 4:00 P.M. tomorrow.

9. *Sono futari wa hatachi de fūfu ni natta.* The two got married at the age of twenty.

10. *Imōto no kazoku wa niwa no aru ie ni sumitagatte imasu.* My younger sister's family wants to live in a house with a garden.

11. *Katei no shufu wa toshi no kure ni wa totemo isogashii desu.* Housewives are very busy at the end of the year.

12. *Sofu wa mago o tsurete, Dizunīrando e itta.* My grandfather took his grandchild to Disneyland.

13. *Kanai no chichioya wa hachijussai made hitorigurashi deshita.* My wife's father lived alone until he was eighty years old.

14. *O-kāsan, kyō wa Haha no Hi da kara, doko e demo o-tomo shimasu yo.* Mother! Today is Mother's Day, so I'll go with you anywhere you wish.

15. *Kodomo no koro, tokidoki ryōshin to shinrui no ie e ikimashita.* When I was a child, I sometimes went to our relatives' houses with my parents.

■ Reading Exercises 10 (p.56) ■

1. *Ani wa gaijin no tomodachi ga gorokunin arimasu.* My older brother has five or six foreign friends.

2. *Mizuki-san wa imōto no mukashi kara no shiriai desu.* Miss Mizuki is my younger sister's old acquaintance.
3. *Ano hito wa kyōdai mo shinrui mo chijin mo arimasen.* He has no siblings, no relatives, and no acquaintances.
4. *Ane wa shin'yū no kodomo o yōshi ni shimashita.* My older sister adopted a child of her close friend.
5. *Senshūmatsu, furui nakama to gorufu o shimashita.* Last weekend, I played golf with my old companions.
6. *Miki-san wa mada imasu ga, ta no hitobito wa mō kaerimashita.* Mr. Miki is still here, but other people have already gone.
7. *Ano futari wa tanin na noni, shimai no yō ni naka ga ii.* Although the two are not related, they are close like sisters.
8. *Sumisu-fujin no kawari ni hoka no hito ga kimashita.* Someone else came in place of Mrs. Smith.
9. *Ano hito ga gaibu no hito ka naibu no hito ka shirimasen.* I don't know whether he is an outsider or an insider.
10. *Kare wa chimeijin dake atte, doko e itte mo yūjin ya chijin ga imasu.* As you might expect of a noted person, he has friends and acquaintances everywhere he goes.

■ Reading Exercises 11 (p.60) ■

1. *Ano kata wa donata-sama de irasshaimasu ka.* May I ask who is that person?
2. *Kimi-tachi wa Tomu-kun o shitte imasu ka.* Do you all know Tom?
3. *Shokun no aida de nani ka ii aidia wa arimasen ka.* Aren't there any good ideas among you people?
4. *Watashi-tachi wa shūmatsu igai ni wa gaishutsu shimasen.* We don't go out except on weekends.
5. *Wareware no gorufu nakama ni wa dansei mo josei mo imasu.* There are both men and women among our golf companions.
6. *Otōto no chōnan wa mada yonsai desu ga, nan demo jibun de yarita-garimasu.* My younger brother's oldest son is still four years old, but he wants to do everything by himself.
7. *Ano otoko wa jiko mo shirazu, jiga bakari tsuyoi.* That man doesn't even know himself, and he's just egoistic.
8. *Miki-shi wa kyonen no natsu, sankagetsu Kanada de kurashita.* Mr. Miki lived in Canada for three months last summer.

1. *Sengetsu, yūjin no imōto-san ni nibanme no onna no ko ga umaremashita.* Last month, a second baby girl was born to my friend's younger sister.

2. *Ima ya, jinsei hachijūnen no jidai ni natta.* Now we live in an age when the span of human life is eighty years old.

3. *Sono josei wa oya no nai yōji no yōiku ni seimei o sasagemashita.* The woman gave her life to bring up parentless infants.

4. *Ano rōjin wa jibun no namae mo seinen gappi mo shiranai.* That old man knows neither his own name nor birth date.

5. *Raishū no mokuyōbi ni watashi-tachi no sensei no tanjōbi o iwaimasu.* We will celebrate our teacher's birthday on Thursday next week.

6. *Sono kyōdai wa shōnenki o Doitsu de sugoshita.* The brothers spent their boyhood in Germany.

7. *Kono kurabu no menbā no kahansū wa wakai josei desu.* The majority of the membership of this club is young women.

8. *Jakunen nagara otōto wa ōkii hoteru no manējā desu.* Young as he is, my younger brother is the manager of a big hotel.

9. *Koko wa otona shika hairemasen. Miseinensha wa dame desu.* This place admits adults only. No minors.

10. *Chichi wa rokujussai de nakunari, haha wa gojūnisai de mibōjin ni natta.* My father died at the age of sixty, and my mother became a widow at the age of fifty-two.

11. *Kinō no akushidento de, shisha no kazu wa hyakunin ijō ni tasshimashita.* Due to yesterday's accident, the number of the dead reached over a hundred.

12. *Ani no musuko wa futari tomo ima ga shishunki desu.* My older brother's sons are both at puberty now.

13. *Ane wa kodomo-tachi ga seichō shita ato, seishun no omoide no aru Pari e satta.* After her children had grown up, my older sister left for Paris where the memories of her youth were.

■ **Reading Exercises 13 (p.74)** ▬▬▬▬▬▬▬▬▬▬

1. *Osanai kodomo ga koinu to asonde imasu.* A young child is playing with a puppy.

2. *Wagaya de ōkii banken o katte imasu.* We keep a big watchdog in our home.
3. *Kono ushi mo sono uma mo chichi ga sodateta no desu.* My father raised both this cow and that horse.
4. *Sofu wa naganen gyūba no shiiku o yatte imashita.* My grandfather raised oxen and horses many years.
5. *Afurika ni wa zō ya suigyū nado no dōbutsu ga imasu.* In Africa there are animals such as elephants and water buffaloes.
6. *Watatshi-tachi wa dōbutsuen made arukimashita.* We walked to the zoo.
7. *Niwa no doko ka de mushi ga naite imasu.* Insects are chirping somewhere in the garden.
8. *Jinan wa kesa hayaku, tomodachi to konchū o tori ni dekaketa.* Early this morning, my second son went out to catch insects with his friend.
9. *Hitsuji no mure ga yukkuri to ugoite imasu.* A flock of sheep are moving slowly.
10. *Sakana no taigun ga mizu no naka o oyoide imasu.* A large shoal of fish are swimming in water.
11. *Kono hon ni wa mezurashii gyorui ya kairui no koto ga dete iru.* This book has information about rare fish and shellfish.
12. *Tori ga sanba tonde iru. Hikōki wa niki tonde iru.* Three birds are flying. Two airplanes are flying.
13. *Aru chōrui wa maitoshi furusu ni kaeru sō desu.* I hear that certain birds return to their old nests every year.
14. *Mukashi wa kaiko o katte imashita ga, genzai yōsan wa okonawarete imasen.* They raised silkworms long ago, but sericulture is not carried out at present.
15. *Kono suizokukan wa getsuyō kyūkan desu.* This aquarium is closed on Mondays.

■ Reading Exercises 14 (p.81) ■

1. *Niwa ni kusa ga haete imasu.* The garden is covered with weeds.
2. *Kodomo ga take o futatsu ni orimashita.* A child broke off a bamboo.
3. *Otoko no hito ga matsu no eda o kitte imasu.* A man is cutting a branch of the pine tree.
4. *Ume no hana ga chitte, sakura no hana no kisetsu ga kita.* Plum blos-

soms have gone, and the cherry blossom season has come.

5. *Konshūmatsu hanami ni ikimasen ka.* Shall we go cherry-blossom viewing this weekend?

6. *Shōgatsu ya sono ta no medetai ori ni shōchikubai o kazarimasu.* Pines, bamboos and plums are used as decorations for happy occasions such as the New Year.

7. *Ki no miki ni ōkii mushi ga tomatte iru.* There is a big bug on the trunk of the tree.

8. *Aki ni wa ko no ha ga ochimasu.* Tree leaves fall in autumn.

9. *Ha no ochiru ki o rakuyōju to iimasu.* A tree whose leaves fall is called a deciduous tree.

10. *Shiyō ni kodawarazu, konkan o tadasu koto ga taisetsu desu.* It is important to correct fundamentals without being particular about unessentials.

11. *Daikon no tane o uemashita ga, mada me ga demasen.* I planted Japanese radish seeds, but they haven't sprouted yet.

12. *Kono mi wa mada jukushite inai ga, sochira wa mō jūbun urete iru.* This fruit hasn't ripened yet, but that one has rippened enough.

13. *Shuju no kusaki/sōmoku ya jumoku o minagara, shokubutsuen no naka o sanpo shita.* I walked through the botanical garden, while looking at all kinds of plants and trees.

■ Reading Exercises 15 (p.85) ■

1. *Hanazono ni iroiro no iro no hana ga saite imasu.* Flowers of various colors are in bloom in the flower garden.

2. *Wakaba ni kin'iro/konjiki no hi ga sashite imasu.* The golden sunlight shines upon the young leaves.

3. *Shōjo ga akai hana o otte kimashita.* A girl picked a red flower and brought it back.

4. *Shiroi tori ga matsu no eda ni tomatte imasu.* A white bird perches on the branch of a pine tree.

5. *Hakuchō ga aoi mizu no ue o oyoide iku.* Swans are swimming away on the blue water.

6. *Kurenai no yūhi ga jitsu ni utsukushii.* The crimson evening sun is truly beautiful.

7. *Teien no kōbai ga chirimashita.* The red plum blossoms in the garden have gone.

8. *Aki ni wa ko no ha ga kōyō shimasu.* Tree leaves turn red in autumn.
9. *Midori no kusa no ue o chairo no kouma ga aruite iru.* A brown pony is walking on the green grass.
10. *Watashi wa kōcha ga ii desu ga, haha wa ryokucha no hō ga ii desu.* I would like black tea, but my mother would prefer green tea.
11. *Kono mi wa ureru to, kiiro ni henshoku shimasu.* This fruit turns yellow, when it ripens.
12. *Sumisu-fujin wa koganeiro/ōgonshoku no burausu ni kuro no sukāto o haite iru.* Mrs. Smith is wearing a golden blouse and a black skirt.
13. *Amerika ni wa samazama na jinshu ga sunde iru. Hakujin mo, kokujin mo, ōshoku jinshu mo iru.* All kinds of races live in America. There are the white, the black, and the yellow race.

■ Reading Exercises 16 (p.93) ■

1. *Yama no itadaki kara, mori ya hayashi ga miemasu.* From the top of the mountain, we can see woods and a forest.
2. *Shinrin ni shuju no dōbutsu ya tori ga sunde iru.* All kinds of animals and birds live in the forest.
3. *Rainen wa Ebersuto-san ni noboritai.* I'd like to climb Mt. Everest next year.
4. *Kyonen no natsuyasumi ni, shigonin no nakama to tozan shita.* During summer vacation last year, I climbed a mountain with my four or five companions.
5. *Sanchō kara tanizoko o mioroshita.* We looked down the valley from the mountain top.
6. *Suitei o chiisai sakana ga oyoide iru.* Small fish are swimming at the bottom of the water.
7. *Tahata o tagayashite iroiro no kokumotsu o tsukuru. Suiden ni kome o, hatake ni mugi o tsukuru.* They cultivate fields and grow various grains. They grow rice in paddies and wheats in dry fields.
8. *Sono tochi no menseki no hanbun ijō wa kōchi desu.* More than half of the area of that land is cultivated fields.
9. *Kono chihō de wa ichinen ni nido beisaku o okonatte iru.* They grow rice twice a year in this region.
10. *Nohara de yachō ga naite iru.* Wild birds are singing in the field.
11. *Hiroi kusahara/sōgen o ichigun no uma ga hashitte iru.* A herd of horses is running in the large grassy plain.

12. *Tonneru o deru to, me no mae ni kōdai na heiya ga hirogatta.* When we got out of the tunnel, a vast plain spread in front of our eyes.
13. *Midori no makiba/bokujō de hitsuji ga kusa o tabete imasu.* Sheep are eating grass in the green pasture.
14. *Kono shokubutsu wa, sunaji de mo ishi ya iwa no aru jimen de mo sodatanai.* This plant can grow neither in sandy nor rocky ground.
15. *Dosha ya ganseki ga tsumikasanatte chisō ga dekiru.* A land stratum is formed with a pile of earth, sand and rocks.

■ Reading Exercises 17 (p.99) ■

1. *Kawagishi ni midori no matsu ga haete iru.* There are green pine trees on the riverbanks.
2. *Kawara de kodomo ga sūnin asonde iru.* Several children are playing in the dry riverbed.
3. *Haru to aki ni wa sanga ga utsukushii.* Mountains and rivers are beautiful in spring and autumn.
4. *Natsu ni wa, hitobito wa umi de oyoidari, kaigan o sanpo shitari suru.* In summer, people do things like swimming in the ocean and walking along the seashore.
5. *Genseirin no naka ni izumi ga wakidete iru.* Fountains gush out in the virgin forest.
6. *Niwa no sensui ni akai kingyo ga iru.* There are red goldfish in the pond in the garden.
7. *Kono shokubutsu wa fukai ike ni wa mirareru ga, asai ike ni wa mirarenai.* This plant is seen in deep ponds but not in shallow ponds.
8. *Ano hito-tachi wa kawa ya, umi ya, mizuumi no shinsen o shirabete iru.* Those people survey the depth of rivers, seas and lakes.
9. *Chosuichi no mizu ga hanbun shika nai.* The water of the reservoir is half full.
10. *Sono itsutsu no mizuumi no naka de, Yamanaka-ko ga ichiban ōkii.* Among those 5 lakes, Lake Yamanaka is the biggest.
11. *Nihon kairyū wa Taiheiyō o nagarete iru.* The Japan Current flows in the Pacific Ocean.
12. *Michishio no toki ni wa, suishin ga jū-mētoru ijō ni naru.* The depth of water becomes above 10 meters at full tide.
13. *Kanchō wa gogo rokuji goro de, jakkan no hito ga kai o hiroi ni deru.* The ebb tide is about 6:00 P.M., and some people go out to pick up

shells.

14. *Umizoi ni sūko no ie ga sanzai shite iru.* Several houses are found here and there along the sea.

15. *Tokidoki, sono engan chihō ni mezurashii shizen genshō ga okotte iru.* Sometimes, an unusual natural phenomenon occurs in the districts along the seashore.

■ Reading Exercises 18 (p.107) ■

1. *Chiri no hon ni sekai no omo na kuni no chizu ga dete iru.* The maps of the main countries in the world are in geography books.

2. *Chiseizu de Nihon zenkoku no tochi ya yama no yōsu o miru.* We look at the condition of flat land and mountains in all Japan on a topographic map.

3. *Chikyūjō ni wa nanatsu no tairiku ga aru.* There are seven continents on the earth.

4. *Nihon wa kita hankyū ni, Ōsutoraria wa minami hankyū ni kurai suru.* Japan lies in the northern hemisphere and Australia in the southern hemisphere.

5. *Hokkyoku to Nankyoku no umi ni kakushu no sakana ya dōbutsu ga iru.* There are various fish and animals in the seas of the North and South poles.

6. *Minami Taiheiyō ni kazu ōku no shima ga sanzai suru.* Many islands lie scattered in the South Pacific.

7. *Nettai no shimajima ni wa tasū no mezurashii shokubutsu ga haete iru.* Many rare plants grow on tropical islands.

8. *Nihon rettō ni wa ikutsu ka no kazanmyaku ga hashitte iru.* Several volcanic mountain ranges run through the Japanese archipelago.

9. *Hiroi kawa ga futatsu no shū no sakai ni natte iru.* The wide river forms the boundary between the two states.

10. *Kono michi wa Kanada no kokkyō made tsuzuku.* This road leads to the Canadian border.

11. *Nihon wa Honshū, Kyūshū, Hokkaidō, Shikoku to sono ta no chiisai shima kara natte iru.* Japan consists of Honshu, Kyushu, Hokkaido, Shikoku and other small islands.

12. *Sono chihō no yaku hanbun wa shinrin chitai de aru.* About half of that region is a forest zone.

13. *Chūō Amerika wa Mekishiko to Koronbia no aida no semai chiiki de*

aru. Central America is the narrow region between Mexico and Co-
lombia.

14. *Chūgoku wa Ajia Tairiku ni ichi shi, Tōyō de ichiban kōdai na ryōdo
o motte iru.* China is located in the Asian Continent, and has the
largest territory in the Orient.

15. *Haru ni wa zenkoku kakuchi kara, ōzei no hito ga kono hantō ni aso-
bi ni kuru.* Many people come to visit this peninsula in spring from
all parts of the country.

■ Reading Exercises 19 (p.114) ■■■■■■■■■

1. *Shi wa ikutsu ka no ku ni kugirarete iru.* The city is divided into
several wards.

2. *Kuyakusho no kinjo ni yūbinkyoku ga aru.* There is a post office in
the vicinity of the ward office.

3. *Mura no kōminkan made basu no ben ga aru.* A bus service is avail-
able as far as the citizen's hall of the village.

4. *Sakuya, sanson no yakuba de kaji ga okotta.* Last night, a fire broke
out at the public office in a mountain village.

5. *Kinnen, sono machi no kingō de wa kosū ga nibai ni natta.* In recent
years, the number of houses doubled in neighboring districts of the
city.

6. *Gunnai o hiroi kawa ga tōzai ni nagarete iru.* A wide river runs from
east to west through the county.

7. *Tōkyō wa Nihon de ichiban ōkii tokai de aru.* Tokyo is the largest
city in Japan.

8. *Tōkyō-to ni wa issenman ijō no hito ga sunde iru.* More than 10 million people live in Tokyo Metropolis.

9. *Kyōto wa Nihon no furui miyako de ari, meisho ga ōku, kenbutsunin
ga ōzei kuru.* Being the old capital of Japan, Kyoto has many noted
places and a great number of sight-seers come.

10. *Tochō ya fuchō ya kenchō nado no yakusho wa machi no chūshinchi
ni aru.* Public offices such as the Tokyo Metropolitan Government
Office and prefectural offices are located at the center of each city.

11. *To-dō-fu-ken no chiji wa kokumin ni yotte erabareru.* The governors
of urban and rural prefectures are chosen by the people.

12. *Nihon no sōjinkō wa yaku ichioku nisenmannin de aru.* The total
polulation of Japan is about 120 million.

1. *Sora ni kurai kumo ga hirogatte iru.* Dark clouds spread in the sky.
2. *Kyō wa tenki wa yoi ga, kūki wa tsumetai.* Although the weather is fine today, the air is cold.
3. *Kono hantō wa kikō ga ondan de, fuyu demo atatakai.* This peninsula has a mild climate, and it's warm even in winter.
4. *Akutenkō no tame, yamamichi de doshakuzure ga atta.* Due to the bad weather, there was a landslide on the mountain road.
5. *Gozenchū wa ame ga futta ga, gogo wa hareta.* It rained in the morning, but cleared up in the afternoon.
6. *Nihon de mottomo kōuryō no ōi tsuki wa rokugatsu de aru.* The month of June has the largest amount of rainfall in Japan.
7. *Kotoshi no Tōkyō no saitei kion wa heinen yori godo mo takai.* The lowest temperature in Tokyo this year is five degrees higher than the average year.
8. *Kyūshū no nigatsu no heikin kion wa kyonen yori sūdo hikukatta.* The average temperature of Kyushu in Feburary was several degrees lower than last year.
9. *Kōkiatsu no tame, seiten ga tsuzuite iru.* Due to the high atomospheric pressure, we have a long spell of fine weather.
10. *Tenki yohō ni yoru to, asu, Kyōto-fu hokubu ni yuki ga furu sō da.* According to the weather forecast, it will snow tomorrow in the northern part of Kyoto Prefecture.
11. *Nihonkai engan chihō de wa, mainen, taryō no kōsetsu ga aru.* In the districts along the coast of the Japan Sea, there is a large amount of snowfall every year.
12. *Samui kisetsu ni wa, ōzei no hito ga atsui Hawai ni dekakeru.* In the cold season, many people go to Hawaii where it is warm.
13. *Sono toshi wa tairiku no chūōbu ni ichi shi, kansho no sa ga ōkii.* The city is located in the central part of the continent, so the difference in cold and heat is great.
14. *Hokkyoku no umi kara hyōzan ga nagarete kuru.* Icebergs flow in from the seas around the North Pole.
15. *Yowai kaze ga kyōfū ni kawatta.* A gentle wind turned into a strong wind.
16. *Sono tochi no jūmin wa hideri ya kōgai ni nayande iru.* The inhabitants of the region suffer from droughts and environmental pollution.

17. *Kishōchō wa takanami chūihō ya bōfū keihō nado o dasu.* The Meteorological Agency issues high-wave warnings and storm warnings, etc.

■ Reading Exercises 21 (p.131) ■

1. *Yozora ni sūsen no hoshi ga kirakira hikatte iru.* Thousands of stars are twinkling in the night sky.
2. *Kagami no yō na tsuki ga komen ni utsutte iru.* A moon like a mirror is reflected upon the surface of the lake.
3. *Hareta ban, bōenkyō de seiza o mita.* On a clear night, I looked at the constellation through a telescope.
4. *Taiyō no kōsen ga kōen no kigi ni sashite iru.* The sunlight shines upon the trees in the park.
5. *Taiyōkei wa taiyō ya, chikyū ya, sono ta ōku no hoshi kara natte iru.* The solar system consists of the sun, the earth, and many other stars.
6. *Jinkō eisei ga chikyū no mawari o mawatte iru.* A man-made satellite is going round the earth.
7. *Chikyū wa yaku sanbyaku rokujūgonichi de taiyō no shūi o kaiten suru.* The earth makes a rotation round the sun in about 365 days.
8. *Tenmondai de tentai no kansoku o okonau.* They make observations of the heavenly body at an astronomical observatory.
9. *Tsuki no inryoku de kanchō ya manchō ga okoru.* The ebb and flow of the tide are due to the gravitation of the moon.
10. *Uchū hikōshi ga kasei e tobu hi wa amari tōkunai darō.* The day will not be far distant when astronauts will fly to Mars.

■ Reading Exercises 22 (p.137) ■

1. *Maiasa, hachiji ni asagohan o taberu.* Every morning, I eat my breakfast at 8 o'clock.
2. *Kesa, chōshoku ni tamago o niko, tōsuto o nimai, ringo o hitotsu tabeta.* This morning, I ate two eggs, two pieces of toast and an apple for breakfast.
3. *Yūhan wa washoku ni suru ka yōshoku ni suru ka mada mitei da.* I haven't decided yet whether I'll have Japanese or Western-style food for supper.

4. *"Yamato" to iu shokudō de, teishoku o chūmon shita.* I ordered a set meal at the restaurant called Yamato.
5. *Ie de hayame ni karui shokuji o shite dekaketa.* I had a light meal earlier at home and went out.
6. *Saikin, asa to hiru wa keishoku ni shite iru.* Recently, I have a light meal for breakfast and lunch.
7. *Kono gyūniku wa katakute taberarenai.* This beef is too tough to eat.
8. *Akachan no tabemono ga kokeishoku ni kawatta.* The baby's diet has changed to solid food.
9. *Mame ya, yasai ya, sakana nado no eiyō ni tomu shokumotsu o toru koto ga taisetsu da.* It is important to have nutritious food such as beans, vegetables and fish.
10. *Aru kuni de wa, eiyō busoku de tasū no yōji ga shibō site iru.* In some countries, many young children die from undernourishment.
11. *Aki wa kajitsu no kisetsu dake atte, iroiro no shurui no kudamono ga aru.* As you might expect from autumn being the season for fruits, there are all kinds of fruits in autumn.
12. *Nikagetsu sesshoku shite mita ga, amari yoi seika wa agaranakatta.* I tried a low-intake diet for two months, but didn't get very good results.
13. *Sono engan chihō wa umi no sachi ni mo yama no sachi ni mo megumarete iru.* The districts along the coast are blessed with both sea and land products.

▬ Reading Exercises 23 (p.140) ▬▬▬▬▬▬▬▬▬▬▬▬▬▬

1. *Kōhī ni kona-miruku o irete nonda.* I had coffee with powdered milk.
2. *Shiranai tochi de wa inshokubutsu ni chūi shita hō ga ii.* You should be careful about food and drink in unknown places.
3. *Gyūnyū no kawari ni tōnyū o nomu koto ga aru.* There are times when I drink soybean milk in place of cow's milk.
4. *Anata no suki na nomimono wa nan desu ka.* What is your favorite drink?
5. *Aru gaijin wa yōshu yori Nihon no sake o konomu yō da.* Some foreigners seem to prefer Japanese sake to foreign liquors.
6. *Kono shima no meibutsu no himono wa watashi no kōbutsu da.* Dried fish, a noted product of this island, is my favorite food.

7. *Kono suimono ni wa tamago to aona ga haitte iru.* This soup has eggs and greens in it.
8. *Insutanto sūpu wa nettō o sosogu dake de dekiru.* Instant soup is made by just pouring in boiling water.
9. *Samui asa wa, atsui kōhī ka kōcha ga hoshii.* I like to have hot coffee or tea on cold mornings.
10. *Atsui kisetsu ni wa, dare demo tashō shokuyoku ga teika suru.* One's appetite falls off more or less in the hot season.

■ Reading Exercises 24 (p.147) ■

1. *Kono ryōri wa ajitsuke ga warui desu ne.* This food isn't seasoned well, is it?
2. *Sakana ni remon o kuwaeru to, fūmi ga yoku naru.* If you add lemon to fish, it tastes better.
3. *Kakō shita mono wa dekiru dake tsukawanai yō ni shite iru.* I try as much as possible not to use processed food.
4. *Kudamono ga garasu no utsuwa ni irete aru.* There are some fruits in the glass vessel.
5. *Ōku no shufu wa daidokoro de atarashii kigu o shiyō shite iru.* Many housewives are using new utensils in their kitchens.
6. *Asu no pātī ni tsukau shokki o shirabete kudasai.* Please check the tableware used for tomorrow's party.
7. *Zairyō ga yokute mo, chōmiryō ga warui to dame da.* Good materials won't do without good seasoning.
8. *Komugiko ni tamago to satō o mazeru.* I mix eggs and sugar with flour.
9. *Maiasa, irorio no yasai o kongō shita jūsu o nomu.* Every morning, I drink mixed vegetable juice.
10. *Hiroi sakagura ni kakushu no sake ga aru.* There are all kinds of wine in the large wine cellar.
11. *Reizōko no naka ni tabemono ya nomimono ga haitte iru.* Food and drink are put in the refrigerator.
12. *Kono sakana wa shioyaki ni shitari, mushiyaki ni shitari suru.* I sometimes broil this fish with salt and sometimes bake it in a casserole.
13. *Konban rokuji ni mukashi no tomodachi to shokuji no yakusoku ga aru.* I have a dinner engagement with my old friend at 6 o'clock this evening.

14. *Haha ga yūhan no yoī o shi, watashi ga saraarai o shita.* My mother prepared supper and I washed the dishes.
15. *Ryōri no jōzu na ane wa yoku jibun no tsukutta teryōri ni chijin o shōtai suru.* My older sister who is a good cook often invites her acquaintances to a dinner prepared by herself.

■ Reading Exercises 25 (p.154) ■

1. *Fukuya de sūtsu o itchaku chūmon shita.* I ordered a suit at the tailor.
2. *Ano mise no ten'in wa wakakute shinsetsu da.* The clerk at that store is young and kind.
3. *Denkiya ni atarashii kigu ga iroiro dete iru.* Various new models are shown in the electric appliances store.
4. *Tokeiten no shō uindō no hi ga tsuitari kietari shite iru.* The lights in the shop window of a watchmaker's go on and off.
5. *Kono tōri wa gaitō ga hitobanjū tsuite ite akarui.* This street is bright all night with the street lights on.
6. *Ano tsūro wa semakute, basu wa tōrenai.* That passage is too narrow to let a bus go through.
7. *Sakaya no mae no dōro wa ima kōji o shite iru.* The street in front of the liquor store is under construction now.
8. *Hyakkaten no jukkai ni wa kakushu no inshokuten ga narande iru.* On the 10th floor of the department store, all kinds of eating places stand in a line.
9. *Biru no okujō kara namikiro o sanpo suru hitobito ga mieru.* From the roof of the building you can see people walking along the tree-lined street.
10. *Kaguya no migigawa ni yakkyoku ga ari, hidarigawa ni kamera-ya ga aru.* There is a pharmacy to the right of the furniture store and a camera shop to the left of it.
11. *Ano yotsukado o sasetsu suru to, migite ni hon'ya ga aru.* Turning to the left at that cornor, you will find a bookstore on the right side.
12. *Sono shoten no sayū ni resutoran ga aru.* There are restaurants on both sides of the bookstore.
13. *Chikagai no mise wa asa jūji ni aite, yoru hachiji ni shimaru.* The stores in the underground shopping mall open at 10 o'clock in the morning and close at 8 o'clock in the evening.

14. *Ano kudamonoya wa sengetsu kaiten shita bakari da.* That fruit store just opened last month.
15. *Heiten made ni mada sanjuppun hodo aru.* There are still 30 minutes or so left before the store closes.
16. *Machi ni wa samazama na shōten ga atsumatte iru.* Various stores are concentrated in town.
17. *Sūmei no shufu ga shōtengai no iriguchi de shūgō shita.* Several housewives gathered at the entrance of the shopping district.

■ **Reading Exercises 26 (p.162)** ▬▬▬▬▬▬▬▬▬▬▬

1. *Kono shina wa yasukute hinshitsu ga yoi.* This article is inexpensive and good in quality.
2. *Kono futatsu wa yoku nite iru ga, kochira wa kōkyūhin de sochira wa yasumono da.* These two are very similar, but this one is a quality article and that one is a cheap stuff.
3. *Akushitsu no shōhin ya ruijihin ni chūishite kudasai.* Please beware of bad-quality goods and imitations.
4. *Aru yakuhin wa jōyō shinai hō ga ii.* Certain medicines should not be used habitually.
5. *Hijōyō no shokuryō ga ano hako ni haitte iru.* That box has the food for emergencies in it.
6. *Yōsōten no manekin ga haru no yosooi ni koromogae shita.* The mannequins at the dressmaking shop have been changed to spring wear.
7. *Gaikoku de, kazukazu no minzoku ishō ya mingeihin o mite mawatta.* In foreign countries, I went around looking at numerous folk costumes and handcrafts.
8. *Ano mise wa yōfuku no nunoji ya keito nado o oite iru.* That store carrys dress materials and woolen yarns, etc.
9. *Daidokoro yōhin wa kono hyakkaten no gokai ni, mōfu wa hachikai ni aru.* Kitchen utensils are on the 5th floor and blankets are on the 8th floor of this department store.
10. *Kotoshi wa dantō de kegawa no kōto o kiru kikai ga nakatta.* Due to a warm winter, I had no chance to wear my fur coat this year.
11. *Chikagai ni kawaseihin no kōkyūten ga kaiten shita.* A high-quality store of leather products opened in the underground shopping mall.
12. *Hōsekibako ni kingin no yubiwa ya burōchi ga irete aru.* Gold and silver rings and brooches have been put in the jewel box.

13. *Natsu no kisetsu ni wa kinu yori menseihin ga konomareru.* Cotton products are prefered to silk in the summer season.
14. *Garasu no kēsu no naka ni, kōkyū na jiki ga narande iru.* Quality pieces of porcelain are displayed in the glass case.
15. *Ten'in ga ningyō o hako ni irete, kiiro no hōsōshi de tsutsunde kureta.* A store clerk put the doll in a box and wrapped it up with yellow paper for me.

■ Reading Exercises 27 (p.171) ■

1. *Shōten no yasuuri ya fukubiki ni ōzei no kaimonokyaku ga atsumatta.* Many shoppers thronged to the bargain sales and raffles in the stores.
2. *Watashi no yūjin wa tochi ya kaoku no baibai o shite iru.* My friend deals in land and houses.
3. *Kono shina wa hinshitsu wa yoi ga, nedan ga takasugiru.* The article is good in quality, but the price is too high.
4. *Aru yūbin kitte wa ichiman'en no kachi ga aru.* Certain postage stamps are worth 10,000 yen.
5. *Kotoshi no denki seihin ni takai kakaku ga tsuite iru.* The electric appliances produced this year are high-priced.
6. *Kono kigu wa tanka nisen'en de sanmandai ureta.* This apparatus sold 30,000 units at 2,000 yen apiece.
7. *Ginza no hōsekiten de, kōka na yubiwa o hangaku de katta.* I bought an expensive ring at half price at a jeweler's on the Ginza.
8. *Chichi wa zaimoku no shōbai de ōki na rieki o eta.* My father made a big profit in his lumber business.
9. *Maitsuki/maigetsu, getsumatsu ni torihiki no sontoku o keisan suru.* We calculate the loss and gain of transactions at the end of every month.
10. *Chūmon o uke shidai, shinamono o hatchū suru.* On receipt of the orders, we'll ship the merchandise.
11. *Aru mise wa shū ni nanoka, denwa de juchū shite iru.* Some stores receive orders by telephone seven days a week.
12. *Ten'in ga nyūka shita shōhin o sōko ni hakonde iru.* The clerks are carrying the newly arrived goods to the warehouse.
13. *Yasai ya kudamono o torakku de machi e shukka suru.* We ship vegetables and fruits to town by truck.

14. *Kono unchin ni wa niwari no waribiki ga aru.* This fare gives you a 20% discount.
15. *Bunkatsu barai de reizōko o katta.* I bought a refrigerator on the installment plan.
16. *Ani wa fukin no yakusho ni shinamono o nōnyū shite iru.* My older brother supplys goods to the public offices in the vicinity.
17. *Nichiyōbi to saijitsu ni wa yūbin no haitatsu wa nai.* There is no postal delivery on Sundays and holidays.
18. *Rainendo no yosan ga kimatta.* The budget for the next fiscal year has been decided.
19. *Wareware wa ichinen ni nido, shūnyū to shishutsu no kessan o suru.* We settle accounts (earnings and expenses) twice a year.
20. *Sūjitsu mae kara dōro kōji no nyūsatsu kōkoku ga dete iru.* A bid for road construction has been advertised for several days.

■ Reading Exercises 28 (p.180) ■

1. *Shōgakkō wa gozen hachiji ni hajimatte, gogo sanji-han ni owaru.* Elementary schools start at 8:00 A.M. and ends at 3:30 P.M.
2. *Watashi-tachi no ukemochi no sensei wa Tanaka-sensei desu.* Our homeroom teacher is Miss Tanaka.
3. *Chōjo mo jijo mo kyōgaku no daigaku de mananda.* My oldest and second daughters studied at a coeducational university.
4. *Ani no chijin wa yūmei na gakusha de, genzai Kyōdai no daigakuin de oshiete iru.* My older brother's acquaintance is a famous scholar, and presently he is teaching a graduate course at Kyoto University.
5. *Chōnan wa Nihon de kyōiku o uketa ga, jinan wa ima Pari ni ryūgaku shite iru.* My oldest son was educated in Japan, but my second son is studying in Paris now.
6. *Aru kōtō gakkō wa daigaku no yobikō da to kangaerarete iru.* Certain high schools are considered to be preparatory schools for universities.
7. *Imōto wa hoikuen de osanai kodomo-tachi no sewa o shite iru.* My younger sister is taking care of young children at a nursery school.
8. *Aru chiiki de wa, gakkō o yameru jidō ya seito no sū ga ōku natta.* In some districts, the number of schoolchildren and pupils who have quit school has increased.
9. *Tsukue no ue ni jisho ga sansatsu to mannenhitsu ga nihon oite aru.* There are three dictionaries and two fountain pens on the desk.

10. *Sankōsho ya hyakka jiten de iroiro na koto o shiraberu.* I check various items in reference books and encyclopedias.
11. *Kyōshitsu no kokuban ni Hokkaidō no chizu ga kaite aru.* A map of Hokkaido is drawn on the blackboard in the classroom.
12. *Yamada-sensei wa shijū atarashii kyōzai o tsukai, oshiekata mo jōzu da.* Mr. Yamada is a good teacher who is always using new materials.
13. *Kono kyōkasho wa naiyō ga sukoshi furui desu ne.* The contents of this textbook are somewhat old, aren't they?
14. *Kōsha no ushiro ni ōkii toshokan ga tatta.* A big library was built behind the school building.
15. *Kōmon o hairu to, migite ni sangaidate no tatemono ga mieru.* Entering the school gate, you can see a three-storied building on the right.
16. *Atsui kara, mado o akete kudasai.* It's warm, so please open the windows.
17. *Watashi to Haruko-san wa kōkō de onaji kumi datta.* Haruko and I were in the same class at high school.
18. *Mainen gogatsu no dōsōkai ni wa, mukashi no dōkyūsei ga nijūnin ijō atsumaru.* At the class reunion every May, more than twenty old classmates get together.

■ Reading Exercises 29 (p.193) ■

1. *Maiban ie de, gakka no yoshū ya fukushū o shimasu.* I review and prepare my lessons every night at home.
2. *Watashi no ukemochi no seito wa sengetsu, kōkō no katei o shūgyō shita.* The pupils under my charge completed the high school course last month.
3. *Jugyō ga kyūkō ni natta node, jimu de undō o shita.* Because the class was cancelled, I exercised at the gymnasium.
4. *Miki-jokyōju no kōgi ni wa gakusei ga ōzei atsumatte kuru.* Assistant Professor Miki's lectures attract many students.
5. *Ano Amerika-jin no kōshi wa Nihon bungaku no kenkyū de yoku shirareteiru.* That American lecturer is well known for his study of Japanese literature.
6. *Shiken ni sonaete yoku benkyō shita node, seiseki ga agatta.* Because I prepared myself for examinations and studied hard, my grades improved.

7. *Wakarimasen. Mō ichido itte kudasai.* I don't understand. Please say it again.
8. *Tēpu o kikinagara, gaikoku no kotoba o renshū shimasu.* I practice foreign languages while listening to tapes.
9. *Shinbun de kyūjin no kōkoku o mite, gansho o teishutsu shita.* I saw a want ad in the newspaper, and sent in an application.
10. *Ano ryūgakusei wa Nihonjin no yō ni hanaseru ga, yomikaki wa heta da.* That foreign student can speak like a Japanese but cannot read or write well.
11. *Dokusho ya taiken o tsūjite, jinsei no igi o tankyū suru.* We search for the meaning of life through our reading and personal experiences.
12. *Kono toi no kotae wa kyōkasho no ushiro ni tsuite iru.* The answers to these questions are provided at the back of the textbook.
13. *Sūgaku wa watashi no senmon de wa nai kara, sono shitsumon ni wa kaitō dekimasen.* Because mathematics is not my speciality, I am not able to answer the question.
14. *Tōan o saiten shita tokoro, manten o totta gakusei wa hitori mo in-akatta.* When I marked the examination papers, there was no student who attained full marks.
15. *Shukudai o wasurete, sensei ni chūi sareta.* I forgot my homework and was cautioned by my teacher.
16. *Riron wa tan ni shitte iru dake de naku, ōyō suru koto gu taisetsu da.* It it important not only to know a theory but also to put it into practice.
17. *Kono hon wa omoshiroi desu ga, shiso wa asai desu.* This book is entertaining but shallow in thought.
18. *Ano hito wa chishiki wa hiroi ga, jōshiki ga kakete iru.* Although well-informed, he/she is lacking in common sense.
19. *Jidō wa sensei ni insotsu sarete ensoku ni itta.* Led by their teacher, the children went on an excursion.
20. *Sotsugyōshiki ni tochi no meishi, narabi ni ōzei no fukei ga shusseki shita.* Local celebrities and many parents attended the graduation ceremony.

■ Reading Exercises 30 (p.200) ■

1. *Sumisu-san wa Amerika no shūritsu daigaku de Nihongo o mananda.* Mr. Smith learned Japanese language at a state university in U.S.A.

2. *Wakai Kanada-jin no sensei ga Tōkyō no shiritsu kōkō de eikaiwa o oshiete iru.* A young Canadian teacher is teaching English conversation at a private high school in Tokyo.
3. *Maiban yūhan no ato de, tēpu o kikinagara hatsuon no renshū o shite imasu.* Every evening after supper, I practice the pronunciation while listening to the tapes.
4. *Hiragana to katakana wa yomeru ga, kanji wa mada sukoshi shika yomenai.* I can read hiragana and katakana but only a few kanji yet.
5. *Kotoba wa meishi, dōshi, keiyōshi, fukushi nado shuju no hinshi ni wakerareru.* Words are divided into various parts of speech such as nouns, verbs, adjectives, adverbs and so forth.
6. *Iroiro no tatoe o hiite oshieru to, seito wa hayaku rikai shimasu.* If you teach by giving various instances, pupils will understand easily.
7. *Bunpō ni wa kanarazu reigai ga aru.* There is no grammar without exceptions.
8. *Kanji no hitsujun o narau koto wa hitsuyō da.* It is necessary to learn the stroke order of kanji.
9. *Kono bunshō wa goku no junjo o kaete kutōten o tadashiku utsu to, yomiyasuku naru.* A change of word order and the proper punctuation will make this composition more readable.
10. *Ano gakusei wa gaikokugo o oboeru nōryoku ga nai to jikaku shite iru yō da.* That student seems to realize his own inability to learn a foreign language.
11. *Gogaku no sainō ga atte mo doryoku shinakereba, seiseki wa agaranai.* Even if you have linguistic talent, you can't make good grades without effort.
12. *Jōkyūsei wa muzukashii shiken ya shukudai ga ōkute komatte iru.* Senior students are having a hard time with a lot of difficult examinations and homework.
13. *Ryūgaku shita toki, kotoba ga muzukashikute, arayuru konnan ni atta.* When I studied abroad, the language was hard, and I met with all sorts of difficulties.
14. *Kono bunshō ni ayamari ga attara, naoshite kudasai.* If there are any mistakes in this composition, please correct them.
15. *Gaikokugo de hanashite iru to, tabitabi gokai ga okoru.* Speaking in a foreign language often causes misunderstanding.

1. *Mainichi, asa to hiru ni rajio taisō o shite imasu.* Every morning and afternoon, I do radio gymnastic exercises.
2. *Mainen, Bosuton no marason kyōsō ni ōzei no hito ga sanka suru.* Every year, many people participate in the Boston marathon.
3. *Tōki Orinpikku de Doitsu-jin ya Amerika-jin no senshu ga kakushu no kyōgi de katta.* In the Winter Olympics German and American players won in various events.
4. *Suiei no kyōsō de Honda-kun to ichii o arasotta ga, futari tomo san'iika ni natta.* Honda and I contended for first place in the swimming competition, but both of us finished below third.
5. *Koko wa "Yakyū no Machi" to shite fukkō shi, shōgyō mo okotta.* This place was reconstructed as a "Baseball Town," and its commerce also flourished.
6. *Kankyaku wa nessen ni ōi ni kōfun shita.* The spectators got very excited about the hot contest.
7. *Goban dasha no Yamashita ga battā bokkusu ni tatsu to, dotto kansei ga okotta.* When the fifth batter Yamashita stood in the batter's box, a great cry arose.
8. *Ōku no gaikokujin ga Nihon no budō ni kyōmi o motte iru yō da.* Many foreigners seem to have an interest in the Japanese martial arts.
9. *Hoketsu no senshu no shippai de aite ni santen mo torareta.* The substitute player's error resulted in the opponent gaining as many as three points.
10. *Hidarikiki no tōshu ga kesshōsen de sugureta ginō o miseta.* The left-handed pitcher displayed excellent skills in the final match.
11. *Yūshō dekinakute zannen datta ga, zen'in saigo made dōdō to tatakatta.* We regretted that we couldn't win the victory, but we all fought with dignity to the end.
12. *Tsuyoi chīmu to no taisen ni san tai go no tokuten de maketa.* We lost the match against the strong team by the score of 3 to 5.
13. *Ryō-chīmu tomo yoku funsen shita ga, kyūkai no ura no hōmuran de shōbu ga kimatta.* Both teams fought desperately, but the game was over with the home run in the second half of the 9th inning.

14. *Shiai wa enchōsen to nari, jukkai no omote de pinchi hittā no namae ga happyō sareta.* The game went into an extra inning, and the name of the pinch hitter was announced in the first half of the 10th inning.

15. *Zenjitsu yabureta rikishi ga ashi ni hōtai o shite dohyō ni arawareta.* The sumo wrestler who had been defeated the day before appeared in the ring with his foot in a bandage.

16. *Kyūdō o hajimeta bakari de mada heta desu.* I just started archery, so I'm still poor at it.

17. *Sono musha wa yumi no meijin de kanarazu mato o itta sō da.* I hear that the warrior was an expert archer and never missed the target.

18. *Koko wa shateki no renshū ni risōteki na basho da.* This is an ideal place for target practice.

19. *Sutajiamu ni kakkoku no kokki — Amerika no hata mo hi no maru mo tatte iru.* The national flags of various countries — the American flag, the Rising Sun flag and others are hoisted in the stadium.

■ Reading Exercises 32 (p.215) ■

1. *Sumisu-kyōju wa Tōyō no geijutsu ni fukai kyōmi o motte iru.* Professor Smith has deep interest in Oriental art.

2. *Asu kara machi no bijutsukan de kaiga no tenrankai ga hirakareru.* An exhibition of paintings will be held at the art museum in the city starting tomorrow.

3. *Ane wa saikin aburae ni netchū shite iru.* My older sister is absorbed in oil painting recently.

4. *Ano gaka wa seibutsuga yori fūkeiga no hō ga tokui da.* That painter has a forte for landscapes rather than still lifes.

5. *Atatakai hi ni, kaigan no keshiki o shasei shita.* On a warm day, I made a shetch of a coastal landscape.

6. *Kinō no bijutsuten de furui Nihon no hanga ga tenji sarete ita.* Some old Japanese woodblock prints were displayed at yesterday's art exhibition.

7. *Bankokuhaku de kakkoku no pabirion o mite mawatta.* We went around looking at the pavilions of various countries at the World's Fair.

8. *Shizuka na mizuumi no suimen ni marui tsuki ga utsutte iru.* A round moon is reflected on the calm surface of the lake.

9. *Utsukushii yūbae o utsushite, shashin o genzō shita.* I photographed a beautiful evening glow and developed the film.
10. *Hakubutsukan no mae no hiroba ni shiroi sekizō ga tatte iru.* A white stone statue is erected in the plaza in front of the museum.
11. *Gogo sanji kara kōdō de eiga no shishakai ga okonawareru.* The preview of a movie will be held in the auditorium at 3:00 P.M.
12. *Ukemochi no sensei ni eishaki no tsukaikata o osowatta.* I learned how to use a movie projecter from my homeroom teacher.

■ Reading Exercises 33 (p.219) ■

1. *Kōkō de wakai onna no sensei ni ongaku o naratta.* In high school I took music lessons from a young woman teacher.
2. *Shōka kyōshitsu kara kodomo-tachi no tanoshisō na utagoe ga kikoete kuru.* The voices of children joyfully singing are heard from the singing room.
3. *Zen'in kiritsu shite chikarazuyoku kokka o utatta.* They all stood up and sang the national anthem vigorously.
4. *Gakkō no pātī de, jidō ga kurisumasu kyaroru o gasshō shita.* At the school party, children sang Christmas carols together.
5. *Sakuya no konsāto de, kokujin no kashu ga kazukazu no meikyoku o dokushō shita.* At last night's concert, a black singer sang solo a great number of famous work of music.
6. *Rajio kara yūbi na piano kyōsōkyoku ga nagarete kuru.* The sound of an elegant piano concerto flows from the radio.
7. *Jūsansai no shōjo ga baiorin no dokusōkai de sugureta sainō o hakki shita.* The thirteen-year-old girl exhibited excellent talent at the violin recital.
8. *Jōnai no dentō ga kiete, shikisha no takuto no moto ni shizuka na zensōkyoku ga nagaredashita.* The lights in the house went off, and under the baton of the conductor, a quiet overture started.
9. *Gakudan ni wa furūto ya ōboe nado no kangakki mo hitsuyō da.* Wind instruments such as flutes, oboes and the like are also essential to the orchestra.
10. *Shōnen ga kuchibue o fukinagara hayashi no naka o aruite iru.* A boy is whistling as he walks through the woods.
11. *Patokā ga keiteki o narashinagara hashirisatta.* The patrol car sped away, its siren blowing.

1. *Gekijō ni tsuitara, kaimaku no gofun mae datta.* When we arrived at the theater, it was five minutes before the rising of the curtain.
2. *Daisanmaku no makugire wa jitsu ni gekiteki datta.* The end of the third acts was truly dramatic.
3. *Kanashii bamen ni josei no kankyaku ga naite ita.* Woman in the audience wept at the sad scenes.
4. *Ano hito wa waraibanashi o kiite mo, shōgeki o mite mo, waratta koto ga nai.* He/she has never laughed at a funny story nor a farce.
5. *Kore wa kazokuzure de mirareru karui kigeki desu.* This is a light comedy that you can see with your family.
6. *Yūmei na seikaku haiyū ga Shēkusupia no higeki no shuyaku o enjite iru.* The famous character actor is playing the leading role of a Shakespearian tragedy.
7. *Watashi wa engeki no sekai ni haitta bakari de, mada sono shūkan ni naremasen.* I just entered the theatrical world, so I haven't got used to its ways yet.
8. *Kono geki wa gendai no wakamono no seikatsu ya fūzoku o yoku arawashite iru.* This play expresses well the lives and customs of the young people of today.
9. *Ano joyū wa hageshii kanjō no hyōgen ga sugurete iru.* That actress is superb in expressing violent emotions.
10. *Rōren na haiyū no subarashii engi ni kangeki shita.* I was deeply moved by the splendid performance of the veteran actor.
11. *Tsuki ni ichido, engeki aikōsha ga atsumatte, jōhō o teikyō shiatte iru.* Once a month, theater lovers get together and trade information.
12. *Kimura-san wa gakusei jidai ni engeki ni muchū ni nari, gekisakka o yumemite ita sō da.* I hear that in his student days Mr. Kimura was absorbed in plays and dreamed of becoming a playwright.
13. *Hajimete jōen sareta sono geki wa seikō ni owari, chikai shōrai saien ga yotei sarete iru.* The play that had been staged for the first time ended with success, and will be repeated in the near future.

■ **Reading Exercises 35 (p.232)** ▬▬▬▬▬▬▬▬▬▬▬▬▬

1. *Shijin ga jibun no shi o rōdoku shita.* The poet read his own poems aloud.

2. *Sono shōjo no nikki wa hyakumanbu ijō mo ureta.* The diary by that girl sold more than 1 million copies.
3. *Mōtsuaruto no denki o yonde kandō shita.* The biography of Mozart moved me profoundly.
4. *Kono Amerika ryokōki wa omoshiroi bakari de naku, totemo yaku ni tatsu.* This book of travel in America is not only interesting but also useful.
5. *Kono kaisōroku ni wa chosha no fukai jinruiai ga nijimidete iru.* This book of memoirs is permeated with the author's deep love for humanity.
6. *Yamada-san wa shinbun kisha o yamete zasshi no henshū o shite iru.* Mr. Yamada quit his job as a journalist and is editing a magazine.
7. *Sono sakka no tanpen wa itsumo hanashi no suji ga kantan da.* The writer's short stories always have a simple plot.
8. *Rekishi shōsetsu no naka ni wa shijitsu to mattaku chigatta mono mo aru.* Among historical novels there are some which are quite different from historical facts.
9. *Nōberu Shō o jushō shita sakuhin wa iroiro no kotoba ni yakusarete, sekai kakkoku de kankō sarete iru.* Works which received the Nobel Prize have been translated into various languages and published throughout the world.
10. *Shōsetsu no eigaka ga junbungaku o tsūzoku na mono ni shita to iwarete iru.* It is said that the filming of novels popularized serious literature.
11. *Kono kikanshi ni shinkansho no bungei hihyō ga dete iru.* Literary criticism of new books appears in this quarterly magazine.
12. *Hyōronku ni yotte bunshō no kaishaku ga chigau koto wa tabitabi aru.* Depending on the critic, the interpretation of writings differs quite often.
13. *Kono kōseizuri ni wa goji ya kutōten no ayamari ga ōi.* This proof has many wrong words and punctuation mistakes.
14. *Sono suiri shōsetsu wa shohan ga ichimanbu insatsu sareta.* Ten thousand copies of that detective story were printed in its first edition.
15. *Aru sakuhin wa kishō kachi de chūmoku o atsumete iru.* Some works hold attention by the value of their scarcity.
16. *Sakka shibō no Tanaka-san wa saisho no shōsetsu o kansei shita bakari da.* Miss Tanaka who wishes to be a writer has just completed her first novel.

1. *Ano gakusei wa mi mo kokoro mo benkyō ni uchikonde iru.* That student puts his heart and soul into his study.

2. *Kodomo wa shintai mo seishin mo tsuyoi ningen ni sodate tai.* I want to bring up my child as a person strong in both body and mind.

3. *Sofu wa saikin, mimi ga tōku natta yō da.* My grandfather seems to be hard of hearing recently.

4. *Sobo wa ha ga warui node, katai mono wa taberarenai.* My grandmother has bad teeth, so she can't eat hard food.

5. *Yōji wa umarete kara hantoshi gurai de nyūshi ga haehajimeru.* An infant begins to have milk teeth about a half year after birth.

6. *Ani no musuko wa ichō ga yowai kara, tsune ni kaoiro ga yokunai.* My older brother's son has poor digestion, so he always looks pale.

7. *Koronda toki, hana o utte hanaji ga deta.* When I fell, I got hit on the nose and had a bloody nose.

8. *Buraun-fujin wa kubi ga hosokute shisei ga yoku, jitsu ni yōshi ga utsukushii.* Mrs. Brown has a slender neck and fine posture, and her face and figure are truly beautiful.

9. *Shujin wa hai ya shinzō o tsuyoku suru tame, mainichi karui undō o shite iru.* My husband does light exercise every day, in order to make his heart and lungs strong.

10. *Kanai no chichioya wa kyonen nōsotchū de shibō shita.* My wife's father died of cerebral apoplexy(accident) last year.

11. *Watashi-tachi no sensei wa hidoi kingan de, atsui megane o kakete iru.* Our teacher is extremely shortsighted and wears thick eyeglasses.

12. *Sono rōjin wa me no shujutsu o ukete, shiryoku o kaifuku shita.* The old man had eye surgery and recovered his sight.

13. *Kaze no tame netsu ga ari, atama ga itaku shita mo arete iru.* Due to a cold, I have a temperature and a headache and my tongue is rough, too.

14. *Sakuya no pātī de nomisugite, kesa kara zutsū ga suru.* I drank too much at a party last night, so I have had a headache since this morning.

15. *Omoi mono o hakonda ato de, mune to senaka ni itami o kanjita.* After carrying something heavy , I felt a pain in my chest and back.

16. *Kinō wa ichinichijū fukutsū de kurushinda ga, kyō wa mō kutsū wa nai.* I suffered from a stomachache all day long yesterday, but I have no more pain today.

17. *Sei ga onaji gurai no chōnan to jinan wa yoku seikurabe o shite iru.* My two oldest sons who are just about the same in stature often compare their heights.

18. *Kono gurafu wa shinchō to taijū no hirei o shimeshite iru.* This graph shows the average proportion of height to weight.

19. *Sono senshu wa ashi no kossetsu no tame, shiai ni derarenakatta.* The player couldn't take part in the game due to a broken leg.

20. *Kurinikku de ketsuatsu o hakattari, ketsueki o shirabetari shite moratta.* I had my blood pressure checked and my blood tested at the clinic.

■ Reading Exercises 37 (p.249) ■

1. *Haha wa aikawarazu genki desu ga, chichi wa kotoshi no shigatsu irai byōki desu.* My mother is well as usual, but my father has been ill since April this year.

2. *Kimura-san no o-tōsan wa shinzōbyō de nyūin shite iru.* Miss Kimura's father is in the hospital with heart disease.

3. *Akiko-san no o-nēsan wa daigaku no fuzoku byōin no kangofu desu.* Akiko's older sister is a nurse at the hospital attached to a university.

4. *Ano kyōdai wa futari tomo Amerika de igaku o manande isha ni natta.* Both of the brothers studied medicine in America and became doctors.

5. *Ishi ga hitai ni atatte kizu o otta node, chikaku no iin de teate o uketa.* A stone hit me on the forehead and I got hurt, so I received a treatment at a nearby doctor's office.

6. *Gekai wa kizuguchi o shōdoku shite itsuhari nutta.* The surgeon disinfected the wound and made five stitches.

7. *Kinō no doshakuzure de sūnin no shishōsha ga deta.* The landslide yesterday turned out several casualties.

8. *Isha wa kokyū konnan no byōnin ni sanso kyūnyū o okonatta.* The doctor gave oxygen to the patient who had difficulty breathing.

9. *Nyūyoku suru jikan no nai toki wa, kawari ni shawā o abimasu.* When I have no time to take a bath, I take a shower instead.

10. *Chijin no musuko-san wa byōki ga kaifuku shite, isshūkan mae ni taiin shita.* The son of my acquaintance recovered from his illness, and left the hospital a week ago.

11. *Kono kusuri wa kōka ga hayai.* This medicine takes effect quickly.

12. *Nando mo kensa o okonatta ga, byōki no gen'in wa mada fumei de aru.* We have conducted many tests, but the cause of the illness is still unknown.

13. *Senshū shintai kensa o ukete, ima sono kekka o matte imasu.* I underwent a physical examination last week and am waiting for the results now.

14. *Karada o seiketsu ni tamotsu koto ga kenkō e no daiippo de aru.* Keeping oneself clean is the first step to maintaining one's health.

15. *Sakuya made kiken na jōtai ni atta byōnin wa kesa kara shōkō o eta.* The sick person who had been in a dangerous condition until last night was better this morning.

16. *Isha ya byōin no hiyō ga kasanda ga, saiwai kenkō hoken ga hotondo kabā shita.* Although doctor's and hospital expenses piled up, fortunately most of them were covered by health insurance.

■ Reading Exercises 38 (p.256) ■

1. *Aru gakusei wa kuruma de gakkō ni kayotte iru.* Some students come to school by car.

2. *Furui jidōsha ga yukkuri to sakamichi o agatte iku.* An old car is going up the slope slowly.

3. *Shinjuku de jōkyaku no kahansū ga densha o orita.* The majority of passengers got off the train at Shinjuku.

4. *Ame no furu hi ni wa, takushī noriba ni hito ga nagai retsu o tsukutte iru.* On rainy days, people form a long line at the taxi stand.

5. *Kita no hōkō ni mukatte gojū-mairu hodo kuruma o unten shita.* I drove the car north for about fifty miles.

6. *Shingō ga ao ni kawatte kara, tōri o mukōgawa e yokogitta.* After the traffic light turned green, I crossed the street to the other side.

7. *Jidō no ichigun ga ōdan hodō o watatte iru.* A group of children are walking across the pedestrian crossing.

8. *Kono machi no chūshin ni wa dōro ga tateyoko/jūō ni hashitte iru.* In the center of this city the streets run vertically and horizontally.

9. *Shiranai tochi de michi ni mayotte taihen komatta.* I lost my way in a strange place and had a terrible time.
10. *Kurai meiro o tōrinukeru to, gaitō de akarui ōdōri ni deta.* After going through a dark maze, I came out to the main road bright with street lights.
11. *Kono michi wa sukoshi saki de, kaidō to suichoku ni majiwatte iru.* A little way ahead this road crosses the highway at right angles.
12. *Kōtsū ga hageshii kōsaten de yoku jiko ga okoru.* Accidents often occur at the intersection where traffic is busy.
13. *Akai supōtsu kā ga jisoku hachijū-mairu de kōsoku dōro o tobashite iru.* A red sports car is speeding up the expressway eighty miles per hour.
14. *Hashi no ue de yūran-basu ga koshō shita.* The sight-seeing bus broke down on the bridge.
15. *Rikkyō wa genzai kōji shite iru node, tōmawari shinakereba naranai.* Because the bridge over road is under construction at present, we must make a long detour.
16. *Kōtsū anzen no tame, dōro hyōshiki ni chūi subeki da.* For traffic safety, you should look at signposts carefully.
17. *Senri no michi mo ippo yori hajimaru.* A journey of a thousand miles starts with but a single step.
18. *Gaido bukku ni kono basu wa "ji Tōkyō shi Chiba" to dete iru.* The guidebook says that this bus runs from Tokyo to Chiba.
19. *Izen wa kono atari ni basu no teiryūjo ga atta to omou.* I think there was a bus stop in this vicinity before.
20. *Kyōto shūhen wa ima demo midori no kigi ga ōi.* There are many green trees in the environs of Kyoto even now.

■ **Reading Exercises 39 (p.261)** ■

1. *Nihonjū, itaru tokoro ni tetsudō ga tsūjite iru.* Railways run everywhere throughout Japan.
2. *Sanji no ressha ni ma ni au yō ni isoide eki e itta.* I went to the station in a hurry to catch the 3 o'clock train.
3. *Kyōto-eki de kyūkō o orite, junkyū ni norikaeta.* I got off the express (train) and took the semi-express at Kyoto Station.

4. *Tokkyū wa niban hōmu kara, kakueki teisha wa gaban hōmu kara hassha shimasu.* Super express trains depart from platform number two and local (slow) trains from platform number five.

5. *Madoguchi de tokkyūken to jōshaken o motometa.* I bought a super express ticket and a passenger ticket at a window.

6. *Kono kenbaiki de wa ōfuku jōshaken wa kaemasen.* You can't buy roundtrip tickets from this ticket vending machine.

7. *Kisha ga nagai tonneru o deru to, hidarite ni massao na umi ga hirogatta.* When the steam train got out of the long tunnel, the deep-blue ocean spread out on our left.

8. *Kaigan ni nozonda hoteru kara utsukushii yakei o tanoshinda.* We enjoyed the beautiful night view from the hotel facing the seashore.

9. *Sukī no kisetsu ni wa rinji ressha ga nanbon mo deru.* Many special trains are put on in the skiing season.

10. *Saikin, sono shitetsu no unchin ga aratamatta. Jikokuhyō mo kaisei sareta.* Recently, the fares of the private railway were revised. The timetable was also revised.

11. *Kaisatsuguchi o tōtte eki no hōmu ni agaru ya ina ya, densha no doa ga shimatta.* As soon as I passed through the ticket barrier and went up to the platform of the station, the doors of the train closed.

12. *Aru hareta hi ni, shiroi ōkina fune ga minato ni haitta.* One fine day, a big white ship entered the harbor.

13. *Amerika no tomodachi ni funabin de hon o okutta.* I sent a book by seamail to my friend in America.

14. *Kishōchō no keikoku de kisen no shukkō ga enki ni natta.* The departure of the steamship was postponed due to the warning of the Meteorological Agency.

15. *Subarashii kyakusen de Taiheiyō o kōkai shita.* We sailed the Pacific by a wonderful passenger ship.

■ Reading Exercises 40 (p.271) ■

1. *Kinnen, Chūgoku no keizai wa ichijirushiku shinpo shita.* In recent years, the Chinese economy has made remarkable progress.

2. *Nyū-yōku wa zaikai no chūshin de aru.* New York is the center of finance.

3. *Kare wa kiken na jigyō ni ōku no shihon o tōshi shita.* He invested a large sum of capital in a risky enterprise.

4. *Kono kuni wa tennen shigen ga yutaka de aru.* This country is rich in natural resources.
5. *Sekiyu no hōfu na kokka ga sekai kakkoku ni nenryō o kyōkyū shite iru.* The oil-rich countries supply the world's nations with fuel.
6. *Jinkō ga fuete, jūtaku no juyō ga zōka shita.* The population increased, then the demand for houses rose.
7. *Kōba/kōjō wa shinamono no juyō ga hetta node, seisan o genshō shita.* Because the demand for goods decreased, the factory curtailed production.
8. *Shi wa yatto dōro no kakuchō kōji ni noridashita.* The city finally embarked on expansion work of the roads.
9. *Shōgyō ga susumu ni shitagatte, shimin no seikatsu suijun ga kōjō shita.* As commerce advanced, the living standard of the citizens has improved.
10. *Zōsengyō ga kudarizaka ni nari, jūgyōin no shukushō ga okonawareta.* The shipbuilding industry declined, and a reduction of employees was carried out.
11. *Kono mura no jūmin wa nōgyō ka gyogyō ni jūji shite iru.* The inhabitants of this village are engaged either in agriculture or the fishing industry.
12. *Nōsanbutsu no seichō o tasukeru tame ni, kagaku hiryō ya sekkai ya gyohi nado ga tsukawareru.* In order to help agricultural products grow, chemical fertilizer, lime, fish fertilizer, etc. are used.
13. *Kōgyō ga sakan na sono chihō wa tetsu ya dō ya sekitan nado no sanchi to shite shirarete iru.* The region where the mining industry flourishes is known as a producing center for iron, copper and coal, etc.
14. *Kono machi wa tekkōgyō ga sakan de ari, kōjō wa subete kindaiteki setsubi o sonaete iru.* The iron and steel industry flourishes in this city, and all the factories are equipped with modern facilities.
15. *Kensetsugyō wa gojūnendai no Nihon no fukkō ni taisetsu na yakume o hatashita.* The construction industry played an important role in the rebuilding of Japan in the 1950s.
16. *Nihonsei no seimitsu kikai wa gaikoku shijō de juyō ga takai.* The precision machinery made in Japan is in great demand on the foreign market.

17. *Tōchi no omo na sangyō wa orimono kōgyō de, toku ni kinuorimono wa yūmei de aru.* The main industry of this place is textiles, and silk fabrics are especially famous.

18. *Senshoku kōjō no haigo ni ōkii sōko o kenchiku shite iru.* They are building a big warehouse behind the dye works.

19. *Chikkō kōji ga owatte, seidai na shukuten o okonatta.* The harbor works were completed, and a grand celebration was held.

20. *Sugureta gijutsu ya atarashii kikai no hatsumei ga sangyō kakumei o motarashita.* Superior technology and the inventions of new machinery brought about an industrial revolution.

■ Reading Exercises 41 (p.275) ■

1. *Nihon wa sekai no ōku no kuni to bōeki o okonatte iru.* Japan conducts trade with many countries in the world.

2. *Shigen ya genryō o gaikoku kara yunyū shite, seihin ya gijutsu nado o kaigai e yushutsu suru.* They import resources and materials from foreign countries, and export their products, technology and other things abroad.

3. *Kono machi wa bōekikō de shirare, yunyūhin no kōkyūten ga ōi.* This city is known as a trade port and has many high-class stores for imports.

4. *Mitsuyunyūhin ga fusei na keiro o hete, yasune de shijō ni demawatte iru.* Smuggled goods are put on the market at lower prices through unlawful channels.

5. *Zaimoku o tsunda kamotsusen ga Hawai keiyu de kesa nyūkō shita.* The cargo ship loaded with lumber entered port via Hawaii this morning.

6. *Zeikin ni wa chokusetsuzei to kansetsuzei ga aru.* There are two kinds of taxes, direct and indirect.

7. *Kanzei wa gaikoku kara yunyū sareru shinamono ni taishite kokka ga kazei suru.* The country imposes tariffs on the goods imported from foreign countries.

8. *Kanzei seido no kaikaku o nozomu koe ga takamatte iru.* A cry for the reform of the tariff system is on the rise.

9. *Zeikan de nyūkoku tetsuzuki o sumasete kara, nimotsu no kensa ga aru.* After you finish the formalities for entry at customs, you go through a baggage inspection.

10. *Izen, akushitsu na yunyūhin ga zokushutsu shita koto ga aru.* Some years ago, we had a crop of imports of bad quality.
11. *Zeikan de gaikoku de katta shōhin o shinkoku shita.* I made a declaration at customs of articles purchased in foreign countries.
12. *Kūkō no mise de muzeihin o utte iru.* Some stores in the airport sell duty-free goods.
13. *Sekai keizai o hatten saseru tame, jiyū bōeki wa hitsuyō de aru.* Free trade is necessary to promote the world economy.
14. *Yunyū o seigen shitari, tokubetsu na kanzei o kakeru no wa hogo bōeki de aru.* Placing restrictions on imports or imposing special tariffs is protective trade.
15. *Nikoku no aida de shijō o jiyū ni hiraku tame no bōeki kyōtei ga hossoku/hassoku shita.* The trade agreement to create a free market started between the two countries.

■ Reading Exercises 42 (p.285) ■

1. *Chōnan wa Ginza de inshokuten o keiei shi, jinan wa Kyūshū de kaisha ni kinmu shite iru.* My oldest son runs a restaurant on the Ginza, and my second son is employed by a company in Kyushu.
2. *Anata wa donna shokugyō ni tsukitai no desu ka.* What kind of occupation do you want to take up?
3. *Ane no musuko wa kotoshi daigaku o sotsugyō shite, shinbunsha ni shūshoku shita.* My older sister's son graduated from college this year and found employment in a newspaper company.
4. *Sono jimusho de wa mada kyūshiki no kikai o tsukatte iru.* They are still using an old-fashioned apparatus in that office.
5. *Gozenchū ni kono shiryō o seiri shite kudasai.* Please take care of these materials before noon.
6. *Shachō hisho wa jibun no shigoto o umaku shori shite iru.* The secretary to the president manages her job well.
7. *Kakariin no annai de atarashii kikai no mokei o mite mawatta.* Led by the person in charge, we went around looking at the new models of the machines.
8. *Sono koto nara, jinjika no Yamada-san ga tantō shite imasu.* For that matter, Mrs. Yamada in the personnel section is in charge of it.
9. *Rōryoku ga fusoku shite, seisan ga genshō shita.* A shortage of labor resulted in a decrease in production.

10. *Rōdō kumiai wa keieishagawa ni chingin no neage o yōkyū shita.* The labor union demanded a wage increase from the management.

11. *Kaisha no sōritsu gojusshūnen o iwatte, seidai na pātī ga hirakareta.* In celebration of the fiftieth anniversary of the founding of the company, a magnificent party was held.

12. *Ano hito wa achi-kochi no ginkō ni kane o azukete, tsūchō o nansatsu mo motte iru.* He/she deposits money with various banks and has many passbooks.

13. *Kono teiki yokin wa roku-pāsento no fukuri o umu.* This time deposit account bears compound interest at 6 percent.

14. *Watashi no chijin wa ginkō kara kane o karite, shōbai o hajimeta.* My acquaintance borrowed money from the bank and started his business.

15. *Kare wa motode ni ana o akete, shakkin no hensai ni komatte iru.* He ran a deficit in his capital and has a hard time paying back the debt.

16. *Tomodachi no aida de wa kinsen no kashikari/taishaku o shinai hō ga ii.* It is better not to borrow or to lend money between friends.

17. *Yobun no shihon ga atta node, yūjin no kankoku ni shitagatte kabu ni tōshi shita.* Because I had surplus funds, I invested in stocks on the recommendation of my friend.

18. *Shinamono o sutene de utte ōkina son o shita.* I sold goods at a sacrifice price and suffered a heavy loss.

19. *Kono repōto no sūji wa subete shisha gonyū shite arimasu.* All the figures in this report are rounded to the nearest whole number.

■ Reading Exercises 43 (p.293) ■

1. *Kokumin wa seifu ni seiketsu na seiji o kitai shite iru.* The people expect clean politics from the government.

2. *Nihon no tennō wa kokka no shinboru de ari, seiji ni wa chokusetsu ni kankei shinai.* The emperor of Japan is the symbol of the nation and does not directly engage in politics.

3. *Konnichi, ōsei o okonatte iru kuni wa hotondo nai.* Today, there are very few countries which have a monarchy.

4. *Showa jidai wa senkyūhyaku nijūrokunen ni hajimari, rokujū-yo-nen mo tsuzuita.* The Showa era began in 1926 and lasted more than sixty years.

5. *Anata no shiji suru seitō wa kakushintō desu ka.* Is the political party you support a reformist party?
6. *Amerika Gasshūkoku de wa, yonen goto ni daitōryō no senkyo ga okonawareru.* In the United States of America, a presidential election is held every four years.
7. *Nihon no gikai wa Shūgiin to Sangiin kara nari, kokkai giin wa kokumin ni yotte erabareru.* The Japanese Diet consists of the House of Representatives and the House of Councilors, and their members are chosen by the people.
8. *Naikaku wa sōri daijin to sono ta no kokumu daijin de soshiki suru.* The cabinet consists of the prime minister and other ministers of state.
9. *Murayama-shi wa Ōkurashō ni sanjūnen kinmu shite kyonen intai shita.* Mr. Murayama worked for the Ministry of Finance for thirty years and retired last year.
10. *Kono kinpen ni wa kanchō ga atsumatte iru.* Many government offices are located in this area.
11. *Yamanaka-shi wa gaikōkan to shite naganen no keiken ga aru.* Mr. Yamanaka has long experience as a diplomat.
12. *Nijussai/hatachi ijō no danjo zen'in ni tōhyō no kenri ga aru.* All men and women who are twenty years of age or over have the right to vote.
13. *Kenpō ni motozuite, kojin no kihonteki jinken ga hogo sarete iru.* In conformity with the Constitution, an individual's fundamental human rights are protected.
14. *Moto gakuchō no Ogawa-hakase ga monbu daijin ni ninmei sareta.* Dr. Ogawa, former university president, was appointed the minister of education.
15. *Kono shigoto ni wa kare ga saikō no tekininsha da.* He is the best-qualified person for this job.
16. *Sakunen no gogatsu irai, sōri daijin ga gaimu daijin o kennin shite iru.* Since last May, the prime minister has been concurrently serving as the foreign minister.
17. *Iinkai de keizai seisaku o tōgi shite iru.* The economic policy is being discussed in a committee.
18. *Iin no kahansū ga bukka taisaku ni hantai shita.* The majority of the committee members objected to the price policy.

19. *Hōan wa zen'in no sansei o ete kaketsu sareta.* Supported by all members, the bill was passed.
20. *Sono teian wa yonju-ttai-jū de hiketsu sareta.* The proposal was rejected by a vote of 40 to 10.

■ Reading Exercises 44 (p.298) ■

1. *Amerika de wa Rikugun, Kaigun, Kūgun, narabi ni Kaiheitai ga kokubō no yakume o hatashite iru.* The Army, the Navy, the Air Force and the Marine Corps perform the duties of national defense in America.
2. *Tomu wa kōkō o sotsugyō suru to sugu, guntai ni haitta.* As soon as he graduated from high school, Tom joined the army.
3. *Bōeihi o setsuyaku shite gunbi no shukushō o okonatta.* They cut down defense expenses and carried out the reduction of armaments.
4. *Jieitai no omo na ninmu wa Nihon no heiwa to dokuritsu o mamori, kōkyō no chian o tamotsu koto de aru.* The main mission of the Self-Defense Forces is to protect the peace and independence of Japan and to maintain public order.
5. *Jieitai ni wa, Rikujō, Kaijō, Kōkū Jieitai ga ari, taiin wa subete shiganhei de aru.* The Self-Defense Forces contain the Ground Self-Defense Force, the Maritime Self-Defense Force and the Air Self-Defense Force, and all members of the Forces are volunteers.
6. *Aru kuni de wa shōnen shōjo ga heitai ni natte teki to tatakatte iru.* In certain countries boys and girls are recruited to fight the enemy.
7. *Shireikan no meirei ni shitagatte butai wa kōshin shita.* At the commander's order, the troops marched.
8. *Sono chiiki ni heiwa o kaifuku suru tame ni, Kokurengun ga shubi ni tsuite iru.* In order to restore peace to the region, the United Nations forces are taking to the field.
9. *Taichō wa senryaku no shippai ni sekinin o kanjite jishoku shita.* The commander resigned from a sense of responsibility for the strategic failure.
10. *Tsumetai sensō wa owatta ga, sekai no itaru tokoro de nairan ga hito-bito o kurushimete iru.* Although the cold war ended, rebellions are tormenting people everywhere in the world.
11. *Sono shōgun wa rikugun o yūtai shite seikai ni haitta.* The general retired from the army voluntarily and entered the political world.

12. *Waga butai wa tekigun no keiryaku ni kakatte kusen shita ga, saigo made isamashiku tatakatta.* Our troops fell prey to the enemy's stratagem and met stiff resistance, and fought bravely to the end.
13. *Sono kassen de kōseki o tateta gunjin wa yūshi no naka no yūshi de aru to shōsan sareta.* The soldiers who had rendered distinguished service in the battle were praised as the bravest of the brave.
14. *Ōzei no wakamono ga kokka ni chūsei o chikatte senjō ni nozonda.* Many young men pledged loyalty to the country and went to the front.
15. *Hanchō no gōrei de, heisotsu zen'in ga hassha shita.* At the word of command by the squad leader, all the privates fired.
16. *Shuzaihan wa kaigai no kiken chitai ni mukatte shuppatsu shita.* The reportage team departed for a danger spot abroad.
17. *Katana no tenjikai de Nihontō no meitō ga toku ni ōku no kanshin o atsumete ita.* The well-known Japanese swords were gazed at with special interest by many people at the sword exhibition.

■ Reading Exercises 45 (p.305) ■

1. *Kokusai Rengō wa senkyūhyaku yonjūgonen, sekai heiwa o tamotsu tame ni soshiki sareta.* The United Nations was organized in 1945 to maintain world peace.
2. *Kokuren wa tasū no kuni ga kuwawatte tsukurareta kokusai kikō de aru.* The U.N. is an international organization formed by many nations.
3. *Nikokukan de tsūshō jōyaku ga musubareta.* A commercial treaty was concluded between the two countries.
4. *Seifu wa shokuminchi no dokuritsu o shōnin shita.* The government recognized the independence of the colony.
5. *Ōkura daijin wa Amerika daitōryō to no kaidan de bōeki mondai o tōgi shita.* The minister of the finance discussed the trade problems in the conference with the president of the United States.
6. *Kono jōrei ni wa nisan zesei subeki ten ga aru.* There are two or three points which should be corrected in these regulations.
7. *Nihon no kokubō ni kansuru koto wa kenpō daikyūjō ni kijutsu sarete iru.* Matters regarding the national defense of Japan are described under Article 9 of the Constitution.

8. *Sono kuni wa busō o kaijo shite, eisei chūritsukoku ni natta.* The nation carried out disarmament, and became a permanent neutral country.
9. *Yoki sarete ita gaimu daijin no jishoku ga kakunin sareta.* The resignation of the foreign minister that was anticipated has been confirmed.
10. *Eien no heiwa wa zenjinrui no nengan de aru.* Eternal peace is the prayer of humanity.
11. *Kokka no shichū to iwareta seijika no gyōseki wa eikyū ni tsutaerareru darō.* The achievements of the stateman who had been regarded as the mainstay of the nation would be talked about forever.
12. *Watashi ga kodomo no toki, Yamanaka-san no kazoku wa Burajiru e ijū shita.* When I was a child, the Yamanaka family emigrated to Brazil.
13. *Iminhō no kaisei ni wa dare mo igi ga nai.* No one objects to revising the immigration law.
14. *Seifu no kyoka nashi ni nyūkoku suru gaikokujin no sū ga mainen zōka shite iru.* The number of the foreigners who enter the country without the government's permission is increasing every year.
15. *Ryōkoku wa kokkō danzetsu o chūshi shite, yūkō kankei o kaifuku shi, keizai dōmei o musunda.* The two countries put an end to the severance of their diplomatic relations, restored friendly relations, and concluded an economic alliance.
16. *Nihon wa Ajia no kakuchiiki de gijutsu no shidō o okonatte iru.* Japan conducts technical guidance in various parts of Asia.
17. *Hinmin o gyakkyō kara kyūjo suru tame ni, kyūsai kikin ga hitsuyō de aru.* A relief fund is needed in order to relieve the poor from adversity.
18. *Fukuzatsu na shakai kikō no naka de, kōsei jigyō o seikō saseru no wa jitsu ni konnan de aru.* In the complex structure of society, it it truly difficult to conduct welfare projects successfully.
19. *Tennō-Kōgō-ryōheika wa shinzen no tame Amerika o hōmon sareta.* Their Majesties the Emperor and Empress made a good-will visit to America.
20. *Kare wa gaikō mondai ni kansuru kichō na kenkyū de hakushi/hakase no shōgō o sazukatta.* He was granted a doctor's degree for his valuable study on diplomatic affairs.

1. *Shakai no chian o tamotsu tame ni, shuju no hōritsu ga seitei sarete iru.* In order to maintain public peace and order, various laws are established.
2. *Kare wa hōritsu o yabutte saiban ni kakerareta.* He broke the law and faced a trial.
3. *Kodomo no nageta bōru ga atatte, mado-garasu ga hason shita.* A ball thrown by a child hit the window pane and broke it.
4. *Seinen wa kōtsū kisoku o mushi shite jiko o okoshita.* The young man disregarded traffic regulations and caused an accident.
5. *Shōnen shōjo o kiritsu no aru seikatsu ni michibiku koto ga mottomo taisetsu de aru.* It is a matter of prime importance to guide boys and girls to lead disciplined lives.
6. *Gakkō tōkyoku wa fusei na katsudō ni sanka shita gakusei ni seisai o kuwaeta.* The school authorities inflicted punishment upon the students who had participated in delinquent activities.
7. *Sono otoko wa chōsa no tame keisatsusho ni ryūchi sareta.* The man was detained at the police station for investigation.
8. *Jiken wa keisatsu kara kensatsuchō e mawasareta.* The case was sent from the police station to the public procecutors office.
9. *Miseinensha ga sake o nomu koto wa hōritsu de kinshi sarete iru.* Minors are prohibited by law from drinking.
10. *Kare wa omoi tsumi o okashite seken kara misuterareta.* He committed a grave crime and was forsaken by the world.
11. *Kan'i saibansho wa karui hanzai o shori suru.* The summary court deals with minor offenses.
12. *Saibankan wa sono onna ni yūzai no hanketsu o kudashita.* The judge pronounced the woman guilty.
13. *Aribai ga nai tame utagawarete tonda sainan o uketa.* Having no alibi, I was suspected and suffered an unexpected misfortune.
14. *Richigi na ano sensei ga kyōkasho jiken ni kankei ga aru ka dō ka gimon da.* It is doubtful whether a honest teacher like him has something to do with the textbook scandal.
15. *Shōnin wa yōgisha no muzai o shōgen shita.* The witness testified to the suspect's innocence.

16. *Wakai bengoshi ga satsujin jiken o tantō shita.* A young lawyer took charge of the murder case.

17. *Sakuya no shōtengai no kasai wa hōka datta.* The fire last night at the shopping street was incendiary.

18. *Keisatsukan ga ōtobai de hannin o otte iru.* A motorcycle policeman is chasing a criminal.

19. *Sono yakunin wa ōryō no utagai de kōshoku kara tsuihō sareta.* The official was banished from public office on suspicion of usurpation.

20. *Rusu no aida ni, ie ni dorobō ga haitte tokei ya, hōseki ya, sono ta iroiro no mono ga nusumareta.* While I was away, my house was robbed, and my watches, jewels and many other things were stolen.

■ Reading Exercises 47 (p.318) ■■■■■■■■■■■■■■■■

1. *Nihon no omo na shūkyō ni wa shintō, bukkyō, kirisuto-kyō ga aru.* The principal religions in Japan are Shinto, Buddhism and Christianity.

2. *Aru kuni de wa konnichi demo shūha no arasoi ga tsuzuite iru.* Sectarian strifes continue even today in some countries.

3. *Furui miyako no Kyōto ni wa, tera ya jinja ga ōku, kankōkyaku ga taenai.* In Kyoto, an old capital, there are many temples and shrines, and tourists never stop coming.

4. *Ganjitsu ni kazokuzure de Meiji Jingū ni sanpai shita.* I visited the Meiji Shrine with my family on New Year's Day.

5. *Tōdaiji wa Nihon ichi no daibutsu de yūmei de aru.* The Todaiji Temple is famous for the largest image of Buddha in Japan.

6. *Watashi-tachi no sosen no haka wa koyama no ue no hiroi bochi ni aru.* The graves of our ancestors are in the large cemetery on the hill.

7. *Sono kyōdai wa chichioya no yuigon ni shitagatte isan o kinbun shita.* In accordance with their father's will, the brothers divided the inheritance equally.

8. *Zenkoku kakuchi ni bakufu jidai ni kizukareta rippa na shiro ga nokotte iru.* Fine castles built in the days of the shogunate remain in various parts of the country.

9. *Tennō tanjōbi ni ōzei no hito ga kyūjō ni sanga shita.* Many people went to the Imperial Palace and offered their congratulations on the Emperor's Birthday.

10. *Ryūgakusei no Tomu-kun kara Nihongo de kaita nengajō ga kita.* I received a New Year's card written in Japanese from Tom, a foreign student.

11. *Kurisuchan no Haruko-san wa mainichiyōbi, kanarazu kyōkai no reihai/raihai ni shusseki suru.* Haruko, a Christian, attends church service every Sunday without fail.

12. *Nichiyō gakkō de seisho o yondari, sanbika o utattari shita.* We did things like reading the Bible and singing hymns at Sunday school.

13. *Buraun-shinpu wa senkyōshi to shite zenseiki ni rainichi shi, isshō o Nihon de oeta.* Father Brown came to Japan as a missionary in the previous century, and ended his life here.

14. *Sotsugyōsei ga onshi no tame ni shaonkai o hiraite, kansha no kokoro o arawashita.* The graduates held a thank-you party for their respected teacher to express their gratitude.

15. *Osanai kodomo ni wa kyōkun no aru monogatari o yomasetai.* I wish young children read the kind of stories which carry lessons.

16. *Dōtoku ga teika suru ni shitagatte, hanzai ga zōka shita.* As morality lowered, crimes increaed.

17. *Kare wa kibishii sensei datta ga, nani yori mo jingi o sonchō shi gakusei kara sonkei sarete ita.* A strict teacher, he valued humanity and justice above all and was respected by his students.

18. *Genkaku na katei ni sodatta Honda-san wa oya ni totemo kōkō da.* Miss Honda who was brought up in a well-ordered home is very dutiful to her parents.

19. *Watashi wa kami no sonzai o shinjita toki, bukkyō o sutete, kirisuto-kyō ni kaishū shita.* When I came to believe in the existence of God, I abandoned Buddhism and converted to Christianity.

20. *Furui mokuzō no kyōkai o kaichiku suru tame ni kifu o atsumete iru.* Donations are being collected to rebuild the old, wooden church.

INDEX by Readings

A

aba(ku)	暴	#353
aba(reru)	暴	353
a(biru)	浴	774
a(biseru)	浴	774
abu(nai)	危	776
abura	油	657
a(garu)	上	90
a(geru)	上	90
	挙	912
AI	愛	689
ai-	相	634
aida	間	65
aji	味	422
aji(wau)	味	422
aka	赤	231
aka(i)	赤	231
a(kari)	明	47
aka(rui)	明	47
a(keru)	明	47
	空	346
	開	454
aki	秋	75
akina(u)	商	456
aki(raka)	明	47
AKU	悪	339
a(ku)	空	346
	開	454
ama	天	335
	雨	340
ama(ru)	余	898
ama(su)	余	898
ame	天	335

	雨	#340
a(mu)	編	709
AN	安	469
	案	571
	暗	348
	行	54
ana	穴	896
ane	姉	131
ani	兄	129
ao	青	179
ao(i)	青	179
araso(u)	争	624
ara(ta)	新	114
arata(maru)	改	815
arata(meru)	改	815
ara(u)	洗	439
arawa(reru)	表	637
	現	116
arawa(su)	表	637
	現	116
	著	714
a(ru)	在	117
	有	146
aru(ku)	歩	189
asa	朝	93
asa(i)	浅	277
ashi	足	33
aso(bu)	遊	186
atai	価	497
	値	495
atama	頭	734
atara(shii)	新	114
ata(ri)	辺	806
ata(ru)	当	765

atata(kai)	暖	#365
	温	359
atata(meru)	暖	365
	温	359
a(teru)	当	765
ato	後	86
ATSU	圧	356
atsu(i)	厚	964
	暑	364
	熱	310
atsu(maru)	集	465
atsu(meru)	集	465
a(u)	会	321
	合	100
a(waseru)	合	100
ayama(chi)	過	176
ayama(ri)	誤	614
ayama(ru)	誤	614
	謝	1008
ayama(tsu)	過	176
ayatsu(ru)	操	621
aya(ui)	危	776
ayu(mu)	歩	189
aza	字	606
azu(karu)	預	887
azu(keru)	預	887

B

BA	馬	188
ba	場	259
BAI	倍	38
	売	492
	梅	219

Reading	Kanji	No.
	買	#491
ba(kasu)	化	723
ba(keru)	化	723
BAKU	博	668
	暴	353
	幕	687
	麦	256
BAN	万	13
	晩	96
	板	540
	番	22
	判	976
BATSU	末	59
-be	辺	806
BEI	米	255
BEN	勉	563
	便	330
	弁	985
beni	紅	232
BETSU	別	812
BI	備	529
	美	654
	鼻	735
BIN	便	330
	貧	967
BO	模	886
	母	125
	墓	997
	暮	149
BŌ	亡	184
	忘	575
	暴	353
	棒	992
	望	388
	貿	857
	防	929
BOKU	木	70
	牧	#258
	目	23
BU	不	405
	武	644
	分	81
	歩	189
	無	868
	部	30
BUN	分	81
	文	387
	聞	568
BUTSU	仏	1000
	物	205
BYAKU	白	230
BYŌ	平	247
	病	758
	秒	82

C

Reading	Kanji	No.
CHA	茶	234
CHAKU	着	37
CHI	値	495
	地	246
	池	271
	治	900
	知	153
	置	295
	質	467
chi	千	12
	乳	415
	血	753
chichi	乳	415
	父	124
chii(sai)	小	171
chiji(meru)	縮	836
chiji(mu)	縮	836
chika(i)	近	#110
chikara	力	385
CHIKU	竹	217
	築	848
CHIN	賃	521
chi(ru)	散	226
CHO	著	714
	貯	272
CHŌ	丁	92
	重	729
	兆	15
	帳	888
	庁	327
	張	835
	潮	279
	町	313
	朝	93
	腸	750
	調	431
	長	103
	頂	239
	鳥	198
CHOKU	直	615
CHŪ	昼	94
	中	88
	仲	152
	宙	374
	忠	939
	柱	968
	注	368
	虫	201

D

Reading	Kanji	No.
DA	打	633
DAI	内	140
	代	107

弟 #130

台 32
大 170
題 572
第 21

DAN 団 676
断 797
暖 365
段 496
男 118
談 950

da(su) 出 105
-date 建 534
DE 弟 130
DEN 伝 702
田 251
電 450
de(ru) 出 105
DO 土 72
度 35
努 618
DŌ 働 882
同 549
動 204
導 960
堂 400
童 532
道 301
銅 845
DOKU 毒 767
独 672
読 567

E

E 会 321
回 34

絵 #655
-e 重 729
eda 枝 212
EI 永 956
営 870
衛 383
映 663
栄 403
泳 197
英 598
EKI 益 503
役 316
易 856
液 754
駅 814
e(mu) 笑 685
EN 円 24
園 206
塩 424
延 631
沿 275
演 682
遠 112
era(bu) 選 635
e(ru) 得 500

F

FU 不 405
夫 135
付 423
婦 137
富 404
布 484
府 322
父 124
負 626

風 #350
歩 189
FŪ 夫 135
富 404
風 350
fuda 札 516
fude 筆 542
fue 笛 680
fu(eru) 増 832
fuka(i) 深 276
fu(keru) 老 182
FUKU 副 604
復 565
福 506
服 449
腹 741
複 892
fumi 文 387
FUN 分 81
奮 646
粉 416
funa 船 820
fune 船 820
fu(ru) 降 341
furu(i) 古 115
furu(u) 奮 646
fuse(gu) 防 929
fushi 節 79
futata(bi) 再 693
futa(tsu) 二 2
futo(i) 太 270
futo(ru) 太 270
fu(yasu) 増 832
fuyu 冬 76

				限	#862	**GYŪ**	牛	#187
				験	579			
G			**GETSU**	月	52	**H**		
GA	画	#656	**GI**	疑	984			
	我	159		技	623	**HA**	波	354
	芽	211		義	557		派	994
	賀	1006		議	908		破	980
GA'	合	100	**GIN**	銀	479	**HA'**	法	599
GAI	外	155	**GO**	五	5	ha	羽	42
	害	355		午	85		葉	210
	街	457		後	86		歯	737
GAKU	学	523		期	174	habu(ku)	省	915
	楽	669		誤	614	**HACHI**	八	8
	額	504		語	597	ha(e)	栄	403
GAN	丸	651		護	764	ha(eru)	映	663
	願	587	**GŌ**	業	555		生	166
	元	757		合	100	hagane	鋼	846
	岸	274		号	799	hage(shii)	激	691
	岩	264		強	351	haha	母	125
	眼	744		郷	325	**HAI**	俳	695
	顔	733	**GOKU**	極	293		拝	1001
GATSU	月	52	**GON**	厳	1010		肺	748
GE	下	91		勤	872		背	742
	夏	74		権	917		敗	627
	外	155		言	566		配	517
	解	576	**GU**	具	433	hai	灰	840
GEI	芸	488	**GŪ**	宮	996	hai(ru)	入	106
GEKI	劇	681	**GUN**	軍	930	haji(maru)	始	536
	激	691		群	193	haji(me)	初	58
GEN	厳	1010		郡	324	haji(meru)	始	536
	元	757	**GYAKU**	逆	970	haji(mete)	初	58
	原	249	**GYO**	漁	842	haka	墓	997
	減	833		魚	195	haka(ru)	図	284
	源	826	**GYŌ**	業	555		量	342
	現	116		形	402		測	390
	眼	744		行	54		計	99
	言	566	**GYOKU**	玉	409	hako	箱	476

Reading	Kanji	No.	Reading	Kanji	No.	Reading	Kanji	No.
hako(bu)	運	#520	HATSU	発	#518	hikari	光	#379
HAKU	博	668	hatsu-	初	58	hika(ru)	光	379
	白	230	haya(i)	早	98	hiki(iru)	率	594
HAN	半	83		速	792	hi(ku)	引	386
	判	976	hayashi	林	242	hiku(i)	低	358
	反	927	hazu(su)	外	155	hiku(maru)	低	358
	坂	793	HEI	平	247	hiku(meru)	低	358
	板	540		兵	932	hi(meru)	秘	878
	版	658		並	458	HIN	貧	967
	犯	983		病	758		品	466
	班	944		閉	455	hira	平	247
	飯	399		陛	904	hira(keru)	開	454
hana	花	209	HEN	変	237	hira(ku)	開	454
	鼻	735		片	609	hiro(garu)	広	250
hanashi	話	514		編	709	hiro(i)	広	250
hana(su)	放	987		辺	806	hiro(maru)	広	250
	話	514		返	891	hiro(u)	拾	19
hana(tsu)	放	987	he(rasu)	減	833	hiru	昼	94
hane	羽	42	he(ru)	減	833	hi(ru)	干	281
hara	原	249		経	822	hisa(shii)	久	957
	腹	741	HI	否	925	hitai	額	504
hara(su)	晴	345		批	719	hito	人	25
hare(ru)	晴	345		比	743	hito(ri)	独	672
hari	針	102		皮	482	hito(shii)	等	526
haru	春	73		秘	878	hito(tsu)	一	1
ha(ru)	張	835		肥	839	HITSU	必	619
hashi	橋	801		費	785		筆	542
hashira	柱	968		非	472	hitsuji	羊	192
hashi(ru)	走	190		悲	684	hi(yasu)	冷	366
hata	旗	650		飛	200	HO	保	527
	機	36	hi	氷	367		歩	189
	畑	252		日	44		補	636
hatake	畑	252		火	68	HO'	法	599
hatara(ku)	働	882		灯	451	ho	火	68
ha(tasu)	果	411	hidari	左	462	HŌ	包	489
ha(te)	果	411	hi(eru)	冷	366		報	370
ha(teru)	果	411	higashi	東	289		宝	475

	方	#160		委	#910	isa(mashii)	勇	#938
	放	987		移	958	isa(mu)	勇	938
	法	599		衣	473	ishi	石	263
	訪	966		遺	998	iso(gu)	急	809
	豊	855		意	369	ita	板	540
hodo	程	553	ICHI	一	1	itadaki	頂	239
hoga(raka)	朗	700		壱	16	itada(ku)	頂	239
hoka	外	155	ichi	市	312	ita(i)	痛	738
HOKU	北	292	ichijiru(shii)	著	714	ita(meru)	傷	766
HON	本	27	ie	家	139		痛	738
	反	927	ike	池	271	ita(mu)	傷	766
hone	骨	752	IKI	域	311		痛	738
hoshi	星	381	iki	息	134	ita(ru)	至	805
ho(shii)	欲	420	ikio(i)	勢	286	ito	糸	485
hoso(i)	細	732	i(kiru)	生	166	itona(mu)	営	870
hos(suru)	欲	420	IKU	育	169	ITSU	一	1
ho(su)	干	281	i(ku)	行	54	itsu(tsu)	五	5
hotoke	仏	1000	ikusa	戦	630	i(u)	言	566
HOTSU	発	518	ima	今	45	iwa	岩	264
HYAKU	百	11	imōto	妹	132	iwa(i)	祝	50
HYŌ	表	637	IN	印	724	iwa(u)	祝	50
	氷	367		員	446	izumi	泉	278
	兵	932		因	779			
	俵	645		引	386	**J**		
	標	803		院	528			
	票	911		音	601	JAKU	弱	352
	評	718		飲	413		着	37
			ina	否	925		若	181
I			inochi	命	167	JI	事	326
			inu	犬	185		仕	873
I	以	89	i(reru)	入	106		似	470
	位	294	iro	色	229		児	173
	医	759	i(ru)	入	106		次	123
	囲	394		居	147		寺	995
	易	856		要	620		地	246
	胃	749		射	642		字	606
	異	953	isagiyo(i)	潔	773		持	551

Reading	Kanji	No.
	時	#80
	治	900
	磁	480
	示	666
	耳	730
	自	157
	辞	545
	除	954
JI'	十	10
ji	路	459
JIKI	直	615
	食	395
JIN	人	25
	仁	1012
	神	756
	臣	914
JITSU	実	224
	日	44
JO	助	559
	女	119
	序	611
	除	954
JŌ	乗	787
	上	90
	城	999
	場	259
	条	947
	定	397
	常	471
	情	690
	成	177
	状	778
	盛	841
	蒸	429
	静	659
JU	就	875
	従	837

Reading	Kanji	No.
	授	#554
	樹	216
	受	515
	需	829
JŪ	重	729
	住	148
	十	10
	従	837
	拾	19
	縦	796
JUKU	熟	225
JUN	準	810
	順	610
	純	716
JUTSU	術	653
	述	952

K

Reading	Kanji	No.
KA	下	91
	可	924
	夏	74
	果	411
	化	723
	仮	608
	何	63
	価	497
	加	426
	家	139
	歌	670
	河	267
	火	68
	科	543
	花	209
	荷	522
	課	552
	貨	445

Reading	Kanji	No.
	過	#176
KA'	合	100
-ka	日	44
kabu	株	893
kado	角	460
	門	535
kaeri(miru)	省	915
kae(ru)	帰	55
	返	891
ka(eru)	変	237
	代	107
kae(su)	返	891
kagami	鏡	389
kagi(ru)	限	862
KAI	会	321
	灰	840
	回	34
	改	815
	街	457
	快	783
	械	850
	海	268
	界	287
	絵	655
	解	576
	開	454
	階	43
kai	貝	196
kaiko	蚕	202
kakari	係	876
kaka(ru)	係	876
ka(keru)	欠	561
kako(mu)	囲	394
kako(u)	囲	394
KAKU	画	656
	各	306
	客	493

Reading	Kanji	No.
	拡	#834
	格	499
	確	955
	覚	616
	角	460
	閣	913
	革	828
ka(ku)	欠	561
	書	447
kama(eru)	構	946
kama(u)	構	946
kami	上	32
	神	756
	紙	490
KAN	看	763
	勧	894
	幹	213
	完	722
	官	916
	寒	363
	巻	29
	干	281
	刊	707
	感	688
	慣	697
	歓	649
	漢	607
	管	678
	簡	991
	観	391
	間	65
	関	864
	館	207
kan	神	765
kana	金	71
kana(deru)	奏	673
kanara(zu)	必	619
kana(shii)	悲	#684
kana(shimu)	悲	684
)		
kane	金	71
ka(neru)	兼	922
kanga(eru)	考	544
kao	顔	733
kara	空	346
karada	体	376
kari	仮	608
ka(riru)	借	889
karo(yaka)	軽	398
karu(i)	軽	398
kasa(naru)	重	729
kasa(neru)	重	729
kashira	頭	734
ka(su)	貸	890
kata	型	885
	形	402
	方	160
kata-	片	609
katachi	形	402
kata(i)	固	401
	難	612
kataki	敵	935
kata(maru)	固	401
kata(meru)	固	401
katana	刀	941
kata(ru)	語	597
KATSU	割	505
	活	694
ka(tsu)	勝	625
katsu(gu)	担	877
ka(u)	買	491
	飼	191
kawa	側	463
	川	266
	河	#267
	皮	482
	革	828
kawa(ri)	代	107
ka(waru)	代	107
	変	237
ka(wasu)	交	789
kayo(u)	通	464
kaza	風	350
kaze	風	350
kazo(eru)	数	20
kazu	数	20
KE	化	723
	仮	608
	家	139
	気	336
	景	660
ke	毛	483
KEI	系	378
	京	319
	係	876
	兄	129
	型	885
	境	307
	形	402
	径	860
	敬	1014
	景	660
	経	822
	計	99
	警	372
	軽	398
KEN	件	977
	健	760
	兼	922
	券	817
	憲	928

Reading	Kanji	No.
	県	#323
	建	534
	検	781
	権	917
	犬	185
	研	589
	絹	487
	見	221
	険	775
	験	579
	間	65
ke(su)	消	452
KETSU	欠	561
	決	511
	潔	773
	穴	896
	結	780
	血	753
kewa(shii)	険	775
KI	危	776
	器	432
	基	918
	喜	683
	寄	1016
	己	158
	希	726
	帰	55
	揮	677
	旗	650
	机	541
	機	36
	気	336
	汽	808
	季	78
	紀	109
	期	174
	規	973

Reading	Kanji	No.
	記	#701
	貴	971
	起	87
ki	木	70
	黄	233
ki-	生	166
kibi(shii)	厳	1010
ki(eru)	消	452
ki(koeru)	聞	568
ki(ku)	効	771
	利	502
	聞	568
ki(maru)	決	511
ki(meru)	決	511
kimi	君	162
KIN	今	45
	勤	872
	均	361
	禁	981
	筋	713
	近	110
	金	71
kinu	絹	487
ki(re)	切	223
ki(reru)	切	223
ki(ru)	切	223
	着	37
kishi	岸	274
kiso(u)	競	622
kita	北	292
kiwa	際	945
kiwa(meru)	極	293
	究	590
kiwa(mi)	極	293
kiyo(i))	清	772
kiyo(maru)	清	772
kiyo(meru)	清	772

Reading	Kanji	No.
kiza(mu)	刻	#816
kiza(shi)	兆	15
kiza(su)	兆	15
kizu	傷	766
kizu(ku)	築	848
KO	個	39
	古	115
	呼	770
	固	401
	去	61
	己	158
	庫	437
	戸	40
	故	790
	湖	273
ko	子	121
	木	70
	黄	233
	粉	416
ko-	小	171
KŌ	向	788
	后	903
	交	789
	候	337
	公	318
	興	647
	効	771
	孝	1011
	厚	964
	口	332
	幸	412
	好	419
	光	379
	工	384
	功	698
	広	250
	康	761

Reading	Kanji	No.
	後	#86
	格	499
	校	525
	構	946
	港	819
	皇	902
	紅	232
	考	544
	耕	253
	航	821
	行	54
	講	556
	鉱	843
	鋼	846
	降	341
	高	357
	黄	233
kō	神	756
koe	声	648
	肥	839
ko(eru)	肥	839
kokono(tsu)	九	9
kokoro	心	328
kokoro (miru)	試	578
kokoroyo(i)	快	783
kokorozashi	志	727
kokoroza (su)	志	727
KOKU	刻	816
	告	507
	国	299
	穀	257
	谷	244
	黒	236
	石	263
koma(kai)	細	732
koma(ru)	困	#613
kome	米	255
KON	今	45
	困	613
	建	534
	根	214
	混	427
	金	71
kona	粉	416
kono(mu)	好	419
kōri	氷	367
koro(bu)	転	392
koro(garu)	転	392
koro(gasu)	転	392
koromo	衣	473
koro(su)	殺	988
kota(e)	答	570
kota(eru)	答	570
koto	事	326
	言	566
koto(naru)	異	953
kotowa(ru)	断	797
KOTSU	骨	752
kowa-	声	648
ko(yashi)	肥	839
ko(yasu)	肥	839
KU	九	9
	久	957
	供	122
	句	602
	区	314
	口	332
	宮	996
	工	384
	功	698
	庫	437
	紅	232
	苦	#739
KŪ	空	346
kuba(ru)	配	517
kubi	首	731
kuchi	口	332
kuda	管	678
kuda(ru)	下	91
kumi	組	548
kumo	雲	347
ku(mu)	組	548
KUN	君	162
	訓	1007
kuni	国	299
kura	倉	513
	蔵	436
kura(beru)	比	743
kurai	位	294
kura(i)	暗	348
ku(rasu)	暮	149
ku(re)	暮	149
kurenai	紅	232
ku(reru)	暮	149
kuro	黒	236
kuro(i)	黒	236
ku(ru)	来	53
kuruma	車	786
kuru(shii)	苦	739
kuru (shimeru)	苦	739
kuru (shimu)	苦	739
kusa	草	208
kusuri	薬	453
ku(u)	食	395
kuwa(eru)	加	426
kuwa(waru)	加	426
KYAKU	客	493

M

KYO	去	#61	
	居	147	
	挙	912	
	許	959	
KYŌ	京	319	
	供	122	
	共	524	
	興	647	
	協	675	
	兄	129	
	境	307	
	強	351	
	教	538	
	橋	801	
	競	622	
	経	822	
	胸	740	
	郷	325	
	鏡	389	
KYOKU	曲	674	
	局	329	
	極	293	
KYŪ	旧	884	
	求	593	
	九	9	
	久	957	
	休	48	
	吸	414	
	宮	996	
	弓	640	
	急	809	
	救	962	
	泣	686	
	球	288	
	究	590	
	級	468	
	給	830	

ma	目	#23
	間	65
	真	662
	馬	188
machi	街	457
	町	313
mado	窓	550
mae	前	84
ma(garu)	曲	674
ma(geru)	曲	674
mago	孫	133
MAI	妹	132
	枚	41
	毎	66
	米	255
mai(ru)	参	18
ma(jiru)	交	789
	混	427
maji(waru)	交	789
maka(seru)	任	920
maka(su)	任	920
ma(kasu)	負	626
ma(keru)	負	626
maki	巻	29
	牧	258
makoto	誠	940
MAKU	幕	687
ma(ku)	巻	29
mame	豆	410
mamo(ru)	守	936
MAN	万	13
	満	282
mana(bu)	学	523
manako	眼	744

mane(ku)	招	#441
maru	丸	651
maru(i)	丸	651
	円	24
maru(meru)	丸	651
masa(ni)	正	56
masa(ru)	勝	625
ma(su)	増	832
mato	的	643
MATSU	末	59
matsu	松	218
ma(tsu)	待	442
matsu(ri)	祭	49
matsurigoto	政	899
matsu(ru)	祭	49
matta(ku)	全	305
mawa(ri)	周	393
mawa(ru)	回	34
mawa(su)	回	34
mayo(u)	迷	794
ma(zaru)	混	727
ma(zeru)	混	727
mazu(shii)	貧	967
me	目	23
	芽	211
	女	119
MEI	命	167
	鳴	203
	名	26
	明	47
	盟	963
	迷	794
MEN	綿	486
	面	260
meshi	飯	399
MI	未	178
	味	422

mi	実	#224	mo(eru)	燃	#854	muku(iru)	報	#370
	身	728	mō(keru)	設	849	muna	胸	740
michi	道	301	MOKU	木	70	mune	胸	740
michibi(ku)	導	960		目	23	mura	村	315
mi(chiru)	満	282	MON	文	387		群	193
mida(reru)	乱	942		門	535	mura(garu)	群	193
mida(su)	乱	942		問	569	mu(re)	群	193
midori	緑	235		聞	568	mu(reru)	群	193
mi(eru)	見	221	mono	物	205	muro	室	539
migi	右	461		者	161	mushi	虫	201
mijika(i)	短	104	mori	守	936	mu(su)	蒸	429
miki	幹	213		森	243	musu(bu)	結	780
mimi	耳	730	mo(ru)	盛	841	mu(tsu)	六	6
MIN	民	333	mo	若	181	mutsuka	難	612
minami	南	291	(shikuwa)			(shii)		
minamoto	源	826	mō(su)	申	865	mut(tsu)	六	6
minato	港	819	moto	下	91	muzuka	難	612
mino(ru)	実	224		本	27	(shii)		
mi(ru)	見	221		元	757	MYAKU	脈	241
misao	操	621		基	918	MYŌ	命	167
mise	店	444	motoi	基	918		名	26
mi(seru)	見	221	moto(meru)	求	593		明	47
mi(tasu)	満	282	MOTSU	物	205			
mito(meru)	認	948	mo(tsu)	持	551	**N**		
MITSU	密	851	motto(mo)	最	360			
mi(tsu)	三	3	mo(yasu)	燃	854	NA	南	291
mit(tsu)	三	3	MU	武	644		納	512
miya	宮	996		無	868	NA'	納	512
miyako	都	320		務	871	na	名	26
mizu	水	69		夢	692		菜	407
mizuka(ra)	自	157	mugi	麦	256	naga(i)	永	956
mizuumi	湖	273	mui	六	6		長	103
MO	模	886	mukashi	昔	111	naga(re)	流	280
MŌ	亡	184	mu(kau)	向	788	naga(reru)	流	280
	毛	483	mu(keru)	向	788	naga(su)	流	280
	望	388	mu(kō)	向	788	nage(ru)	投	632
mochi(iru)	用	434	mu(ku)	向	788	nago(mu)	和	396

Reading	漢字	No.
nago(yaka)	和	#396
NAI	内	140
na(i)	亡	184
	無	868
naka	中	88
	仲	152
naka(ba)	半	83
na(ku)	鳴	203
	泣	686
nama	生	166
nami	並	458
	波	354
NAN	南	291
	男	118
	納	512
	難	612
nan	何	63
nana	七	7
nana(tsu)	七	7
nani	何	63
nano	七	7
nao(ru)	直	615
	治	900
nao(su)	直	615
	治	900
nara(beru)	並	458
nara(bi ni)	並	458
nara(bu)	並	458
na(rasu)	慣	697
nara(u)	習	564
na(reru)	慣	697
na(ru)	鳴	203
	成	177
nasa(ke)	情	690
na(su)	成	177
natsu	夏	74
ne	値	495
	根	#214
	音	601
nega(u)	願	587
NEN	年	60
	念	652
	然	283
	燃	854
ne(ru)	練	577
NETSU	熱	310
NI	弐	17
	二	2
	仁	1012
	児	173
ni	荷	522
NICHI	日	44
niga(i)	苦	739
nii-	新	114
NIKU	肉	406
NIN	人	25
	任	920
	認	948
nina(u)	担	877
ni(ru)	似	470
nishi	西	290
niwa	庭	142
no	野	248
NŌ	能	617
	納	512
	脳	751
	農	838
no(basu)	延	631
no(beru)	述	952
no(biru)	延	631
nobo(ru)	上	90
	登	240
nochi	後	86
noko(ri)	残	344
noko(ru)	残	#344
noko(su)	残	344
no(mu)	飲	413
no(ru)	乗	787
no(seru)	乗	787
nozo(ku)	除	954
nozo(mi)	望	388
nozo(mu)	望	388
	臨	813
nuno	布	484
nushi	主	138
NYAKU	若	181
NYO	女	119
NYŌ	女	119
NYŌ	乳	415
	入	106

O

Reading	漢字	No.
O	悪	339
	和	396
o-	小	171
Ō	央	302
	応	580
	往	818
	桜	220
	横	795
	王	901
	皇	902
	黄	233
ō-	大	170
obi	帯	309
o(biru)	帯	309
obo(eru)	覚	616
o(chiru)	落	228
o(eru)	終	537
oga(mu)	拝	1001

ogina(u)	補	#636		織	#852		礼	#1002
ogoso(ka)	厳	1010	osa(maru)	治	900	REKI	歴	712
ō(i)	多	303		納	512	REN	練	577
o(iru)	老	182	osa(meru)	修	588		連	51
oka(su)	犯	983		収	508	RETSU	列	298
ō(kii)	大	170		治	900	RI	裏	638
o(kiru)	起	87		納	512		理	285
okona(u)	行	54	osana(i)	幼	172		利	502
oko(ru)	興	647	oshi(eru)	教	538		里	804
o(koru)	起	87	oso(waru)	教	538	RICHI	律	972
oko(su)	興	647	o(su)	推	710	RIKI	力	385
o(kosu)	起	87	oto	音	601	RIKU	陸	296
OKU	億	14	otoko	男	118	RIN	林	242
	屋	448	o(tosu)	落	228		臨	813
o(ku)	置	295	otōto	弟	130		輪	478
oku(reru)	後	86	otozu(reru)	訪	966	RITSU	率	594
oku(ru)	送	519	otto	夫	135		律	972
omo	面	260	o(u)	生	166		立	77
omo(i)	重	729		負	626	RO	路	459
omo(na)	主	138		追	990	RŌ	労	881
omote	表	637	o(waru)	終	537		老	182
	面	260	oya	親	126		朗	700
omo(u)	思	180	ōyake	公	318	ROKU	六	6
ON	恩	1005	oyo(gu)	泳	197		緑	235
	温	359					録	704
	遠	112	**R**			RON	論	584
	音	601				RU	流	280
ona(ji)	同	549	RAI	来	53		留	531
onna	女	119		礼	1002	RUI	類	144
onoono	各	306	RAKU	楽	669	RYAKU	略	937
onore	己	158		落	228	RYO	旅	703
o(reru)	折	227	RAN	卵	408	RYŌ	両	127
ori	折	227		乱	942		量	342
o(riru)	下	91		覧	667		漁	842
	降	341	REI	令	933		料	421
o(rosu)	降	341		例	605		良	338
o(ru)	折	227		冷	366		領	308

Reading	Kanji	No.
RYOKU	力	#385
	緑	235
RYŪ	流	280
	留	531
	立	77

S

Reading	Kanji	No.
SA	再	693
	作	254
	左	462
	査	782
	砂	265
	差	362
	茶	234
SA'	早	98
saba(ku)	裁	975
sachi	幸	412
sada(maru)	定	397
sade(meru)	定	397
sa(garu)	下	91
saga(su)	探	592
sa(geru)	下	91
	提	574
sagu(ru)	探	592
SAI	再	693
	才	31
	切	223
	裁	975
	妻	136
	災	989
	採	582
	最	360
	殺	988
	済	823
	祭	49
	細	732
	菜	#407
	西	290
	財	824
	際	945
saiwa(i)	幸	412
saka	坂	793
	酒	417
saka(e)	栄	403
saka(eru)	栄	403
sakai	境	307
saka(n)	盛	841
sakana	魚	195
saka(rau)	逆	970
saka(sa)	逆	970
sake	酒	417
saki	先	57
SAKU	冊	28
	作	254
	昨	46
	策	919
sa(ku)	割	505
sakura	桜	220
sama	様	163
sa(masu)	覚	616
sa(meru)	冷	366
	覚	616
samu(i)	寒	363
SAN	三	3
	蚕	202
	参	18
	山	238
	散	226
	産	827
	算	510
	賛	926
	酸	768
sara	皿	438
sa(ru)	去	#61
sasa(eru)	支	509
sa(su)	指	477
	差	362
sato	里	804
SATSU	冊	28
	刷	725
	察	978
	札	516
	殺	988
sawa(ru)	障	791
sazu(karu)	授	554
sazu(keru)	授	554
SE	世	108
se	背	742
SECHI	節	79
SEI	正	56
	世	108
	省	915
	制	861
	勢	286
	声	648
	性	120
	情	690
	成	177
	政	899
	星	381
	晴	345
	整	879
	清	772
	聖	1003
	生	166
	盛	841
	精	755
	製	481
	西	290
	誠	940

	青	#179	SHA	舎	#533	視	#745
	静	659		写	661	私	156
sei	背	742		捨	897	糸	485
SEKI	夕	97		砂	265	紙	490
	席	560		社	869	自	157
	昔	111		者	161	至	805
	石	263		謝	1008	詞	603
	積	261		射	642	詩	699
	績	583		車	786	試	578
	責	943	SHAKU	借	889	誌	705
	赤	231		尺	679	資	825
seki	関	864		昔	111	飼	191
se(meru)	責	943		石	263	歯	737
SEN	千	12		赤	231	shiawa(se) 幸	412
	宣	1004		釈	721	SHICHI 七	7
	先	57	SHI	史	711	質	467
	専	585		師	558	shi(iru) 強	351
	川	266		市	312	SHIKI 式	596
	戦	630		仕	873	織	852
	染	853		使	435	色	229
	浅	277		次	123	識	586
	洗	439		司	934	shima 島	297
	泉	278		四	4	shi(maru) 閉	455
	線	380		志	727	shi(meru) 閉	455
	船	820		士	375	shime(su) 示	666
	選	635		姉	131	shi(mi) 染	853
	銭	895		始	536	shi(miru) 染	853
se(ri)	競	622		子	121	shimo 下	91
se(ru)	競	622		指	477	SHIN 申	865
SETSU	切	223		支	509	信	800
	折	227		枝	212	真	662
	接	867		止	101	心	328
	殺	988		死	183	新	114
	節	79		氏	164	森	243
	設	849		思	180	深	276
	説	708		矢	641	神	756
	雪	343		示	666	臣	914

	親	#126
	身	728
	進	831
	針	102
shina	品	466
shi(nu)	死	183
shio	塩	424
	潮	279
shira	白	230
shira(be)	調	431
shira(beru)	調	431
shirizo (keru)	退	784
shirizo(ku)	退	784
shiro	代	107
	城	999
	白	230
shiro(i)	白	230
shi(ru)	知	153
shirushi	印	724
shiru(su)	記	701
shita	下	91
	舌	736
shitaga(u)	従	837
shita(shii)	親	126
shita (shimu)	親	126
SHITSU	失	628
	室	539
	質	467
shizu(ka)	静	659
shizu(maru)	静	659
shizu(meru)	静	659
SHO	処	880
	所	317
	署	364
	署	979

	書	#447
	初	58
	諸	165
SHŌ	正	56
	少	175
	承	949
	省	915
	商	456
	傷	766
	上	90
	唱	671
	声	648
	小	171
	賞	717
	従	837
	性	120
	招	441
	政	899
	昭	905
	星	381
	松	218
	相	634
	消	452
	清	772
	焼	428
	照	349
	将	113
	生	116
	称	969
	笑	685
	精	755
	勝	625
	装	474
	証	986
	象	194
	障	791
	青	179

	章	#600
SHOKU	植	222
	織	852
	職	874
	色	229
	食	395
SHU	主	138
	衆	909
	修	588
	守	936
	手	440
	酒	417
	種	215
	取	494
	首	731
SHŪ	州	300
	衆	909
	就	875
	修	588
	周	393
	収	508
	宗	993
	拾	19
	祝	50
	秋	75
	終	537
	習	564
	週	64
	集	465
SHUKU	宿	573
	縮	836
	祝	50
SHUN	春	73
SHUTSU	出	105
SO	想	591
	祖	128
	素	769

SŌ

Reading	Kanji	No.
SŌ	組	#548
	巣	199
	争	624
	倉	513
	創	883
	奏	673
	宗	993
	層	262
	想	591
	操	621
	早	98
	相	634
	窓	550
	総	334
	草	208
	装	474
	走	190
	送	519
soda(teru)	育	169
soda(tsu)	育	169
soko	底	245
soko(nau)	損	501
soko(neru)	損	501
SOKU	束	443
	側	463
	測	390
	息	134
	則	974
	足	33
	速	792
so(maru)	染	853
so(meru)	染	853
-so(meru)	初	58
somu(keru)	背	742
somu(ku)	背	742
SON	尊	1015
	存	1013
sona(eru)	供	122
	備	529
sona(waru)	備	529
sono	園	206
sora	空	346
so(rasu)	反	927
sōrō	候	337
so(ru)	反	927
soso(gu)	注	368
soto	外	155
SOTSU	卒	595
	率	594
so(u)	沿	275
SU	主	138
	子	121
	守	936
	数	20
	素	769
su	州	300
	巣	199
SŪ	数	20
su(beru)	統	906
sue	末	59
sugata	姿	746
su(giru)	過	176
su(gosu)	過	176
sugu(reru)	優	629
SUI	出	105
	垂	798
	推	710
	水	69
su(i)	酸	768
suji	筋	713
suke	助	559
suko(shi)	少	#175
suko(yaka)	健	760
su(ku)	好	419
suku(nai)	少	175
suku(u)	救	962
su(masu)	済	823
sumi	炭	844
sumi(yaka)	速	792
su(mu)	住	148
	済	823
SUN	寸	720
suna	砂	265
su(ru)	刷	725
susu(meru)	勧	894
	進	831
susu(mu)	進	831
su(teru)	捨	897
su(u)	吸	414
suwa(ru)	座	382

T

Reading	Kanji	No.
TA	他	154
	多	303
	太	270
ta	手	440
	田	251
taba	束	443
ta(beru)	食	395
tabi	度	35
	旅	703
-tachi	達	151
tada(chi ni)	直	615
tada(shii)	正	56
tada(su)	正	56
ta(eru)	絶	961

tagaya(su)	耕	#253	tano(shii)	楽	#669		停	#802
TAI	代	107	tano(shimu)	楽	669		弟	130
	体	376	ta(rasu)	垂	798		定	397
	台	32	ta(reru)	垂	798		底	245
	大	170	ta(riru)	足	33		庭	142
	太	270	ta(ru)	足	33		提	574
	帯	309	tashi(ka)	確	955		程	553
	待	442	tashi	確	955	TEKI	敵	935
	態	777	(kameru)				的	643
	対	639	tas(suru)	達	151		笛	680
	貸	890	ta(su)	足	33		適	921
	退	784	tasu(karu)	助	559	TEN	天	335
	隊	931	tasu(keru)	助	559		典	546
tai(ra)	平	247	tataka(u)	戦	630		点	581
taka	高	357	tate	縦	796		展	665
taka(i)	高	357	ta(teru)	建	534		店	444
taka(maru)	高	357		立	77		転	392
taka(meru)	高	357	tato(e)	例	605	tera	寺	995
takara	宝	475	tato(eru)	例	605	te(rasu)	照	349
take	竹	217	TATSU	達	151	te(ru)	照	349
TAKU	宅	143	ta(tsu)	裁	975	TETSU	鉄	807
	度	35		建	534	TO	図	284
tama	玉	409		断	797		土	72
	球	288		立	77		度	35
tamago	卵	408		絶	961		徒	530
tame(su)	試	578	tatto(bu)	尊	1015		登	240
tami	民	333		貴	971		頭	734
tamo(tsu)	保	527	tatto(i)	尊	1015		都	320
TAN	単	498		貴	971	to	十	10
	炭	844	tawara	俵	645		戸	40
	担	877	ta(yasu)	絶	961	TŌ	東	289
	探	592	tayo(ri)	便	330		島	297
	短	104	tazu(neru)	訪	966		刀	941
	誕	168	te	手	440		冬	76
	反	927	TEI	丁	92		当	765
tane	種	215		体	376		党	907
tani	谷	244		低	358		投	632

	湯	#418	tomi	富	#404	tsuka(u)	使	#435
	灯	451	tomo	供	122	tsu(keru)	付	423
	登	240		共	524	tsuki	月	52
	答	570		友	150	tsu(ku)	就	875
	等	526	to(mu)	富	404		付	423
	糖	425	TON	団	676		着	37
	納	512	ton	問	569	tsukue	机	541
	統	906	tona(eru)	唱	671	tsuku(ru)	作	254
	討	923	tori	鳥	198		造	847
	読	567	to(ru)	採	582	tsuma	妻	136
	豆	410		取	494	tsume(tai)	冷	366
	頭	734	tō(ru)	通	464	tsumi	罪	982
	道	301	toshi	年	60	tsu(mori)	積	261
tō	十	10	tō(su)	通	464	tsu(moru)	積	261
to(basu)	飛	200	tōto(bu)	尊	1015	tsu(mu)	積	261
to(bu)	飛	200		貴	971	tsune	常	471
todoke	届	562	tōto(i)	尊	1015	tsuno	角	460
todo(keru)	届	562		貴	971	tsura	面	260
todo(ku)	届	562	totono(eru)	整	879	tsura(naru)	連	51
to(gu)	研	589		調	431	tsu(re)	連	51
to(i)	問	569	totono(u)	整	879	tsu(reru)	連	51
tō(i)	遠	112		調	431	tsuta(eru)	伝	702
to(jiru)	閉	455	to(u)	問	569	tsuta(waru)	伝	702
to(keru)	解	576	TSU	通	464	tsuto(meru)	努	618
toki	時	80		都	320		勤	872
toko-	常	471	TSU	痛	738		務	871
tokoro	所	317		通	464	tsutsu(mu)	包	489
TOKU	得	500	tsuchi	土	72	tsuyo(i)	強	351
	徳	1009	tsudo(u)	集	465	tsuyo(maru)	強	351
	特	811	tsu(geru)	告	507	tsuyo(meru)	強	351
	読	567	tsugi	次	123	tsuzu(keru)	続	866
to(ku)	解	576	tsu(gu)	次	123	tsuzu(ku)	続	866
	説	708		接	867	**U**		
to(maru)	止	101	TSUI	追	990			
	留	531		対	639	U	右	461
to(meru)	止	101	tsui(yasu)	費	785		宇	373
	留	531	tsuka(eru)	仕	873			

	羽	#42	utsuku(shii)	美	#654		**Y**		
	有	146	utsu(ru)	写	661				
	雨	340		映	663				
ubu	産	827		移	958	**YA**		夜	#95
uchi	内	140	utsu(su)	写	661			野	248
ue	上	90		映	663	ya		八	8
u(eru)	植	222		移	958			屋	448
ugo(kasu)	動	204	utsuwa	器	432			矢	641
ugo(ku)	動	204	uwa-	上	90			家	139
ui-	初	58	uyama(u)	敬	1014	yabu(reru)		破	980
uji	氏	164						敗	627
u(keru)	受	515	**W**			yabu(ru)		破	980
uketamawa	承	949				yado		宿	573
(ru)			**WA**	和	396	yado(ru)		宿	573
uma	馬	188		話	514	ya(keru)		焼	428
u(mareru)	生	166	wa	輪	478	**YAKU**		益	503
	産	827	wa(ga)	我	159			役	316
ume	梅	219	waka(i)	若	181			約	304
umi	海	268	wa(kareru)	分	81			薬	453
u(mu)	生	166	waka(reru)	別	812			訳	715
	産	827	wa(karu)	分	81	ya(ku)		焼	428
UN	運	520	wake	訳	715	yama		山	238
	雲	347	wa(keru)	分	81	yamai		病	758
uo	魚	195	warabe	童	532	ya(meru)		辞	545
ura	裏	638	wara(u)	笑	685	ya(mu)		病	758
u(reru)	売	492	ware	我	159	yasa(shii)		優	629
	熟	225	wa(reru)	割	505			易	856
u(ru)	売	492	wari	割	505	yashina(u)		養	145
	得	500	wa(ru)	割	505	yashiro		社	869
ushi	牛	187	waru(i)	悪	339	yasu(i)		安	469
ushina(u)	失	628	wasu(reru)	忘	575	yasu(mi)		休	48
ushi(ro)	後	86	wata	綿	467	yasu(mu)		休	48
uta	歌	670	watakushi	私	156	ya(tsu)		八	8
utaga(u)	疑	984	watashi	私	156	yat(tsu)		八	8
uta(u)	歌	670	waza	業	555	yawa(ragu)		和	396
u(tsu)	打	633		技	623	**YO**		予	371
	討	923	wazawa(i)	災	989			余	898

	預	#887
yo	世	108
	夜	95
	代	107
YŌ	容	547
	幼	172
	曜	67
	様	163
	洋	269
	用	434
	羊	192
	養	145
	葉	210
	要	620
	陽	377
yō	八	8
yo(bu)	呼	770
yo(i)	善	965
	良	338
yoko	横	795
YOKU	浴	774
	翌	62
	欲	420
yo(mu)	読	567
yon	四	4
yoroko(bi)	喜	683
yoroko(bu)	喜	683
yoru	夜	95
yo(ru)	因	779
	寄	1016
yo(seru)	寄	1016
yoshi	由	858
yosoo(u)	装	474
yo(tsu)	四	4
yot(tsu)	四	4
yowa(i)	弱	352
yowa(maru)	弱	352

yowa(meru)	弱	#352
yowa(ru)	弱	352
YU	由	858
	油	657
	輸	859
	遊	186
yu	湯	418
YŪ	由	858
	優	629
	勇	938
	友	150
	右	461
	遊	186
	有	146
	郵	331
yū	夕	97
yubi	指	477
yue	故	790
YUI	由	858
	遺	998
yuki	雪	343
yu(ku)	行	54
yume	夢	692
yumi	弓	640
yuru(su)	許	959
yuta(ka)	豊	855
yu(u)	結	780

Z

ZA	座	382
ZAI	在	117
	材	430
	罪	982
	財	824
ZAN	残	344
ZATSU	雑	706

ZE	是	#951
ZEI	税	863
	説	708
ZEN	全	305
	前	84
	善	965
	然	283
zeni	銭	895
ZETSU	絶	961
	舌	736
ZŌ	像	664
	増	832
	臓	747
	蔵	436
	象	194
	造	847
	雑	706
ZOKU	俗	696
	属	762
	族	141
	続	866
ZON	存	1013
ZU	事	326
	図	284
	豆	410
	頭	734

INDEX by Stroke Count

1 stroke

一	#1

2 strokes

丁	92
九	9
七	7
二	2
人	25
入	106
八	8
刀	941
力	385
十	10

3 strokes

万	13
三	3
下	91
久	957
丸	651
千	12
才	31
亡	184
上	90
口	332
土	72
士	375
夕	97
大	170
女	119
子	121
小	171

山	#238
川	266
工	384
己	158
干	281
弓	640

4 strokes

五	5
天	335
不	405
中	88
内	140
午	85
夫	135
少	175
予	371
元	757
六	6
仁	1012
化	723
仏	1000
今	45
分	81
公	318
円	24
切	223
区	314
反	927
友	150
収	508
太	270
尺	679
引	386

心	#328
戸	40
手	440
支	509
文	387
方	160
日	44
月	52
木	70
欠	561
止	101
比	743
毛	483
氏	164
水	69
火	68
父	124
片	609
牛	187
犬	185
王	901

5 strokes

可	924
民	333
平	247
正	56
央	302
冊	28
由	858
史	711
申	865
旧	884
世	108

本	#27
出	105
必	619
永	956
氷	367
半	83
包	489
末	59
失	628
未	178
市	312
主	138
以	89
令	933
他	154
仕	873
付	423
代	107
写	661
加	426
句	602
北	292
古	115
圧	356
弁	985
台	32
兄	129
司	934
右	461
号	799
四	4
去	61
冬	76
処	880

外	#155	曲	#674	守	#936	束	#443
功	698	后	903	安	469	卵	408
左	462	争	624	光	379	我	159
布	484	危	776	当	765	兵	932
刊	707	年	60	式	596	来	53
幼	172	多	303	成	177	忘	575
庁	327	交	789	早	98	似	470
広	250	件	977	机	541	位	294
打	633	任	920	列	298	住	148
札	516	仲	152	死	183	体	376
母	125	伝	702	毎	66	低	358
犯	983	休	48	気	336	作	254
玉	409	会	321	池	271	余	898
生	166	仮	608	灯	451	何	63
用	434	合	100	竹	217	児	173
田	251	全	305	米	255	弟	130
白	230	先	57	糸	485	冷	366
皮	482	共	524	羊	192	判	976
皿	438	同	549	耳	730	別	812
目	23	兆	15	羽	42	努	618
矢	641	次	123	老	182	助	559
石	263	灰	840	考	544	労	881
示	666	吸	414	肉	406	医	759
礼	1002	因	779	有	146	孝	1011
穴	896	団	676	自	157	君	162
立	77	回	34	至	805	告	507
辺	806	寺	995	舌	736	囲	394

6 strokes

		在	117	虫	201	困	613
		地	246	血	753	図	284
弐	17	声	648	行	54	壱	16
百	11	各	306	衣	473	坂	793
両	127	名	26	西	290	志	727
再	693	好	419			均	361
州	300	存	1013			売	492
色	229	宅	143			条	947
向	788	宇	373			完	722
印	724	字	606			局	329

7 strokes

否	925
求	593
系	378

災	#989	走	#190	効	#771	招	#441
改	815	足	33	協	675	拝	1001
希	726	身	728	直	615	放	987
序	611	車	786	参	18	易	856
応	580	返	891	味	422	昔	111
形	402	近	110	呼	770	明	47
役	316	里	804	固	401	枚	41
快	783	防	929	国	299	林	242
批	719	麦	256	幸	412	枝	212
技	623			並	458	松	218

8 strokes

折	227	画	656	妹	132	板	540
投	632	武	644	妻	136	歩	189
対	639	果	411	姉	131	毒	767
材	430	表	637	始	536	泳	197
村	315	承	949	学	523	沿	275
汽	808	刷	725	宣	1004	治	900
決	511	垂	798	宙	374	波	354
状	778	東	289	宝	475	河	267
町	313	乳	415	宗	993	注	368
男	118	事	326	官	916	泣	686
杜	869	卒	595	定	397	油	657
利	502	京	319	実	224	法	599
私	156	育	169	届	562	受	515
究	590	夜	95	居	147	版	658
臣	914	価	497	岸	274	牧	258
乱	942	舎	533	岩	264	物	205
良	338	念	652	府	322	的	643
芸	488	例	605	底	245	具	433
花	209	命	167	店	444	知	153
初	58	供	122	延	631	季	78
見	221	使	435	径	860	委	910
角	460	典	546	往	818	和	396
言	566	周	393	忠	939	空	346
谷	244	券	817	性	120	者	161
豆	410	刻	816	所	317	取	494
貝	196	制	861	拡	834	肥	839
赤	231			担	877	服	449

芽 #211
若 181
英 598
苦 739
述 952
金 71
長 103
門 535
雨 340
青 179
非 472

9 strokes

昼 94
単 498
省 915
看 763
乗 787
重 729
変 237
係 876
便 330
俗 696
信 800
保 527
前 84
軍 930
勇 938
南 291
点 581
里 804
厚 964
品 466
型 885
城 999
奏 673
姿 746

室 #539
宣 1004
客 493
専 585
県 323
屋 448
炭 844
巻 29
度 35
建 534
律 972
待 442
後 86
急 809
拾 19
持 551
指 477
故 790
政 899
昭 905
映 663
昨 46
是 951
星 381
春 73
査 782
柱 968
栄 403
染 853
相 634
段 496
派 994
浅 277
洋 269
洗 439
活 694
海 268

畑 #252
独 672
界 287
胃 749
思 180
発 518
泉 278
皇 902
研 589
砂 265
祖 128
祝 50
神 756
秒 82
科 543
秋 75
級 468
紀 109
約 304
紅 232
美 654
肺 748
背 742
草 208
茶 234
要 620
計 99
負 626
則 974
迷 794
送 519
退 784
逆 970
追 990
限 862
面 260
革 828

音 #601
風 350
飛 200
食 395
首 731

10 strokes

蚕 202
夏 74
師 558
勉 563
島 297
俵 645
候 337
倍 38
俳 695
倉 513
値 495
個 39
借 889
修 588
益 503
兼 922
弱 352
真 662
原 249
能 617
員 446
純 716
孫 133
害 355
案 571
容 547
宮 996
家 139
党 907
展 665

帯	#309	紙	#490	停	#802	球	#288
庫	437	素	769	側	463	理	285
席	560	差	362	健	760	現	116
庭	142	耕	253	貧	967	略	937
座	382	書	447	副	604	異	953
帰	55	朗	700	動	204	盛	841
従	837	脈	241	唱	671	眼	744
徒	530	胸	740	域	311	務	781
恩	1005	息	134	基	918	祭	49
挙	912	航	821	婦	137	視	745
救	962	荷	522	密	851	移	958
旅	703	討	923	宿	573	窓	550
時	80	訓	1007	寄	1016	産	827
桜	220	記	701	常	471	笛	680
株	893	財	824	堂	400	組	548
梅	219	起	87	帳	888	終	537
格	499	射	642	康	761	細	732
校	525	速	792	張	835	経	822
根	214	造	847	強	351	絶	961
残	344	連	51	術	383	翌	62
殺	988	通	464	得	500	習	564
浴	774	郡	324	情	690	脳	751
酒	417	配	517	捨	897	船	820
消	452	針	102	授	554	第	21
流	280	陸	904	採	582	菜	407
将	113	院	528	探	592	著	714
特	811	除	954	推	710	葉	210
班	944	降	341	教	538	票	911
留	531	馬	188	断	797	規	973
病	758	骨	752	族	141	許	959
破	980	高	357	械	850	設	849
称	969			済	823	訪	966
秘	878	**11 strokes**		液	754	訳	715
笑	685	悪	339	混	427	欲	420
料	421	巣	199	清	772	責	943
粉	416	率	594	深	276	貨	445
納	512	商	456	望	388	敗	627

転	#392	寒	#363	筋	#713	隊	#931
週	64	属	762	等	526	階	43
郷	325	順	610	筆	542	陽	377
部	30	街	457	統	906	集	465
郵	331	復	565	絵	655	雲	347
都	320	揮	677	給	830	悲	684
進	831	提	574	結	780	飯	399
釈	721	敬	1014	買	491	飲	413
野	248	散	226	着	37	歯	737
間	569	暑	364	群	193		

13 strokes

閉	455	量	342	期	174	業	555
険	775	景	660	勝	625	裏	638
陸	296	晴	345	朝	93	働	882
雪	343	晩	96	落	228	傷	766
章	600	最	360	衆	909	勢	286
頂	239	森	243	装	474	勧	894
魚	195	棒	992	補	636	幹	213
鳥	198	植	222	覚	616	準	810
黄	233	検	781	詞	603	園	206
黒	236	湖	273	評	718	塩	424
		港	819	証	986	想	591
		測	390	象	194	感	688

12 strokes

		湯	418	費	785	戦	630
就	875	温	359	貿	857	損	501
備	529	満	282	賀	1006	数	20
善	965	減	833	貯	272	新	114
尊	1015	然	283	貸	890	暖	365
創	883	焼	428	貴	971	暗	348
割	505	無	868	軽	398	極	293
勤	872	痛	738	達	151	楽	669
博	668	登	240	過	176	源	826
裁	975	短	104	道	301	漢	607
営	870	程	553	運	520	照	349
場	259	税	863	遊	186	愛	689
報	370	童	532	番	22	聖	1003
喜	683	策	919	間	65	盟	963
富	404	答	570	開	454		

禁	#981	疑	#984	酸	#768	誕	#168
福	506	歴	712	銅	845	談	950
節	79	鳴	203	銀	479	課	552
絹	487	境	307	閣	913	論	584
続	866	増	832	関	864	調	431
義	557	察	978	聞	568	諸	165
署	979	層	262	際	945	賛	926
罪	982	徳	1009	障	791	質	467
置	295	態	777	雑	706	輪	478
腸	750	慣	697	需	829	選	635
腹	741	旗	650	静	659	遺	998
辞	545	様	163	領	308		
蒸	429	構	946	駅	814		

16 strokes

幕	687	模	886	鼻	735	興	647
墓	997	歌	670			奮	646
夢	692	穀	257			憲	928

15 strokes

解	576	漁	842	劇	681	操	621
誠	940	演	682	億	14	樹	216
話	514	磁	480	器	432	橋	801
詩	699	種	215	導	960	機	36
試	578	算	510	賞	717	整	879
豊	855	管	678	敵	935	激	691
賃	521	精	755	暴	353	燃	854
資	825	緑	235	標	803	積	261
路	459	練	577	権	917	築	848
農	838	綿	486	横	795	糖	425
遠	112	総	334	歓	649	縦	796
鉱	843	暮	149	潔	773	薬	453
鉄	807	製	481	潮	279	親	126
銭	895	複	892	熟	225	頭	734
電	450	誌	705	熱	310	輸	859
意	369	認	948	確	955	録	704
預	887	誤	614	箱	476	鋼	846
飼	191	説	708	線	380	館	207
		語	597	編	709		

14 strokes

17 strokes

像	664	読	567	養	145	厳	1010
		適	921	蔵	436		

優	#629
績	583
縮	836
覧	667
謝	1008
講	556

18 strokes

曜	67
題	572
簡	991
織	852
職	874
臨	813
観	391
難	612
額	504
類	144
顔	733
験	579

19 strokes

願	587
臓	747
識	586
警	372
鏡	389

20 strokes

競	622
護	764
議	908

Subject-Grouped 1016 KANJI IN CONTEXT
A Guide to Reading Japanese
分野別 1016 漢字ブック

1997年12月10日　初版発行

著　者　Taeko Kamiya

発行者　株式会社 北星堂書店

代表者　山 本 雅 三

〒 113 東 京 都 文 京 区 本 駒 込 3-32-4

検印省略

Tel（03）3827-0511　Fax（03）3827-0567

THE HOKUSEIDO PRESS
32-4, Honkomagome 3-chome, Bunkyo-ku, Tokyo 113 Japan

◆落丁・乱丁本はお取替いたします。

About the Author

Taeko Kamiya was born in Japan and graduated from Doshisha Women's College in Kyoto. She holds two master's degrees——in education from the University of San Francisco, and in linguistics from the Monterey Institute of International Studies. She has taught Japanese for twenty-fiye years at one of the top language schools in the United States, the Defense Language Institute in Monterey, California. Her publications include *Speak Japanese Today* (Tuttle), *Japanese for Fun* (Tuttle), *Tuttle New Dictionary of Loanwords in Japanese* (Tuttle) and *Japanese Particle Workbook* (Weatherhill).